McGRAW-HILL

5 Steps to a 5

11 Practice Tests
for the AP Exams

Books in McGraw-Hill's *5 Steps to a 5* Series include:

AP Biology
AP Calculus AB
AP Chemistry
AP Computer Science
AP English Language
AP English Literature
AP Microeconomics/Macroeconomics
AP Physics B&C
AP Psychology
AP Spanish Language
AP Statistics
AP U.S. Government and Politics
AP U.S. History
AP World History
Writing the AP English Essay

McGRAW-HILL

5 Steps to a 5

11 Practice Tests
for the AP Exams

McGRAW-HILL

New York   Chicago   San Francisco   Lisbon   London   Madrid   Mexico City
Milan   New Delhi   San Juan   Seoul   Singapore   Sydney   Toronto

1 2 3 4 5 6 7 8 9 0 QPD/QPD 0 9 8 7 6 5

ISBN 0-07-146463-8

"The Origins of Stories" by Margaret Atwood, an excerpt from "Reading Blind," first appeared in *The Best American Short Stories 1989,* copyright © 1989 by O. W. Toad, Ltd. Reprinted by permission of the author.

"The Writer" from *The Mind-Reader,* copyright © 1971 by Richard Wilbur. Reprinted by permission of Harcourt, Inc.

"The Flowers" from *In Love & Trouble: Stories of Black Women,* copyright © 1973 by Alice Walker. Reprinted by permission of Harcourt, Inc.

"The Naked and the Nude" by Robert Graves from *The Complete Poems: In One Volume* by Robert Graves et al., 2001. Reprinted by permission of Carcanet Press Limited, Manchester, England, on behalf of the Trustees of the Robert Graves Copyright Trust.

McGraw-Hill books are available at special quantity discounts to use as premiums and sales promotions, or for use in corporate training programs. For more information, please write to the Director of Special Sales, Professional Publishing, McGraw-Hill, Two Penn Plaza, New York, NY 10121-2298. Or contact your local bookstore.

♲ This book is printed on recycled, acid-free paper containing a minimum of 50% recycled, de-inked fiber.

Library of Congress Cataloging-in-Publication Data

11 practice tests for the advanced placement exams.

   p. cm.
  ISBN 0-07-146463-8 (alk. paper)

1. Advanced placement programs (Education)—Examinations—Study guides.
I. Title: Eleven practice tests for the advanced placement exams.

LB2353.62.A14 2005

378.1'664—dc22

                               2005029524

Contents

Contributing Authors

Mark Anestis (Biology) is a private test preparation tutor and coauthor of *McGraw-Hill's SAT 1.*

Stephen Armstrong (U.S. History) is a social studies teacher and an adjunct professor of history at Central Connecticut State University.

Duane C. Hinders, Ed.D. (Statistics), teaches statistics at Foothill College in Los Altos Hills, CA. He has also presented extensively on AP Statistics and published several articles on mathematics.

Greg Jacobs (Physics) teaches both the B and C levels of AP Physics at Woodberry Forest School in central Virginia. He is also a reader and consultant for the College Board's AP Physics program.

Pamela K. Lamb (U.S. Government and Politics) teaches AP U.S. Government and Politics at Del Rio High School and is a reader of AP tests in history, government, and economics.

Richard Langley, Ph.D. (Chemistry), has graded AP Chemistry exams for the past three years and is a chemistry professor at Stephen F. Austin State University.

William Ma (Calculus) is the lead math department chair of the Herrick's school system in New York. He is also the author of online review guides for New York State mathematics exams.

Laura Lincoln Maitland (Psychology) teaches AP Psychology at the Bellmore-Merrick Central High School District and is the science chairperson.

John T. Moore, Ed.D. (Chemistry), is the author of *Chemistry for Dummies* and is a professor of chemistry at Stephen F. Austin State University.

Barbara Murphy (English Language, English Literature, English Essay) has taught AP English Language and Composition for over 20 years and has been a reader of the AP English Language and Composition exam since 1993.

Estelle Rankin (English Language, English Literature, English Essay) taught AP English Literature at Jericho High School for over 25 years and was honored with the AP Literature Teacher of the Year Award by the College Board in 1996.

Joshua Schulman (Physics) is a U.S. Physics Team semifinalist, currently attending Harvard Medical School.

Preface

Are you one of the many students who will be taking two or more AP exams? If so, this book was designed with you in mind. Here, in one volume, are practice tests for the AP exams that consistently draw the highest enrollments.

Taken from the bestselling 5 STEPS TO A 5 series, each of the 11 practice tests is modeled on recent AP exams. If you follow the directions carefully and do not exceed the stated time limits, you will have the invaluable experience of previewing what is going to happen on the day of the actual exam. Then read the correct answers and score your results. This will not only give you some idea of how you might fare if you took the exam today, but it will also let you pinpoint those areas where you need additional work, which could help improve your grades on the day of the actual test.

McGRAW-HILL

5 Steps to a 5

11 Practice Tests for the AP Exams

Chapter 1

Preparing for an AP Exam

INTRODUCTION TO THE FIVE-STEP PLAN

The five-step program is designed to provide you with the knowledge, skills, and strategies to help lead you to the highest score you can earn on the AP exam. Each step is designed to provide you with the opportunity to get closer and closer to the "Holy Grail" score of 5.

STEP ONE leads you through a brief process to help determine which type of exam preparation you want to commit yourself to:

1. Month-by-month: September through May
2. The calendar year: January through May
3. Basic training: six weeks before the exam

STEP TWO helps you develop the knowledge you need to succeed on the exam:

1. A comprehensive review of the content of the course. Use your classroom text, or you might find it more convenient to acquire a concise text (like the course review included in each volume of the 5 STEPS TO A 5 series).
2. Try to access a Diagnostic Exam that you can go through step by step and question by question to determine the areas in which you need more work.*
3. Use a glossary of terms related to the AP subject(s) you are studying.*
4. Check out the list of useful related Web sites in the Appendix of this book.

STEP THREE helps you develop the skills necessary to take the exam and do well:

1. Practice multiple-choice questions
2. Practice free-response questions

STEP FOUR helps you develop strategies for taking the exam:

1. Learning about the test itself
2. Learning to read multiple-choice question
3. Learning how to answer multiple-choice questions, including whether or not to guess
4. Learning how to plan and write the free-response answers

---

*A Diagnostic Exam and a Glossary are included in each volume of the 5 Steps to a 5 series.

STEP FIVE helps you develop your confidence in using the skills demanded on the AP exam:

1. Time management techniques and skills
2. A practice exam that tests how well honed your skills are

THREE APPROACHES TO PREPARING FOR AN AP EXAM

No one knows your study habits, likes, and dislikes better than you. You are the only one who can decide which approach you want or need to adopt to prepare for an Advanced Placement examination. Look at the brief profiles below. These may help you determine a particular prep mode.

You're a full-year prep student if:

1. You are the kind of person who likes to plan for everything very far in advance.
2. You like to plan for a graduation party or vacation a year in advance.
3. You arrive at the airport three hours before your flight because you never know when something may happen.
4. You like detailed planning and everything in its place.
5. You feel you must be thoroughly prepared.
6. You are always early for appointments.
7. You hate surprises.

You're a one-semester prep student if:

1. You begin to plan for a graduation party or vacation four to five months before the event.
2. You get to the airport at least two hours before your flight is scheduled to leave.
3. You are willing to plan ahead to feel comfortable in stressful situations, but are okay with skipping some details.
4. You feel more comfortable when you know what to expect, but a surprise or two is fine.
5. You are always on time for appointments.

You're a six-week prep student if:

1. You plan a graduation party or vacation a week before the big day.
2. You get to the airport just as final boarding for your plane is being announced.
3. You work best under pressure and tight deadlines.
4. You feel very confident with the knowledge and skills you've learned in your AP class.
5. You decided late in the year to take the exam.
6. You feel okay if you arrive a little late for an appointment.
7. Surprises energize and please you.

General Outline of Three Different Study Schedules*

Month	Year-Long Plan	Semester-Long Plan	Six-Week Plan
September–October	Introduction to material	—	—
November	Chapters 1–3	—	—
December	Chapters 4–5	—	—
January	Chapters 6–7	Chapters 1–5	—
February	Chapters 8–9	Chapters 1–5	—
March	Chapters 10–12	Chapters 6–10	—
April	Chapters 13–15; Take Practice Exam; note weaknesses	Chapters 11–15; Take Practice Exam; note weaknesses	Skim Chapters 1–15; Take Practice Exam; note weaknesses
May	Review everything, concentrating on weaknesses	Review everything, concentrating on weaknesses	Review everything, concentrating on weaknesses

*The schedules are based on a hypothetical 15-chapter classroom text and/or concise review text. Adjust the schedules up or down as necessary.

BACKGROUND OF THE AP PROGRAM

The Advanced Placement program was begun by the College Board in 1955 to construct standard achievement exams that would allow highly motivated high school students the opportunity to be awarded advanced placement as first-year students in colleges and universities in the United States. Today, there are 33 college-level high school courses, with more than a million students from every state in the nation and from foreign countries taking the annual AP exams in May.

WHO WRITES THE AP EXAMS

Each of the AP exams is created by a group of college and high school instructors, who teach the particular subject, known as the AP Development Committee. The committee's job is to ensure that the annual exam reflects what is being taught and studied in AP classes at high schools throughout the United States.

The committees write a large number of multiple-choice questions, which are pretested and evaluated for clarity, appropriateness, and range of possible answers. The committee also generates a pool of free-response questions, pretests them, and chooses those questions that best represent the full range of the scoring scale, which will allow the AP readers to evaluate the free-response answers equitably.

It is important to remember that every AP exam is thoroughly evaluated after it is administered each year. This way, the College Board can use the results to make course suggestions and to plan future tests.

THE AP GRADES AND WHO RECEIVES THEM

Once you have taken the exam and it has been scored, your test will be graded with one of five numbers by the College Board:

- A 5 indicates that you are extremely well qualified.
- A 4 indicates that you are well qualified.
- A 3 indicates that you are adequately qualified.
- A 2 indicates that you are possibly qualified.
- A 1 indicates that you are not qualified to receive college credit.

A grade of 5, 4, 3, 2, or 1 will usually be reported by early July.

REASONS FOR TAKING THE AP EXAMS

Why put yourself through a year of intensive study, pressure, stress, and preparation? Only you can answer that question. Following are some of the reasons that students have indicated to us for taking the AP exam:

- For personal satisfaction
- To compare themselves with other students across the nation
- Because colleges look favorably on the applications of students who elect to enroll in AP courses
- To receive college credit or advanced standing at their colleges or universities
- Because they love the subject
- So that their families will be really proud of them

There are plenty of other reasons, but no matter what they might be, the primary reason for your enrolling in an AP course and taking the exam in May is to feel good about yourself and the challenges that you have met.

QUESTIONS FREQUENTLY ASKED ABOUT THE AP EXAMS

Here are some common questions student have about the AP exams and some answers to those questions.

If I don't take an AP course, can I still take the AP exam?

Yes. Although the AP exams are designed for students who have had a year's course at the college level, some high schools do not offer such courses. Many students in these high schools have also done well on the exam although they have not taken the course. However, if your high school does offer AP courses, by all means take advantage of them and the structured background that they will provide you.

How are the AP exams organized?

AP exams generally have two parts and are scheduled to last two to three hours. The first section is a set of multiple-choice questions. After you complete this section, you will hand in your test booklet and scan sheet, and you will be given a brief break. The length of this break depends on the particular administrator. You will not be able to return to the multiple-choice questions when you resume the examination.

The second section of the exam is a writing or calculating segment consisting of mandatory, free-response questions or problems that cover broad topics.

Must I check the box at the end of the essay booklet that allows AP staff to use my essays as samples for research?

No. This is simply a way for the College Board to make certain that it has your permission if they decide to use one or more of your essays as a model. The readers of your essays pay no attention to whether or not that box is checked. Checking the box will not affect your grade.

How is the multiple-choice section scored?

The scan sheet with your answers is run through a computer, which counts the number of wrong answers and subtracts a fraction of that number from the number of correct answers. If there are five choices, the fraction is one fourth. A question left blank receives a zero. The formula for this calculation looks something like this (where N = the number of answers):

$$N_{right} - (N_{wrong} \times 0.25) = \text{raw score rounded up or down to nearest whole number}$$

How are my free-response answers scored?

Each of your answers is read by a different, trained AP reader called a *faculty consultant*. The AP/College Board members have developed a highly successful training program for their readers, together with many opportunities for checks and double checks of essays or problems to ensure a fair and equitable reading of each free-response answer.

The scoring guides are carefully developed by a chief faculty consultant, a question leader, table leaders, and content experts. All faculty consultants are then trained to read and score just *one* free-response question on the exam. They actually become experts in that one question. No one knows the identity of any writer. The identification numbers and names are covered, and the exam booklets are randomly distributed to the readers in equal packets of randomly chosen answers. Table leaders and the question leader review samples of each reader's scores to ensure that quality standards are constant.

Each free-response answer is scored on a scale from 1 to 10. Once your answers are graded on this scale the next set of calculations is completed.

Additional details on scoring the free-response section may be found in the chapter dealing with each specific exam.

How is my composite score calculated?

Your total composite score for the exam is determined by adding the score from the multiple-choice section to the score from the free-response section and rounding that sum to the nearest whole number. Additional details are given in each of the chapters.

How is my composite score turned into the grade that is reported to my college?

Keep in mind that the total composite scores needed to earn a 5, 4, 3, 2, or 1 change each year. These cutoffs are determined by a committee of AP, College Board, and Educational Testing Service (ETS) directors, experts, and statisticians. The same exam that is given to the AP high school students is given to college students. The various college professors report how the college students fared on the exam. This provides information for the chief faculty consultant on where to draw the lines for a 5, 4, 3, 2, or 1 score. A score of 5 on an AP exam is set to represent the average score received by the college students who scored an A on the exam. A score of a 3 or a 4 is the equivalent of a college grade B, and so on.

What should I bring to the exam?

Here are some suggestions:

- Several pencils and an eraser
- Several black pens (black ink is easier on the eyes)
- A watch (no beeping or alarm watches)
- A calculator (for Physics, Chemistry, Statistics, and Calculus*)
- Something to drink—water is best
- A quiet snack, such as Lifesavers
- Tissues

*Visit *www.collegeboard.com/ap* for a list of approved calculators.

Is there anything else I should be aware of?

You should

- Allow plenty of time to get to the test site.
- Wear comfortable clothing.
- Eat a light breakfast or lunch.
- Remind yourself that you are well prepared and that the test is an enjoyable challenge and a chance to share your knowledge. Be proud of yourself! You worked hard all year. Once test day comes, there is nothing further you can do. It is out of your hands, and your only job is to answer as many questions correctly as you possibly can.

What should I do the night before the exam?

Although few instructors vigorously support last-minute cramming, there may be some value to some last-minute review. Spending the night before the exam relaxing with family or friends is helpful for many students. Watch a movie, play a game, gab on the phone, then find a quiet spot to study. While you're unwinding, flip through your own notebook and review sheets. As you are approaching the date of the exam, you might want to put together a list of topics that have troubled you and review them briefly the night before the exam. Then turn off the light when you're ready to drift off. Pleasant dreams.

TIPS FOR TAKING THE AP EXAMS

The AP exam is a timed exam; keep this in mind as you prepare. When taking the various tests presented in this book, you should follow the AP exam rules as closely as possible. Anyone can improve his or her score by using notes, books, or an unlimited time. You will have none of these on the AP exam, so resist the temptation to use them on practice exams. Carefully time yourself; do not use other materials; and only use a calculator when expressly allowed to do so. After you have finished an exam, you may use other sources to go over questions you missed or skipped. We have seen many students get into trouble because the first time they attempted a test under "test conditions" was on the day of the AP exam itself.

Following are some suggestions for taking the multiple-choice and free-response parts of an exam.

Multiple-Choice Questions

Here are a few rules of thumb:

1. *Don't outthink the test.* It is indeed possible to be too smart for your own good. If you happen to know the answer immediately, this does not mean that the question is too easy. First, give yourself credit for knowing a fact. They asked you something, you knew it, and *wham,* you fill in the bubble. Do not overanalyze the question and assume that your answer is too obvious for that question. Just because you get it doesn't mean that it was too easy.

2. *Don't be afraid to leave questions blank.* This exam penalizes the random guess. Generally, it will take off $\frac{1}{4}$ point for *each* wrong answer you give. For this reason, do not wildly guess at questions simply because you don't want to leave anything blank. However, although a random guess is bad, an educated guess is good. If you can eliminate

answers that you know for sure are not the right answer, and get it down to two or three choices, go for it! Take a stab! But no random pick guesses, please!

3. *Be on the lookout for trick wording!* Always pay attention to words or phrases such as "least," "most," "not," "incorrectly," and "does not belong." Do not answer the wrong question. There are few things as annoying as getting a $\frac{1}{4}$ point off on this test simply because you didn't read the question carefully enough, especially if you know the right answer.

4. *Use your time carefully.* You usually have a minute or less per question on the multiple-choice section of the exam. If you find yourself struggling on a question, try not to waste too much time on it. Circle it in the booklet, and come back to it later if time permits. This test should be an exercise in window shopping. It does not matter *which* questions you get correct. What is important is that you answer enough questions correctly. Find the subjects that you know the best, answer those questions, and save the others for review later on.

5. *Be careful about changing answers!* If you have answered a question already, but come back to it later on and get the urge to change it . . . make sure that you have a real *reason* to change it. Often an urge to change an answer is the work of exam "elves" in the room who want to trick you into picking a wrong answer. Change your answer only if you can justify your reasons for making the switch.

Free-Response Questions

Here are a few basic guidelines:

1. *The makeup of the question.* The free-response questions tend to be multipart questions. The test preparers are not unrealistic, and they recognize that nobody knows everything about every topic. Therefore, they show a touch of kindness on the free-response section by often constructing the questions so that the test-taker must answer *two* of three, or *three* of four.

2. *Budget your time wisely.* As an example, let's say that you have 90 minutes to answer four free-response questions. This translates into 22.5 minutes per essay or problem. It would be fair to say that you will probably spend 1–3 minutes reading the question to figure out what the exam graders want to know. The next 2 minutes should be used to ponder your answer. For an essay, use 2–4 minutes to construct a basic outline of what you want to write for each question. The remaining 14–19 minutes should be spent writing your response. If it is a two-part question, spend approximately half of the time on each section. If it is a three-part question, divide your time up three ways and spend approximately 5 minutes per section.

3. *Spread the wealth!* The free-response questions are graded in a way that forces the student to provide information for each section of the question. You can receive only a set maximum number of points for each subquestion. For example, in a question that asks you to answer *three* of the following four choices, most likely the grader's guidelines will say something along the lines of "You can give the student a maximum of only three points for part A, a maximum of three points for part B, and a maximum of four points for part C." This is a very important point for you to realize as a test-taker. This means that it is more important for you to attempt to answer every question than to try to stuff every little fact you know about part A into that portion of the essay. You could write the most fantastic essay ever submitted on the subject matter found in part A, and yet receive only a 3 out of 10 on the question if you ignore parts B and C. No matter how great your essay may be, the grader can give you only the maximum points allowed.

Also, be sure to write the various answers to the different parts of the question in separate paragraphs so that the essay reader is definitely able to give you as many points as you deserve.

4. *If you will be writing an essay, make an outline.* When you have read the question and know what the exam is asking you, it is time to make a quick outline. Don't write the most elaborate outline—just jot down enough notes so that you have an idea of how you are going to construct your essay. While the reader is not grading you according to how well the essay is constructed, it will not hurt your score to attempt to write it in a well-organized and grammatically correct fashion. A quick outline can help you organize your thoughts more clearly, and also help you make sure that you do not leave out any important information.

5. *Two wrongs can still make a right.* An interesting twist to the free-response section of many AP exams is that wrong information in an essay is simply ignored. You do not lose points for saying things that are incorrect, but you do not *get* points for saying things that are incorrect either. So, if you are unsure about something, and *think* it may be right, give it a shot, and include it in your essay. It certainly cannot hurt. This is called "positive scoring."

Chapter 2

AP U.S. History

Answer Sheet for Multiple-Choice Questions

1. _____	21. _____	41. _____	61. _____
2. _____	22. _____	42. _____	62. _____
3. _____	23. _____	43. _____	63. _____
4. _____	24. _____	44. _____	64. _____
5. _____	25. _____	45. _____	65. _____
6. _____	26. _____	46. _____	66. _____
7. _____	27. _____	47. _____	67. _____
8. _____	28. _____	48. _____	68. _____
9. _____	29. _____	49. _____	69. _____
10. _____	30. _____	50. _____	70. _____
11. _____	31. _____	51. _____	71. _____
12. _____	32. _____	52. _____	72. _____
13. _____	33. _____	53. _____	73. _____
14. _____	34. _____	54. _____	74. _____
15. _____	35. _____	55. _____	75. _____
16. _____	36. _____	56. _____	76. _____
17. _____	37. _____	57. _____	77. _____
18. _____	38. _____	58. _____	78. _____
19. _____	39. _____	59. _____	79. _____
20. _____	40. _____	60. _____	80. _____

Scoring Formula:

$$\underline{\hspace{3cm}} - \underline{\hspace{4cm}} = \underline{\hspace{3cm}}$$
number right   (number wrong × .25)   raw score

AP U.S. HISTORY

Section I

Time—55 minutes

80 questions

Directions: Each of the questions or incomplete statements below is followed by five suggested answers or completions. Select the one that is best in each case and write your answer neatly on the answer sheet.

1. The headright system

   A. enabled wealthy property owners to acquire more land by paying the passage of indentured servants
   B. gave farmers in New England a greater share of the town commons for each head of cattle they raised
   C. placed restrictions on the mobility of slaves in colonial Virginia
   D. outlawed capital punishment for most criminal offenses in British North America
   E. made women in colonial New England subordinate to men in all legal matters

2. The Eisenhower Doctrine attempted to

   A. improve relations with Latin American countries
   B. undermine the government of Fidel Castro
   C. arrest the spread of communism in the Middle East
   D. funnel millions of dollars of business investments into Africa and Asia
   E. lower international tariffs

3. "Abolish slavery in all its forms and aspects, advocate universal emancipation, exalt the standard of public morality, and promote the moral and intellectual improvement of the colored people, and hasten the day of freedom to the Three Millions of our enslaved fellow countrymen."

   The preceding quotation comes from the masthead of the abolitionist newspaper *The North Star*. Its founder was

   A. William Lloyd Garrison
   B. Frederick Douglass
   C. Phyllis Wheatley
   D. Harriet Tubman
   E. Angelina Grimke

4. Demonstrating a significant shift in government policy toward organized labor, which of the following presidents sided with anthracite coal miners in their strike against mine owners?

   A. Grover Cleveland
   B. Woodrow Wilson
   C. William H. Taft
   D. Theodore Roosevelt
   E. Benjamin Harrison

5. Which of the following was a women's rights advocate who published *The Feminine Mystique* in 1963?

   A. Phyllis Schlafly
   B. Geraldine Ferraro
   C. Shirley Chisolm
   D. Gloria Steinem
   E. Betty Friedan

6. Which of the following best explains why President Andrew Jackson resisted annexing Texas during his administration?

   A. He feared that annexation would strengthen the Whig party.
   B. He knew annexation would lead to war with France, which possessed land along the Texas border.
   C. He believed that the addition of another agricultural state would hurt the developing commercial economy.
   D. He had consistently opposed westward expansion.
   E. He feared that debates over annexation would exacerbate sectional strife.

7. The Nineteenth Amendment achieved one of the goals of the Progressives by

   A. granting women the right to vote
   B. establishing Prohibition

    C. providing for the direct election of senators

    D. ensuring citizenship rights for African-Americans

    E. establishing term limits for elected officials

8. Which of the following statements best captures public sentiment about the Great Railroad Strike of 1877?

    A. The strike only affected people along the Pacific Coast and thus only met with regional opposition.

    B. The American public sided with the African-American sleeping car porters.

    C. Applauding the intervention of President Theodore Roosevelt, the American people sided with the railway workers' union throughout the strike.

    D. Public opinion shifted from sympathy to condemnation as people blamed the strikers for looting and violence.

    E. Rendered apathetic by their belief in "laissez-faire," the American public expressed no opinion on the strike.

9. The *Chesapeake* Incident (1807) involved

    A. the sinking of a British ship off the coast of Maryland

    B. an Anglo-American conflict over the issue of impressment

    C. an investigation of illegal smuggling of slaves into the United States

    D. the seizure of an American merchant ship by the French navy in the English Channel

    E. an attack by the Iroquois on an American fort near the Great Lakes

10. During the Civil War, the Peninsular Campaign (1862) revealed

    A. Ulysses S. Grant's determination to destroy Robert E. Lee's Army of Northern Virginia

    B. Henry Halleck's jealousy of Grant's success on the battlefield

    C. George McClellan's tentativeness

    D. William T. Sherman's application of "total warfare"

    E. the Confederate resolve to keep New Orleans and Vicksburg from falling under Union control

11. Which of the following methods of colonial resistance achieved the greatest success in reversing Parliamentary legislation before the Revolutionary War?

    A. Petitions to King George III

    B. The Sons of Liberty

    C. Boycotts of British goods

    D. The intercession of colonial governors

    E. Contradictory legislation passed by the colonial assemblies

12. The "Saturday Night Massacre" refers to

    A. the death of four students at Kent State in 1970

    B. President Hoover's attempt to remove the Bonus Marchers from Washington, DC in 1932

    C. the assassination of President John F. Kennedy

    D. the clash between civil rights marchers and the Alabama state police on the Edmund Pettus Bridge

    E. President Richard Nixon's attempts to remove special prosecutor Archibald Cox from the Watergate investigation

13. The Dred Scott decision

    A. undermined the authority of Congress to limit the expansion of slavery into the territories

    B. overturned the Fugitive Slave Law

    C. emphasized the supremacy of civilian courts in response to President Lincoln's suspension of habeas corpus in Maryland

    D. silenced the abolitionist press by limiting the proliferation of antislavery newspapers in the South

    E. expanded Congress's naturalization powers

14. As governor of the state of Wisconsin, which of the following instituted Progressive reforms such as the initiative, referendum, and state income tax?

    A. Charles Evans Hughes

    B. Woodrow Wilson

    C. Eugene Debs

    D. Hiram Johnson

    E. Robert La Follette

15. The Constitution provided for both the federal government and the states to share the power to

A. coin money
B. regulate interstate commerce
C. establish post offices
D. control the state militias
E. admit new states

16. Which of the following statements best describes Chief Justice Roger B. Taney's decision in *Charles River Bridge* v. *Warren Bridge* (1837)?

   A. Taney overturned John Marshall's decision in *McCulloch* v. *Maryland*.
   B. Taney expanded economic opportunity and the powers of a state government.
   C. Taney supported Jackson's opposition to using federal funds on internal improvements.
   D. Taney granted the Charles River Bridge Company exclusive rights to control toll bridges into Boston.
   E. Taney rejected the principle of nullification.

17. At the turn of the nineteenth century, the emergence of Wild West shows and vaudeville demonstrated

   A. an effort by wealthy Americans to recapture a mythic past
   B. the rejection of the early movie industry
   C. a declining emphasis on outdoor recreation
   D. the growing importance of popular culture
   E. a popularization of immigrant traditions brought to the United States

18. Which of the following presidents sent federal troops to Little Rock, Arkansas, when Governor Orval Faubus attempted to stop the integration of Central High School?

   A. Harry S Truman
   B. John F. Kennedy
   C. Dwight D. Eisenhower
   D. Lyndon B. Johnson
   E. Richard M. Nixon

19. Which of the following technological innovations contributed the most to the economic development of the United States during the first four decades of the nineteenth century?

   A. Cotton gin
   B. Rubber
   C. Chilled steel plow
   D. Electricity
   E. Barbed wire

20. Which of the following statements best supports Charles Beard's interpretation of the Constitution?

   A. The authors of the Constitution emphasized libertarian over conservative interests.
   B. The Constitution reflected the interests of the upper class of American society.
   C. The authors of the Constitution remained deliberately vague on the issue of slavery.
   D. The Constitution reflected the local or regional interests of the signers.
   E. The Constitution captured a broad consensus of American society.

21. Which of the following statements best summarizes Abraham Lincoln's views on John Brown's raid at Harper's Ferry in 1859?

   A. He distanced his party from Brown and his followers.
   B. He criticized Southerners who wanted to execute Brown.
   C. He supported Brown as a fellow Republican.
   D. He supported Brown's method but not his goal.
   E. He praised Brown's goal but criticized his failure to motivate more slaves to join him.

22. "Stagflation," an economic problem characterized by high inflation at a time of slow economic growth, plagued the administration of

   A. Dwight D. Eisenhower
   B. Richard M. Nixon
   C. Franklin D. Roosevelt
   D. Harry S Truman
   E. Ronald Reagan

23. In an effort to thwart Progressive state legislation, the Supreme Court reinterpreted

   A. its original ruling in *Plessy* v. *Ferguson*
   B. the theory of Social Darwinism
   C. its earliest antitrust suit in the *E. C. Knight* v. *United States* case
   D. the property clause of the Sixteenth Amendment
   E. the "due-process" clause of the Fourteenth Amendment.

24. Which of the following best describes the Hartford Convention?

A. It expressed Southern concerns over the Fugitive Slave Act.

B. It established the foundations of the Whig party.

C. It produced a series of non-importation agreements among Britain's North American colonies.

D. It led to the demise of the Federalists.

E. It nominated Andrew Jackson for president.

25. Medicaid provided

A. medical insurance for the elderly

B. medical relief under the Marshall Plan

C. medical insurance for the impoverished

D. a regulatory agency of the health profession

E. a medical corps for soldiers during the Vietnam War

26. During the first half of the nineteenth century, the expansion of suffrage increased popular interest in presidential elections. Partisan politics often shifted the voters' attention from issues to images. The "log cabin, hard cider" campaign helped which candidate win the presidency?

A. James Monroe in 1820

B. John Quincy Adams in 1824

C. Andrew Jackson in 1828

D. William Henry Harrison in 1840

E. James K. Polk in 1844

27. McCarthyism spawned a hysteria that swept over the nation during the early Cold War. Accusations of links to communism ruined numerous people and their careers. The decline of Joe McCarthy came after his televised hearings with

A. the House Un-American Activities Committee

B. the Army

C. Edward R. Murrow

D. the State Department

E. the FBI

28. All of the following statements about President Thomas Jefferson's administration are true *except*

A. Jefferson waged an undeclared war on the Barbary pirates

B. Jefferson sought to influence the conviction of Aaron Burr for treason

C. Jefferson kept in place many Federalist economic policies

D. Jefferson moved to cut government expenditures

E. Jefferson consistently acted as strict constructionist

29. In 1676, Bacon's Rebellion signaled that

A. colonial taxes fell more heavily on eastern counties than western counties

B. Nathaniel Bacon's extremist views were only supported by the younger sons of Virginia's wealthy planters

C. supposedly docile, loyal slaves could, in fact, turn on their masters

D. colonial governors struggled to contain domestic unrest

E. excise taxes on whiskey were unpopular with western farmers

30. Although criticized by 1960s conservatives, the Supreme Court case of *Gideon* v. *Wainwright* ensured that those accused of crimes

A. were informed of the specific charges drawn against them

B. were entitled to a lawyer even if they could not afford one

C. had the right to remain silent

D. did not have to testify against family members

E. were protected against illegal "searches and seizures"

31. The paintings of Charles Willson Peale and Gilbert Stuart

A. represent the emerging nationalism of the post-Revolutionary era

B. reflected the sentiments of the Transcendentalists of the 1840s

C. were connected to the Ashcan school of painting

D. were sponsored by the Works Progress Administration (WPA)

E. focused upon classical rather than modern themes

32. In response to the sinking of the USS *Panay* and three American commercial vessels in 1937,

the American public urged President Franklin Roosevelt to

A. impose economic sanctions on Japan
B. declare war on Germany
C. withdraw American ships from China
D. prohibit the sale of arms and munitions to belligerent nations
E. extend Lend-Lease to the Soviet Union

33. Which of the following statements best expresses the outcome of the French and Indian War (1754 to 1763)?

A. It restored a balance of power between the French, British, and native tribes of North America.
B. It ended Indian resistance to white expansion east of the Mississippi River.
C. It opened the trans-Appalachia west to American trade.
D. It demonstrated the political unity of Britain's North American colonies.
E. It forced Great Britain to reevaluate the administration of its colonial affairs.

34. Jane Addams was significant for

A. voting against a congressional declaration of war in 1917
B. writing the book *Silent Spring*, which raised concerns about the pollution of American waters
C. founding Hull House, a settlement house in Chicago
D. establishing the National Organization of Women
E. helping organize the Populist party in Kansas

35. In order to limit opposition to his liberal domestic programs, which of the following presidents attempted to expand the size of the Supreme Court from 9 to 12 justices?

A. Theodore Roosevelt
B. Woodrow Wilson
C. Harry S Truman
D. Franklin D. Roosevelt
E. John F. Kennedy

36. As settlers from various nations arrived in North America, they interacted differently with the native tribes. A major difference between French and British settlers was that

A. French treated natives with more respect and intermarried with some tribes
B. the French fur traders waged more bloody wars with native tribes before 1720
C. British settlers were less interested in establishing permanent settlements
D. only the French attempted to convert the natives
E. the French outnumbered the British before 1754

37. Which of the following individuals founded Standard Oil Trust, which dominated the oil refining industry in the late nineteenth century?

A. Leland Stanford
B. Andrew Carnegie
C. J. P. Morgan
D. Henry George
E. John D. Rockefeller

38. Which of the following statements about the antebellum mining frontier is *not* true?

A. Few miners were interested in permanently settling in the West.
B. In spite of the hardships, women flocked to California in large numbers.
C. Miners persecuted the native tribes of the West.
D. Mining towns were often disorderly, lawless communities.
E. Some foreign miners competed with Americans for gold.

39. What best explains the decline in immigration during the years pictured in the graph on the following page?

A. Postwar recession ruined the agricultural economy.
B. Slow industrial expansion limited available job opportunities.
C. Nativistic legislation restricted immigration from certain nations.
D. Government land policy favored speculators over individual purchasers.
E. Better employment opportunities existed in Europe rather than in the United States.

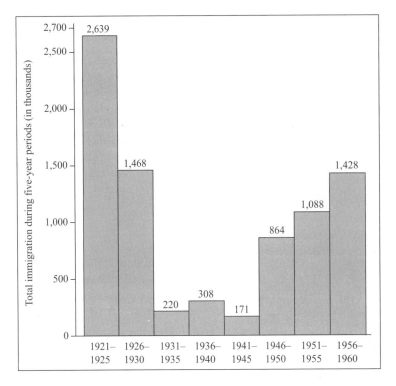

TOTAL IMMIGRATION, 1920–1960

40. Which of the following was a foreign affairs issue during the administration of President Jimmy Carter?

A. Iranian hostage crisis
B. Iran-Contra affair
C. North American Free Trade Agreement (NAFTA)
D. Invasion of Panama to arrest Manuel Noriega
E. Fall of Saigon

41. The Annapolis Convention succeeded in

A. resolving a boundary dispute between Maryland and Pennsylvania
B. uniting British colonists against the French
C. convincing Confederation leaders to call a constitutional convention
D. resolving tariff issues
E. settling disputes over the slave trade in North America

42. In the antebellum period, the largest number of women working outside of the home could be found in which of the following professions?

A. Nursing
B. Education
C. Secretarial
D. Textiles
E. Law

43. As part of his "Square Deal," which president signed the Pure Food and Drug Act and the Hepburn Act?

A. Benjamin Harrison
B. Grover Cleveland
C. William McKinley
D. Woodrow Wilson
E. Theodore Roosevelt

44. The Dawes Severalty Act of 1887 attempted to

A. provide economic aid to war-torn European nations
B. force Native Americans to assimilate into white society
C. set lower railroad rates
D. promote western land sales to railroad companies
E. lower tariffs on foreign industrial goods

45. Arthur and William Levitt were responsible for which of the following icons of the 1950s?

A. Standardized suburban communities
B. Polio vaccine

C. *Leave It to Beaver*
D. Hydrogen bomb
E. Electric refrigerators

46. When Congress gained control of Reconstruction policy, Radical Republican leaders

A. hastened the readmission of the seceded states according to President Abraham Lincoln's "10 Percent Plan"
B. redistributed thousands of acres of land formerly owned by slave masters
C. divided the South into military districts to be occupied by the Union army until loyal governments could be created
D. sought only to limit the involvement of the highest Confederate leaders in postwar governments
E. prohibited Northern business investments in the Southern economy as a means of punishing the former Confederacy for secession

47. The "*Sussex* pledge" was

A. President Nixon's promise to release the Watergate tapes
B. President Franklin Roosevelt's promise to provide relief to American farmers
C. a protest statement written by the SDS (Students for a Democratic Society)
D. a plan for postwar Europe stemming from the Yalta Conference
E. a statement by Germany promising to stop unrestricted U-boat warfare

48. Which of the following statements about the Whig party is true?

A. Party members universally opposed the expansion of slavery into the territories.
B. The party succeeded in winning only one election.
C. Party members tended to advocate nationalistic economic policies.
D. The party emerged immediately after the demise of the Federalists.
E. Party members sought to enlist the votes of immigrants.

49. In the late nineteenth century, the growth of cities was caused in part by the

A. settlement house movement
B. rise of public education
C. absence of nativism

D. expansion of industry
E. increasing importance of political machines

50. Racial tensions and fears of espionage led President Franklin D. Roosevelt to issue Executive Order 9066. As a result, which of the following groups were forced into "relocation" camps?

A. Italian-Americans
B. Japanese-Americans
C. German-Americans
D. Mexican immigrants
E. Socialists

51. The Tet Offensive (1968)

A. demonstrated that the United States was no closer to ending the Vietnam War
B. revealed the success of Nixon's Vietnamization plans
C. temporarily reversed the rising popular opposition to the war
D. improved Johnson's bid for reelection
E. enabled American forces to enter North Vietnam

52. American colonists opposed the passage of the Stamp Act (1765) primarily because it

A. severely limited colonial commerce
B. followed the passage of the unpopular Townshend Acts
C. was too expensive for average colonists
D. did not receive the endorsement of the king
E. imposed a revenue tax

53. Beginning in 1872, mail-order catalogs

A. ruined small businesses
B. promoted the sale of industrial goods in rural areas
C. replaced billboards as the primary means of business advertisement
D. expanded American markets overseas
E. caused the reorganization of the postal system

54. Which of the following statements best asserts the principle of "popular sovereignty?"

A. Congress has the authority to decide where slavery may or may not exist.
B. Political parties provided the best forum for the resolution of the slavery issue.

C. The American people shall decide where slavery will exist by creating a national law in a special legislative convention.

D. The settlers in a given territory have the sole right to decide whether or not slavery will be permitted there.

E. Individual states have the right to reject congressional decisions concerning slavery.

55. All of the following were means of slave resistance during the antebellum period *except*

A. running away
B. breaking tools and slowing down the pace of work
C. field songs
D. adaptations of slave religion
E. frequent bloody slave revolts

56. The Servicemen's Readjustment Act, popularly known as the GI Bill of Rights, granted financial assistance and opened new educational opportunities for veterans. It was passed by

A. Woodrow Wilson.
B. Warren G. Harding
C. Franklin D. Roosevelt.
D. Harry S Truman.
E. Richard Nixon.

57. The Monroe Doctrine (1823) intended to

A. reverse George Washington's neutrality policy
B. eliminate British influence in North America
C. restrict European involvement in the Western Hemisphere
D. facilitate the expansion of American trade in the West Indies
E. open South America to American colonization

58. The federal government promoted the settlement of the Great Plains in the nineteenth century through the passage of the

A. Reclamation Act
B. Homestead Act
C. Gadsden Purchase
D. Webster-Ashburton Treaty
E. Soil Conservation and Domestic Allotment Act

59. One difference between the Middle Colonies and the other British colonies in North America was that

A. residents of the Middle Colonies represented more diverse nationalities
B. the Middles Colonies outstripped their neighbors in the production of tobacco
C. the Middle Colonies developed a primarily industrial economy
D. the residents of the Middle Colonies had little interaction with the native tribes
E. no settlers in the Middle Colonies owned slaves

60. Which of the following was *not* an issue associated with the Kennedy administration?

A. Integration of the University of Mississippi
B. Bay of Pigs Invasion
C. Construction of the Berlin Wall
D. Trade Expansion Act
E. U-2 incident

61. At the turn of the century, the United States favored the Open-Door policy in order to

A. encourage trade among its overseas colonies
B. protect the governments of Latin America
C. ensure that it would have its share in China's trade
D. promote the use of the Panama Canal
E. cripple the Nazi war effort

62. The Northwest Ordinances

A. provided a means to establish new states in the territory ceded in the Treaty of Paris (1783)
B. admitted Oregon and Washington to the Union
C. sanctioned the exploration of the Louisiana Purchase
D. restricted westward expansion
E. were supported mostly by farmers and railroad companies seeking the removal of Indian tribes

63. Breaking with precedent, President Woodrow Wilson went abroad to negotiate a treaty to end World War I. He supported the Treaty of Versailles because it

A. banned submarine warfare
B. blamed Germany for starting the war

C. divided Germany into occupation zones
D. provided for the creation of the League of Nations
E. gave the United States trading privileges in Great Britain

64. The intent of the Alien and Sedition Acts was to

A. weaken the opponents of John Adams
B. expand the meaning of the First Amendment
C. protect the rights of recent immigrants
D. expel French residents of the Louisiana Purchase
E. require all newspapers to be printed in English

65. Which of the following statements about the First Great Awakening is true?

A. It led to the founding of new colonies in North America.
B. It splintered existing congregations and churches.
C. It found most of its converts in the commercial cities of the East Coast.
D. It strengthened the authority of established religious figures.
E. It cemented the ties between colonial governments and religious denominations.

66. The WPA

A. supported Prohibition during the 1920s
B. was a conservation organization started by John Muir
C. promoted rationing during World War I
D. addressed unfair hiring practices during World War II
E. attempted to revive the economy by creating jobs in the 1930s

67. Harriet Beecher Stowe was notable for

A. organizing an early women's rights convention
B. promoting the reform of prisons and asylums
C. writing the abolitionist novel *Uncle Tom's Cabin*
D. leading slaves to freedom along the Underground Railroad
E. founding a utopian community at New Harmony

68. Which of the following statements is true about the election of 1972?

A. Nixon was the first Republican candidate to carry the "Solid South."
B. Nixon's opponent, Democrat George McGovern, had reunited a party divided since 1968.
C. Nixon benefited from the first economic boom since 1945.
D. Nixon placed Gerald Ford on the ballot to win votes from the Midwest.
E. Nixon struggled to defeat challenger Ronald Reagan in the Republican primary.

69. The term "Dust Bowl" refers to which area of the nation ravaged by drought during the Great Depression?

A. The West Coast
B. South Carolina to Mississippi
C. New England
D. Texas to the Dakotas
E. The Mississippi Delta

70. After the War of 1812, the United States government sought to

A. stimulate trade by lowering tariffs
B. improve commerce with Great Britain in a series of favorable treaties
C. slow the pace of westward expansion
D. redistribute British property seized during the war
E. renew the charter of the Bank of the United States

71. The passage of the first graduated income tax enabled the federal government to rely less upon which of its traditional sources of income?

A. The sale of public lands
B. High tariffs
C. Sale of war bonds
D. Bank loans
E. Corporate taxes

72. In the post-Reconstruction South, white Southerners attempted to circumscribe the citizenship rights of African-Americans by restoring the social customs of the "Old South." Which of the following means of limiting black freedom found its predecessor in the antebellum period?

A. The Ku Klux Klan
B. "Grandfather clause"
C. National legalized segregation
D. "Black Codes"
E. Literacy tests for voting

73. The Strategic Defense Initiative ("Star Wars"), which intended to use lasers and satellites to counter Soviet nuclear weapons, was proposed under

A. Gerald Ford
B. Jimmy Carter
C. Ronald Reagan
D. George Bush
E. Bill Clinton

74. "It was the best of nationally advertised and quantitatively produced alarm clocks, with all modern attachments, including cathedral chime, intermittent alarm, and phosphorescent dial. Babbitt was proud of being wakened by such a rich device. Socially, it was almost as creditable as buying expensive cord tires."

In *Babbitt*, which of the following authors criticized the shallow materialism of his or her contemporaries?

A. Sinclair Lewis
B. John Steinbeck
C. Ida Tarbell
D. Bruce Barton
E. Jack London

75. The intent of British mercantile legislation before 1750 was to

A. cripple the colonial economy in North America
B. promote favorable trade between Great Britain and its colonies
C. give special trade privileges to its North American colonies
D. limit the growth of a merchant class in the colonies
E. prevent the founding of new colonies west of the Appalachian mountains

76. Which of the following diplomatic initiatives during the Cold War best matches the goal of Franklin D. Roosevelt's "Good Neighbor" policy?

A. Eisenhower Doctrine
B. Alliance for Progress

C. Mann Doctrine
D. SALT II
E. Warsaw Pact

77. Reform legislation, including stricter building codes and factory inspection acts, followed a horrendous fire in 1911 that claimed 146 lives at the

A. Triangle Shirtwaist Company (New York)
B. International Harvester Corporation (Chicago)
C. Swift meatpacking plant (Chicago)
D. U.S. Steel Corporation (Pittsburgh)
E. Bessemer Steel Corporation (New York)

78. Which of the following was *not* a provision of the Compromise of 1850?

A. Admission of California as a free state
B. No congressional restriction on slavery in the Mexican Cession
C. Settlement of the Texas and New Mexico boundary issue
D. Prohibition of the slave trade in Washington, DC
E. Appropriation of federal funds for railroad construction in the Southwest

79. Which of the following Supreme Court cases could be viewed as a victory for the opponents of reform?

A. *Swift and Company* v. *United States*, 1905
B. *Lochner* v. *United States*, 1905
C. *National Securities Company* v. *United States*, 1904
D. *Standard Oil of NJ* v. *United States*, 1911
E. *American Tobacco Company* v. *United States*, 1911

80. The cartoon, on the following page, by Thomas Nast

A. called for reform of American prisons
B. opposed imperialism
C. attacked political corruption
D. demanded improvements in the educational system
E. criticized new child labor laws

The political cartoon, "Tweed-le-dee and Tilden-dum,"
Harper's Weekly, July 1, 1876; courtesy of the Library
of Congress.

END OF SECTION I

AP U.S. HISTORY

Section II

Part A

Time—45 minutes

Directions: The following question requires you to construct a coherent essay that integrates your interpretation of Documents A to H *and* your knowledge of the period referred to in the question. High scores will be earned only by essays that both cite key pieces of evidence from the documents and draw on outside knowledge of the period.

1. At the turn of the century, several nations were competing for international empires. After the Spanish-American War, the United States government sought to extend and solidify its influence in the Western Hemisphere. Analyze the effects of American foreign policy in Latin America in the period 1899 to 1917.

Document A
Source: Platt Amendment, May 22, 1903

> *Article III. The Government of Cuba consents that the United States may exercise the right to intervene for the preservation of Cuban independence, the maintenance of a government adequate for the protection of life, property, and individual liberty, and for discharging the obligations with respect to Cuba imposed by the Treaty of Paris on the United States, now to be assumed and undertaken by the Government of Cuba.*

Document B
Source: Hay-Bunau-Varilla Treaty, November 18, 1903

> *The Republic of Panama grants to the United States in perpetuity, the use, occupation and control of a zone of land and land under water for the construction . . . of said canal. . . . The Republic of Panama further grants to the United States in perpetuity, the use, occupation and control of any other lands and waters outside the zone . . . which may be necessary and convenient for the construction . . . and protection of the said Canal.*

Document C
Source: John Wilson Bengough, "Autonomy," *The Public*, January 23, 1904; courtesy of BoondocksNet.com.

Document D
Source: Theodore Roosevelt, Annual Message to Congress, December 6, 1904

> *If a nation shows that it knows how to act with reasonable efficiency and decency in social and political matters, if it keeps order and pays its obligations, it need fear no interference from the United States. Chronic wrongdoing, or an impotence which results in a general loosening of the ties of civilized society, may . . . ultimately require intervention by some civilized nation, and in the Western Hemisphere the adherence of the United States to the Monroe Doctrine may lead the United States, . . . in flagrant cases of such wrongdoing or impotence, to exercise an international police power.*

Document E
Source: W. A. Rogers, "The Full Dinner Pail," *Harper's Weekly,* April 13, 1907; courtesy of Theodore-Roosevelt.com.

Document F

Source: William Howard Taft, Fourth Annual Message to Congress, December 3, 1912

> *The diplomacy of the present administration has sought to respond to modern ideas of commercial intercourse. This policy has been characterized by substituting dollars for bullets. . . . It is an effort frankly directed to the increase of American trade upon the axiomatic principle that the government of the United States shall extend all proper support to every legitimate and beneficial American enterprise abroad.*

Document G

Source: Erving Winslow, "Aggression in South America," excerpt from Report of the Thirteenth Annual Meeting of the Anti-Imperialist League, 1912

> *It is proposed that in the Honduras and Nicaragua . . . the United States government should be authorized to secure the collection and disbursement of the revenue in the interest of American capitalists who contemplate making loans to those countries. This involves serious risk of complications which may lead to further interferences and ultimate control.*
>
> *The delicacy of these and other foreign relations of the United States is such as should put our citizens upon their guard and confirm their determination to treat with justice all their neighbors and to recognize generally their independent right to govern (or misgovern) their own countries.*

Document H
Source: Nelson Harding, "Uncle Sam: 'I Smell Oil!,'" *Brooklyn Eagle,* reprinted from *American Review of Reviews,* January 1914; courtesy of BoondocksNet.com.

Document I
Source: Woodrow Wilson, Address to Congress, April 20, 1914

> *A series of incidents have recently occurred which cannot but create the impression that the representatives of General Huerta were willing to go out of their way to show disregard for the dignity and rights of this government, . . . making free to show in many ways their irritation and contempt.*
>
> *I, therefore, come to ask your approval that I should use the armed forces of the United States in such ways . . . as may be necessary to obtain from General Huerta and his adherents the fullest recognition of the rights and dignity of the United States, even amidst the distressing conditions now unhappily obtaining in Mexico.*

AP U.S. HISTORY

Section II

Part B and Part C

Time—70 minutes

Part B

Directions: Choose *one* question from this part. You are advised to spend 5 minutes planning and 30 minutes writing your answer. Cite relevant historical evidence in support of your generalizations, and present your arguments clearly and logically.

2. Evaluate the impact of *two* of the following in diffusing domestic tensions during the nineteenth century:

Compromise of 1820

Compromise of 1833

Compromise of 1877

3. Explain the impact of the Kansas-Nebraska Act upon national politics, 1854 to 1860.

Part C

Directions: Choose *one* question from this part. You are advised to spend 5 minutes planning and 30 minutes writing your answer. Cite relevant historical evidence in support of your generalizations, and present your arguments clearly and logically.

4. Analyze the causes of the Great Depression.

5. Evaluate the success of the containment policies of the Truman administration, 1945 to 1953.

END OF SECTION II

ANSWERS TO MULTIPLE-CHOICE QUESTIONS

Answer Key

1.	A	21.	A	41.	C	61.	C
2.	C	22.	B	42.	D	62.	A
3.	B	23.	E	43.	E	63.	D
4.	D	24.	D	44.	B	64.	A
5.	E	25.	C	45.	A	65.	B
6.	E	26.	D	46.	C	66.	E
7.	A	27.	B	47.	E	67.	C
8.	D	28.	E	48.	C	68.	A
9.	B	29.	D	49.	D	69.	D
10.	C	30.	B	50.	B	70.	E
11.	C	31.	A	51.	A	71.	B
12.	E	32.	C	52.	E	72.	D
13.	A	33.	E	53.	B	73.	C
14.	E	34.	C	54.	D	74.	A
15.	D	35.	D	55.	E	75.	B
16.	B	36.	A	56.	D	76.	B
17.	D	37.	E	57.	C	77.	A
18.	C	38.	B	58.	B	78.	E
19.	A	39.	C	59.	A	79.	B
20.	B	40.	A	60.	E	80.	C

Explanations of Answers to the Multiple-Choice Questions

1. **A.** The headright system stimulated population growth in colonial Virginia. Planters who helped bring more settlers to the colony received "headrights" of 50 acres. Any planter who imported indentured servants could accumulate sizable tracts of land. The system conferred some political privileges to the holders of large estates.

2. **C.** Similar to the Truman Doctrine, President Eisenhower's policies intended to halt the spread of communism and limit the influence of pan-Arab nationalism. In the wake of the Suez crisis, Eisenhower offered economic and military aid to pro-Western governments. American aid and presence helped Jordan's King Hussein suppress internal strife. In 1958, American marines landed in Lebanon to protect the government of Camile Chamoun.

3. **B.** Garrison, Douglass, Tubman, and Grimke were antebellum abolitionists. Both Garrison and Douglass established newspapers with wide circulations. Douglass established *The North Star;* Garrison founded *The Liberator.*

4. **D.** Before the twentieth century, the labor movement had yet to build significant public support. Government officials at the state and federal level often sent troops to disperse labor strikes. Theodore Roosevelt, William Howard Taft, and Woodrow Wilson resided in the White House during part of the Progressive era. The United Mine Workers, led by John Mitchell, struck against anthracite mine operators in 1902 for higher wages, an eight-hour work day, and, most importantly, recognition of the union. When mine operators refused to compromise, Roosevelt threatened to send in federal troops. The president's position forced operators to agree to arbitration.

5. **E.** Betty Friedan published her attack upon sexism and spurred the modern feminist movement. Gloria Steinem also emerged as one of the principal proponents of women's rights. A conservative journalist, Phyllis Schlafly campaigned against the Equal Rights Amendment. Shirley Chisolm was the first African-American woman to serve in Congress. Geraldine Ferraro ran as the Democratic vice presidential candidate in 1984.

6. **E.** Although many Southerners advocated the annexation of Texas, Jackson was fully aware of the simmering slave controversy. During the last year of his administration, Congress adopted a "gag rule" to prevent discussion of abolitionist petitions. Most Whigs opposed annexation out of fear that it would add another state committed to Jackson. Jackson's land sales policy promoted westward expansion. He saw merit in promoting both the commercial and agricultural economies.

7. **A.** The Nineteenth Amendment established women's suffrage. Prohibition began with the Eighteenth Amendment. The Seventeenth Amendment changed the process for electing senators. The Fourteenth Amendment protected the citizenship rights of African-Americans.

8. **D.** The Great Railway Strike of 1877 began in West Virginia and rapidly spread to other states east of the Mississippi. Still feeling the effects of the Panic of 1873, some Americans embraced the workers' demands for higher wages. However, as union members fought local authorities in a series of highly publicized clashes, public opinion turned against the strikers. Many Americans applauded President Hayes's use of federal troops to quell the violence in West Virginia.

9. **B.** In the early nineteenth century, Great Britain and France resumed hostilities. Sailors deserted British ships to escape the low pay and harsh conditions. The British navy soon began to stop and search American ships for escaped sailors. Impressment often forced native-born Americans into service aboard British ships. James Barron, captain of the *Chesapeake,* refused to allow Admiral Berkley of the HMS *Leopard* to search his ship for deserters. Berkley ordered his men to open fire, killing three and wounding eighteen. Barron relented and the British impressed four of his men. The *Chesapeake* Incident sparked national outrage.

10. **C.** President Lincoln hoped that a successful strike against Richmond would bring the yearlong war to an end. From the beginning of the campaign, McClelland complained that he lacked sufficient men. At Yorktown, a small detachment of Confederate soldiers (12,000) slowed the advance of McClellan's force of over 110,000 men. McClellan believed that the men marching behind the Confederate earthworks constituted a much larger force. McClellan's trudging pace toward Richmond confirmed Lincoln's assessment that his general "had a bad case of the slows."

11. **C.** After passage of the unpopular Stamp Act, many colonists in New England stopped purchasing British goods. The boycott soon spread to other colonies. British merchants and manufacturers lost considerable profits and urged Parliament to repeal the act. Petitions to the king typically fell on deaf ears. Most colonial governors executed British laws in spite of colonial protest. Although the Sons of Liberty intimidated governors and colonists loyal to the Crown, they had little effect upon parliamentary legislation.

12. **E.** Archibald Cox demanded that President Nixon relinquish the Watergate tapes. Nixon ordered his Attorney General, Elliot Richardson, to fire Cox. Richardson promptly resigned, as did Deputy Attorney General William Ruckelshaus. Nixon's desperate measures raised public indignation and prompted the House of Representatives to pursue impeachment charges.

13. **A.** The slave of an army surgeon, Dred Scott had lived with his master in Illinois and Wisconsin, both which banned slavery. As a result, Scott sued for his freedom after his master's death. Chief Justice Taney wrote one of the majority positions in which he stated that Scott could not sue because he was not a citizen. Taney further ruled that the Missouri Compromise line, imposed by Congress, was "not warranted by the Constitution and is therefore void."

14. **E.** Robert La Follette served as three terms as governor of Wisconsin. Charles Evans Hughes (NY), Woodrow Wilson (NJ), and Hiram Johnson (CA) also instituted progressive reforms as governor. Eugene Debs ran as the Socialist candidate for president in 1912.

15. **D.** The Constitution granted Congress the sole power to coin money, establish post offices, regulate interstate commerce, and admit new states. While the state government retained the authority to raise a militia, the federal government may nationalize state troops to enforce federal law and maintain order.

16. **B.** The Charles River Bridge Company held a Massachusetts state charter to operate a toll bridge between Boston and Cambridge. The company asserted that the charter ensured a monopoly over bridge traffic. The Warren Bridge Company applied to the state legislature for permission to construct a second bridge. The Charles River Bridge Company argued that John Marshall's Dartmouth College decision prevented the state from violating contracts. Nevertheless, Chief Justice Roger Taney sided with the Warren Bridge Company and the state of Massachusetts. He argued that the vagueness of the original charter did not specifically confer monopoly rights. Thus, new charters could be granted to expand economic opportunities for the wider community.

17. **D.** Americans of the late nineteenth century embraced new forms of leisure and entertainment. Urban dwellers particularly flocked to vaudeville houses and theaters. Working-class Americans often attended these shows. The movie industry thrived during this era.

18. **C.** The *Brown* v. *Board of Education* decision ordered the desegregation of public schools in 1954. In 1957, nine African-American students attempted to integrate Little Rock Central High School. Governor Orval Faubus ordered the state militia to prevent the students from enrolling. He later withdrew the troops, and an angry mob filled the void. President Eisenhower used federal troops to protect the students and enforce the desegregation of Little Rock Central.

19. **A.** The mass production of the cotton gin increased demand for the Southern staple. Cotton production increased dramatically during the antebellum period. The chilled steel plow and barbed wire helped Great Plains settlers of the late nineteenth century farm and raise cattle.

20. **B.** In *An Economic Interpretation of the Constitution* (1913), Beard asserted that the framers created a government in order to protect private property and promote commerce. Wealthy Americans, who bought bonds during the Revolutionary War, also had a vested interest in the repayment of the public debt.

21. **A.** Lincoln advocated the containment of slavery, not immediate abolition. Although some notable figures such as Wendell Phillips and Ralph Waldo Emerson praised Brown, most Northerners and Republicans condemned his attack on the federal arsenal. In his Cooper Union Speech, Lincoln claimed that "John Brown was no Republican" and assured his listeners that no one could "implicate a single Republican in his Harper's Ferry enterprise."

22. **B.** Roosevelt, Truman, Eisenhower, and Reagan presided over years in which the American economy experienced significant growth. Some had to deal with

intermittent problems of inflation. During the early 1970s, Nixon had to battle both inflation and a stagnant economy.

23. **E.** In the late nineteenth century, various state legislatures passed Progressive legislation ranging from child labor regulations to maximum hours. The Fourteenth Amendment forbade states from depriving "any person of life, liberty, or property without due process of law." The Supreme Court construed the meaning of the term "person" to include corporations. If state laws appeared to deprive corporations of property, the Court reasoned, then those acts violated the "due process" clause. For example, the Supreme Court struck down a state law regulating railroad rates. The *E. C. Knight* decision undermined the Sherman Antitrust Act by exempting manufacturing companies from antimonopoly legislation.

24. **D.** Federalists from the New England States met in Hartford in December 1814 to discuss the impact of the War of 1812 on their section. New England opposed war with England because of its impact on commerce. During the war, Federalists did not support the sale of war bonds or federal use of state militias. Moderates at the convention rejected the extremists' proposal for secession and a separate peace. The delegates agreed to a list of grievances and constitutional amendments aimed at protecting the power of the states. However, the signing of the Treaty of Ghent and Jackson's victory at New Orleans turned public opinion against the Federalists.

25. **C.** President Lyndon B. Johnson waged a "War on Poverty" with his "Great Society" legislation. Johnson attempted to extend health care benefits. Medicare provided federally funded medical insurance for the elderly. Medicaid funded medical care for impoverished Americans of all ages.

26. **D.** The Whig party emerged in 1836 to challenge Andrew Jackson's hand-picked successor, Martin Van Buren. Van Buren won the election but soon faced the Panic of 1837. Persistent economic problems affected the next election. The Whigs cast Van Buren as an aristocrat who spent money lavishly while average Americans suffered from the privations of the depression. Furthermore, Whig partisans portrayed their candidate, Indiana Governor William Henry Harrison, as a man of the people. Banners and leaflets pictured Harrison living in a rustic log cabin, consuming hard cider rather than champagne like Van Buren. Harrison defeated Van Buren in the election of 1840.

27. **B.** Many Republicans hoped that the election of Dwight D. Eisenhower would erode the position of Senator McCarthy. However, McCarthy ensured his own fall in 1954. McCarthy's accusations against Secretary of the Army Robert Stevens led to a special congressional inquiry. Television stations broadcasted the Army-McCarthy hearings to a national audience. Viewers witnessed the senator's intimidation tactics. By the end of the year, the Senate censured McCarthy for his conduct.

28. **E.** After his inauguration in 1801, Jefferson refused to renew the Alien and Sedition Acts but did not move to dismantle many economic measures of his Federalist predecessors. Jefferson did not eliminate the national debt but oversaw significant cuts in military and administrative spending. In 1807 Aaron Burr was arrested for an alleged conspiracy to seize lands in the Southwest. Jefferson helped manage the federal government's case against Burr and urged a conviction for treason. Jefferson refused to pay bribe money to ensure American commerce in the Mediterranean. Without a declaration of war, he ordered the American navy to protect ships in the region. The Louisiana Purchase represents another example of Jefferson interpreting the Constitution loosely.

29. **D.** Colonial assemblies often represented the interests of eastern over western counties. Taxes sometimes fell heavily upon those underrepresented in the legislature.

In colonial Virginia, Governor Berkeley sought to restrict white expansion in order to avoid bloody conflicts with Indian tribes. After a number of conflicts with the natives, Bacon raised a rebel army composed mainly of former indentured servants and other unemployed men. The rebels twice marched on Jamestown and evoked a lawlessness Berkeley struggled to contain. Bacon's Rebellion dissipated with the arrival of British troops and Bacon's death from dysentery. The social unrest alarmed propertied Virginians. The Whiskey Rebellion occurred in 1794. Major slave rebellions occurred in 1739, 1800, 1822, and 1832.

30. **B.** The Warren Court made a number of landmark decisions protecting the rights of those accused of crimes. In 1961, Clarence Gideon was arrested for a crime he did not commit. Gideon could not afford a lawyer; the presiding judge refused to provide one. Gideon was subsequently sentenced to five years in prison. He petitioned the Supreme Court, claiming that the judge's refusal to provide a lawyer denied him "due process of law" under the Fourteenth Amendment. The Supreme Court's decision in *Gideon* v. *Wainwright* overturned the conviction and ensured legal representation for the impoverished. The *Escobedo* decision extended access to a lawyer prior to questioning by the authorities. The *Miranda* decision required the police to inform suspects of these rights. Critics argued that the Court protected the rights of the accused at the expense of law-abiding citizens. The Fourth Amendment protects against "unreasonable search and seizures."

31. **A.** Peale and Stuart contributed to emerging cultural nationalism of the early republic. Peale painted several portraits of George Washington and other Revolutionary War heroes. Stuart also produced a wide array of portraits. The "Ashcan school" focused upon the grim realities of urban poverty and city life during the Progressive era.

32. **C.** Americans embraced isolationism in response to world events in the 1930s. Franklin Roosevelt's "quarantine speech" met with extremely mixed emotions. Congress passed a series of laws intended to ensure American neutrality. Japanese airplanes attacked the USS *Panay* and three Standard Oil tankers. Public opinion favored accepting reparations from Japan and removing American ships from foreign waters rather than punitive action. The Neutrality Act of 1935, prohibiting the sale of arms and munitions to belligerent nations, preceded the *Panay* Incident.

33. **E.** During the French and Indian War, American colonists continued to trade with Britain's enemies. Colonial assemblies did not always relinquish control of local militias. However, the colonial governments often failed to cooperate with their neighbors. Parliament began to reexamine its ability to control its North American colonies and passed new regulatory and taxation laws that contributed to the American Revolution. The war weakened France and the Indian tribes. Parliament attempted to check white expansion and limit the colonial trade west of the Appalachians with the Proclamation of 1763. Nevertheless, Indian resistance east of the Mississippi increased as whites migrated across the mountains.

34. **C.** The settlement house movement emerged to address the unhealthy conditions in industrial cities. Jane Addams established Hull House in Chicago, which served as a model for urban reformers. Workers at Hull House strove to help immigrant families adapt to the language and traditions of the United States. Representative Jeannette Rankin voted against the declaration of war in 1917 and 1941. Rachel Carson published *Silent Spring* in 1962. Betty Friedan was the founder and first president of the National Organization of Women. Mary Elizabeth Lease gave several speeches supporting Populist reforms.

35. **D.** President Franklin D. Roosevelt perceived his reelection in 1936 as a popular mandate to extend his New Deal programs. The Supreme Court overturned his

Agricultural Adjustment Act and National Industrial Recovery Act in that same year. Roosevelt proposed to raise the number of justices ostensibly to alleviate the workload of older justices. Most people saw the measure as a transparent effort to increase the number of Democrats on the bench. His proposal caused some Democrats to bolt the party and undergirded conservative opposition to the New Deal.

36. **A.** British settlers in North America established permanent settlements in order to take advantage of economic opportunities. The French attempted to exploit trade but did not found as many settled communities. Thus, British settlers outnumbered the French throughout the colonial period. British farmers continually clashed with natives along the frontier. The French tried to form alliances to promote the fur trade and often married native women. Both French and British missionaries attempted to convert the native tribes.

37. **E.** Rockefeller, Carnegie, Stanford, and Morgan each forged lucrative business enterprises in the late nineteenth century. Rockefeller's Standard Oil Trust cornered the refining industry. Carnegie created a vast steel empire. Stanford attempted to monopolize the railroad industry in the West. Morgan dominated the field of banking and investments.

38. **B.** The gold rush drew thousands of immigrants to the West between 1848 and 1852. Prospectors came from abroad, as well as from eastern states. Many hoped to strike it rich and return home. Most fortune-seekers decided to remain in the West. Miners often clashed with Indian tribes as they staked claims. Some tried to force the native population to work in the mines; others killed local tribes. The population of mining towns remained predominantly male; few women or families traveled to the West. Crime and violence permeated these communities.

39. **C.** Industrial expansion in the late nineteenth century drew millions of immigrants to American cities. While many factory owners sought cheap labor, nativists continually urged Congress to preserve opportunities for American workers. Congress responded with a variety of restrictive laws between 1882 and 1921. The Immigration Restriction Act of 1924 established extremely low quotas for certain nationalities, thus barring numerous immigrants from the United States. Congress extended the act in 1929. The Great Depression paralleled a worldwide economic crisis.

40. **A.** Nationalists and religious fundamentalists forced Shah Reza Pahlevi to flee Iran in January 1979. The deposed Shah sought medical treatment in the United States. An angry mob stormed the American embassy in November, demanding the return of Pahlevi. The militants held 53 American diplomats and service personnel hostage for over a year. A failed rescue attempt exacerbated public frustration with the Carter administration. The United States withdrew from Saigon in 1975. Congress began investigations into the Iran-Contra Affair in 1987. American troops invaded Panama and arrested Manuel Noriega in 1989. Congress ratified the North American Free Trade Agreement in 1993.

41. **C.** In 1786, delegates from five states met in Annapolis to discuss methods to improve interstate commerce. States retained significant power under the Articles of Confederation and often passed high tariffs on each other's goods. Realizing the weaknesses of the existing political structure, the delegates asked Congress to call a general convention in Philadelphia to revise the Articles. The Albany Congress attempted to promote intercolonial unity in 1754.

42. **D.** Enterprises in Lowell and Waltham, Massachusetts, began a trend of employing women in the textile industry in the 1830s. Many women did not enter the fields of education and nursing until after the Civil War. Secretarial work

remained a province for men until World War II. Few women made inroads into the law profession until later in the twentieth century.

43. **E.** Roosevelt adopted a more reform-minded domestic program than his Republican predecessors Harrison and McKinley. In 1906, he signed the Hepburn Act to increase the powers of the Interstate Commerce Commission. The Pure Food and Drug Act passed that same year after public outcry against the food and patent medicine industries.

44. **B.** The Dawes Severalty Act intended to dissolve the tribal system by dividing reservations into 160-acre homesteads. Indian families were encouraged to live on their own farms and abandon native customs. In reality, much of the reservation land was sold to white speculators. The Dawes Plan (1924) provided loans to enable Germany to repay reparations to France after World War I.

45. **A.** The return of World War II soldiers and postwar "baby boom" caused a severe housing shortage. The Levitts introduced mass-produced houses to accommodate the demand. Standardized suburban communities sprang up in New York, New Jersey, and Pennsylvania. Jonas Salk developed a polio vaccine in the 1950s.

46. **C.** Before the Radical Republicans gained control of Reconstruction, the former Confederate states reentered the Union under the moderate conditions imposed by Lincoln and Johnson. New state legislatures enacted "Black Codes" circumscribing the rights of freedmen. Furthermore, most Southern states rejected the Fourteenth Amendment. As a result, Congress passed the Military Reconstruction Act of 1867. The act disbanded the governments created under Lincoln's "Ten Percent Plan" and under Johnson. Military occupation would last until loyal governments ratified the Fourteenth Amendment and registered African-Americans to vote. The act fell short of the hopes of many Radicals by not redistributing land to the freedmen.

47. **E.** During World War I, German submarines sank ships heading to British ports. The German government announced that U-boats would sink all enemy ships. In 1915, a German submarine sank the British luxury liner *Lusitania,* killing nearly 1200 people, including 128 Americans. President Wilson, like many Americans, angrily condemned German actions. He warned Germany not to continue unrestricted U-boat warfare. When an attack on the French ship *Sussex* injured several American passengers, Wilson repeated his warning. In order to keep the United States out of the war, the German government gave assurances that it would stop attacking ships without warning.

48. **C.** The Whigs emerged in the 1830s as an anti-Jackson party. The party absorbed elements of the nativistic American ("Know-Nothing") party. They supported the maintenance of the Bank of the United States, road construction, and tariffs to protect American industries. The Whigs found adherents in every region. The Whig presidential candidate won the elections of 1840 and 1848. However, the slavery issue troubled the party. By the 1850s, many Southern Whigs supported the expansion of slavery into the territories, while their Northern counterparts opposed expansion.

49. **D.** After the Civil War, rapid industrial growth created significant demand for labor in American factories. Millions of immigrants, especially from Southern and Eastern Europe, flocked to the cities seeking employment. Nativism increased as Americans feared competition for jobs and the spread of non-Protestant religions.

50. **B.** In response to Pearl Harbor and long-standing racial prejudice, local authorities in the West urged Roosevelt to address the presence of Japanese-Americans (Nisei). Roosevelt issued Executive Order 9066, which allowed military officials

to remove the Nisei to relocation centers. No similar policy was followed for first-generation Americans of German or Italian descent.

51. **A.** In late 1967, General William Westmoreland assured President Johnson that American victories portended the surrender of the Vietnamese communists. In reality, North Vietnamese leaders were planning a massive invasion of South Vietnam. The communist offensive began in January 1968 during the Tet holiday. North Vietnamese forces struck 41 cities, including Saigon. The Tet Offensive revealed that the United States was no closer to victory than earlier in the war. As a result, the antiwar movement intensified.

52. **E.** After the French and Indian War, Parliament imposed the Stamp Act to defray the costs of colonial defense. However, the colonists had become accustomed to paying revenue taxes passed by their assemblies. Many believed that Parliament legitimately retained the right to regulate trade but not to raise revenue. Although the tax was not extremely burdensome, it sparked fiery rhetoric and boycotts throughout the colonies. Parliament later rescinded the act but would try to raise revenue with the Townshend Acts in 1767.

53. **B.** Advertising changed in the late nineteenth century to expand the markets of American industries. Chain stores challenged small merchants to market mass-produced goods at a lower price. However, farmers often could not obtain similar products in local country stores. Catalogs such as Montgomery Ward and Sears Roebuck made new items available in rural areas. Farmers soon embraced the newest tools, technologies, and fashions displayed in the catalogs.

54. **D.** The acquisition of new territories in the antebellum period exacerbated the controversy over the expansion of slavery. The Constitutional Convention had banned the further importation of slaves after 1808. Congress established the Missouri Compromise line to limit the expansion of slavery in the Louisiana territory. The Mexican Cession became the target of new debates. Some argued that Congress could extend the Missouri Compromise line to California. Others argued the people residing in a territory should decide the question of slavery. Stephen Douglas and other Democratic politicians promoted "popular sovereignty" as a solution to the slavery question.

55. **E.** Slaves resisted oppressive conditions in many ways. Although laws did not recognize slave marriages, slaves frequently held their own ceremonies. Slaves merged African traditions with Christianity and practiced their own forms of religion. Field songs and religious music challenged the dominance of whites through coded messages. Slaves resisted the pace of work set by masters and drivers by breaking tools or working more slowly. Others ran away from their plantations, especially in the upper South. However, slave revolts did not occur frequently.

56. **C.** Roosevelt signed the GI Bill in 1944. This act provided loans for purchasing homes and grants for education. Millions of veterans took advantage of government funding to pursue higher education and job training. The GI Bill helped fuel postwar prosperity in the 1940s and 1950s.

57. **C.** The United States adopted an official policy of neutrality in the conflicts between Spain and its Latin American colonies. Nevertheless, American businesses supplied the rebels in those colonies. The United States became the first nation to recognize the newly independent governments. Wary of European involvement in the Western Hemisphere, Secretary of State John Quincy Adams urged President James Monroe to adopt a more forceful policy. The Monroe Doctrine opposed future European colonization and efforts to undermine existing governments. Furthermore, it reiterated a traditional policy of noninterference in European affairs.

58. **B.** Congress passed the Homestead Act in 1862. This act offered prospective settlers 160-acre homesteads in the West for a nominal fee if they resided on the land for five years. Thousands of settlers streamed west with hopes of establishing farms on the Great Plains. The Gadsden Purchase provided a potential railroad route in the Southwest. The Webster-Ashburton Treaty settled a boundary dispute along the Maine border. Congress passed the Reclamation Act (1902) to fund irrigation projects in the West. The Soil Conservation and Domestic Allotment Act replaced provisions of the Agricultural Adjustment Act during the New Deal.

59. **A.** English, Scotch-Irish, Dutch, and German settlers resided in the Middle Colonies (New York, New Jersey, and Pennsylvania). The region sustained a thriving agricultural and commercial economy. Although the Quakers of Pennsylvania opposed slavery, some colonists in the region owned slaves. Virginia produced more tobacco than any other colony.

60. **E.** The Soviet Union shot down an American U-2 airplane during the last year of the Eisenhower administration. The Soviets captured the pilot and displayed photographic equipment after the administration denied Soviet charges of espionage. Although the plans for an invasion of Cuba began under Eisenhower, the Bay of Pigs affair occurred during the first few months of the Kennedy administration. The Berlin Wall was constructed in 1961. In October 1962, Kennedy sent federal troops to protect James Meredith, the first African-American to attend the University of Mississippi. The 1962 Trade Expansion Act lowered tariffs to promote trade between the United States and European nations.

61. **C.** In the late nineteenth century, several European nations established "spheres of influence" in China. These nations protected their provincial commerce with discriminatory port duties, tariffs, and railroad rates. Secretary of State John Hay issued the "Open-Door Notes" in order to convince the European powers to provide equal access to Chinese markets.

62. **A.** The Confederation government passed the Northwest Ordinances to resolve problems with territory ceded by Great Britain at the end of the Revolutionary War. As settlers migrated across the Appalachian Mountains, Congress sought the means to include the region in the new republic. The ordinances established plans for orderly settlement and creation of new state governments.

63. **D.** Wilson traveled to France to ensure passage of his Fourteen Points. Wilson hoped that the conference would not impose a punitive peace treaty upon Germany. However, Allied leaders agreed only to a few his points. The treaty included the creation of the League of Nations, which Wilson believed would prevent future wars. At the end of World War II, the Potsdam Conference finalized plans to divide Germany into occupation zones.

64. **A.** Recent immigrants frequently joined the Jeffersonian Republicans at the close of the eighteenth century. During the "quasi-war" with France, Republican newspapers excoriated the policies of John Adams. Federalists in Congress searched for ways to weaken the opposition. The Alien Act made naturalization of immigrants more difficult. The Sedition Act empowered the federal government to arrest those who printed libelous material. The acts alarmed many who saw them as a direct assault on the Constitution.

65. **B.** The First Great Awakening swept across the colonies in the 1730s and 1740s. Preachers urged people to reestablish a direct relationship with God. Established ministers rejected the message of the evangelicals, splitting denominations between "New Lights" and "Old Lights." The religious revivals were particularly popular along the frontier. The Great Awakening undermined the authority of established churches by diversifying American religion.

66. **E.** One of Franklin Roosevelt's New Deal programs, the Works Progress Administration expanded relief efforts. It financed diverse activities from road and building construction to projects for writers and artists. The Fair Employment Practices Committee (FEPC) investigated discriminatory hiring practices during World War II.

67. **C.** Stowe wrote *Uncle Tom's Cabin,* the most widely read antebellum novel. Its strident abolitionist message intensified the sectional conflict. However, she did not participate in the organization of the Seneca Falls Convention. Dorothea Dix advocated prison and asylum reform. Harriet Tubman helped other slaves escape to the North. Robert Owen founded New Harmony.

68. **A.** The Republican party stuck with the Nixon-Agnew ticket in 1972. The president had little difficulty winning the primaries. His conservative "Southern strategy," emphasizing his opposition to busing, enabled him to win votes in the solidly Democratic South. Nixon's reelection campaign benefited from lingering divisions within the Democratic party. Nixon won every state except Massachusetts.

69. **D.** Severe drought contributed to widespread erosion on the Great Plains. Windstorms stripped away the rich topsoil, leaving many hard-pressed farmers few options but to move off their land. This ecological distress spawned new cultivation and conservation efforts during the New Deal.

70. **E.** The War of 1812 revealed an array of problems that Republican administrations strove to address. Circulation of state bank notes and fluctuating currency values led Congress to charter the second Bank of the United States. Merchants and manufacturers grew alarmed as Great Britain began to flood American marts with cheap industrial goods. They pleaded with Congress to raise tariffs to protect domestic industries and commerce.

71. **B.** The sale of public lands had diminished by the early twentieth century. Woodrow Wilson used passage of the national income tax as a springboard for tariff reform. Progressives had long demanded reduction of tariffs, which seemed to enrich only the industrialists. Wilson signed the Underwood Tariff, since the federal government gained a new source of income with the Sixteenth Amendment. The government continued to rely upon loans and war bonds.

72. **D.** The "Black Codes" passed in the postwar era resembled the antebellum state laws that restricted the freedoms of African slaves. The Ku Klux Klan menaced African-Americans who challenged the old order during and after Reconstruction. Southern states enacted literacy tests and "grandfather clauses" in order to limit black suffrage. *Plessy* v. *Ferguson* (1896) legalized segregation.

73. **C.** The Strategic Defense Initiative escalated Cold War tensions during the Reagan administration. The Soviets argued that it undermined arms control agreements. In the United States and Europe, a "nuclear freeze" movement urged the superpowers to halt the construction of nuclear weapons.

74. **A.** Sinclair Lewis mocked the material aspirations of society in the 1920s. Tarbell and London were turn-of-the-century muckrakers. Steinbeck's work addressed the social dislocations of the Great Depression. A prominent advertising executive, Barton published *The Man Nobody Knows* (1925), which portrayed Jesus as a salesman.

75. **B.** Great Britain prospered when goods flowed freely between the colonies and the mother country. The seventeenth-century Navigation Acts attempted to ensure that all colonial trade went to Great Britain. The Woolen Act (1699), Hat Act (1732), and Iron Act (1750) discouraged domestic manufacturing so that colonists would purchase British goods.

76. **B.** Roosevelt attempted to improve relations with Latin American nations by rejecting the policy of sending American troops to resolve internal problems. Kennedy's Alliance for Progress also aimed to improve relations by offering economic aid to Latin American nations. The Eisenhower Doctrine offered economic and military aid to Middle Eastern nations. Eisenhower sent troops to restore order in Lebanon. During the 1960s, the Mann Doctrine led to American military intervention to support a right-wing regime in the Dominican Republic.

77. **A.** The disaster at the Triangle Shirtwaist Company heightened public awareness of industrial abuses. Triangle employed mostly women workers. Many perished in the blaze or leapt to their deaths trying to avoid the flames. Investigations revealed that locked exits and the collapse of the main fire escape trapped the women inside.

78. **E.** The rapid increase in California's population escalated sectional tensions. Southerners in Congress agreed to admit California as a free state and ban the slave trade in Washington, DC as long as Congress imposed no direct ban on slavery in the Mexican Cession. Furthermore, they required the passage of a stricter fugitive slave law. The compromise resolved the boundary dispute between Texas and New Mexico but did not provide funding for railroad construction.

79. **B.** The Supreme Court overturned a state maximum-hours law in *Lochner* v. *New York*. However, the Court supported antitrust legislation by ordering the dissolution of monopolies in the other four decisions.

80. **C.** Thomas Nast published cartoons in many of the leading journals of the nineteenth century. He criticized Andrew Johnson and the treatment of African-Americans during Reconstruction. No individual figure incurred Nast's wrath more than Tammany Hall boss William M. Tweed. Nast continually addressed corruption in New York City during the Tweed years.

RATING THE ESSAYS

Summary Response to the Document-Based Question

1. Students might begin the essay with a brief discussion of the Treaty of Paris (1898) and its impact upon Cuba. American military occupation under General Leonard Wood followed ratification of the treaty. Wood oversaw the construction of infrastructure, revamped Cuba's political administration, and pioneered health reforms. However, the United States violated the Teller Amendment by not affording Cuba complete independence. Congress retained the right to intervene in Cuban affairs and curbed Cuban autonomy in the Platt Amendment (Document A). Students may note that the United States sent troops into Cuba in 1906 and 1912 to quell rebellions and maintained a naval base at Guantanamo. Students may also refer to "dollar diplomacy" by discussing how American corporations came to dominate the oil, railroad, and, most importantly, sugar industries. Some might compare American involvement in Cuba to a different policy towards Puerto Rico (Foraker Act of 1900, Jones Act of 1917). Students should identify the policies of Theodore Roosevelt, William H. Taft, and Woodrow Wilson. They should examine how the Venezuela crisis (1902) precipitated the announcement of the "Roosevelt Corollary" to the Monroe Doctrine (Document D). Students will apply their knowledge of this policy to American intervention in the Dominican Republic in 1905. Some might note that U.S. control of Dominican customs undermined the nation's independence. Students might speculate on the results of involvement in the internal

affairs of nations. A discussion of American interests in constructing an isthmian canal should include Secretary of State John Hay and overtures to Colombia. Students may discuss Philippe Bunau-Varilla, the USS *Nashville*, and Panamanian Revolution. Students will note how Panama reacted to the Hay-Bunau-Varilla Treaty (Document B). Students may interpret Document C as an allegation that the United States orchestrated the Panamanian Revolution. Others might argue that the Hay-Bunau-Varilla Treaty enabled the United States to direct Panamanian affairs. An examination of "dollar diplomacy" under Taft (Document F) may touch upon his Secretary of State Philander C. Knox. Students will note how the growing influence of American mining companies in Nicaragua resulted in military intervention in 1909. Others might note that American banks financed and owned Nicaragua railroads. American troops returned in 1912 to help maintain the government of Adolfo Diaz. Students might state that Document E reflects the belief that the United States used its military to open or preserve economic opportunities. Some might point to future problems with the Sandinistas or Contras. Students may use Document G to indicate that American imperialism did not enjoy universal support in the United States. Students could observe how the United States continued its involvement in the Dominican Republic and Nicaragua (Bryan-Chamorro Treaty, 1914) under Wilson. They may also touch upon how intervention in Haiti in 1915 paralleled involvement with its neighbor. Most students will discuss Wilson's relationship with Mexico. Some might begin with the transfer of power from Porfirio Diaz to Francisco Madero to General Victoriano Huerta and Wilson's refusal to recognize the Huerta regime. Students might observe that American businesses wanted to promote stability in Mexico in order to establish favorable trade (Document H). Students should examine the instability related to conflicts between Huerta and Venustiano Carranza. Students should discuss the effects of the Tampico affair (Document I) and seizure of Veracruz. Students should also refer to the tenuous relationship between Wilson and Carranza and the issue of recognition. Some may touch upon Pancho Villa and raids in the American Southwest that caused Wilson to send General John Pershing and an expeditionary force across the border. Students will note that the United States and Mexico approached war and should speculate about the long-term effects of American policy.

Summary Responses to the Standard Free-Response Questions

2. Students might observe that immigration into the Louisiana Territory raised the issue of the expansion of slavery. When Missouri applied for statehood, New York Representative James Tallmadge Jr. proposed an amendment that banned the future importation of slaves into the state and provided for the gradual emancipation of existing bondsmen. The Tallmadge amendment touched off a rancorous sectional debate. Students may comment that this debate revolved around moral issues, political power, or which economic system (slave versus free labor) would predominate. Maine's application for statehood complicated the questions over Missouri. Students may touch upon leading political figures: Henry Clay, John C. Calhoun, and Jesse B. Thomas. The Compromise of 1820 admitted Missouri as a slave state, Maine as a free state, and banned slavery north of the 36° 30′ line. Students might argue that the Missouri Compromise resolved the immediate debate but revealed potential divisions. Domestic tensions over the tariff issue began during Andrew Jackson's first administration. South Carolinians blamed their economic distress on the "tariff of abominations" (tariff of 1828). Some asserted that secession would provide relief from the despised legislation. John C. Calhoun, Democratic vice presidential candidate, hoped to avert secession by asserting the theory of nullification in his anonymously published *South Carolina Exposition and Protest*. He believed a strong statement would induce the federal government

to reduce tariff rates. Some students might touch upon the Webster-Hayne debate or Jackson's Jefferson Day dinner speech as evidence of the rift between nationalists and states' rights advocates. The Tariff of 1832 did little to reduce tariff rates or the frustrations of South Carolinians. The South Carolina legislature passed an "ordinance of nullification" and ordered state officials not to enforce the tariff law. Jackson called nullification treason in his *Proclamation to the People of South Carolina* and made military preparations to enforce the law. Congress approved a "force bill" empowering Jackson to use the military to achieve compliance. Passage of the Compromise of 1833, which gradually lowered tariff rates, avoided armed conflict between South Carolina and the federal government. Students might discuss the issue of states' rights versus national supremacy. Electoral irregularities during the election of 1876 raised sectional tensions. Democrat Samuel Tilden held a slight edge in the popular vote over Republican Rutherford B. Hayes. However, electoral votes from Oregon, Louisiana, South Carolina, and Florida remained disputed between both parties. No constitutional provision offered a solution to the problem. Tensions ran high as newspapers and private citizens speculated about the renewal of civil war. Congress appointed a special election commission that awarded the election to Hayes. In exchange, Republicans promised to remove federal troops from the South and made other concessions. Students may observe that the crisis and compromise spelled an end to Reconstruction.

3. The Kansas-Nebraska Act (1854) divided part of the Louisiana territory into two new territories and repealed the congressional ban on slavery above the Missouri Compromise line. Passage of the act sparked bitter sectional debate. Students might discuss the Sumner-Brooks affair to illustrate the rising passions. The Kansas-Nebraska destroyed the Whig party, which could not breach the divide between its antislavery and pro-slavery factions. Some Southern Whigs crossed party lines in support of the act. Others remained opposed to the legislation and ran against Democrats in local elections. The Whig party disintegrated as a national partisan unit. Students should discuss how Northern Whigs organized the sectional Republican party. The act caused some Northern Democrats to bolt the party. However, the Democratic party preserved a tenuous alliance between its Southern faction and some Northern constituents. Pennsylvania Democrat James Buchanan defeated Republican John C. Fremont in 1856. Sectional strife over "bleeding Kansas," the *Dred Scott* decision, and the Lecompton Constitution stemmed from the act and further unsettled the political atmosphere. Students should discuss how the Democratic party failed to contain sectional tensions during the election of 1860. The nomination of Stephen Douglas caused delegates from the Deep South to leave the national convention and nominate John C. Breckinridge. John Bell won the nomination of the Constitutional Union party, which drew significant support from former Southern Whigs. Students will observe how the division among the Democrats led to the election of Abraham Lincoln, who had opposed the Kansas-Nebraska Act.

4. Students should assess the factors leading to the Great Depression and broaden the discussion beyond the stock market crash. World War I and government policy led to an overproduction that depressed the farm economy early in the 1920s. Many farmers struggled to meet mortgage payments. Over the course of the decade, farmers stopped purchasing industrial goods. The industrial economy would also suffer from overproduction. Students might note how advertising and mass production fostered a consumer mania. Automobiles and construction were the leading industries. Those who could not afford items could purchase them through installment buying. Many people overextended their personal finances. A maldistribution of wealth also contributed to the Depression. Half of all Americans barely made subsistence wages, while 5 percent earned one-third of the nation's income. The Supreme Court overturned minimum-wage legislation in *Adkins* v. *Children's*

Hospital in 1923. Students should discuss the importance of money in circulation to maintain the nation's economy. Government policies contributed to the Depression. Students should touch upon the three Republican presidents (Harding, Coolidge, and Hoover) and their administrations. High tariffs (Fordney-McCumber, Hawley-Smoot) led to retaliatory responses from foreign nations. Some students might discuss reparations policy, particularly in relation to Germany. Europe also began producing its own food at the end of the decade. Students should note that domestic production increased, while foreign markets were constricted. Coolidge (Revenue Act of 1926) and Treasury Secretary Andrew Mellon cut taxes on the highest income brackets but not on middle incomes. Banks lowered interest rates, making loans easily available. Consumers and businesses took out loans. Businesses expanded their facilities, but laid off workers if the expansion did not turn a profit. As a result, consumers had less purchasing power by the end of the decade. Many banks kept little reserve as they made loans and speculated on the stock market. When private citizens, farmers, or businesses defaulted on loans, banks closed their doors. The growth of the stock market reflected the false prosperity of the greater economy. Students will observe how overspeculation, reckless investments, and the failure of some investment banks contributed to the stock market crash. Although a large percentage of the population did not invest on the stock market, numerous businesses and banks saw the bulk of their assets disappear. Factories closed; bank failures caused runs on banks. Over a half million people lost their homes. Unemployment rose to over 25 percent of the population.

5. Students might begin a discussion of the early Cold War by examining the Yalta and Potsdam Conferences. Yalta seemed to provide for free elections in nations formerly occupied by the Nazis. Potsdam divided Germany into occupation zones with the intent of reuniting the nation at a later date. Some students might refer to George Kennan's "long telegram" or X Article. Students should focus upon the Marshall Plan and Truman Doctrine as the foundation of containment policy. The Marshall Plan provided over $13 billion to rebuild European industries, combat inflation, and increase European production. Great Britain, France, Germany, Italy, and the Netherlands received the largest amount of American grants and loans, but several smaller nations also received aid. Most of those nations did not succumb to internal strife or ally with the Soviet Union. The Truman Doctrine had a $400 million budget to provide economic or military assistance to "nations facing armed aggression." Greece received American assistance and suppressed a communist revolt. Turkey solidified its defenses along its border with the Soviet Union. Neither nation fell under Soviet influence during the Truman administration. Stalin perceived a threat to Soviet control of Eastern Europe when the Allies merged their occupation zones in 1948. He imposed a blockade around Berlin in June to force the city to join the Soviet zone. Truman authorized the Berlin Airlift ("Operation Vittles") in order to provide the beleaguered with food and medical supplies. The Soviets lifted the blockade in May 1949. Some students might discuss the formation of NATO. Students might argue that Truman's efforts at containment achieved more success in Europe than in Asia. A discussion of Asian containment policy should address the Chinese Civil War. Some students might refer to George Marshall's mission to China. Chiang Kai-shek was unable to stop the peasants' revolt led by Mao Tse-tung. Chiang fled to Formosa (Taiwan); the Truman administration recognized his government as the legitimate Chinese government. Truman refused to recognize Mao's government. NSC-68 followed Truman's call for a reevaluation of American foreign policy. Truman responded to the North Korean invasion and resolution by the U.N. Security Council by sending American forces under General Douglas MacArthur. Students might discuss the restrictions of "limited warfare" but that American forces kept South Korea from falling under the control of the communist North.

Rubric for Essays

Essays for free-response and document-based questions (DBQs) are both scored on a 9 to 0 scale, with 9 being the highest grade.

The 8–9 Essay:
Contains and supports a well-developed thesis
Presents and effective analysis of the topic
Presents substantial and relevant outside information
May contain minor errors
Is clearly organized and well written
For DBQs: Effectively uses a substantial number of documents

The 5–7 Essay:
Contains a thesis
Presents a limited analysis of the topic
Supports thesis with some relevant outside information
May have errors that do not seriously detract from the quality of the essay
Shows acceptable organization and writing
For DBQs: Effectively uses some documents

The 2–4 Essay:
Contains a limited or underdeveloped thesis
Deals with the topic in a general or simplistic manner
Contains little outside information
May have major errors
May be poorly organized and/or poorly written
For DBQs: Merely refers to or quotes documents

The 0–1 Essay:
Contains no thesis or a thesis that does not addrss the question
Exhibits an incorrect understanding of the topic
Has numerous errors
Is written poorly, with grammatical errors that inhibit understanding
For DBQs: Shows no understanding of documents or makes no reference to them

SCORING AND INTERPRETATION

Multiple-Choice Questions = 50% of your grade
Free-Response Essays = 50% of your grade

Within the Free-Response Essay Section:

The DBQs = 45% of your grade
The two standard essays = 55% of your grade

Chapter 3

AP English Language

Answer Sheet for Multiple-Choice Questions

1. _____	19. _____	37. _____
2. _____	20. _____	38. _____
3. _____	21. _____	39. _____
4. _____	22. _____	40. _____
5. _____	23. _____	41. _____
6. _____	24. _____	42. _____
7. _____	25. _____	43. _____
8. _____	26. _____	44. _____
9. _____	27. _____	45. _____
10. _____	28. _____	46. _____
11. _____	29. _____	47. _____
12. _____	30. _____	48. _____
13. _____	31. _____	49. _____
14. _____	32. _____	50. _____
15. _____	33. _____	51. _____
16. _____	34. _____	52. _____
17. _____	35. _____	53. _____
18. _____	36. _____	54. _____

Scoring Formula:

$$\underset{\text{number right}}{\underline{\hspace{3cm}}} - \underset{\text{(number wrong} \times .25)}{\underline{\hspace{4cm}}} = \underset{\text{raw score}}{\underline{\hspace{2cm}}}$$

AP ENGLISH LANGUAGE

Section I

Time—1 hour

54 Questions

Carefully read the following passages and answer the questions that follow.

Questions 1–10 are based on the following passage
excerpted from Charles Dickens's *Pictures from Italy*.

Magnificently stern and sombre are the streets of beautiful
Florence; and the strong old piles of building make such heaps of
shadow, on the ground and in the river, that there is another and
different city of rich forms and fancies, always lying at our feet.
Prodigious palaces, constructed for defence, with small distrustful   5
windows heavily barred, and walls of great thickness formed of huge
masses of rough stone, frown, in their old sulky state, on every street.
In the midst of the city—in the Piazza of the Grand Duke, adorned with
beautiful statues and the Fountain of Neptune—rises the Palazzo Vecchio,
with its enormous overhanging battlements, and the Great Tower that   10
watches over the whole town. In its court-yard—worthy of the Castle of
Otranto in its ponderous gloom—is a massive staircase that the heaviest
wagon and the stoutest team of horses might be driven up. Within it, is a
Great Saloon, faded and tarnished in its stately decorations, and mouldering
by grains, but recording yet, in pictures on its walls, the triumphs of the   15
Medici and the wars of the old Florentine people. The prison is hard by, in
an adjacent court-yard of the building—a foul and dismal place, where some
men are shut up close, in small cells like ovens; and where others look through
bars and beg; where some are playing draughts, and some are talking to their
friends, who smoke, the while, to purify the air and some are buying wine and   20
fruit of women-vendors; and all are squalid, dirty, and vile to look at. "They are
merry enough, Signor," says the Jailer. "They are all blood-stained here," he
adds, indicating, with his hand, three-fourths of the whole building. Before the
hour is out, an old man, eighty years of age, quarrelling over a bargain with a
young girl of seventeen, stabs her dead, in the market-place full of bright   25
flowers; and is brought in prisoner, to swell the number.
Among the four old bridges that span the river, the Ponte Vecchio—
that bridge which is covered with the shops of Jewellers and Goldsmiths—
is a most enchanting feature in the scene. The space of one house, in the
center, being left open, the view beyond is shown as in a frame; and that   30
precious glimpse of sky, and water, and rich buildings, shining so quietly
among the huddled roofs and gables on the bridge, is exquisite. Above it,
the Gallery of the Grand Duke crosses the river. It was built to connect the
two Great Palaces by a secret passage; and it takes its jealous course among
streets and houses, with true despotism: going where it lists, and spurning   35
every obstacle away, before it.

1. The purpose of the passage is to

   A. condemn the squalor of Florence
   B. entice visitors to Florence
   C. praise the Grand Duke
   D. present the dichotomy existing in Florence
   E. reveal the author's worldliness

2. The primary rhetorical strategy used by the author is

   A. narration
   B. description
   C. analysis
   D. process
   E. argument

3. In developing his purpose, the author uses all of the following rhetorical devices <u>except</u>

   A. spatial organization
   B. metaphor and simile
   C. comparison and contrast
   D. imagery
   E. chronological order

4. Which of the following lines contains an example of paradox?

   A. line 20
   B. line 22
   C. lines 5, 6
   D. line 31
   E. line 34

5. The most probable function of the selected detail which focuses on the murder of the young girl by the old man (23–26) is

   A. to emphasize the brutality of the citizens
   B. to establish a tone of pathos
   C. to criticize the city's government
   D. to warn visitors about the dangers of the city
   E. to emphasize the contrasts evident in the city

6. The abrupt shift caused by a lack of transition between paragraphs 1 and 2 serves to do all of the following <u>except</u>

   A. re-emphasize the unexpected nature of murder
   B. reinforce the idea that there is no connection between the two paragraphs
   C. reinforce the element of contrast
   D. reinforce author's style
   E. to immediately whisk the reader to a place of safety away from the murder scene

7. What can be inferred from the following details taken from the passage

   — *"small distrustful windows" (5, 6)*
   — *"walls of great thickness" (6)*
   — *"enormous overhanging battlements" (10)*
   — *"secret passage" (34)*

   A. Florence was not architecturally sound.
   B. Florence was designed to protect its artwork.
   C. Florence had experienced both warfare and intrigue.
   D. Florence was unsuited for habitation.
   E. Florence was preparing for war.

8. Lines 14–26 contain examples of which of the following rhetorical device?

   A. antithetical images
   B. anecdotal evidence
   C. parallel structure
   D. denotation
   E. inversion

9. If one were building a house of horrors, which of the following would be best suitable as a model or inspiration?

   A. Piazza of the Grand Duke (8)
   B. Palazzo Vecchio (9)
   C. The Castle of Otranto (11, 12)
   D. Ponte Vecchio (27, 28)
   E. Galley of the Grand Duke (33)

10. Which of the following terms has most probably undergone a shift in meaning from Dickens' time to its current usage?

    A. "stately" (14)
    B. "squalid" (21)
    C. "enchanting" (29)
    D. "jealous" (34)
    E. "obstacle" (36)

Questions 11–20 are based on the following
passage from Margaret Atwood's "Origins of Stories."

Our first stories come to us through the air. We hear voices. 1

Children in oral societies grow up within a web of stories; but so do all chil- 2
dren. We listen before we can read. Some of our listening is more like listening in,
to the calamitous or seductive voices of the adult world, on the radio or the television or in our daily lives. Often it's an overhearing of things we aren't supposed to
hear, eavesdropping on scandalous gossip or family secrets. From all these scraps of
voices, from the whispers and shouts that surround us, even from ominous silences,
the unfilled gaps in meaning, we patch together for ourselves an order of events, a
plot or plots; these, then, are the things that happen, these are the people they happen to, this is the forbidden knowledge.

We have all been little pitchers with big ears, shooed out of the kitchen when 3
the unspoken is being spoken, and we have probably all been tale-bearers, blurters
at the dinner table, unwitting violators of adult rules of censorship. Perhaps this is
what writers are: those who never kicked the habit. We remained tale-bearers. We
learned to keep our eyes open, but not to keep our mouths shut.

If we're lucky, we may also be given stories meant for our ears, stories 4
intended for us. These may be children's Bible stories, tidied up and simplified and
with the vicious bits left out. They may be fairy tales, similarly sugared, although
if we are very lucky it will be left in. In any case, these tales will have deliberate,
molded shapes, unlike stories we have patched together for ourselves. They will
contain mountains, deserts, talking donkeys, dragons; and, unlike the kitchen stories, they will have definite endings. We are likely to accept these stories being on
the same level of reality as the kitchen stories. It's only when we are older that we
are taught to regard one kind of story as real and the other kind as mere invention.
This is about the same time we're taught to believe that dentists are useful, and
writers are not.

Traditionally, both the kitchen gossips and the readers-out-loud have been 5
mothers or grandmothers, native languages have been mother tongues, and the
kinds of stories that are told to children have been called nursery tales or old wives'
tales. It struck me as no great coincidence when I learned recently that, when a
great number of prominent writers were asked to write about the family member
who had the greatest influence on their literary careers, almost all of them, male as
well as female, had picked their mothers. Perhaps this reflects the extent to which
North American children have been deprived of the grandfathers, those other great
repositories of story; perhaps it will come to change if men come to
share in early child care, and we will have old husbands' tales. But as things are,
language, including the language of our earliest-learned stories, is a verbal matrix,
not a verbal patrix . . .

11. One reason Atwood gives for the presence of
stories in children's lives is

A. scandalous gossip
B. family secrets
C. supernatural influences
D. listening
E. radio and television

12. The close association between the reader and
the author is immediately established by

A. a first person, plural point-of-view
B. placing the reader into a family situation
C. using accessible diction and syntax
D. being emotional
E. appealing to the child in the reader

13. The last sentence of paragraph 2, "From all these scraps . . ." to "forbidden knowledge," contains all of the following except

    A. parallel structure
    B. a periodic sentence
    C. prepositional phrases
    D. a compound-complex sentence
    E. an ellipsis

14. The phrase "forbidden knowledge" in the last sentence of the second paragraph can best be categorized as

    A. a paradox
    B. a biblical allusion
    C. hyperbole
    D. antithesis
    E. understatement

15. According to the author, the writer is like a child because

    A. "We are likely to accept these stories as being of the same level of reality as the kitchen stories" paragraph 4
    B. ". . . we are taught to regard one kind of story as real . . ." (paragraph 4, next to last line)
    C. "We have remained tale-bearers" (paragraph 3)
    D. "We will have old husbands' tales" (paragraph 5)
    E. ". . . the kinds of stories that are told to children have been called nursery tales . . ." (paragraph 5)

16. A careful reading of the last two paragraphs of the excerpt can lead the reader to infer that

    A. society does not value the story teller
    B. women should be the story tellers
    C. story telling should be left to children

    D. men can never be story tellers
    E. the author is a mother herself

17. The predominant tone of the passage is best stated as

    A. scathingly bitter
    B. sweetly effusive
    C. reverently detailed
    D. wistfully observant
    E. aggressively judgmental

18. The author makes use of which of the following rhetorical strategies?

    A. narration and description
    B. exposition and persuasion
    C. process and analysis
    D. anecdote and argument
    E. cause and effect

19. A shift in the focus of the passage occurs with which of the following?

    A. "If we're lucky" (paragraph 4)
    B. "Perhaps, this is what writers are . . ." (paragraph 5)
    C. "Traditionally, . . ." (paragraph 5)
    D. "Perhaps this reflects the extent to which children have been deprived of their grandfathers . . ." (paragraph 5)
    E. "But, as things are, language, including the language of the earliest-learned stories . . ." (paragraph 5)

20. The primary purpose of the passage is to

    A. plead for men to tell more stories
    B. criticize censorship
    C. idealize children
    D. analyze story telling
    E. look at the sources of story telling

Questions 21–32 are based on the following passage from Herman Melville's "Nantucket."

Nantucket! Take out your map and look at it. See what a real corner of the world it occupies; how it stands there, away off shore, more lonely than the Eddystone lighthouse. Look at it—a mere hillock, and elbow of sand; all beach, without a background. There is more sand there than you would use in twenty years as a substitute for blotting paper. Some gamesome wights* will tell you that they have to plant weeds there, they don't grow naturally; they import Canada thistles; they have to send beyond seas for a spile† to stop a leak in an oil cask; that pieces of wood in Nantucket are carried about like bits of the true cross in Rome; that people there plant toadstools before their houses, to get under the shade in summer time; that one blade of grass makes an oasis, three blades a day's walk in a prairie; that they wear quicksand shoes, something like Laplander snowshoes; that they are so shut up, belted about, every way inclosed, surrounded, and made an utter island of by the ocean, that to their very chairs and tables small clams will sometimes be found adhering, as to the backs of sea turtles. But these extravaganzas only show that Nantucket is no Illinois.

Look now at the wondrous traditional story of how this island was settled by the red-men. Thus goes the legend. In olden times an eagle swooped down upon the New England coast, and carried off an infant Indian in his talons. With loud lament the parents saw their child borne out of sight over the wide waters. They resolved to follow in the same direction. Setting out in their canoes, after a perilous passage they discovered the island, and there they found an empty ivory casket,—the poor little Indian's skeleton. 2

What wonder, then, that these Nantucketers, born on a beach, should take to the sea for a livelihood! They first caught crabs and quahogs in the sand; grown bolder, they waded out with nets for mackerel; more experienced, they pushed off in boats and captured cod; and at last, launching a navy of great ships on the sea, explored this watery world; put an incessant belt of circumnavigations round it; peeped in at Behring's Straits; and in all seasons and all oceans declared everlasting war with the mightiest animated mass that has survived the flood; most monstrous and most mountainous! That Himmalehan, salt-sea Mastodon, clothed with such portentousness of unconscious power, that his very panics are more to be dreaded than his most fearless and malicious assaults! 3

And thus have these naked Nantucketers, these sea hermits, issuing from their ant-hill in the sea, overrun and conquered the watery world like so many Alexanders; parceling out among them the Atlantic, Pacific, and Indian oceans, as the three pirate powers did Poland. Let America add Mexico to Texas, and pile Cuba upon Canada; let the English overswarm all India, and hang out their blazing banner from the sun; two thirds of this terraqueous globe are the Nantucketer's. For the sea is his; he owns it, as Emperors own empires; other seamen having but a right of way through it. Merchant ships are but extension bridges; armed ones but floating forts; even pirates and privateers, though following the sea as highwaymen the road, they but plunder other ships, other fragments of the land like themselves, without seeking to draw their living from the bottomless deep itself. The Nantucketer, he alone resides and riots on the sea; he alone, in Bible language, goes down to it in ships; to and fro ploughing it as his own special plantation. *There* is his home; *there* lies his business, which a Noah's flood would not interrupt, though it overwhelmed all the millions in China. He lives on the sea, as prairie dogs in the prairie; he hides among the waves, he climbs them as mountain goats climb the Alps. For years he knows not the land; so that when he comes to it at last, it smells like another world, more strangely than the moon would to an Earthsman. With the landless gull, that as sunset folds her wings and is rocked to sleep between billows; so at nightfall, the Nantucketer, out of sight of land, furls his sail, and lays him to his rest, while under his very pillow rush herds of walruses and whales. 4

* wights: human beings
† spile: a small plug

21. The controlling analogy of the passage is

    A. Nantucket: Illinois
    B. sea: land
    C. Noah: Nantucket
    D. moon: Earthsman
    E. legends: reality

22. Melville describes Nantucketers as all of the following except

    A. conquerors
    B. natives of the sea
    C. farmers of the sea
    D. strangers to the land
    E. exploiters of the Native American

23. The tone of the passage can best be described as

    A. self-congratulatory and confident
    B. formal and pompous
    C. admiring and hyperbolic
    D. informal and cynical
    E. pedantic and objective

24. The shift in the focus of the piece occurs in which line?

    A. The first sentence of paragraph 2
    B. The first sentence of paragraph 3
    C. The first sentence of paragraph 4
    D. The third sentence in paragraph 4
    E. The last sentence

25. The first paragraph contains an extended example of

    A. parallel structure
    B. anecdote
    C. periodic sentence
    D. generalization
    E. argument

26. Melville retells the legend of how the island was settled in order to

    A. have his audience identify with the Native American population
    B. make the passage seem like a parable
    C. contrast with the reality of the Nantucketers
    D. bring a mythic quality to the subject
    E. highlight the plight of the islanders

27. The development of paragraph 3 is structured around

    A. spatial description
    B. selection of incremental details
    C. central analogy
    D. parallel structure
    E. paradox

28. Based on a careful reading of the passage, complete the following analogy:
    NANTUCKET : ILLINOIS ::

    A. merchant ships : pirate ships
    B. Native American : eagle
    C. ivory casket : skeleton
    D. backs of sea turtles : chairs and tables
    E. walrus : prairie dog

29. One may conclude from paragraph 3 that "himmalehan salt-sea mastedon" refers to

    A. the ocean
    B. the whale
    C. the power of nature
    D. Biblical vengeance
    E. emperors

30. The purpose of the passage is to

    A. encourage people to settle on Nantucket
    B. use Nantucket as a model of ecological conservation
    C. honor the indomitable spirit of the Nantucketers
    D. plead for the return of Nantucket to the Native Americans
    E. present a nostalgic reminiscence of the writer's birthplace

31. The subtle humor of the first paragraph is dependent upon

    A. paradox
    B. hyperbole
    C. juxtaposition
    D. irony
    E. ad hominem argument

32. The last sentence of the passage continues the analogy between

    A. reality: illusion
    B. night: day
    C. man: animal
    D. gull: walrus
    E. sea: land

Questions 33–43 are based on the following passage from Ralph Waldo Emerson's Oration before the
Phi Beta Kappa society, at Cambridge University, August 31, 1837,
entitled "The American Scholar."

It is remarkable, the character of the pleasure we derive from the best books.   1
They impress us with the conviction that one nature wrote and the same reads.
We read the verses of one of the great English poets, of Chaucer, of Marvell, of
Dryden, with the most modern joy,—with a pleasure, I mean, which is in great part
caused by the abstraction of all *time* from their verses. There is some awe mixed   5
with the joy of our surprise, when this poet, who lived in some past world, two or
three hundred years ago, says that which lies close to my own soul, that which I
also had well-nigh thought and said. But for the evidence thence afforded to the
philosophical doctrine of the identity of all minds, we should suppose some pre-
established harmony, some foresight of souls that were to be, and some preparation   10
of stores for their future wants, like the fact observed in insects, who lay up food
before death for the young grub they should never see.

It would not be hurried by any love of system, by an exaggeration of instincts,
to underrate the Book. We boil grass and the broth of shoes, so the human mind
can be fed by any knowledge. And great and heroic men have existed who had   15
almost no other information than by the printed page. I only would say that it
needs a strong head to bear that diet. One must be an inventor to read well. As the
proverb says, "He that would bring home the wealth of the Indies, must carry out
the wealth of the Indies." There is then creative reading as well as creative writing.
When the mind is braced by labor and invention, the page of whatever book we   20
read becomes luminous with manifold allusion. Every sentence is doubly significant, and the sense of our author is as broad as the world. We then see, what is
always true, that as the seer's hour of vision is short and rare among heavy days
and months, so is its record, perchance, the least part of his volume. The discerning
will read, in his Plato or Shakespeare, only the least part,—only the authentic utter-   25
ances of the oracle;—all the rest he rejects, were it never so many times Plato's and
Shakespeare's.

Of course, there is a portion of reading quite indispensable to a wise man.
History and exact science he must learn by laborious reading. Colleges, in like manner, have their indispensable office,—to teach elements. But they can only highly   30
serve us when they aim not to drill, but to create; when they gather from far every
ray of various genius to their hospitable halls, and by the concentrated fires, set the
hearts of their youth on flame. Thought and knowledge are natures in which apparatus and pretension avail nothing. Gowns and pecuniary foundations, though of
towns of gold, can never countervail the least sentence or syllable of wit. Forget   35
this, and our American colleges will recede in their public importance, whilst they
grow richer every year.

33. In context, the word "oracle" in line 26 can
best be interpreted to mean the

A. visionary writer
B. inventive writer
C. popular writer of a time
D. intuitive writer or
E. writer as critic

34. In line 17, the word "diet" refers to

A. "Broth of shoes" (paragraph 2, sentence 2)
B. "Boiled grass" (paragraph 2, sentence 2)
C. "Any knowledge" (paragraph 2, sentence 2)
D. "Any love" (paragraph 2, sentence 1)
E. "Printed page" (paragraph 2, sentence 3)

35. The speaker characterizes the great writers as being able to

    A. surprise the reader
    B. present universal truths
    C. create harmony in their writing
    D. be philosophical
    E. write about nature

36. The speaker's attitude toward great writers in the fourth sentence of paragraph 1 [lines 5–8] might best be described as

    A. skeptical
    B. confused
    C. accusative
    D. validated
    E. patronizing

37. The speaker's tone in the passage can best be described as

    A. pretentious
    B. analytical
    C. satirical
    D. ambiguous
    E. servile

38. All of the following lines use figurative language except

    A. "It is remarkable, the character of the pleasure we derive from the best books. They impress us with the conviction that one nature wrote and the same reads."
    B. ". . . and some preparation of stores for their future wants, like the fact observed in insects . . ."
    C. "We boil grass and the broth of shoes, so the human mind can be fed by any knowledge."
    D. "I would only say that it needs a strong head to bear that diet. One must be an inventor to read well."
    E. "Gowns and pecuniary foundations, though of towns of gold, can never countervail the least sentence or syllable of wit."

39. After reading the passage, the reader can infer that the author desires to

    A. praise the work of current writers

    B. change the curriculum of the college
    C. change college administration
    D. warn against relying on academic appearances
    E. criticize the cost of college

40. The pronoun "this" in the last line of the passage refers to

    A. "But they can only highly serve us when they aim not to drill but to create . . ."
    B. "History and exact science he must learn by laborious reading."
    C. "Thought and Knowledge are natures in which apparatus and pretension avail nothing."
    D. "Forget this, and our American colleges will recede in their public importance . . ."
    E. "When the mind is braced by labor and invention, the page of whatever book we read becomes luminous with manifold allusion."

41. According to the speaker, the characteristics of the discerning reader include all of the following except

    A. brings himself to the work
    B. makes connections with the past
    C. discards irrelevancies
    D. approaches difficult readings willingly
    E. aspires to be a writer

42. Paragraphs 1 and 2 develop their ideas by means of
    I. metaphor and simile
    II. allusion
    III. paradox

    A. I
    B. II
    C. III
    D. I and II
    E. I, II, and III

43. The purpose of the third paragraph is to

    A. defend the role of reading
    B. praise history and science
    C. Delineate the qualities of an ideal college
    D. inspire student scholars
    E. honor college instructors

Questions 44–54 are based on the following
excerpt from Joseph Conrad's *The Secret Sharer*.

   On my right hand there were lines of fishing stakes resembling a mysterious
system of half-submerged bamboo fences, incomprehensible in its division of the
domain of tropical fishes, and crazy of aspect as if abandoned forever by some
nomad tribe of fishermen now gone to the other end of the ocean; for there was no
sign of human habitation as far as the eye could reach. To the left a group of barren   5
islets, suggesting ruins of stone walls, towers, and blockhouses, had its foundations
set in a blue sea that itself looked solid, so still and stable did it lie below my feet;
even the track of light from the westering sun shone smoothly, without that animated glitter which tells of an imperceptible ripple. And when I turned my head to
take a parting glance at the tug which had just left us anchored outside the bar, I   10
saw the straight line of the flat shore joined to the stable sea, edge to edge, with a
perfect and unmarked closeness, in one leveled floor half brown, half blue under
the enormous dome of the sky. Corresponding in their insignificance to the islets of
the sea, two small clumps of trees, one on each side of the only fault in the impecca-
ble joint, marked the mouth of the river Meinam we had just left on the first   15
preparatory stage of our homeward journey; and, far back on the inland level, a
larger and loftier mass, the grove surrounding the great Paknam pagoda, was the
only thing on which the eye could rest from the vain task of exploring the monoto-
nous sweep of the horizon. Here and there gleams as of a few scattered pieces of silver marked the windings of the great river; and on the nearest of them, just within   20
the bar, the tug steaming right into the land became lost to my sight, hull and funnel and masts, as though the impassive earth had swallowed her up without an
effort, without a tremor. My eye followed the light cloud of her smoke, now here,
now there, above the plain according to the devious curves of the stream, but
always fainter and farther away, till I lost it at last behind the miter-shaped hill of   25
the great pagoda. And then I was left alone with my ship, anchored at the head of
the Gulf of Siam.

44. Within the passage, the long, sinuous sentences
emphasize the

A. narrator's sense of anticipation
B. objectivity of nature
C. insecurity of the narrator
D. passive nature of the journey
E. fearful tone of the passage

45. In the next to last sentence of the passage
[lines 23–26], "devious curves" most likely is
used to reinforce

A. the unpredictability of the water
B. the hidden nature of the stream
C. the concept of the complexity of what lies
   beneath the surface of the story
D. the mystery of nature
E. all of the above

46. The passage as a whole can best described as

A. an interior monologue
B. a melodramatic episode
C. an evocation of place
D. an historical narrative
E. an allegory

47. The first sentence of the passage helps to
establish tone by means of

A. structure that reflects the strangeness of the
   experience described
B. parallel structure that contrasts with the
   chaos of the situation
C. alliteration to heighten the imagery
D. irony to create a sense of satire
E. hyperbole that exaggerates the danger of
   the situation

48. Which of the following ideas can be supported based on the third sentence [lines 9–13] beginning with "And when I . . . "?

    A. The speaker enjoys watching boats sailing on the horizon.
    B. The speaker wants to revel in the beauty and grace of nature.
    C. The speaker responds to the symmetry and balance of nature.
    D. The speaker realizes how vulnerable man is in the universe.
    E. The speaker is fearful of the earth and sea.

49. All of the following contribute to the feeling of solitude except

    A. ". . . the impassive earth had swallowed her up without an effort . . ."
    B. "the group of barren islets"
    C. "the groves surrounding the great Paknam pagoda"
    D. "the monotonous sweep of the horizon"
    E. "ruins of stone walls, towers, and blockhouses"

50. The passage is organized primarily by means of

    A. spatial description
    B. definition
    C. chronological order
    D. order of importance
    E. parallelism

51. In the third to last sentence of the passage [lines 19–23] beginning with "Here and there . . . ," the figure of speech used to describe "the windings of the great river" is

    A. personification
    B. simile
    C. apostrophe
    D. antithesis
    E. symbol

52. The writer emphasizes his solitude by using all of the following rhetorical techniques except

    A. heavy descriptive emphasis placed on setting
    B. overt statement of the absence of other people
    C. tracking the departure of the tugboat
    D. diction that emphasizes desertion and neglect
    E. contrasting the present situation with previous times

53. A characteristic of the author's style is

    A. succession of allusions
    B. the use of emotional language
    C. terse sentence structure
    D. vividness of contrasting images
    E. shifts in points of view

54. The tone of the passage can best be described as

    A. cynical
    B. reflective
    C. sarcastic
    D. elegiac
    E. apathetic

END OF SECTION I

AP ENGLISH LANGUAGE

Section II

Time—2 hours
(Suggested time for each question is 40 minutes. Each question counts
as one-third of the total score for Section II.)

Question 1

Carefully read Chief Seattle's oration to Governor Isaac I. Stevens who had just returned from Washington, DC with orders to buy Indian lands and create reservations. In a well-written essay identify Chief Seattle's purpose and analyze the rhetorical strategies he uses to convey his purpose. Consider such items as figurative language, organization, diction, and tone.

. . . Yonder sky that has wept tears of compassion upon my people for centuries untold, and which to us appears changeless and eternal, may change. Today is fair. Tomorrow it may be overcast with clouds. My words are like the stars that never change. Whatever Seattle says the great chief at Washington can rely upon with as much certainty as he can upon the return of the sun. The White Chief says that Big Chief at Washington sends us greetings of friendship and goodwill. This is kind of him for we know he has little need of our friendship in return. His people are many. They are like the grass that covers vast prairies. My people are few. They resemble the scattering trees of a storm-swept plain. The great, and I presume—good White Chief sends us word that he wishes to buy our lands but is willing to allow us enough to live comfortably. This indeed appears just, even generous, for the Red Man no longer has rights that he need respect, and the offer may be wise, as we are no longer in need of an extensive country. 1

There was a time when our people covered the land as the waves of a wind-ruffled sea cover its shell-paved floor, but that time long since passed away with the greatness of tribes that are now but a mournful memory. I will not dwell on, nor mourn over, our untimely decay, nor reproach my paleface brothers with hastening it as we too may have been somewhat to blame. 2

Youth is impulsive. When our young men grow angry at some real or imaginary wrong, and disfigure their faces with black paint, it denotes that their hearts are black, and our old men and old women are unable to restrain them. Thus it was when the white men first began to push our forefathers further westward. But let us hope that the hostilities between us may never return. We would have everything to lose and nothing to gain. 3

Our good father at Washington—for I presume he is now our father as well as yours—our great and good father, I say, sends us word that if we do as he desires he will protect us. But can that ever be? Your God is not our God! Your God loves your people and hates mine. He folds his strong protecting arms lovingly about the pale face—but he has forsaken his red children—if they really are his. Our God, the Great Spirit, seems also to have forsaken us. Our people are ebbing away like a rapidly receding tide that will never return. How then can we be brothers? We are two distinct races with separate origins and separate destinies. 4

To us the ashes of our ancestors are sacred and their resting place is hallowed ground. You wander far from the graves of your ancestors and seemingly without regret. Your dead cease to love you and the land of your nativity as soon as they 5 pass the portals of the tomb and wander away beyond the stars. Our dead never forget the beautiful world that gave them being . . . and often return to visit, guide, console, and comfort the lonely hearted living.

It matters little where we pass the remnant of our days. They will not be many. 6
The Indians' night promises to be dark. Not a single star of hope hovers above his horizon. Tribe follows tribe, and nation follows nation like the waves of the sea. It is the order of nature, and regret is useless. Your time of decay may be distant, but it will surely come, for even the white man whose God walked and talked with him as friend with friend, cannot be exempt from the common destiny. We may be brothers after all. We will see.

And when the Last Red Man shall have perished, these shores will swarm with 7
the invisible dead of my tribe, and when your children's children think themselves alone, they will not be alone. At night when you think your cities are deserted, they will throng with the returning hosts that once filled them and still love this beautiful land. The White Man will never be alone.

Let him be just and deal kindly with my people, for the dead are not 8
powerless.

Question 2

In "At the Funeral" from *An Unfinished Burlesque of Books on Etiquette*, Mark Twain pokes fun at the social norms surrounding a very serious subject. In a well-written essay analyze Twain's attitude toward his subject and how he creates the humor in the piece. Consider such items as tone, diction, selection of detail, and use of the unexpected.

At the Funeral

Do not criticize the person in whose honor the entertainment is given. 1

Make no remarks about his equipment. If the handles [of the encasement] are plated, it is best to not observe it. 2

If the odor of the flowers is too oppressive for your comfort, remember that they were not brought there for you, and that the person for whom they were brought suffers no inconvenience from their presence. 3

Listen, with as intense an expression of attention as you can command, to the official statement of the character and history of the person in whose honor the entertainment is given; and if these statistics should seem to fail to tally with the facts, in places, do not nudge your neighbor, or press your foot upon his toes, or manifest, by any other sign, your awareness that taffy is being distributed. 4

If the official hopes expressed concerning the person in whose honor the entertainment is given are known to you to be oversized, let it pass—do not interrupt. 5

At the moving passages, be moved—but only according to the degree of your intimacy with the parties giving the entertainment, or with the party in whose honor the entertainment is given. Where a blood relation sobs, an intimate friend should choke up, a distant acquaintance should sigh, a stranger should merely fumble sympathetically with his handkerchief. Where the occasion is military, the emotions should be graded according to military rank, the highest officer present taking precedence in emotional violence, and the rest modifying their feelings according to their position in the service. 6

Do not bring your dog. 7

Question 3

In his essay "The Wilderness Idea," Wallace Stegner states the following.

Without any remaining wilderness we are committed wholly, without chance for even momentary reflection and rest, to a headlong drive into our technological termite-life, the Brave New World of a completely man-controlled environment.

Write a well-constructed essay that defends, challenges, or qualifies Stegner's statement using your own knowledge, experience, observation, or reading.

END OF SECTION II

ANSWERS TO MULTIPLE-CHOICE QUESTIONS

Answer Key

1. D	19. C	37. B
2. B	20. E	38. A
3. E	21. B	39. D
4. A	22. E	40. C
5. E	23. E	41. E
6. B	24. D	42. D
7. C	25. A	43. C
8. A	26. D	44. D
9. C	27. D	45. E
10. D	28. C	46. C
11. D	29. B	47. A
12. A	30. A	48. C
13. E	31. C	49. C
14. B	32. E	50. A
15. C	33. A	51. B
16. A	34. E	52. E
17. D	35. B	53. D
18. B	36. D	54. B

Explanations of Answers to the Multiple-Choice Questions

The Dickens Passage

1. **D.** The very first sentence indicates the author's purpose. Here, the reader is told directly that Florence is both fanciful and somber, rich and stern.

2. **B.** This selection is based on a quite specific description of Florence and an area within the city. To correctly answer this question, the student needs to be familiar with the different types of rhetorical strategies.

3. **E.** The reader is brought from the general street scene to a specific prison and then to a specific scene outside the prison. Metaphors, similes, and imagery are found throughout the selection, such as "small cells like ovens" and "distrustful windows." Contrast and comparison are provided when a phrase such as "faded and tarnished Great Saloon" is placed next to the "walls which record the triumphs of the Medici." The passage does *not* follow a specific time line.

4. **A.** The test taker needs to know the definition of paradox and must be able to recognize it in a given text. Here, smoke is being used to purify the air even though it is in itself a pollutant.

5. **E.** Dickens is not warning people away from Florence, nor is he criticizing its government. What the text and its selection of details do is to reinforce the idea of Florence being a city of contrast (youth and age, life and death, bright flowers and squalid prisons).

6. **B.** There is no support from a close reading of the text that will allow you to defend choice B, which sees no connection between the two scenes described. Obviously both reveal aspects of Florence. Both are descriptive, with the second paragraph containing the selective contrast with the first paragraph.

7. **C.** Distrustful and secret are indicative of "intrigue" and building thick walls and huge battlements point to the need for protection from aggression. No other choice provides these same inferences.

8. **A.** A close look at each of the selected lines reveals opposites being placed side by side. This is the nature of antithesis.

9. **C.** The Castle of Otranto is described using such terms as "ponderous gloom," "faded" and "tarnished" and "mouldering." These are evocative of a place that is creepy and frightening. None of the other choices projects these qualities.

10. **D.** In Dickens' time, "jealous" was used to indicate the state of being watchful or closely guarded. If you look at the context of the line, you can see that "jealous" has nothing to do with our current use of the word.

The Atwood Passage

11. **D.** Although you might be inclined to accept A, B, or E as possible correct choices, you should be aware that these are specific things the child hears. Each of these would cancel the other out, because they would be equally valid. Choice C is nowhere to be found in the selection. Therefore, the appropriate choice is D, listening.

12. **A.** The very first word of the selection is "Our." This immediately links the writer and the reader. Both are vested with this choice of pronoun.

13. **E.** If you look carefully, you find examples of all of the choices except E. An ellipsis is punctuation comprising three periods. You find none in this sentence. Its function is to notify the reader that a piece of the text has been omitted.

14. **B.** The question makes reference to wanting or seeking something not permitted, such as Adam and Eve being warned not to eat of the forbidden fruit from the tree of knowledge. The other choices are simply not appropriate to the relationship between *forbidden* and *knowledge*.

15. **C.** This is a rather easy question. The entire third paragraph supports this idea.

16. **A.** The answer is clearly supported in the last sentence of paragraph 4. That which is immediately practical and helpful in a very tangible way is the more valuable.

17. **D.** Words, phrases used, and specific details given in this passage support the adjective "wistful" (paragraphs 3 and 4). She is observant throughout the passage as she provides details of the child acquiring her stories. The writer's wistfulness is reiterated in the last paragraph as she states her yearning for men to share in the language of story telling.

18. **B.** The only choice that presents two strategies actually present in the text is B. The entire passage employs exposition to support the author's purpose. Even the final paragraph, which attempts to persuade, uses exposition to strengthen the appeal to have men welcomed into the language of story telling. (If you are not crystal clear about the terminology used in the choices, this may be one of those questions you choose to skip, because it can be time consuming trying to determine the correct choice.)

19. **C.** The abruptness of "Traditionally," provides no real connection with the previous paragraph or the previous sentence. It is an obvious break that grabs the reader's attention and leads him or her to Atwood's point.

20. **E.** Throughout the passage, Atwood is taking a close look at the beginnings of story telling. Although she does attempt to persuade us of the need to encourage men to tell their stories, this is not the primary purpose of the piece. It is important to also notice that the title is a clue to this answer.

The Melville Passage

21. **B.** Throughout the passage, Melville builds his description on the comparison between items connected to the sea and those related to the land. Choices A and C are examples of this controlling analogy. D is another specific detail provided, and E is an example used by Melville to reinforce his description of the Nantucketer.

22. **E.** Paragraph 4 supports choices A, B, C, and D. The only choice not supported in the text is E.

23. **C.** The diction and selection of detail all support the tone of admiration. The hyperbole can easily be seen in paragraph 1 and the end of paragraph 3.

24. **B.** Here, pronouns are very important. In paragraph 2, *this* refers the reader to paragraph 1, which is about the island. *These* in paragraph 4 refers to the previous paragraph, which is about the inhabitants of Nantucket. The last sentence of the passage, while quite moving, indicates, again, a reference to Nantucketers. However, *these* in the first sentence of paragraph 3 is a definite shift in focus from the island to its inhabitants.

25. **A.** The only choice appearing in the first paragraph is parallel structure that is used throughout the listing of "extravaganzas" that Melville bestows on Nantucket. Many of the items in the listing begin with the word *that*.

26. **D.** Keeping in mind the central focus of the passage, Melville's retelling of the Native American legend is not to highlight or focus on Native Americans, but to reinforce his attitude toward the Nantucketer whom he perceives in mythic proportions. He compares them to Noah, to Alexander the Great, and to Emperors.

27. **B.** The question requires the reader to be aware of the consecutive details that build in size and importance: from the clam to the whale.

28. **E.** The analogy established with Nantucket to Illinois is that of an island to a land-locked state. The only choice given that illustrates the same relationship is walrus to prairie dog. Here a walrus lives its life surrounded by the sea; whereas, the prairie dog is surrounded by the land.

29. **B.** The whale is a "mightiest animated mass." This can only refer to the largest creature in the sea. "Himmalehan" and "Mastadon" reinforce the power and size of the creature.

30. **C.** The tone, diction, syntax, and selection of detail all point to Melville's admiration of the fortitude, perseverance, and uniqueness of the Nantucketer.

31. **B.** Beginning with "There is more sand" and continuing to the end of the paragraph, Melville presents examples dependent upon extreme exaggeration.

32. **E.** The paragraph develops an extended analogy that compares the world of the sea to that of the land, such as sea to prairie, sailor to prairie dog. None of the other choices are valid in this context.

The Emerson Passage

33. **A.** If you go back to the next to last sentence of paragraph 2, you will see the phrase "the seer's hour of vision." Your knowledge of synonyms will lead you to choose A.

34. **E.** Using the process of substitution, it is not difficult to eliminate all choices other than "the printed page."

35. **B.** For Emerson, the universal crosses barriers between time and place. This idea is supported in the third sentence of paragraph 1.

36. **D.** Using the process of elimination while looking carefully at the given lines, you will discover that the only answer that correctly relates to Emerson's attitude is D. All the others are negative.

37. **B.** Vocabulary is a key factor in this question. In this passage, Emerson is "taking apart" the qualities of a great writer, book, and college. This is what an analytical essay does.

38. **A.** In the first two sentences of paragraph 1, Emerson is setting up the parameters of his argument. There is no figurative language here.

39. **D.** Carefully reading the last paragraph, especially the last three sentences, can only lead you to choose D. None of the other choices is logical within the context of the passage.

40. **C.** Antecedents come *before* the given pronoun, and as close as possible to that pronoun. With this in mind, the fifth sentence of paragraph 3 is the only choice that correctly and logically fits the criteria.

41. **E.** If you pay close attention to the second paragraph, you will find all the choices, except E.

42. **D.** Emerson alludes to "great English poets" in the first paragraph, to a proverb and other writers in the second paragraph. Similes and metaphors can be found throughout both paragraphs, but no paradox is evident.

43. **C.** Because this is an analytical passage, including the final paragraph, C is the only acceptable choice.

The Conrad Passage

44. **D.** The very nature of sentences that are long and flowing serves to create a corresponding mood of passivity, ease, and timelessness. This lack of tension in the structure is not indicated in any of the other choices.

45. **E.** Each of the choices deals with what is yet unknown to the narrator and the reader. The phrase "devious curves" foreshadows the complexity of the novella itself.

46. **C.** This exemplifies that choosing the correct answer can be dependent on the student's knowing definitions of terms and ability to recognize them in context. No other choice is acceptable in characterizing this passage.

47. **A.** This compound-complex sentence sets the task for the reader with its convoluted structure and imagery. This reflects the very essence the narrator is presenting to the reader of the strangeness of the experience.

48. **C.** The diction, which includes "joined," "edge to edge," and "half brown, half blue" supports the idea of balance and corresponding symmetry.

49. **C.** Choices A, B, D, and E all reinforce the feeling of abandonment and aloneness. Choice C does not contribute to this impression of isolation; it is rather just a descriptive detail.

50. **A.** By its very definition spatial description will provide the reader an opportunity to sense the setting by means of directions, scale, dimension, and color.

51. **B.** Just find the word *as,* and you will easily locate the simile comparing the light to scattered pieces of silver.

52. **E.** A careful reading of the passage uncovers each of the given choices except E. Nowhere in the excerpt does the narrator indicate a contrast between the current situation and a previous one.

53. **D.** The passage contains no allusions, has no real emotional diction, and maintains a constant first person point of view. And, most obviously, it does not rely on short, direct sentences. Therefore, the only choice is D.

54. **B.** The entire passage involves the reader in the narrator's thoughtful and reflective observations about his or her surroundings.

RATING THE ESSAYS

Rubrics for Chief Seattle Passage

High-Range Essay

- Clearly identifies Seattle's purpose and attitude
- Successfully and effectively analyzes the rhetorical strategies used to accomplish the author's purpose
- Effectively cites specifics from the text to illustrate rhetorical devices and their meanings and effects on the oration
- Indicates a facility with organization
- Effectively manipulates language
- Few, if any syntactical errors

Midrange Essay

- Correctly identifies Seattle's purpose and attitude
- Understands the demands of the prompt
- Cites specific examples of rhetorical devices found in the text and effects on oration
- Ideas clearly stated
- Less well-developed than the high-range essays
- A few lapses in diction or syntax

Low-Range Essay

- Inadequate response to the prompt
- Misunderstands, oversimplifies, or misrepresents Seattle's purpose and attitude
- Insufficient or inappropriate use of examples to develop the demands of the prompt
- Lack of mature control of elements of essay writing

Students apparently found the question quite accessible. Most recognized the figurative language used in the passage and were able to incorporate examples into their essays. They were able to recognize the purpose and emotional appeal of Seattle's oration. The more perceptive writers recognized the subtleties of Seattle's manipulation of the situation—his implied sarcasm and his subtle threatening predictions.

Chief Seattle Passage—Student Sample A

In his oration to Governor Isaac I. Stevens, Chief Seattle attempts to convince the whites that they should deal fairly with the Native Americans despite their inferior status. Through the use of rhetorical strategies and devices like figurative language, organization, diction, and tone, he appeals both to the pride and the reason of the Governor, reminding him that, though weak, the Natives are not powerless.

Chief Seattle begins his oration in a friendly manner, appealing to the Governor and the white's pride while recognizing their superior status. He refers to the Governor as "the great" and "the good white chief" throughout the piece, hoping the governor will look favorably on his subordinance despite the mocking that is hidden in his words. Seattle takes responsibility for the plight of the Natives, another strategy that undoubtedly makes him more respectable and admirable to the Governor, although he does not necessarily believe his people are truly at fault. In yet another attempt to get or remain on the Governor's "good side," Seattle says that the young Indian warriors' "hearts are black," blaming them and not the whites for the warfare and distrust that characterizes the Native American-American relationship. To increase his own credibility, Seattle uses the simile "my words are like the stars that never change," once more emphasizing his steadfastness and ability to work with the Americans. By presenting himself as inferior, apologetic, responsible and respectful, Seattle attempts to win Stevens' favor.

In addition to promoting his own respectability, Seattle emphasizes differences between his people and the Americans. Appreciating the Americans' "generosity" and "friendship and goodwill," Seattle points out the differences between the two peoples in a respectful manner. He calls the whites his "pale-face brothers," but is certain to point out that they believe in different supreme beings, have different customs, are "two distinct races with separate origins and separate destinies." With rhetorical questions like "How then can we be brothers?" Seattle suggests that the two peoples cannot intermingle through no fault of their own. Instead of blaming the Americans, he implies that they are just and kind and that the peoples' lack of friendship is just the way it's supposed to be.

Despite his calm, almost compromising attitude throughout his oration, Chief Seattle does, at certain points, warn Governor Stevens of the power of his people. Short of belligerent, these comments are often made in a manner that implies rather than openly affirms Native American strength and lack of fear. With the emotional statement "Indians' night promises to be dark," Seattle almost suggests that his people have nothing to lose if the relationship with the Americans goes sour. They have already lost so much that they will fight to the end. Seattle warns that "these shores will swarm with the invisible dead of my tribe . . . the White Man will never be alone." Thus, he reminds Stevens that, even though his people are but "the scattering trees of a storm-swept plain," they are strong—a force to be reckoned with. In a respectful manner, he manages to threaten Stevens and clearly deliver his message that the tribe will not so easily be destroyed.

In addition to warning the Governor, acting respectfully and emphasizing the inherent differences between the two peoples, Chief Seattle gives a sense of the unfair treatment his tribe has suffered. In his oration so deeply saturated with figurative language, balanced sentences, carefully chosen diction, and hidden implications, the Chief conveys his message loud and clear. Though weak in number, his people are strong in heart; though inferior in legal status, his tribe is superior in customs and values. The governor may buy their land, but, Seattle reminds him, he may never buy their pride or their silence.

Chief Seattle Passage—Student Sample B

Chief Seattle, one of great speakers for the Native Americans, spoke out against Governor Stevens in an attempt to discourage the buying of more Indian land. His style which includes similes, rhetorical questions, and emotional diction, not only gets his point across, but warns and denounces the whites as well.

Right in the beginning, Seattle starts emotionally with "wept tears of compassion" to try to gain a sympathy for his people. Later on in the passage, he exclaims, "Your God is not our God!" and blatantly announces "Your God loves your people and hates mine." These harsh words obviously convey Chief Seattle's anger and disapproval.

To further increase the emotional appeal, Seattle employs rhetorical questions in an attempt to make the reader wonder and empathize. He states ". . . he will protect us. But can that ever be" and "How then can we be brothers . . . we are two distinct races." Since this was addressed to Governor Isaac, what this did was it made the Governor question himself whether the buying of more Indian land and pushing the Indians west are right and moral. In addition, the rhetorical questions allow Chief Seattle to express his anger better.

The use of similes in this piece not only add a poetic touch, but also effectively describe the decrease in Native Americans and the increase in whites. He compares the invasive whites as "grass that covers the prairies" while describing the disappearing Indians as "scattering trees of a storm-swept plain." The storm that swept through clearly also represents the whites that pushed the Native Americans westward or bought their land. By comparing the whites to grass *that grows anywhere they want and as a storm, Chief Seattle subtly establishes the idea that whites are land-hungry and greedy.*

In addition, the Chief denounces certain cultural aspects of whites through a 5 *series of antitheses. As he uses "To us the ashes of our ancestors are sacred . . . You wander from the graves . . . without regret" and "your dead cease to love you . . . Our dead never forget the beautiful world," there seems to be a criticism of whites as loveless people who don't respect the dead. And, as a final warning, Chief Seattle says, "Your time of decay may be distant, but it will surely come . . ." As he tried to tell the whites that what they have done will eventually cause their demise.*

In all, Chief Seattle's speech to Governor Isaac not only achieves his purpose 6 *of discouraging the actions of the whites, but warns and denounces the culture of the whites as well.*

Rating Student Sample A

This is a high-range essay for the following reasons:

- An immediate and clear indication of Seattle's purpose and attitude
- Understanding and discussion of Seattle's attitude and purpose (paragraph 2)
- Demonstration of a mature voice
- Thorough and effective connection between texts and insights (last 2 sentences of paragraph 2)
- Superior use of connective tissue—transitions and echo words ("in addition," "despite his calm," "acting respectfully," "winning favor")
- Refers to a variety of rhetorical strategies and devices to support the writer's assertion (paragraph 3: rhetorical questions), (paragraph 3: cause and effect), (paragraph 4: details), (paragraph 4: figurative language)
- Mature perceptions and insights (paragraph 2, sentence 2), (paragraph 4, sentence 2), (paragraph 5, next to last sentence)
- Mature writing style (last sentence)

This high-range essay indicates the clear voice of a mature writer and reader. Once the writer has committed to Seattle's purpose and attitude, the writer develops in each successive paragraph a supporting aspect of the stated purpose and/or attitude.

Rating Student Sample B

This is a midrange essay for the following reasons:

- Concise, on-target development of prompt
- Indicates an understanding of the oration
- Makes intelligent points, but does not always develop them or defend them (paragraph 3, last sentence)
- Each paragraph deals with a different strategy (paragraph 2: emotional details), (paragraph 3: rhetorical questions), (paragraph 4: simile), (paragraph 5: antithesis)
- Good connective tissue
- A few lapses in syntax and diction (paragraph 3, next to last sentence)

This essay is indicative of a writer who both understands the passage and the prompt. There is an adequate analysis of the rhetorical strategies and devices present in the text, and the student reaches for unique insights (paragraph 4, last sentence). The lack of development of a couple of the cited points places this essay squarely in the midrange.

Rubrics for the Twain Passage

High-Range Essay

- Correctly identifies Twain's purpose and attitude toward his subject
- Effectively discusses/analyzes methods used to create the tone, attitude
- Effectively analyzes devices used to develop the purpose
- Effectively connects the humor to the author's purpose
- Recognizes and discusses the subtleties of the passage
- Good use of connective tissue
- Effectively manipulates language
- Clear organization and topic adherence
- Few, if any, syntactical errors

Midrange Essay

- Correctly identifies the author's purpose and attitude
- Adequately recognizes and analyzes the devices used to create tone and attitude
- Adequately analyzes the devices used to develop the purpose
- Recognition of Twain's subtleties may be missing
- Development not as strong/complete as the high-range essays
- A few syntactical errors

Low-Range Essay

- Inadequate response to the prompt
- May misrepresent or incorrectly identify the author's purpose and attitude toward his subject
- May inaccurately identify and/or analyze rhetorical devices
- Ideas are incompletely developed
- Indicates a lack of control of diction, syntax, and/or organization

Twain Passage—Student Sample A

Do not pick your teeth and lick your fingers while conversing with your dentist.   1

Do not yell out instructions to actors in crowded movie theaters. And if you   2
sleep in the nude, always wear a long, heavy bathrobe when collecting your morning paper.

All of these instructions are rather obvious, I hope—but extremely humorous.   3
I never realized Mark Twain had such a great sense of humor. He makes a funeral, that ordinarily is a remarkably somber occasion, almost bearable with his sarcastic tone. I remember thinking that Tom Sawyer's own funeral in Twain's novel of the same name was amusing, but not quite as funny as "At the Funeral."

Because of the diction and syntax in this passage, the excerpt could easily qualify as a "Miss Manners" column from my local newspaper. It could also fit in with stuffy old British books. The very proper and elegant English used helps to make this piece so ironic. One would expect important matters to be discussed when "the official statement of the character and history of the person in whose honor" is read, but in actuality, one would be more likely to crack up with laughter. Who would even think about a mourner bringing a dog to a funeral, or examining the handles of the coffin to see if they are plated?   4

The things Twain suggests are too ridiculous for anyone to ever consider them as realistic possibilities, but that is exactly what makes this passage hilarious. This twist on such a serious event is positively unexpected, and at first glance, the reader is almost taken aback until he realizes that this is a humorous piece about a funeral. The fact that such a grave subject is touched upon in a jocular fashion is ironic. The whole work is based on irony and sarcasm. Twain provides a series of negative commandments, "do not nudge your neighbor," and "do not bring your dog!" This becomes more ridiculous as the passage progresses Also, the tips Twain gives are so absurd that not one single person on the face of this planet would ever do any of the things Twain warns against.   5

My favorite part of "At the Funeral" is Twain counseling against showing one's acknowledgement of the truth that is being fudged (or the "taffy being distributed") when the person is being eulogized. It's so funny because people are supposed to be respectful at funerals, and this work is all about people being disrespectful.   6

The piece was enjoyable to read because it was so humorous. I would really like to read more of Mark Twain's work now that my eyes have been opened to his comedic side.   7

Twain Passage—Student Sample B

When many enter a funeral home, besides often being overcome with grief, many find themselves lost and wondering how to behave. Here, Mark Twain "conveniently forgets" the grief associated with funerals, and gives a humorous account of how one should act.   1

This passage's humorous tone, that is really sarcastic, reminds us of the first time each of us has entered a funeral home. I can remember my first time in one, wondering how to act or what to say. Twain's "guidelines" wouldn't have been of too much help to me before. But after attending a funeral it is a fresh reminder of what goes on, and of the thoughts that filled my head.   2

Twain uses short sentences and simple diction from the first line, making this a great essay you would find in a small chapter of a book or in an "upbeat" funeral home. At points the reader may think Twain is attempting to be serious, but by the end of the sentence, Twain uses the unexpected to create irony. Nowhere is this   3 more obvious than when he tells us "Do not bring your dog!" at the end of the passage. Twists are placed in every sentence. Twain uses this every time that he states a thought that no refined would ever say, such as referring to the "equipment." Paragraph four ends with an action many of us are guilty of at funeral homes. Many times I have heard untruths at funerals and have seen rude nudging.

Twain creates humor by expressing in words the thoughts people have inside at funeral homes. At every funeral I go to the smell of the flowers is always that same extreme smell. Do I comment to my family? Of course I don't. Here, Twain not only admits the "oppressive" nature of the flowers, but he acts sarcastically by telling of how the honored person cannot smell them. 4

Twain possessed a power to place the intangible feelings of many in words of meaning. He, like many, finds funerals confusing. Yet, he expresses the way he finds best to deal with some common feelings. 5

Rating Student Sample A

This is a high-range essay for the following reasons:

- Obviously understands the tone and intent of the passage
- Recognizes the devices used to create humor
- Presents a clear, controlled, confident voice
- Effectively address the requirements of the prompt
- Catches the subtleties of the passage
- Has good connective tissue
- Shows mature diction and syntax
- Has clear organization and topic coherence
- Has few, if any, syntactical errors

This writer attempts to recreate the tone and attitude of Twain's passage to indicate a true understanding of the prompt and selection! This risk indicates a confident student writer.

Rating Student Sample B

This is a midrange essay for the following reasons:

- Correctly identifies Twain's tone and attitude
- Adequate illustration of the devices used to create and indicate tone and attitude
- Clear and concise analysis of the tone and attitude
- Needs to link observations with the text
- Obvious examples
- Not as subtle as the high-range essays
- Few, if any, lapses in diction and syntax

This solid, midrange essay is developed by a writer who brings personal experience into the presentation. The paper's brevity and need of further development is what keeps this paper from being ranked in the higher range.

Rubrics for the Stegner Essay

High-Range Essay

- Correctly identifies Stegner's position and attitude re: the environment *and* wilderness
- Effectively presents a position about Stegner's position *and* attitude
- Clear writer's voice
- Successfully defends his or her position
- Presents carefully reasoned arguments making reference to specific examples from personal experience, knowledge, reading
- Effectively manipulates language
- Few, if any, syntactical errors

Midrange Essay

- Correctly identifies Stegner's position and attitude about the environment *and* wilderness
- Understands the demands of the prompt
- Clearly states the position of the writer
- Presents a generally adequate argument that makes use of appropriate examples
- Less well-developed than the high-range essay
- Ideas clearly stated
- A few lapses in diction or syntax

Low-Range Essay

- Inadequate response to the prompt
- Misunderstands, oversimplifies, or misrepresents Stegner's position and attitude
- Insufficient or inappropriate use of examples to develop the writer's position
- Lack of mature control of elements of essay writing

This prompt posed some difficulties for students. Many had a tendency to address only one aspect of it: the loss of wilderness. Often, they did not adequately connect this to the "Brave New World" concept of a human-controlled environment. The stronger writers included references to and discussions of the "reflection and rest" in their essays. Many student writers opposed Stegner's position by expanding on the concept of wilderness. Those who agreed with Stegner cited pertinent illustrations ranging from the rain forest to gasoline prices to overpopulation and the ozone layer. Contradictory and qualifying essays relied heavily on humankind's "frontier spirit" and artistic endeavors.

Stegner Passage—Student Sample A

Wallace Stegner writes in an essay, "Without any remaining wilderness we are committed wholly, without chance for even momentary reflection and rest, to a headlong drive into our technological termite-life, the 'Brave New World' of a completely man-controlled environment." This excerpt attempts to convey that humankind is on a direct path to a highly mechanical and technological world; one that is ideal in man's quest for scientific and technological dominance over nature. According to Stegner, man has neglected to stop and smell the proverbial patch of roses. The idea that humankind aims at ultimately dominating the earth with its technological advances can be tenable. However, Stegner's argument is fallacious because people DO pause to observe and introspect.

2   Humans have been in constant search of enlightenment in the world since time immemorial. Like all other organisms, man tends to innovate in order to better adapt to his natural surroundings. As time progresses, man develops more and better ways to survive. From the days of the Enlightenment, to the Scientific Revolution, to the Industrial Revolution, and to the computerized world of today, humankind has persistently been pursuing ways to analyze and control his environment. During the Enlightenment, natural philosopher Francis Bacon developed the scientific method as a set process which experiments ought to follow. His methodology has been adhered to since then in experimentation throughout the world. Using this method, Benjamin Franklin experimented with a kite in a storm and discovered electricity. Other thinkers utilized Franklin's findings and developed ways to use new energy sources. One concept has led to another and another, eventually arriving at our highly evolved world today.

3   These advances serve to benefit man's survival, which is why Stegner sees humans as heading for a man-controlled environment. To relieve nature-related hardships, man seeks ways to make things more comfortable for himself. For instance, air-conditioning was invented to control temperature. Another example of man controlling his environment can be found in the area of transportation: automobiles, trains, airplanes, ships, etc. Man is naturally slow, and to adapt himself to the large world, he creates machines to do the transporting. All of the inventions in the world today demonstrate attempts mankind has made in order to survive and to make life more "livable," and in these efforts, man controls nature.

4   Though Stegner's case that humanity's focus on dominating their environment can be defended, his idea that people ignore the need to rest for reflection is erroneous. While scientific and technological advancement is a commanding aspect of humankind, it is not as if history, art and culture do not exist. These facets of human society contribute to introspection. We create art to express modes of self-examination. Musicians, painters, sculptors, poets, and other artists concentrate on reflecting about man and his world. We study history as a method of introspection, and, in so doing, we essentially examine our past and reflect on it. There exist in this world goals other than the desire to control nature with technology. Humans are not "committed wholly, without chance for even momentary reflection and rest," to dominate the globe.

5   While Stegner's concept of humanity's desire to attain dominance over nature contains truth, his notion that people do not focus on anything else is false. Yes, humans do possess the tendency to explore and conquer. However, humans do not exclude all else in life. We are not always in pursuit of scientific and technological accomplishment. We are also seekers of cultural, artistic and philosophical achievement.

Stegner Passage—Student Sample B

Wallace Stegner wrote that, "Without any remaining wilderness we are committed wholly, without chance for even momentary reflection and rest, to a headlong drive into our technological termite-life, the 'Brave New World' of a completely man-controlled environment." It seems that in writing this, Stegner expresses his concern for the receding forests and other wilderness areas, along with the extinction of the species that populate them. His concern is quite justified, for as we use our natural resources, we destroy those species that we now share this planet with.   1

It has long been known that unlike the other species of the Earth, the one known as Homo Sapiens does not adapt well to its environment. Instead, this species adapts the environment to it, and the Devil take anything that stands in its way. Homo Sapiens cannot bear the fierce winters of New England or the hot summers of the Caribbean, so it chops down trees to build houses. It does this without the slightest concern for the other species that call the forest home. Many terrible injuries have been dealt to the eco-system of this planet because of the lack of concern Homo Sapiens has shown. Holes in the ozone layer, which let terrible amounts of ultra-violet radiation bombard the earth. The constant growth of the Sahara Desert, and the destruction of the rainforests are painful examples of Homo Sapiens' ignorance, painful not just to other species, but to Homo Sapiens itself. It seems as though Homo Sapiens does not realize that when all the trees are gone, there will be no oxygen left for anyone. Hopefully before that atrocity is carried out, for it is almost sure that it will be, Homo Sapiens will figure out how to adapt very quickly.   2

When Stegner wrote of a "completely man-controlled environment," he is talking of a world where our species has destroyed the wilderness or at least bent it totally to our will. He writes of a world with cities, inhabited "termite-like" by reflective Homo Sapiens, the size of which no one has ever seen, most likely with rampant air pollution. Let us hope that we are not one day forced, as in "Lost in Space," to seek out other planets to live on because ours is taking its last breath. This is one possibility; Stegner is warning us to change our ignorant ways before it is too late, and he certainly has the right idea. For, if we don't, we will have truly become exactly like our hated enemy, the virus.   3

Rating Student Sample A

This is a high-ranking essay for the following reasons:

- Effectively covers the points made by Stegner in his statement
- Clearly takes a position regarding Stegner's statement

- Thoroughly develops the argument with specific examples and historical references (paragraphs 2 and 3)
- Indicates and discusses the fallacy of Stegner's statement (paragraphs 4 and 5)
- Good topic adherence
- Thorough development of the points of the writer's argument
- Mature voice, diction, and syntax

This high-range essay was written by a student who is both confident and well-versed and one who has balanced the presentation with scientific and introspective illustrations in support of the argument.

Rating Student Sample B

- Clearly understands Stegner's statement and the demands of the prompt
- Creative voice is present
- An interesting objectification of humanity (paragraph 2–"Homo Sapiens")
- Strong conclusion
- Linkage between man's destruction of the wilderness and its consequences needs further development
- Development of the argument needs further support
- A few syntactical errors
- Lacks needed transitions

This student writer has a definite opinion to which he or she gives a strong voice. Although there is a strong, clear opening and conclusion, the body paragraphs containing the argument need further development.

Chapter 4

AP English Literature

Answer Sheet for Multiple-Choice Questions

1. _____	14. _____	27. _____	40. _____
2. _____	15. _____	28. _____	41. _____
3. _____	16. _____	29. _____	42. _____
4. _____	17. _____	30. _____	43. _____
5. _____	18. _____	31. _____	44. _____
6. _____	19. _____	32. _____	45. _____
7. _____	20. _____	33. _____	46. _____
8. _____	21. _____	34. _____	47. _____
9. _____	22. _____	35. _____	48. _____
10. _____	23. _____	36. _____	49. _____
11. _____	24. _____	37. _____	50. _____
12. _____	25. _____	38. _____	51. _____
13. _____	26. _____	39. _____	

Scoring Formula:

$$\underline{\qquad\qquad} - \underline{\qquad\qquad} = \underline{\qquad\qquad}$$
number right (number wrong $\times$ .25) raw score

AP ENGLISH LITERATURE

Section I

Time—1 hour

51 Questions

Carefully read the following passages and answer the questions that follow.

Questions 1–14 are based on the following passage.

Samuel Johnson on Pope, from *The Lives of the English Poets* (1779–1781)

The person of Pope is well known not to have been formed by the nicest model. He has compared himself to a spider, and by another is described as protuberant behind and before. He is said to have been beautiful in his infancy; but he was of a constitution feeble and weak; and as bodies of a tender frame are easily distorted, his deformity was probably in part the effect of his application. But his face was not displeasing, and his   5
eyes were animated and vivid.

By natural deformity, or accidental distortion, his vital functions were so much disordered, that his life was a "long disease."

He sometimes condescended to be jocular with servants or inferiors; but by no merriment, either of others or his own, was he ever seen excited to laughter.   10

Of his domestic character frugality was a part eminently remarkable. Having determined not to be dependent, he determined not to be in want, and therefore wisely and magnanimously rejected all temptations to expense unsuitable to his fortune.

The great topic of his ridicule is poverty; the crimes with which he reproaches his antagonists are their debts and their want of a dinner. He seems to be of an opinion not   15
very uncommon in the world, that to want money is to want everything.

He professed to have learned his poetry from Dryden, whom he praised through his whole life with unvaried liberality; and perhaps his character may receive some illustration, if he be compared with his master.

Integrity of understanding and nicety of discernment were not allotted in a less   20
proportion to Dryden than to Pope. But Dryden never desired to apply all the judgment that he had. He wrote merely for the people; and when he pleased others, he contented himself. He never attempted to mend what he must have known to be faulty. He wrote with very little consideration; and once it had passed the press, ejected it from his mind.

Pope was not content to satisfy; he desired to excel, and, therefore always endeavored   25
to do his best; he did not court the candour, but dared the judgment of his reader, and, expecting no indulgence from others, he showed none to himself. He examined lines and words with minute and punctilious observation, and retouched every part with diligence, till he had nothing left to be forgiven.

Poetry was not the sole praise of either; for both excelled likewise in prose.   30
The style of Dryden is capricious and varied; that of Pope is cautious and uniform. Dryden observes the motions of his own mind; Pope constrains his mind to his own rules of composition. Dryden's page is a natural field, diversified by the exuberance of abundant vegetation. Pope's is a velvet lawn, shaven by the scythe, and leveled by the roller.

If the flights of Dryden are higher, Pope continues longer on the wing. If of Dryden's   35
fire the blaze is brighter, of Pope's the heat is more regular and constant. Dryden is read with frequent astonishment, and Pope with perpetual delight.

1. The passage is primarily a(n)
   A. character sketch of Pope
   B. discussion of poetic style
   C. criticism of Dryden
   D. model for future poets
   E. opportunity for the writer to show off his own skills

2. The passage discusses a contrast between all of the following *except*
   A. prose and poetry
   B. Pope and Dryden
   C. body and mind
   D. poverty and wealth
   E. body and soul

3. "If the flights . . ." (line 35) means
   A. Pope's writing will outlast Dryden's
   B. both Pope and Dryden are equal
   C. Pope is not idealistic
   D. Pope is more wordy
   E. Pope is not as bright as Dryden

4. The character of Pope is developed by all of the following *except*
   A. examples
   B. comparison
   C. contrast
   D. satire
   E. description

5. According to the passage, Pope and Dryden are
   A. rivals
   B. equally intelligent
   C. outdated
   D. equally physically attractive
   E. in debt

6. From the passage, the reader may infer that Pope
   A. was extravagant
   B. was a man of the people
   C. was jealous of Dryden
   D. had a desire to be popular
   E. had a bitter, satirical nature

7. The tone of the passage is
   A. informal and affectionate
   B. formal and objective
   C. condescending and paternalistic

D. laudatory and reverent
E. critical and negative

8. Lines 20–25 indicate that Dryden was what type of writer?
   A. one who labored over his thoughts
   B. one who wrote only for himself
   C. one who wrote only for the critics
   D. one who wrote to please Pope
   E. one who did not revise

9. Using the context of lines 27–29, "punctilious" means
   A. precise
   B. timely
   C. cursory
   D. scholarly
   E. philosophical

10. In the context of the passage, "Till he had nothing left to be forgiven" (lines 28–29) means
    A. Pope outraged his readers
    B. Pope suffered from writer's block
    C. Pope exhausted his subject matter
    D. Pope's prose was revised to perfection
    E. Pope cared about the opinions of his readers

11. "Shaven" and "leveled" in line 34 indicate that Pope's style of writing was
    A. natural
    B. richly ornamented
    C. highly controlled
    D. mechanical
    E. analytical

12. Based upon a close reading of the final paragraph of the passage, the reader could infer that the author
    A. looks on both writers equally
    B. prefers the work of Pope
    C. sees the two writers as inferior to his own writing style
    D. indicates no preference
    E. prefers the work of Dryden

13. Johnson's attitude toward the general public can be best described as
    A. laudatory and respectful
    B. flattering and fearful

C. critical and condescending
D. moralistic and concerned
E. pedantic and taunting

A. "unvaried liberality"
B. "nicety of discernment"
C. "punctilious observation"
D. "excelling likewise in prose" and poetry
E. "integrity of understanding"

14. According to Johnson, the qualities of a great
writer include all of the following *except*

Questions 15–25 are based on the following poem.

The Writer
by Richard Wilbur

In her room at the prow of the house
Where light breaks, and the windows are tossed with linden,
My daughter is writing a story.

I pause in the stairwell, hearing
From her shut door a commotion of typewriter-keys   5
Like a chain hauled over a gunwale.

Young as she is, the stuff
Of her life is a great cargo, and some of it heavy:
I wish her a lucky passage.

But now it is she who pauses,   10
As if to reject my thought and its easy figure.
A stillness greatens, in which

The whole house seems to be thinking,
And then she is at it again with a bunched clamor
Of strokes, and again is silent.   15

I remember the dazed starling
Which was trapped in that very room, two years ago;
How we stole in, lifted a sash

And retreated, not to affright it;
And how for a helpless hour, through the crack in the door,   20
We watched this sleek, wild, dark

And iridescent creature
Batter against the brilliance, drop like a glove
To the hard floor, or the desk-top,

And wait then, humped and bloody,   25
For the wits to try it again; and how our spirits
Rose when, suddenly sure,

It lifted off from a chair-back,
Beating a smooth course for the right window
And clearing the sill of the world.   30

It is always a matter, my darling,
Of life or death, as I had forgotten. I wish
What I wished you before, but harder.

15. The last line of the poem "What I wished for you before, but harder" implies that

    A. the speaker loves his daughter more than at the beginning of the poem
    B. the speaker realizes the intensity of life's challenges
    C. the speaker cannot be as creative as she
    D. the speaker feels he has failed her
    E. the daughter will never be a successful writer

16. Which of the following is used to develop the poem?

    A. cause and effect
    B. argument
    C. general to specific examples
    D. definition
    E. parallel analogy

17. Line 13 is an example of

    A. allusion
    B. alliteration
    C. personification
    D. simile
    E. apostrophe

18. "A smooth course for the right window" in line 29 parallels line(s)

    A. 1
    B. 5–6
    C. 8
    D. 9
    E. 11

19. The poem breaks after line

    A. 3
    B. 6
    C. 8
    D. 15
    E. 27

20. The final stanza serves all the following purposes *except*

    A. to restate the theme
    B. to reemphasize the father's love for his daughter
    C. to solidify the daughter's character
    D. to connect the two major sections of the poem
    E. to allow the father to be more sympathetic

21. Stanzas 1–3 include all the following analogies *except*

    A. the house as a ship
    B. the daughter's room as a ship's cabin
    C. life's problems as a ship's cargo
    D. writing as a safe harbor
    E. life is a sea journey

22. The father's sensitivity is supported by line(s)

    A. 3
    B. 4
    C. 11
    D. 19
    E. 21–22

23. Contrasts developed in the poem include all the following *except*

    A. stillness and clamor
    B. house and cargo
    C. bird and daughter
    D. life and/or death
    E. light and dark

24. According to the poem, the daughter, as young as she is, has

    A. endured hardships
    B. published her writing
    C. fought for her independence
    D. saved a starling
    E. left home and returned

25. The poet alludes to all the following as part of the process of a creative life *except*

    A. "Batter against the brilliance"
    B. "Drop like a glove to the hard floor"
    C. "clearing the sill of the world"
    D. "the wits to try it again"
    E. "Beating a smooth course for the right window"

Questions 26–38 are based on the following passage.

Jane Eyre
by Charlotte Bronte

Miss Temple got up, took her hand and . . . returned to her own seat: as she resumed it, I heard her sigh low. She was pensive a few minutes, then rousing herself, she said cheerfully:—

"But you two are my visitors to-night; I must treat you as such." She rang her bell.

"Barbara," she said to the servant who answered it, "I have not yet had tea; bring   5
the tray, and place cups for these two young ladies."

And a tray was soon brought. How pretty, to my eyes, did the china and bright teapot look, placed on the little round table near the fire! How fragrant was the steam of the beverage, and the scent of the toast! of which, however, I, to my dismay (for I was beginning to be hungry), discerned only a very small portion: Miss Temple discerned it   10
too:—

"Barbara," said she, "can you not bring a little more bread and butter? There is not enough for three."

Barbara went out: she returned soon:—

"Madam, Mrs. Harden says she has sent up the usual quantity."   15

Mrs. Harden, be it observed, was the housekeeper: a woman after Mr. Brocklehurst's own heart, made up of equal parts of whalebone and iron.

"Oh, very well!" returned Miss Temple; "we must make it do, Barbara, I suppose." And as the girl withdrew, she added, smiling, "Fortunately, I have it in my power to supply deficiencies for this once."   20

Having invited Helen and me to approach the table, and placed before each of us a cup of tea with one delicious but thin morsel of toast; she got up, unlocked a drawer, and taking from it a parcel wrapped in paper, disclosed presently to our eyes a good-sized seed-cake.

"I meant to give each of you some of this to take with you," said she; "but as there   25
is so little toast, you must have it now," and she proceeded to cut slices with a generous hand.

We feasted that evening as on nectar and ambrosia; and not the least delight of the entertainment was the smile of gratification with which our hostess regarded us, as we satisfied our famished appetites on the delicate fare she liberally supplied. Tea over and the   30
tray removed, she again summoned us to the fire; we sat one on each side of her, and now a conversation followed between her and Helen, which it was indeed a privilege to be admitted to hear.

Miss Temple had always something of serenity in her air, of state in her mien, of refined propriety in her language, which precluded deviation into the ardent, the excited, the   35
eager: something which chastened the pleasure of those who looked on her and listened to her, by a controlling sense of awe; and such was my feeling now: but as to Helen Burns, I was struck with wonder.

The refreshing meal, the brilliant fire, the presence and kindness of her beloved instructress, or, perhaps, more than all these, something in her own unique mind, had   40
roused her powers within her. They woke, they kindled: first, they glowed in the bright tint of her cheek, which till this hour I had never seen but pale and bloodless; then they shone in the liquid lustre of her eyes, which had suddenly acquired a beauty more singular than that of Miss Temple's—a beauty neither of fine colour nor long eyelash, nor pencilled brow, but of meaning, of movement, of radiance. Then her soul sat on her lips, and language   45
flowed, from what source I cannot tell: has a girl of fourteen a heart large enough, vigorous

enough to hold the swelling spring of pure, full, fervid eloquence? Such was the characteristic of Helen's discourse on that, to me, memorable evening; her spirit seemed hastening to live within a very brief span as much as many live during a protracted existence. 50

They conversed of things I had never heard of! Of nations and times past; of countries far away: of secrets of nature discovered or guessed at: they spoke of books: how many they had read! What stores of knowledge they possessed! They seemed so familiar with French names and French authors: but my amazement reached its climax when Miss Temple asked Helen if she sometimes snatched a moment to recall the Latin her 55 father had taught her, and taking a book from a shelf, bade her read and construe a page of "Virgil"; and Helen obeyed, my organ of Veneration expanding at every sounding line. She had scarcely finished ere the bell announced bedtime: no delay could be admitted; Miss Temple embraced us both, saying, as she drew us to her heart:—

"God bless you, my children!" 60

Well has Solomon said—"Better is a dinner of herbs where love is, than a stalled ox and hatred therewith."

26. From the passage, it can be concluded that Mrs. Harden is

A. in love with Mr. Brocklehurst
B. generous with the girls
C. a confidante of Miss Temple's
D. strong-willed and inflexible
E. Miss Temple's superior

27. Religious imagery in this passage is developed by all the following *except*

A. Miss Temple's name
B. feasting on nectar and ambrosia
C. the taking of tea and toast
D. Miss Temple's benediction
E. being summoned to sit by the fire

28. The "smile of gratification with which our hostess regarded us" (line 29) indicates that Miss Temple derives pleasure from

A. having power over the girls
B. being a role model for the girls
C. keeping secrets
D. outsmarting the girls
E. providing for the girls

29. For the speaker, the most nourishing part of the evening was

A. the seed cake
B. the tea and toast
C. the company of an adult
D. the conversation
E. the brilliant fire

30. The speaker is amazed by

A. Miss Temple's beauty
B. the breadth of Helen's knowledge
C. Miss Temple's generosity
D. her own knowledge
E. her envy of the attention Helen receives

31. "... Her spirit seemed hastening to live within a very brief span as much as many live during a protracted existence" (lines 48–49) is an example of

A. circular reasoning
B. satire
C. foreshadowing
D. denouement
E. digression

32. The reader can infer from lines 45–47 ("Then her soul sat on her lips . . . eloquence") that

A. Helen has traveled the world
B. Helen likes to show off intellectually
C. Miss Temple has been tutoring Helen
D. the speaker is afraid of Helen
E. Helen is an instrument of divine inspiration

33. The last line of the passage may be best interpreted to mean

A. It is better to be rich than poor
B. Everything in moderation
C. The greatest of all riches is love
D. Denial of riches leads to love
F. Riches lead to hatred

34. The pronoun "they" in lines 41–42 refers to
   A. her powers
   B. her unique mind
   C. the meal and the fire
   D. Helen and Miss Temple
   E. Helen's eyes

35. The tone developed in the passage is best described as
   A. amused indifference
   B. subdued admiration
   C. pedantic
   D. reverent wonder
   E. remorseful

36. The reader may infer all the following *except that*
   A. the evening has transformed Helen
   B. the speaker is observant of and sensitive to human nature
   C. the evening is in contrast to their daily lives
   D. Miss Temple will save the two children
   E. love of learning is important to the speaker

37. The description of Miss Temple in lines 34–38 reveals her to be a woman of
   A. religious fervor
   B. restraint and reservation
   C. passionate beliefs
   D. submissive inclinations
   E. dominating sensibilities

38. Based on the passage, all the following can be inferred about Jane's character *except that* she is
   A. cognizant of her limitations
   B. a great observer
   C. of an inquisitive nature
   D. highly impressionable
   E. religious

Questions 39–51 are based on the following poem.

The Pulley
by George Herbert

When God at first made man,
Having a glass of blessings stand by,
Let us, said He, pour on him all we can.
Let the world's riches, which dispersed lie,
Contract into a span.   5

So Strength first made a way,
Then Beauty flowed, then Wisdom, Honor, Pleasure.
When almost all was out, God made a stay,
Perceiving that alone of all his treasure
Rest in the bottom lay.   10

For if I should, said He,
Bestow this jewel also on my creature,
He would adore my gifts instead of me,
And rest in Nature, not the God of Nature:
So both should losers be.   15

Yet let him keep the rest,
But keep them with repining restlessness.
Let him be rich and weary, that at least
If goodness lead him not, yet weariness
May toss him to my breast.   20

(Note: Poem reprinted in its original form.)

39. The "pulley" of the title refers to
    A. the balance between God and nature
    B. the conflict between beauty and riches
    C. the conflict between blessings and curses
    D. God's method of controlling mankind
    E. the conflict between winners and losers

40. In line 9, "alone of all his treasure" refers to
    A. wisdom
    B. honor
    C. pleasure
    D. strength
    E. rest

41. According to the first stanza, God is
    A. totally generous
    B. suspicious of humankind
    C. drunk with power
    D. planning to test humanity
    E. forgiving of human weakness

42. In line 16, "Yet let him keep the rest" refers to
    A. all the gifts, except "rest"
    B. the Sabbath
    C. nature
    D. a glass of blessings
    E. "this jewel"

43. God will control humans by keeping them
    A. away from evil
    B. poor
    C. alone
    D. weak
    E. fatigued

44. The pun in this poem depends upon the reading of which word?
    A. pour
    B. alone
    C. rest
    D. losers
    E. least

45. The dominant imagery concerns
    A. wealth
    B. goodness

C. God
D. nature
E. contracts

46. In line 12, "this jewel" refers to
    A. wisdom
    B. my creature
    C. glass of blessings
    D. rest
    E. nature

47. The first and last lines of each stanza are written in
    A. iambic pentameter
    B. iambic trimeter
    C. trochaic trimeter
    D. spondaic tetrameter
    E. dactylic trimeter

48. The conflict of the poem is best expressed in line
    A. 3
    B. 8
    C. 13
    D. 15
    E. 17

49. For George Herbert, the God of all mankind is
    A. all-forgiving and generous
    B. disappointed and jealous
    C. judgmental and punitive
    D. regretful and plaintive
    E. speculative and manipulative

50. The organization of the first two stanzas depends upon
    A. contrast and comparison
    B. paradox
    C. chronological order
    D. specific to general
    E. description

51. We can infer that the speaker is
    A. heretical
    B. nonmaterialistic
    C. scientific
    D. skeptical
    E. materialistic

END OF SECTION I

Section II

Time–2 hours

(Suggested time for each question is 40 minutes. Each question counts as one-third of the total score for Section II.)

Question 1

In a well-organized essay discuss how Alice Walker conveys the meaning of "The Flowers" and how she prepares the reader for the ending of this short story. Consider at least two elements of the writer's craft such as imagery, symbol, setting, narrative pace, diction, and style.

The Flowers
by Alice Walker

It seemed to Myop as she skipped lightly from her house to pigpen to smokehouse that the days had never been as beautiful as these. The air held a keenness that made her nose twitch. The harvesting of the corn and cotton, peanuts and squash, made each day a golden surprise that caused excited little tremors to run up her jaws.

Myop carried a short, knobby stick. She struck out at random at chickens she liked, and worked out the beat of a song on the fence around the pigpen. She felt light and good in the warm sun. She was ten, and nothing existed for her but her song, the stick clutched in her dark brown hand, and the tat-de-ta-ta-ta of accompaniment. 5

Turning her back on the rusty boards of her family's sharecropper cabin, Myop walked along the fence till it ran into the stream made by the spring. Around the spring, where the family got drinking water, silver ferns and wildflowers grew. Along the shallow banks pigs rooted. Myop watched the tiny white bubbles disrupt the thin black scale of soil and the water that silently rose and slid away down the stream. 10

She had explored the woods behind the house many times. Often, in late autumn, her mother took her to gather nuts among the fallen leaves. Today she made her own path, bouncing this way and that way, vaguely keeping an eye out for snakes. She found, in addition to various common but pretty ferns and leaves, an armful of strange blue flowers with velvety ridges and a sweetsuds bush full of the brown, fragrant buds. 15

By twelve o'clock, her arms laden with sprigs of her findings, she was a mile or more from home. She had often been as far before, but the strangeness of the land made it not as pleasant as her usual haunts. It seemed gloomy in the little cove in which she found herself. The air was damp, the silence close and deep. 20

Myop began to circle back to the house, back to the peacefulness of the morning.

It was then she stepped smack into his eyes. Her heel became lodged in the broken ridge between brow and nose, and she reached down quickly, unafraid, to free herself. It was only when she saw his naked grin that she gave a little yelp of surprise. He had been a tall man. From feet to neck covered a long space. His head lay beside him. When she pushed back the leaves and layers of earth and debris Myop saw that he'd had large white teeth, all of them cracked or broken, long fingers, and very big bones. All his clothes had rotted away except some threads of blue denim from his overalls. The buckles of the overalls had turned green. 25 30

Myop gazed around the spot with interest. Very near where she'd stepped into the head was a wild pink rose. As she picked it to add to her bundle she noticed a raised mound, a ring, around the rose's root. It was the rotted remains of a noose, a bit of shredding plow-line, now blending benignly into the soil. Around the overhanging limb of a great spreading oak clung another piece, frayed, rotted, bleached, and frazzled—barely there—but spinning restlessly in the breeze. Myop laid down her flowers. 35

And the summer was over.

Question 2

In a well-organized essay discuss the distinguishing differences between the connotations of the two main words in the title of the poem "The Naked and the Nude" as they are developed in this poem by Robert Graves. Refer to such literary techniques as tone, style, poetic devices, structure, and imagery.

The Naked and the Nude
by Robert Graves

For me, the naked and the nude
(By lexicographers construed
As synonyms that should express
The same deficiency of dress
Or shelter) stand as wide apart   5
As love from lies, or truth from art.

Lovers without reproach will gaze
On bodies naked and ablaze;
The Hippocratic eye will see
In nakedness, anatomy;   10
And naked shines the Goddess when
She mounts her lion among men.

The nude are bold; the nude are sly
To hold each treasonable eye.
While draping by a showman's trick   15
Their dishabille in rhetoric,
They grin a mock-religious grin
Of scorn at those of naked skin.

The naked, therefore, who compete
Against the nude may know defeat;   20
Yet when they both together tread
The briary pastures of the dead,
By Gorgons with long whips pursued,
How naked go the sometime nude!

Question 3

From your study of full-length works, choose one in which a character or group intentionally dissembles in order to advance a specific agenda. Be sure to discuss the nature of the deceit or misrepresentation and how it contributes to the development of that character or the meaning of the work. You may choose a work from the list below or another novel or play of literary merit.

The Stranger

Oedipus

Jane Eyre

Desire Under the Elms

Heart of Darkness

The Secret Sharer

Beloved

A Streetcar Named Desire

Major Barbara

Hamlet

Twelfth Night

King Lear

The Great Gatsby

The Importance of Being Earnest

Hedda Gabler

A Doll's House

Catch-22

END OF SECTION II

ANSWERS TO MULTIPLE-CHOICE QUESTIONS

Answer Key

1.	A	14.	A	27.	E	40.	E
2.	E	15.	B	28.	E	41.	A
3.	A	16.	E	29.	D	42.	A
4.	D	17.	C	30.	B	43.	E
5.	B	18.	D	31.	C	44.	C
6.	E	19.	D	32.	E	45.	A
7.	B	20.	C	33.	C	46.	D
8.	E	21.	D	34.	A	47.	B
9.	A	22.	D	35.	D	48.	C
10.	D	23.	B	36.	D	49.	E
11.	C	24.	A	37.	B	50.	C
12.	B	25.	B	38.	E	51.	B
13.	C	26.	D	39.	D		

Explanations of Answers to the Multiple-Choice Questions

1. **A.** Although references to poetic style and to Dryden are contained in the passage, they are included to illuminate the character of Pope.

2. **E.** There are no references to body and soul in the passage. We do find references to the prose and poetry of both Pope and Dryden. We are told of Pope's monetary concerns, and we can infer the contrast between Pope's broken body and healthy mind.

3. **A.** This is a fairly straightforward interpretation of a figurative line. The idea of "long on the wing" naturally leads the reader to think of endurance.

4. **D.** A careful reading of this passage will allow you to locate each of the devices, except satire.

5. **B.** Line 20 clearly states that the two men were equally gifted.

6. **E.** Lines 9–10 tell the reader that Pope's humor was condescending. Lines 14–15 allude to his use of ridicule, and the reader may infer that these characteristics were carried over into Pope's writing.

7. **B.** The author never interjects his own feelings, and the diction and syntax remain on a scholarly, elevated level.

8. **E.** Carefully read lines 23–24 and you will see a direct correlation between those lines and choice E.

9. **A.** This is strictly a vocabulary question. You should be able to use the context clues of "minute" and "diligent" to lead you to choose A.

10. **D.** If you go to lines 24–28, you will see that Pope demanded perfection of himself and his writing. This characteristic is further extended with the clause in line 29.

11. **C.** Both words indicate a practiced, continuous, and extreme control of the work at hand. Even the "velvet of the lawn" indicates a tightness, a smoothness, and a richness of form and content.

12. **B.** If it were a contest, Pope would be declared the winner by Johnson. A close reading of both the structure and content of the paragraph leads the reader to Pope. When discussing Dryden and Pope, it is Pope who has the last word. This allows Pope to linger in the reader's mind. "Frequent" with Dryden and "perpetual" with Pope is another indication of Samuel Johnson's preference.

13. **C.** In lines 15–16, Johnson expresses his critical observations and judgments. He dismisses the people with the adverb "merely" in line 22.

14. **A.** A close examination of the text finds Johnson tolerant of differences in style but constant with regard to the qualities of the great writer. "Unvaried liberality" in line 18 refers only to Pope's respect for Dryden and not to the process of writing.

15. **B.** The entire poem hinges on the speaker's epiphany about life and creativity which occurs in the last stanza. It is this realization that points to choice B. Choice A is silly and should be eliminated immediately. There is no discussion of the daughter's talent which eliminates choice E. Although C and D sound plausible and may even be insights raised by the reader, once again there is no concrete evidence in the poem to support these choices.

16. **E.** The careful reader should recognize that the poem introduces a new idea in lines 16–30, and he or she should question the reason for this. It is obvious that the episode of the starling is meant to parallel the intensity of the creative process the daughter is experiencing.

17. **C.** The house is personified as "thinking." This is a question that is really a free-bie if you've done your preparation. The answer depends on your knowledge of simple terms and your ability to identify examples of them in a work.

18. **D.** A question of this type demands that you actually refer to the passage. (You might try highlighting or underlining to emphasize line 29 and the various choices. This will prevent you from losing your place or focus.) Use the process of elimination until you find an "echo" word or phrase. In line 9, "passage" parallels "course" and points to choice D. It is a good idea to follow the choices in order for clarity and continuity because each rereading may give you help with another question.

19. **D.** Question 2 may help you with this answer. Skim the poem from line 1 until you strike a new idea—the dazed bird. The answer has to be D. A, B, and C all describe the daughter and are on topic, while line 27 refers to the previous idea, in this case, the starling introduced earlier.

20. **C.** The perceptive reader will understand that the stanza is not about the daughter at all; whereas, each of the other ideas is valid and can be supported in the context of the stanza.

21. **D.** The use of nautical terms dominates the first section of the poem, establishing the concept of life as a sea journey or passage. The words, "prow" (line 1), "gunwale" (line 6), and "heavy cargo" (line 8), all support choices A, B, C, and E. The only image *not* stated concerns writing as a safe harbor.

22. **D.** This is essentially a reading question and one you should find easy to answer. Start with the first choice and work your way through each of the others. Highlight or underline lines and look for concrete evidence and eliminate unsupported choices. Line 19 indicates the sensitivity shown by the father's consideration for the trapped bird.

23. **B.** This type of question is more complicated than the others because there are many steps involved in finding the answer. Don't just rely on memory. Actually circle or highlight the contrasts as you skim the poem. You may have a quick flash.

If so, look immediately to prove it. If you can't, you have your answer. In this case, B. To illustrate the process, here are the images that prove that the other choices are contained in the poem.

    A. Line 5: commotion; line 12: stillness
    C. Lines 22–23: the implied analogy of child and bird
    D. Line 32: life and death
    E. Line 2: light breaks; line 21: dark

24. **A.** This simple reading question is a giveaway. Stanza three tells the reader that "the stuff of her life is a great cargo, and some of it heavy." You should be able to interpret the metaphor as life's difficulties.

25. **B.** All the choices, with the exception of B, reflect the need to persist in order to achieve a goal—freedom and creation. Only B is grounded to the hard floor.

26. **D.** The answer is obvious if you carefully read lines 15–17. A heart made up of whalebones and iron is synonymous with strong-willed and inflexible.

27. **E.** Temple, feasting, food of the gods, and benediction can all imply religious connotations. Tea and toast can be a direct allusion to taking communion. Being asked to "come sit by the fire" is simply a request, nothing more.

28. **E.** "Gratification" involves thankfulness. And, in this case, Miss Temple is pleased that she is able to give the girls some special foods during their visit.

29. **D.** This is a metaphorical construction. With it, Jane lets the reader know that having the opportunity to be part of engaging and exciting conversation was like food for her mind and soul.

30. **B.** Lines 39–59 of this excerpt are devoted to Helen's mind, knowledge, and eloquence.

31. **C.** This is one of those questions that assumes the student is familiar with the definitions of specific terms. "Seemed hastening" is almost a literal flag waving in front of the reader's eyes signaling that something will happen in the future.

32. **E.** Helen's "soul sitting on her lips," her "secret sources of language," and her "purity and radiance" all relate to the realm of the divine.

33. **C.** Herbs are simple and of small quantity. An ox, on the other hand, is overwhelmingly large and overabundant. Love is better than hate. This analogy is straightforward and obvious.

34. **A.** This is the frequently used antecedent question. All you have to do is substitute each of the choices for the word "they," and it will be obvious that your only viable choice is "her powers."

35. **D.** If you read the passage carefully, Jane's wonder and deference are apparent. Look at lines 39–50 to see her sense of awe. Look at line 39. It clearly states Jane's wonder at Helen.

36. **D.** There is nothing in this passage that indicates either of the two girls needs to be saved.

37. **B.** "Serenity," "state in her mien," "refined propriety" in lines 34–35 are synonymous with one who is restrained. The remainder of the lines illustrates and supports this characterization.

38. **E.** Although there is considerable religious diction and imagery in the passage, none of it directly relates to Jane's character and her being a religious person.

39. **D.** A pulley is a device used to bring something to a particular destination. In this case, man to God.

40. **E.** If you recast lines 9 and 10 into a sentence, you can easily see that "treasure" is the antecedent of "Rest." This is an example of poetic inversion.

41. **A.** Lines 3 and 4 are the indicators. Look carefully at what God is doing—giving all the world's riches away.

42. **A.** Use the process of substitution to help you find the answer. If you place each of the choices in place of "Rest," you will see that the only appropriate choice is A.

43. **E.** Lines 17 and 18 clearly indicate that God intends for man to be without rest.

44. **C.** The pun depends on your knowing that a play on words and their meanings is essential to the understanding of this poem. Choice C refers to both renewal and the remains of the blessings.

45. **A.** Each stanza presents an image to support choice A. "Riches" (line 4), "treasure" (line 9), "jewel" (line 12), and "rich" (line 18) sustain the concept of wealth.

46. **D.** This is another question that benefits from using the process of substitution to locate an antecedent. This procedure will lead you to lines 9 and 10 and choice D.

47. **B.** You should notice immediately that the first and last lines of each stanza are shorter than the other lines. It is a good idea to briefly check to see if the form is iambic (˘ ´) because the iambic foot is the most common one in the English language. Count the number of iambs, and you will come up with three (tri). (*Note*: If meter presents a problem to you, this may be a question you should choose to skip.)

48. **C.** God is wary of man's potential goodness and loyalty and devises another method of ensuring mankind's adoration and reliance on Him.

49. **E.** A, B, C, and D are all partially supported in the poem. But, only E has *both* characteristics evident in the poem's context.

50. **C.** The words "when," "first," "then," and "when" are all indicative of the chronological pattern of the first two stanzas.

51. **B.** The text of the poem, especially in the choice of blessings the speaker presents, indicates that he is interested in the world of the spirit rather than the world of material possessions and investigations. The diction proves he considers these nonmaterial concepts to be the real "riches," "treasure," "jewel," and "gifts."

RATING THE ESSAYS

Rubrics for "The Flowers" by Alice Walker

High-Range Essay

- Indicates complete understanding and support of the prompt.
- Uses appropriate literary techniques to illustrate how Walker prepares the reader for the ending of the story.
- Thoroughly explores the contrasts inherent in the story.
- Fully presents Myop's character.
- Recognizes the underlying theme related to prejudice and innocence.
- Responds insightfully to image, diction, and setting.
- Presents suitable and unique interpretations of the text.
- Demonstrates a mature, sophisticated writing style.

Midrange Essay

- Refers accurately to the prompt.
- Utilizes appropriate devices in the analysis of Walker's preparation for the surprise ending.
- Adequately supports the thesis.
- Uses obvious references and details.
- May miss the subtleties of the story.
- Inferences are based on an acceptable reading of the text.
- Demonstrates writing that is adequate to convey the writer's intent.
- May exhibit a few errors in syntax and/or diction.

Sample Student Essays

Student Essay A

"... the days had never been as beautiful as these ... each day a golden surprise." Surprise is the element Alice Walker presents in her story "The Flowers." It is at the heart of the meaning of this story which is driven forward by imagery, setting, and diction.

In the beginning of the story, Walker utilizes diction that creates an atmosphere of euphoric childhood innocence. Myop, the main character, "skipped lightly." Walker describes the harvests, which evince "excited little tremors" in Myop as she anticipates the new day.

This jocund diction continues into the second paragraph. Specifically, Myop feels "light and good" in the heat of the warm sun. In addition, ten year old Myop creates her own world in which nothing exists "but her song." In line 8, the use of onomatopaeia, "tat-de'ta'ta'ta" reinforces the idea of a happy, carefree youth.

Paragraph three, however, marks a small yet significant shift in the passage. Walker begins the paragraph with "Turning her back on the rusty boards of her family's sharecropper cabin, Myop ... " Myop's world is not behind her, but moves forward to the familiar woods.

As the story progresses, there is a significant shift in paragraphs four and five. Walker begins to prepare the reader for her profound conclusion. While Myop has often explored the woods behind the house with her mother, today she sets out alone and "made her own path." As she walks through the woods, she cautiously keeps an eye out for snakes. The solitude of her journey, and the possibility of danger, builds suspense and prepares the reader for the dark surprise of the ending.

The diction of paragraphs four and five also contributes to the sudden shift in the passage. While the diction in the beginning was blithe, describing "beautiful," the language in paragraph five is negative, foreshadowing the conclusion. Specifically, Myop is disoriented by the, "strangeness of the land."

5

10

15

20

25

It was "not as pleasant" as her usual expeditions. Furthermore, words such as "gloomy" and "damp" reiterate the dark setting and prepare the reader for the grotesque conclusion of the story. 30

Paragraph six, which is only one sentence long, marks a brief transition into the ending of the passage. Myop wants to return to her house, to the "peacefulness of the morning." But, while she was able to turn her back on the reality of her poverty, she will not be able to ignore the next truth that hits her. 35

"Stepping smack into his eyes," Myop encounters death, but is unafraid as she "frees herself." She is filled with innocent curiosity and gazes "around the spot with interest." Ironically, as she picks her "wild pink rose," a symbol of beauty, she spots the noose and has her epiphany.

The transition in image, setting, and diction all propel Walker's theme— 40 the coming of age. In the last paragraph Myop picks up the flowers and places her bouquet in front of the lynched man. It is as if she is at a funeral, as if she has sobered from her carefree state to one of realization. For, in the last line, the images of the beginning are finally crushed. Myop can no longer return to the world of flower-gathering or sun-lit skipping. For Myop, the "summer is over." 45

This is a high-range essay for the following reasons:

- Indicates complete understanding of the prompt (lines 3–4).
- Cites appropriate details to support the thesis:
  - Imagery (lines 15, 25–30, 36)
  - Diction (lines 5–6, 10, 30)
  - Setting (lines 1, 15–16)
- Thoroughly explores contrasts (lines 12, 16–17, 45).
- Presents unique insights into the underlying theme (lines 16–17, 22–23, 41–43).
- Adheres well to topic, exhibits transitions, and connective tissue.
- Has a definite, clear progression of thought and a strong writer's voice.

This high-range essay presents a solid, mature, and insightful discussion and analysis of Myop's "epiphany" and how Walker prepares the reader for it.

Student Essay B

In the short story "The Flowers" by Alice Walker, the author conveys the meaning of the story and prepares the reader for the ending by using various literary techniques. Some of these are symbol, narrative pace, and style.

The narrative pace starts out as slow and relaxed as Myop explores the land around her family's sharecropper cabin. Every little detail is described creating 5 an image of the blissful summer day. Myop's exuberance is portrayed through diction such as "skipped lightly," "she felt light and good," "bouncing," and "she was singing." Her innocence is shown by the way she is able to block out everything but her happiness and her song. The colors used in the beginning of

the story further form the image that is being set up because they are earthy yet 10
shiny colors such as "golden," "silver," and "dark brown."

The fifth paragraph is a transition of narrative pace. The diction and tone
change from peaceful and relaxed to tense and dark. Diction such as "strangeness"
and "gloomy" take over. When describing the new atmosphere, Walker uses syntax
like "the air was damp, the silence close and deep." 15

From here, the story continues to darken and reaches a climax when Myop
steps on a dead man's face. She then discovers his body—in parts and decaying.
Walker's use of colors suddenly changes too. Now, "blue," "green," and "wild pink"
are used. Although these colors can be seen as positive, in this story, they represent
"rotting." Myop finds the noose as she picks up a flower. Such irony. 20

The last paragraph/sentence is brief and compact. It simply reads, "And the
summer was over." The summer can be seen as a symbol of Myop's innocence. With
the end of her summer, when she lays down her flowers, her innocence is gone forever.
She can no longer exist "for nothing but her song." She had seen death in the midst
of her paradise. 25

This is a midrange essay for the following reasons:

- Makes adequate, expedient presentation of the details in developing the thesis.
- Illustrates an understanding of the selected literary devices used in the story, but does not fully link or expand them with regard to the thesis (lines 14–15, 9–10).
- Has unsupported interpretation in lines 18–19.
- In many places, the syntax resembles a list because ideas are not fully developed (lines 16–20).

This midrange essay addresses the prompt and provides details to support the thesis. While the writer obviously understood both the story and the author's process, the subtleties are not fully explored and the syntax lacks fluidity.

Rubrics for "The Naked and the Nude" by Robert Graves

High-Range Essay

- Indicates complete understanding of the requirements for discussing the differences in connotation between "naked" and "nude."
- Recognizes and identifies the many differences between the two words.
- Utilizes appropriate literary techniques to present a coherent distinction between the two words.
- Responds to the irony in the final stanza.
- Perceives Graves's tone and preference for one of the words.
- Interprets allusions, images, symbols, etc.
- Uses smooth transitions and clear connective tissue.
- Demonstrates a mature writing style.

Midrange Essay

- Refers accurately to the thesis involving the contrast in meanings between two words.
- Adequately supports the thesis with appropriate details.

- Is less adept at interpreting the poem.
- May not be sensitive to the complex allusions and images or vocabulary.
- Demonstrates writing that is adequate to convey the writer's intent.

Sample Student Essays

Student Essay A

Many people tend to use the words "naked" and "nude" interchangeably. Yet Robert Graves objects to this misconception in his poem "The Naked and the Nude." Although both words mean "without clothes," Graves interprets them differently with regard to their connotations. He points out that "naked" refers to the body itself, whereas, "nude" refers to a personality or state of mind. Through   5
his use of various allusions and imagery, Graves contrasts the two synonyms.

Graves dedicates one stanza apiece to explain his perception of each word. When describing the "naked," Graves uses several classical allusions. He points out that "the Hippocratic eye will see in nakedness, anatomy." Likewise, "naked shines the Goddess when she mounts her lion among men." It's clear that   10
nakedness only refers to the naked body. However, Graves uses allusions to deception and trickery to explain his concept of the nude. He says, "the nude are bold, the nude are sly . . . they grin a mock religious grin of scorn at those of naked skin." The concept of nude seems to be more of a cunning state of mind—"being naked with attitude."   15

The poet uses these details to create a certain imagery that clearly explains this discrepancy. His use of classical allusions creates images of peace, beauty, and spirituality which imply the inherent beauty of the human body on a physical level. Yet, the imagery created by the second set of details does not deal with the physical body. Graves explains that the nude have a cunning state of mind, "while draping   20
by a showman's trick their dishabille in rhetoric."

The contrast described in the poem, body versus mind, is reinforced when Graves tells us that the naked are physical bodies that are admired by "Lovers without reproach" and men of medicine. The nude, however, are more than that; they "are sly" and "hold each treasonable eye." The writer concludes that the naked, therefore, who   25
compete against the nude may know defeat because the nude are more complex and cynical.

Graves's final stanza transfers the vulnerability of the naked to the nude. "When treading the briary patches of the dead," the nude will not have artifice to protect them from the Gorgons' whips—they will be the naked as well as the nude.   30

This is a high-range essay for the following reasons:

- Shows complete understanding of the prompt.
- Immediately presents an accurate distinction between "naked" and "nude" (lines 4–5).

- Utilizes allusion and imagery correctly and links examples to meaning (lines 8–11, 12–15, 17–18).
- Reinforces the contrast throughout the essay (lines 16, 22, 29–30).
- Indicates perceptive, subtle analysis (lines 20–21, 29).
- Is well organized.
- Demonstrates mature writing style.

This high-range essay is indicative of a confident writer and thinker. The paper is well focused, and it exhibits the writer's facility with literary terminology and analysis.

Student Essay B

The poem "The Naked and the Nude" written by Robert Graves explicitly shows how connotations can change the meaning of a thought or statement through images and other poetic devices. Those who are "naked" and those who are "nude" are not, according to the poem, in the same state of undress.

The speaker of the poem describes the differences between the naked and the 5 nude using a variety of images and descriptions. He feels that one who is naked is hiding nothing while one who is nude is a picture of deception and art. The images of "Lovers without reproach who gaze on bodies naked and ablaze" depicts the honesty and truth that is given with love. Also the "Hippocratic eye will see in nakedness, anatomy." When this "eye" sees a naked person it is seeing what is really there and 10 not what could be held in the deception of a person who is nude.

Although the naked are personified as "love" and "truth," when they "compete against the nude they may know defeat." This statement shows how those that are naked can sometimes be deceived and beaten by those who are artful liars. However, when it comes to the life after death, those who have been nude will also be naked, 15 meaning that no matter what they were in life, when they die there will be no hiding behind the art of the body. Also, the facade that was built in life to hide from the truth will not work when it comes to the end.

Tone is another device that is used to convey the different connotations of naked and nude. When those who are naked are being discussed, the tone is not only 20 positive, it presents an image of those who are happy with their position in life. For example, nakedness is linked with words such as "love," "truth," "shines," and "Goddess." However, when the speaker directs his attention on the nude, the tone is just the opposite. Nude is associated with "scorn," "showman," and "mock-religious." The speaker's tone in the descriptions of the two states of undress presents a clear 25 difference in the connotations of the two words in the title of the poem.

The style and structure of the poem also contribute to conveying the two different connotations of naked and nude. The simple rhyme scheme shows how simplistic those that are naked can be as opposed to the deception and intricacies of those who are nude. The four stanza's each have a theme that it conveys. The first stanza 30 *exhibits the differences between the naked and the nude. The second stanza has the theme of the freedom of the naked, while the third shows the deception of the nude. The fourth and final stanza reinforces the theme that everyone will be naked after death.*

This is a midrange essay for the following reasons:

- Accurately addresses the prompt.
- Understands deception and artifice (lines 6–7).
- Refers to suitable textual material to support the thesis (lines 8–9, 22–24).
- Demonstrates an ability to handle literary analysis (19–25, 27–29).
- Stays on topic.
- Has several awkward sentences and punctuation and agreement errors (lines 10–11, 30).
- Uses transitions and connective tissue.

It's obvious that the writer of this midrange essay understands both the prompt and process of literary analysis. The second half of the paper is not as strong as the first. Perhaps, this writer was feeling the time pressure.

Rubrics for the Free-Response Essay

High-Range Essay

- Effectively and coherently addresses the intentional dissembling of a character or group.
- Effectively and coherently analyzes how the dissembling contributes to character development.
- Effectively and coherently discusses how the dissembling contributes to the meaning of the work.
- Chooses an appropriate novel or play.
- Uses references insightfully to support and illustrate the dissembling.
- Thoroughly discusses the character's nature and its relation to the theme.
- Strongly adheres to topic.
- Substantiates development of the thesis.
- Exhibits mature writing style.

Midrange Essay

- Identifies the intentional dissembling of a character or group.
- Chooses an acceptable novel or play.
- Adequately addresses the prompt with respect to intentional dissembling and how it contributes to both character development and meaning.
- Uses obvious references to support the prompt.
- Discussion of the character's nature and its relation to the theme is less developed.
- Adheres to topic, but may have lapses in coherence.
- Discussion of the theme is less developed.
- Writing style is acceptable but may show lapses in syntax and/or diction.

Sample Student Essays

Student Essay A

"To thine own self be true," advises Polonius in Shakespeare's <u>Hamlet</u>. Too bad he doesn't follow his own counsel when he continually dissembles to advance his own position in Claudius's court. This deceitfulness is the cause of the destruction of the lives of his children, himself, and ultimately the kingdom. His seemingly minor deceits reinforce the theme of betrayal and deception in the play. 5

Our first impression of Polonius is a positive one when we see him supporting Laertes's desire to return to his studies in Paris. However, his fatherly advice, "to not be false to any man" is ironic because he has already hired Reynaldo to spy on his son. He tells Reynaldo to use a "bait of falsehood" to see if Laertes's friends will be faithful 10 and true. Polonius plans for this to include starting rumors and even malicious lies. Later in the play, Shakespeare has Rosencrantz and Guildenstern play out a parallel scene with Hamlet.

As with his son, Polonius seems to be genuinely concerned with the well-being of his daughter Ophelia. He tells her to reject the "love" letters and tokens from Hamlet 15 because he fears Hamlet only wants to take advantage of her and will not and cannot marry her. But soon we see the other side of this paternal schemer when Polonius willingly uses his daughter's emotional connections to Hamlet for his own purpose of furthering his service to Claudius. Hoping to prove that Hamlet's madness is caused by love sickness, he permits himself to advance his own agenda even though he has to 20 know that it will cause pain and distress for both Ophelia and Hamlet.

Inevitably, Polonius's dissembling leads to his own destruction. Ever the deceitful sycophant, he suggests to Claudius that he hide behind the arras in Gertrude's chamber in order to spy on both her and Hamlet. While eavesdropping, he cries out when he believes that Hamlet is attacking the Queen. Believing the voice to be that of 25 Claudius, Hamlet thrusts his sword through the curtain, fatally wounding Polonius. Here, the irony lies in his death resulting from an attempt to protect Gertrude.

It is this act that is the catalyst for the subsequent tragic events: Ophelia's madness and death, Laertes's desire for revenge, and Hamlet's fleeing Denmark. The final tragedies of the play—the deaths of Ophelia, Laertes, Gertrude, Claudius, and 30 Hamlet—are all the results of further dissembling which is foreshadowed by Polonius's deceit.

Although Polonius dies in Act III, he sets the foundation for the theme of deceit and murder throughout the remainder of the drama. Truly, something was rotten in the state of Denmark, and it was Polonius. 35

This is a high-range essay for the following reasons:

- Demonstrates a clear and focused understanding of the prompt and its demands.
- Exhibits solid evidence of the writer's knowledge of the chosen work.

- Demonstrates the ability to garner insights from the work.
- Uses appropriate illustrations and details (lines 8–9, paragraphs 3 and 4).
- Uses strong connective tissue.
- Demonstrates thorough development of ideas that are linked to the meaning of the work (lines 3–6, 11–13, 19–21).
- Strongly adheres to topic and organization.
- Uses mature vocabulary and syntax (lines 22–23, 28).

This high-range essay is strong because of its clear voice and strong organization. The introductory paragraph establishes the premise, which is fully supported in the body paragraphs. Rather than a summary, the concluding paragraph makes an insightful final comment connecting the topic and student interpretation.

Student Essay B

Often, in literature, there is a gap between the appearance of a situation and the meaning of the truth behind it. In Shakespeare's Hamlet, the protagonist assumes the antic disposition as a means of investigating the veracity of the ghost's admonition, "The serpent that did sting thy father's life, now wears his crown." In addition to contributing to the psychological development of Hamlet's character, this deceit augments many of the important themes in the play. In a work whose main topic is the search for truth, Hamlet's misrepresentation acts as a warning to sift through the surface appearance of things to discover purpose in this world. 5

Throughout the play, nothing is really as it seems. Hamlet's feigned madness is perhaps the most egregious example of this pattern. The melancholy Dane becomes a different man behind the mask of insanity. He is free to taunt Polonius regarding his lack of intelligence, or to scold his mother for her sexual improprieties, or to chastise Ophelia for her attempt to trick him. He is free to express himself without the fear of being held responsible for his insolence. This is a psychological coping method for Hamlet to deal with the trauma of a father's death and a mother's betrayal. Hamlet represses his anger and is paralyzed by it. The course of the play is a struggle for Hamlet to overcome his repression and to deal with the problems before him. Pretending to be mad is symbolic of this inner struggle and Hamlet's shield from the world. 10 15 20

Many of the major themes in Hamlet are also embodied in Hamlet's misrepresentation. The pervading irony in the play is that the "madman" is really thinking rationally. He sees what others do not and recognizes that his father was killed at Claudius's hands. Hamlet is a man who can and does make plans to seek the truth, and he carries these plans out. Another major theme is that of appearance versus reality. Connected to and with Hamlet's situation is a king who is a murderer, a mystery involving a ghost, a play within a play, a royal request which will turn into an invasion of Denmark, spying for proof of madness, fatherly advice to his children, 25 and friends who are enemies. Each of these separately and all of them together enhance this theme of the play.

30

<u>Hamlet</u> is a search for truth. Through the protagonist's discovery of self and the revelation of Claudius's guilt, he embodies everyman's striving for understanding. Dissembling as a madman, Hamlet is able to work toward his goal of gaining authentic knowledge of past events and future battles.

This is a solid midrange essay for the following reasons:

- Writer has an obvious voice that engages the reader.
- Uses strong vocabulary.
- Decisively identifies theme and character.
- References are appropriate.
- Uses parallel structure well.
- Indicates cause and effect with supporting details.
- Uses inferences rather than plot.
- Good use of connective tissue.

Here is a paper that shows great promise and strength in the first half, but it loses continuity and lacks development in the second half. It seems that the writer has run out of time and is anxious to complete the essay. This student is a real thinker, but is trapped by time constraints.

Chapter 5

AP Calculus AB

Answer Sheet for Multiple-Choice Questions

Part A

1. _____
2. _____
3. _____
4. _____
5. _____
6. _____
7. _____
8. _____
9. _____
10. _____
11. _____

12. _____
13. _____
14. _____
15. _____
16. _____
17. _____
18. _____
19. _____
20. _____
21. _____
22. _____
23. _____

24. _____
25. _____
26. _____
27. _____
28. _____

Part B

76. _____
77. _____
78. _____
79. _____
80. _____

81. _____
82. _____
83. _____
84. _____
85. _____
86. _____
87. _____
88. _____
89. _____
90. _____
91. _____
92. _____

AP CALCULUS AB

Section I—Part A

Time—55 minutes
Use of calculator *is not* permitted
28 questions

Directions: Use the answer sheet provided on page 105. All questions are given equal weight. There is no penalty for unanswered questions. However, ¼ of the number of incorrect answers will be subtracted from the number of correct answers. Unless otherwise indicated, the domain of a function *f* is the set of all real numbers. The use of a calculator is *not* permitted in this part of the exam.

1. The $\lim\limits_{x \to -\infty} \dfrac{2x - 1}{1 + 2x}$ is

   (A) −1   (B) 0   (C) 1
   (D) 2   (E) nonexistent

2. $\displaystyle\int_{\pi/2}^{x} \cos t \, dt$

   (A) $\cos x$ (B) $-\sin x$ (C) $\sin x - 1$
   (D) $\sin x + 1$ (E) $-\sin x + 1$

3. The radius of a sphere is increasing at a constant of 2 *cm/sec*. At the instant when the volume of the sphere is increasing at $32\pi \ cm^3/sec$, the surface area of the sphere is

   (A) 8π (B) $\dfrac{32\pi}{3}$ (C) 16π

   (D) 64π (E) $\dfrac{256\pi}{3}$

4. Given the equation $A = \dfrac{\sqrt{3}}{4}\left(5s - 1\right)^2$, what is the instantaneous rate of change of A with respect to s at $s = 1$?

   (A) $2\sqrt{3} + 5$ (B) $2\sqrt{3}$ (C) $\dfrac{5}{2}\sqrt{3}$

   (D) $4\sqrt{3}$ (E) $10\sqrt{3}$

5. What is the $\lim\limits_{x \to \ln 2} g(x)$, if $g(x)$

   $= \begin{cases} e^x & \text{if } x > \ln 2 \\ 4 - e^x & \text{if } x \le \ln 2 \end{cases}$?

   (A) −2   (B) ln 2   (C) e^2
   (D) 2   (E) nonexistent

6. The graph of f' is shown in Figure 1.

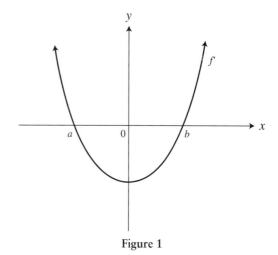

   y

   f

   a   0   *b*   *x*

   Figure 1

   A possible graph of *f* is (see Figure 2):

7. If $g(x) = -2|x + 3|$, what is the $\lim\limits_{x \to -3^-} g'(x)$?

   (A) −6   (B) −2   (C) 2
   (D) 6   (E) nonexistent

8. What is $\lim\limits_{\Delta x \to 0} \dfrac{\sin\left(\dfrac{\pi}{3} + \Delta x\right) - \sin\left(\dfrac{\pi}{3}\right)}{\Delta x}$?

   (A) $-\dfrac{1}{2}$ (B) 0   (C) $\dfrac{1}{2}$

   (D) $\dfrac{\sqrt{3}}{2}$ (E) nonexistent

(A)

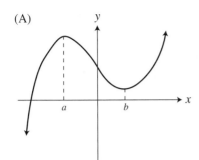

(B)

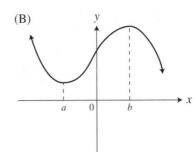

(C)

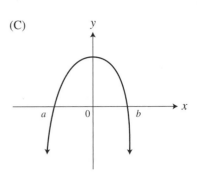

(D)

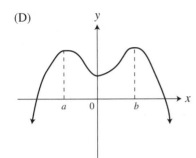

(E)

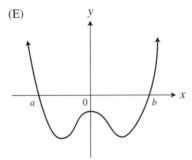

Figure 2

9. If $f(x)$ is an antiderivative of xe^{-x^2} and $f(0) = 1$, then $f(1) =$

(A) $\dfrac{1}{e}$

(B) $\dfrac{1}{2e} - \dfrac{3}{2}$

(C) $\dfrac{1}{2e} - \dfrac{1}{2}$

(D) $-\dfrac{1}{2e} + \dfrac{3}{2}$

(E) $-\dfrac{1}{2e} + \dfrac{1}{2}$

10. If $g(x) = 3\tan^2(2x)$, then $g'\left(\dfrac{\pi}{8}\right)$ is

(A) 6

(B) $6\sqrt{2}$

(C) 12

(D) $12\sqrt{2}$

(E) 24

11. The graph of the function f is shown in Figure 3, which of the following statements are true?

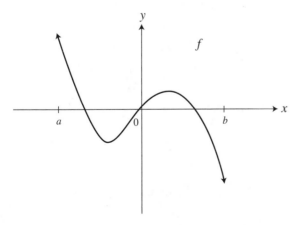

Figure 3

I. $f'(0) = 0$
II. f has an absolute maximum value on $[a, b]$
III. $f'' < 0$ on $(0, b)$

(A) III only
(B) I and II only
(C) II and III only
(D) I and III only
(E) I, II and III

12. $\displaystyle\int \dfrac{1+x}{\sqrt{x}}\,dx =$

(A) $2\sqrt{x} + \dfrac{x^2}{2} + c$

(B) $\dfrac{\sqrt{x}}{2} + \dfrac{3}{2}x^{3/2} + c$

(C) $2\sqrt{x} + \dfrac{2}{3}x^{3/2} + c$

(D) $x + \dfrac{2}{3}x^{3/2} + c$

(E) 0

13. The graph of f is shown in Figure 4 and f is twice differentiable. Which of the following has the smallest value?

I. $f(-1)$
II. $f'(-1)$
III. $f''(-1)$

(A) I   (B) II   (C) III
(D) I and II   (E) II and III

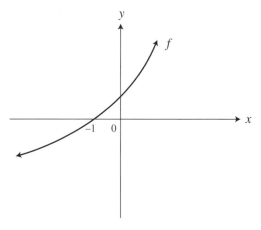

Figure 4

14. If $\dfrac{dy}{dx} = 3e^{2x}$, and at $x = 0$, $y = \dfrac{5}{2}$, a solution to the differential equation is

(A) $3e^{2x} - \dfrac{1}{2}$ (B) $3e^{2x} + \dfrac{1}{2}$ (C) $\dfrac{3}{2}e^{2x} + 1$

(D) $\dfrac{3}{2}e^{2x} + 2$ (E) $\dfrac{3}{2}e^{2x} + 5$

15. The graph of the velocity function of a moving particle is shown in Figure 5 What is the total displacement of the particle during $0 \le t \le 20$?

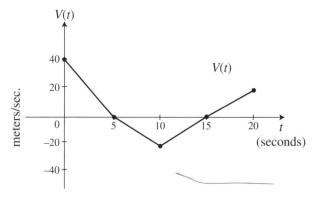

Figure 5

(A) 20m   (B) 50m   (C) 100m
(D) 250m   (E) 500m

16. The position function of a moving particle is

$$s(t) = \dfrac{t^3}{6} - \dfrac{t^2}{2} + t - 3 \quad \text{for } 0 \le t \le 4.$$ What is the maximum velocity of the particle on the interval $0 \le t \le 4$?

(A) $\dfrac{1}{2}$ (B) 1   (C) $\dfrac{14}{6}$ (D) 4   (E) 5

17. If $\displaystyle\int_{-k}^{k} |2x|\, dx = 18$ and $k > 0$, the value(s) of k are

(A) -3 (B) $-3\sqrt{2}$ (C) 3
(D) $3\sqrt{2}$ (E) 9

18. A function f is continuous on $[-1,1]$ and some of the values of f are shown below:

x	-1	0	1
$f(x)$	2	b	-2

If $f(x) = 0$ has only one solution, r, and $r < 0$, then a possible value of b is

(A) 3   (B) 2   (C) 1   (D) 0   (E) -1

19. $\displaystyle\int_{0}^{\ln 2} e^{2x}\, dx =$

(A) $\dfrac{3}{2}$ (B) 3   (C) 4

(D) $e^2 - \dfrac{1}{2}$ (E) $2e^2 - 1$

20. The area of the region enclosed by the graph of $y = \sqrt{9 - x^2}$ and the x-axis is

(A) 36   (B) $\dfrac{9\pi}{2}$ (C) 9π

(D) 18π (E) 36π

21. If a function f is continuous for all values of x, and $a > 0$ and $b > 0$, which of the following integrals always have the same value?

I. $\displaystyle\int_{0}^{a} f(x)\, dx$

II. $\displaystyle\int_{b}^{a+b} f(x - b)\, dx$

III. $\displaystyle\int_{b}^{a+b} f(x + b)\, dx$

(A) I and II only
(B) I and III only
(C) II and III only
(D) I, II, and III
(E) none

22. What is the average value of the function $y = 2\sin(2x)$ on the interval $\left[0, \dfrac{\pi}{6}\right]$?

(A) $-\dfrac{3}{\pi}$ (B) $\dfrac{1}{2}$ (C) $\dfrac{3}{\pi}$ (D) $\dfrac{3}{2\pi}$ (E) 6π

23. Given the equation $y = 3\sin^2\left(\dfrac{x}{2}\right)$, what is an equation of the tangent line to the graph at $x = \pi$?

(A) $y = 3$
(B) $y = \pi$
(C) $y = \pi + 3$
(D) $y = x - \pi + 3$
(E) $y = 3(x - \pi) + 3$

24. The position function of a moving particle on the *x-axis* is given as $s(t) = t^3 + t^2 - 8t$ for $0 \le t \le 10$. For what values of t is the particle moving to the right?

(A) $t < -2$ (B) $t > 0$ (C) $t < \dfrac{4}{3}$

(D) $0 < t < \dfrac{4}{3}$ (E) $t > \dfrac{4}{3}$

25. See Figure 6.

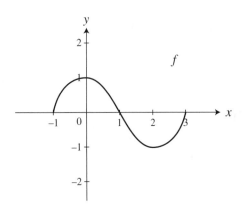

Figure 6

The graph of f consist of two semicircles, for $-1 \le x \le 3$ as shown in Figure 6. What is the value of $\int_{-1}^{3} f(x)\,dx$?

(A) 0   (B) π (C) 2π (D) 4π (E) 8π

26. If $f(x) = \int_{1}^{x} t(t^3 + 1)^{3/2}\,dt$, then $f'(2)$ is

(A) $2^{3/2}$ (B) $54 - 2^{3/2}$ (C) 54

(D) $135 - \dfrac{13\sqrt{2}}{2}$ (E) 135

27. If $\int_{-k}^{k} f(x)\,dx = 2\int_{-k}^{0} f(x)\,dx$ for all positive values of k, then which of the following could be the graph of f? (See Figure 7.)

28. If $h'(x) = k(x)$ and k is a continuous function for all real values of x, then $\int_{-1}^{1} k(5x)\,dx$ is

(A) $h(5) - h(-5)$
(B) $5h(5) + 5h(-5)$
(C) $5h(5) - 5h(-5)$
(D) $\dfrac{1}{5}h(5) + \dfrac{1}{5}h(-5)$
(E) $\dfrac{1}{5}h(5) - \dfrac{1}{5}h(-5)$

(A)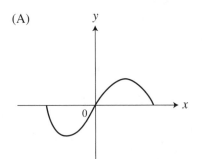

(B)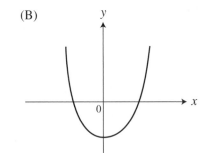

(C)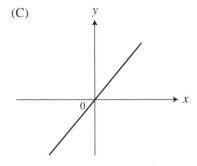

(D)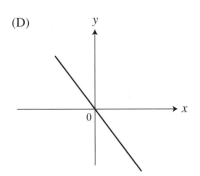

(E)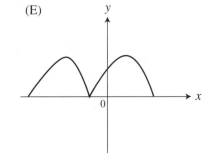

Figure 7

AP CALCULUS AB

Section I—Part B

Time—50 minutes
Use of calculator *is* permitted
17 questions

Directions: Use the answer sheet on page 105. *Please note that the questions begin with number 76.* This is not an error. It is done to be consistent with the numbering system of the actual AP Calculus AB Exam. All questions are given equal weight. There is no penalty for unanswered questions. However, ¼ of the number of incorrect answers will be subtracted from the number of correct answers. Unless otherwise indicated, the domain of a function *f* is the set of all real numbers. If the exact numerical value does not appear among the given choices, select the best approximate value. The use of a calculator is *permitted* in this part of the exam.

76. If $f(x) = \int_0^x -\cos t \, dt$ on $[0, 2\pi]$, then f has a local maximum at $x =$

    (A) 0 (B) $\dfrac{\pi}{2}$ (C) π

    (D) $\dfrac{3\pi}{2}$ (E) 2π

77. The equation of the normal line to the graph $y = e^{2x}$ at the point where $\dfrac{dy}{dx} = 2$ is

    (A) $y = -\dfrac{1}{2}x - 1$

    (B) $y = -\dfrac{1}{2}x + 1$

    (C) $y = 2x + 1$

    (D) $y = -\dfrac{1}{2}\left(x - \dfrac{\ln 2}{2}\right) + 2$

    (E) $y = 2\left(x - \dfrac{\ln 2}{2}\right) + 2$

78. The graph of f', the derivative of f, is shown in Figure 8. At which value of x does the graph of f have a point of inflection?

    (A) 0 (B) x_1 (C) x_2 (D) x_3 (E) x_4

79. The temperature of a metal is dropping at the rate of $g(t) = 10e^{-0.1t}$ for $0 \le t \le 10$ where g is measured in degrees Fahrenheit and

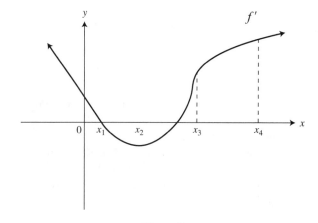

Figure 8

t in minutes. If the metal is initially 100°F, what is the temperature to the nearest degree Fahrenheit after 6 *minutes*?

(A) 37 (B) 45 (C) 55 (D) 63 (E) 82

80. What is the approximate volume of the solid obtained by revolving about the *x-axis* the region in the first quadrant enclosed by the curves $y = x^3$ and $y = \sin x$?

    (A) $0.061\,\pi$ (B) $0.139\,\pi$ (C) $0.215\,\pi$
    (D) $0.225\,\pi$ (E) $0.278\,\pi$

81. Let f be a differentiable function on (a,b). If f has a point of inflection on (a,b), which of the following could be the graph of f'' on (a,b)? See Figure 9.

(A)

(B)

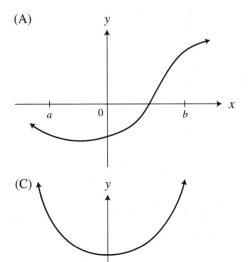

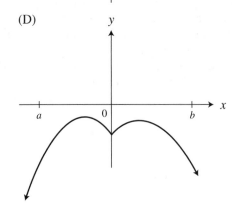

(C)

(D)

Figure 9

(A) A   (B) B   (C) C   (D) D   (E) None

82. The base of a solid is a region bounded by the lines $y = x$, $y = -x$ and $x = 4$ as shown in Figure 10. What is the volume of the solid if the cross sections perpendicular to the x-*axis* are equilateral triangles?

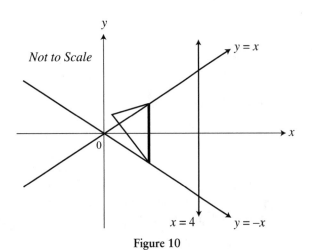

Figure 10

(A) $\dfrac{16\sqrt{3}}{3}$ (B) $\dfrac{32\sqrt{3}}{3}$ (C) $\dfrac{64\sqrt{3}}{3}$

(D) $\dfrac{256\pi}{3}$ (E) $\dfrac{3072\pi}{5}$

83. Let f be a continuous function on $[0, 6]$ and have selected values as shown below.

x	0	2	4	6
$f(x)$	0	1	2.25	6.25

If you use the subintervals $[0,2]$, $[2,4]$ and $[4,6]$, what is the trapezoidal approximation of $\displaystyle\int_0^6 f(x)\,dx$?

(A) 9.5   (B) 12.75   (C) 19
(D) 25.5   (E) 38.25

84. The amount of a certain bacteria y in a petri dish grows according to the equation

$\dfrac{dy}{dt} = ky$, where k is a constant and t is measured in hours.

If the amount of bacteria triples in 10 *hours*, then $k \approx$

(A) −1.204   (B) −0.110   (C) 0.110
(D) 1.204   (E) 0.3

85. The volume of the solid generated by revolving about the y-*axis* the region bounded by the graphs of $y = \sqrt{x}$ and $y = x$ is

(A) $\dfrac{2\pi}{15}$ (B) $\dfrac{\pi}{6}$ (C) $\dfrac{2\pi}{3}$

(D) $\dfrac{16\pi}{15}$ (E) $\dfrac{56\pi}{15}$

86. How many points of inflection does the graph of

$y = \dfrac{\sin x}{x}$ have on the interval $(-\pi, \pi)$?

(A) 0   (B) 1   (C) 2   (D) 3   (E) 4

87. Given $f(x) = x^2 e^x$, what is an approximate value of $f(1.1)$, if you use a tangent line to the graph of f at $x = 1$.

(A) 3.534   (B) 3.635   (C) 7.055
(D) 8.155   (E) 10.244

88. The area under the curve $y = \sin x$ from $x = b$ to $x = \pi$ is 0.2. If $0 \le b < \pi$, then $b =$

(A) −0.927   (B) −0.201   (C) 0.644
(D) 1.369   (E) 2.498

89. At what value(s) of x do the graphs of $y = x^2$
and $y = -\sqrt{x}$ have perpendicular tangent lines?

(A) −1   (B) 0   (C) $\dfrac{1}{4}$

(D) 1   (E) none

90. What is the approximate slope of the tangent to the curve $x^3 + y^3 = xy$ at $x = 1$?

(A) −2.420   (B) −1.325   (C) −1.014
(D) −0.698   (E) 0.267

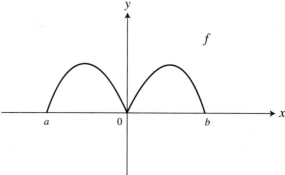

Figure 11

91. The graph of f is shown in Figure 11, and
$g(x) = \displaystyle\int_a^x f(t)\,dt$, $x > a$. Which of the following is a possible graph of g? See Figure 12.

92. If $g(x) = |xe^x|$, which of the following statements about g are true?

I. g has a relative minimum at $x = 0$.
II. g changes concavity at $x = 0$.
III. g is differentiable at $x = 0$.

(A) I only
(B) II only
(C) III only
(D) I and II only
(E) I and III only

(A)

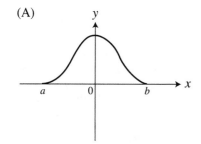

(B)

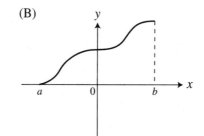

(C)

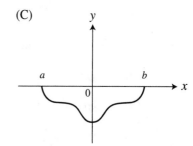

(D)

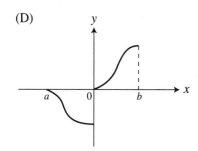

(E)

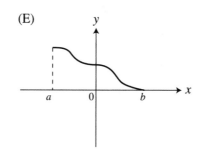

Figure 12

END OF SECTION I

AP CALCULUS AB

Section II—Part A

Time—45 minutes
Use of calculator *is* permitted
3 questions

Directions: You may *not* receive any credit for correct answers without supporting work. You may use an approved calculator to help solve a problem. However, you must clearly indicate the setup of your solution using mathematical notations and *not* calculator syntax. Calculators may be used to find the derivative of a function at a point, compute the numerical value of a definite integral, or solve an equation. Unless otherwise indicated, you may assume the following: (a) the numeric or algebraic answers need not be simplified, (b) your answer, if expressed in approximation, should be correct to 3 places after the decimal point, and (c) the domain of a function *f* is the set of all real numbers.

1. The slope of a function at any point (x, y) is $\dfrac{e^x}{e^x + 1}$. The point $(0, 2 \ln 2)$ is on the graph of f.

   (a) Write an equation of the tangent line to the graph of f at $x = 0$.
   (b) Use the tangent line in part (a) to approximate $f(0.1)$ to the nearest thousandth.
   (c) Solve the differential equation $\dfrac{dy}{dx} = \dfrac{e^x}{e^x + 1}$ with the initial condition $f(0) = 2 \ln 2$.
   (d) Use the solution in part (c) and find $f(0.1)$ to the nearest thousandth.

2. The temperature in a greenhouse from 7:00 *p.m.* to 7:00 *a.m.* is given by $f(t) = 96 - 20 \sin\left(\dfrac{t}{4}\right)$, where $f(t)$ is measured in Fahrenheit and t is measured in hours.

   (a) What is the temperature of the greenhouse at 1:00 a.m. to the nearest degree Fahrenheit?
   (b) Find the average temperature between 7:00 p.m. and 7:00 a.m. to the nearest tenth of a degree Fahrenheit.
   (c) When the temperature of the greenhouse drops below 80°F, a heating system will automatically be turned on to maintain the temperature at a minimum of 80°F. At what value of t to the nearest tenth is the heating system turned on?
   (d) The cost of heating the greenhouse is $0.25 *per hour* for each degree. What is the total cost to the nearest dollar to heat the greenhouse from 7:00 p.m. and 7:00 a.m.?

3. A particle is moving on a straight line. The velocity of the particle for $0 \le t \le 30$ is shown in the table below for selected values of t.

t (sec)	0	3	6	9	12	15	18	21	24	27	30
$v(t)$ (m/sec)	0	7.5	10.1	12	13	13.5	14.1	14	13.9	13	12.2

   (a) Using the midpoints of five subintervals of equal length, find the approximate value of $\displaystyle\int_0^{30} v(t)\,dt.$
   (b) Using the result in part (a), find the average velocity over the interval $0 \le t \le 30$.
   (c) Find the average acceleration over the interval $0 \le t \le 30$.
   (d) Find the approximate acceleration at $t = 6$.
   (e) During what intervals of time is the acceleration negative?

AP CALCULUS AB

Section II—Part B

Time—45 minutes
Use of calculator *is not* permitted
3 questions

Directions: The use of a calculator is *not* permitted in this part of the exam. When you have finished this part of the exam, you may return to the problems in Part A of Section II and continue to work on them. However, you may not use a calculator. You should *show all work*. You may *not* receive any credit for correct answers without supporting work. Unless otherwise indicated, the numeric or algebraic answers need not be simplified, and the domain of a function *f* is the set of all real numbers.

4. See Figure 13.

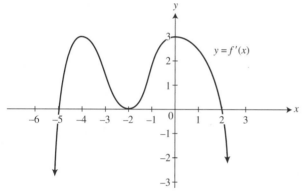

Figure 13

The graph of *f′*, the derivative of a function *f*, for $-6 \le x \le 3$ is shown in Figure 13.

(a) At what value(s) of *x* does *f* have a relative maximum value? Justify your answer.
(b) At what value(s) of *x* does *f* have a relative minimum value? Justify your answer.
(c) At what value(s) of *x* does the function have a point of inflection? Justify your answer.

(d) If $f(-5) = 2$, draw a possible sketch of *f* on $-6 < x < 3$.

5. Given the equation $y^2 - x + 2y - 3 = 0$:

(a) Find $\dfrac{dy}{dx}$.
(b) Write an equation of the line tangent to the graph of the equation at the point $(0, -3)$.
(c) Write an equation of the line normal to the graph of the equation at the point $(0, -3)$.
(d) The line $y = \dfrac{1}{4}x + 3$ is tangent to the graph at point *P*. Find the coordinates of point *P*.

6. Let *R* be the region enclosed by the graph of $y = x^2$ and the line $y = 4$.

(a) Find the area of region *R*.
(b) If the line $x = a$ divides region *R* into two regions of equal area, find *a*.
(c) If the line $y = b$ divides the region *R* into two regions of equal area, find *b*.
(d) If region *R* is revolved about the *x*-axis, find the volume of the resulting solid.

END OF SECTION II

ANSWERS TO MULTIPLE-CHOICE QUESTIONS

Answer Key

Part A	12. C	24. E	81. A
1. C	13. A	25. A	82. C
2. C	14. C	26. C	83. B
3. C	15. B	27. B	84. C
4. E	16. E	28. E	85. A
5. D	17. C		86. C
6. A	18. E	Part B	87. A
7. C	19. A	76. D	88. E
8. C	20. B	77. B	89. D
9. D	21. A	78. C	90. C
10. E	22. C	79. C	91. B
11. C	23. A	80. B	92. D

Solutions to Multiple-Choice Questions

Part A—No calculators.

1. The correct answer is (C).

$$\lim_{x \to -\infty} \frac{2x - 1}{1 + 2x} = \lim_{x \to -\infty} \frac{2 - \frac{1}{x}}{\frac{1}{x} + 2} = 1$$

2. The correct answer is (C).

$$\int_{\pi/2}^{x} \cos t \, dt = \sin t \Big]_{\pi/2}^{x} = \sin x - \left(\sin \frac{\pi}{2} \right)$$
$$= \sin x - 1.$$

3. The correct answer is (C).

$$V = \frac{4}{3} \pi r^3 \text{ and } \frac{dV}{dt} = 4\pi r^2 (2) = 8\pi r^2$$

$$\frac{dV}{dt} = 32\pi \, cm^3/\text{sec}; \ 8\pi r^2 = 32\pi \Rightarrow r = 2$$

Surface Area $= 4\pi r^2 = 4\pi (2)^2 = 16\pi.$

4. The correct answer is (E).

$$A = \frac{\sqrt{3}}{4} (5s - 1)^2, \frac{dA}{ds} = (2) \left(\frac{\sqrt{3}}{4} \right) (5s - 1)(5)$$

$$= \frac{5\sqrt{3}}{2} (5s - 1)$$

$$\frac{dA}{ds} \bigg|_{s=1} = \frac{5\sqrt{3}}{2} (4) = 10\sqrt{3}.$$

5. The correct answer is (D).

$$\lim_{x \to (\ln 2)^+} \left(e^x \right) = e^{\ln 2} = 2 \text{ and } \lim_{x \to (\ln 2)^-} \left(4 - e^x \right)$$
$$= 4 - e^{\ln 2} = 4 - 2 = 2$$

Since the two, one-sided limits are the same,
$$\lim_{x \to \ln 2} g(x) = 2.$$

6. The correct answer is (A).
See Figure S1.
The only graph that satisfies the behavior of f is (A).

7. The correct answer is (C).

$$g(x) = \begin{cases} -2(x + 3) & \text{if } x \geq -3 \\ (-2)[-(x + 3)] & \text{if } x < -3 \end{cases}$$

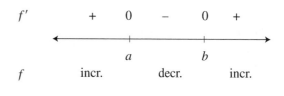

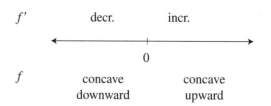

Figure S1

$$= \begin{cases} -2x - 6 & \text{if } x \geq -3 \\ 2x + 6 & \text{if } x < -3 \end{cases}$$

$$g'(x) = \begin{cases} -2 & \text{if } x > -3 \\ 2 & \text{if } x < -3 \end{cases}$$

Thus $\lim\limits_{x \to -3^-} g'(x) = 2.$

8. The correct answer is (C).
The definition of $f'(x)$ is $f'(x)$
$$= \lim_{\Delta x \to 0} \frac{f(x + \Delta x) - f(x)}{\Delta x}.$$

Thus $\lim\limits_{\Delta x \to 0} \dfrac{\sin \left(\frac{\pi}{3} + \Delta x \right) - \sin \left(\frac{\pi}{3} \right)}{\Delta x}$

$$= \frac{d(\sin x)}{dx} \bigg|_{x = \pi/3}$$

$$= \cos \left(\frac{\pi}{3} \right) = \frac{1}{2}.$$

9. The correct answer is (D).

Since $f(x) = \int xe^{-x^2} dx$, let $u = -x^2$,

$$du = -2x \, dx \text{ or } \frac{-du}{2} = x \, dx.$$

Thus $f(x) = \int e^u \left(-\frac{du}{2} \right) = -\frac{1}{2} e^u + c$

$$= -\frac{1}{2} e^{-x^2} + c$$

And $f(0) = 1 \Rightarrow -\frac{1}{2}\left(e^0\right) + c = 1 \Rightarrow -\frac{1}{2} + c$

$= 1 \Rightarrow c = \frac{3}{2}$

Therefore, $f(x) = -\frac{1}{2}e^{-x^2} + \frac{3}{2}$ and

$f(1) = -\frac{1}{2}e^{-1} + \frac{3}{2} = -\frac{1}{2e} + \frac{3}{2}$

10. The correct answer is (E).

$g(x) = 3\left[\tan(2x)\right]^2; g'(x) = 6\left[\tan(2x)\right]\sec^2(2x)2$

$= 12\tan(2x)\sec^2(2x)$

$g'\left(\frac{\pi}{8}\right) = 12\tan\left(\frac{\pi}{4}\right)\sec^2\left(\frac{\pi}{4}\right)$

$= 12(1)^2\left(\sqrt{2}\right)^2 = 24.$

11. The correct answer is (C).

(I) $f'(0) \neq 0$ since the tangent to $f(x)$ at $x = 0$ is not parallel to the x-axis.
(II) f has an absolute maximum at $x = a$.
(III) f'' is less than 0 on $(0,b)$ since f is concave downward.

Thus only statements II and III are true.

12. The correct answer is (C).

$\int \frac{1+x}{\sqrt{x}}\,dx = \int \left(\frac{1}{\sqrt{x}} + \frac{x}{\sqrt{x}}\right) dx$

$= \int \left(x^{-\frac{1}{2}} + x^{\frac{1}{2}}\right) dx$

$= \frac{x^{\frac{1}{2}}}{\frac{1}{2}} + \frac{x^{\frac{3}{2}}}{\frac{3}{2}} + c$

$= 2x^{\frac{1}{2}} + \frac{2}{3}x^{\frac{3}{2}} + c$

$= 2\sqrt{x} + \frac{2}{3}x^{\frac{3}{2}} + c.$

13. The correct answer is (A).

(I) $f(-1) = 0;$
(II) Since f is increasing, $f'(-1) > 0$
(III) Since f is concave upward, $f''(-1) > 0$

Thus $f(-1)$ has the smallest value.

14. The correct answer is (C).

Since $dy = 3e^{2x}dx \Rightarrow \int 1\,dy \Rightarrow \int 3e^{2x}dx \Rightarrow$

$y = \frac{3e^{2x}}{2} + c.$

At $x = 0, \frac{5}{2} = \frac{3\left(e^0\right)}{2} + c \Rightarrow \frac{5}{2} = \frac{3}{2} + c \Rightarrow c = 1$

Therefore, $y = \frac{3e^{2x}}{2} + 1.$

15. The correct answer is (B).

$\int_0^{20} v(t)\,dt = \frac{1}{2}(40)(5) + \frac{1}{2}(10)(-20) + \frac{1}{2}(5)(20)$

$= 50.$

16. The correct answer is (E).

$v(t) = s'(t) = \frac{t^2}{2} - t + 1$ and $a(t) = t - 1$ and $a'(t) = 1.$

Set $a(t) = 0 \Rightarrow t = 1.$ Thus, $v(t)$ has a relative minimum at $t = 1$ and $v(1) = \frac{1}{2}.$ Since it is the only relative extremum, it is an absolute minimum. And since $v(t)$ is continuous on the closed interval $[0,4]$, thus $v(t)$ has an absolute maximum at the endpoints.

$v(0) = 1$ and $v(4) = 8 - 4 + 1 = 5.$

Therefore, the maximum velocity of the particle on $[1,4]$ is 5.

17. The correct answer is (C).

Since $y = |2x|$ is symmetrical with respect to the y-axis,

$\int_{-k}^{k} |2x|\,dx = 2\int_0^k 2x\,dx = 2\left[x^2\right]_0^k = 2k^2$

Set $2k^2 = 18 \Rightarrow k^2 = 9 \Rightarrow k = \pm3.$ Since $k > 0$, $k = 3.$

18. The correct answer is (E).
See Figure S2.

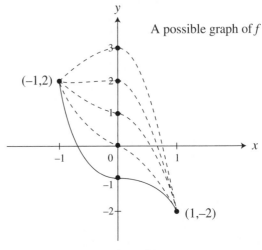

Figure S2

If $b = 0$, then 0 is a root and thus $r = 0$.

If $b = 1, 2,$ or 3, then the graph of f must cross the *x-axis* which implies there is another root. Thus, $b = -1$.

19. The correct answer is (A).

$$\int_0^{\ln 2} e^{2x} dx = \frac{e^{2x}}{2}\Bigg]_0^{\ln 2} = \frac{e^{2(\ln 2)}}{2} - \frac{e^{2(0)}}{2}$$

$$= \frac{\left(e^{\ln 2}\right)^2}{2} - \frac{e^0}{2} = \frac{(2)^2}{2} - \frac{1}{2} = \frac{3}{2}.$$

20. The correct answer is (B).

The graph of $y = \sqrt{9 - x^2}$ is a semicircle above the *x-axis* and whose endpoints are $(-3,0)$ and $(3,0)$. Thus the radius of the circle is $r = 3$.

$$\text{Area} = \frac{1}{2} \pi r^2 = \frac{9\pi}{2}.$$

21. The correct answer is (A).
See Figure S3.
The graphs $f(x - b)$ and $f(x + b)$ are the same as the graph of $f(x)$ shifted b units to the right and left, respectively. Looking at Figure S3, only I and II have the same value.

22. The correct answer is (C).

$$\text{Average value} = \frac{1}{\pi/6 - 0} \int_0^{\pi/6} 2\sin(2x)\,dx$$

$$= \frac{6}{\pi} \left[-\cos(2x)\right]_0^{\pi/6}$$

$$= \frac{6}{\pi} \left[-\cos\left(\frac{\pi}{3}\right) - (-\cos 0)\right]$$

$$= \frac{6}{\pi} \left[-\frac{1}{2} + 1\right] = \frac{3}{\pi}.$$

23. The correct answer is (A).

$$y = 3\sin^2\left(\frac{x}{2}\right); \frac{dy}{dx} = 6\sin\left(\frac{x}{2}\right)\left[\cos\left(\frac{x}{2}\right)\right]\frac{1}{2}$$

$$= 3\sin\left(\frac{x}{2}\right)\cos\left(\frac{x}{2}\right)$$

$$\frac{dy}{dx}\Bigg|_{x=\pi} = 3\sin\left(\frac{\pi}{2}\right)\cos\left(\frac{\pi}{2}\right) = 3(1)(0) = 0.$$

At $x = \pi$, $y = 3\sin^2\left(\frac{\pi}{2}\right) = 3(1)^2 = 3$; $(\pi, 3)$

Equation of tangent at $x = \pi$: $y = 3$.

24. The correct answer is (E).

$s(t) = t^3 + t^2 - 8t$; $v(t) = 3t^2 + 2t - 8$

Set $v(t) = 0 \Rightarrow 3t^2 + 2t - 8$

$$= 0 \Rightarrow (3t - 4)(t + 2)$$

$$= 0 \text{ or } t = \frac{4}{3} \text{ or } t = -2$$

Since $0 \leq t \leq 10$, thus $t = -2$ is not in the domain.

If $t > \frac{4}{3}$, $v(t) > 0 \Rightarrow$ the particle is moving to the right.

25. The correct answer is (A).

$$\int_{-1}^3 f(x)\,dx = \int_{-1}^1 f(x)\,dx + \int_1^3 f(x)\,dx$$

$$= \frac{1}{2}\pi(1)^2 - \frac{1}{2}\pi(1)^2 = 0.$$

26. The correct answer is (C).

$$f'(x) = x\left(x^3 + 1\right)^{3/2}; f'(2) = 2\left(2^3 + 1\right)^{3/2}$$

$$= 2(9)^{3/2} = 54.$$

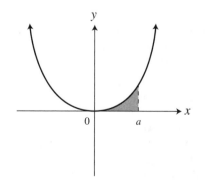
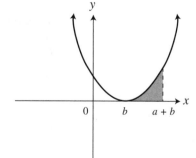
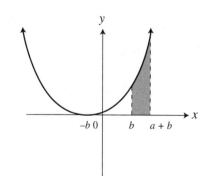

Figure S3

27. The correct answer is (B).

$$\int_{-k}^{k} f(x)\,dx = 2\int_{-k}^{0} f(x)\,dx \Rightarrow f(x) \text{ is an even}$$

function, i.e., $f(x) = f(-x)$.

The graph in (B) is the only even function.

28. The correct answer is (E).

Let $u = 5x$; $du = 5dx$ or $\dfrac{du}{5} = dx$

$$\int k(5x)\,dx = \frac{1}{5}\int k(u)\,du = \frac{1}{5}h(u) + c$$

$$= \frac{1}{5}h(5x) + c$$

$$\int_{-1}^{1} k(5x)\,dx = \frac{1}{5}h(5x)\Big]_{-1}^{1} = \frac{1}{5}h(5) - \frac{1}{5}h(-5).$$

Part B—Calculators are permitted.

76. The correct answer is (D).

$$f(x) = \int_{0}^{x} -\cos t\,dt;\ f'(x) = -\cos x$$

Let $f'(x) = 0$; $-\cos x = 0$.

$$x = \frac{\pi}{2} \text{ or } \frac{3\pi}{2}.$$

See Figure S4.

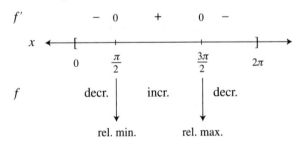

Figure S4

Thus f has a local maximum at $x = \dfrac{3\pi}{2}$.

77. The correct answer is (B).

$$y = e^{2x};\ \frac{dy}{dx} = \left(e^{2x}\right)2 = 2e^{2x}$$

Set $\dfrac{dy}{dx} = 2 \Rightarrow 2e^{2x} = 2 \Rightarrow e^{2x} = 1 \Rightarrow \ln\!\left(e^{2x}\right)$

$$= \ln 1 \Rightarrow 2x = 0 \text{ or } x = 0.$$

At $x = 0$, $y = e^{2x} = e^{2(0)}$

$$= 1;\ (0,1) \text{ or } y = -\frac{1}{2}x + 1.$$

78. The correct answer is (C).
See Figure S5.

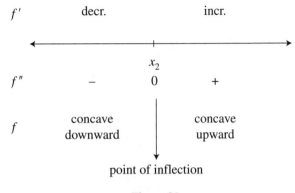

Figure S5

The graph of f has a point of inflection at $x = x_2$.

79. The correct answer is (C).

$$\text{Temperature of metal} = 100 - \int_{0}^{6} 10e^{-0.1t}\,dt$$

Using your calculator, you obtain:

Temperature of metal $= 100 - 45.1188$

$$= 54.8812 \approx 55°\text{F}.$$

80. The correct answer is (B).
See Figure S6.

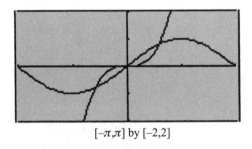

$[-\pi,\pi]$ by $[-2,2]$

Figure S6

Using the Intersection function on your calculator, you obtain the points of intersection: $(0, 0)$ and $(0.929, 0.801)$.

$$v = \pi\int_{0}^{0.929}\left(\left(\sin x\right)^{2} - \left(x^{3}\right)^{2}\right)dx = 0.139\pi.$$

81. The correct answer is (A).
A point of inflection $\Rightarrow$ the graph of f changes its concavity $\Rightarrow f''$ changes signs. Thus, the graph in (A) is the only one that goes from below the x-axis (negative) to above the x-axis (positive).

82. The correct answer is (C).

Area of a cross section = $\dfrac{\sqrt{3}}{4}(2x)^2 = \sqrt{3}x^2$

Using your calculator, you have:

Volume of solid = $\displaystyle\int_0^4 \sqrt{3}(x^2)dx = \dfrac{64\sqrt{3}}{3}$.

83. The correct answer is (B).

$\displaystyle\int_0^6 f(x)dx \approx \dfrac{6-0}{2(3)}\left[0 + 2(1) + 2(2.25) + 6.25\right]$

≈ 12.75.

84. The correct answer is (C).

$\dfrac{dy}{dx} = ky \Rightarrow y = y_0 e^{kt}$

Triple in 10 hours $\Rightarrow y = 3y_0$ at $t = 10$.

$3y_0 = y_0 e^{10k} \Rightarrow 3 = e^{10k} \Rightarrow \ln 3 = \ln\left(e^{10k}\right)$

$\Rightarrow \ln 3 = 10k$ or $k = \dfrac{\ln 3}{10}$

$\approx 0.109861 \approx 0.110$.

85. The correct answer is (A).
See Figure S7.

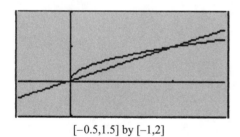

[−0.5,1.5] by [−1,2]

Figure S7

Points of intersection: (0, 0) and (1, 1)

Volume of solid = $\pi\displaystyle\int_0^1 \left(y^2 - \left(y^2\right)^2\right)dy$

Using your calculator, you obtain:

Volume of solid = $\dfrac{2\pi}{15}$.

86. The correct answer is (C).
See Figure S8.
Using the Inflection function on your calculator, you obtain $x = -2.08$ and $x = 2.08$. Thus, there are two points of inflection on $(-\pi, \pi)$.

87. The correct answer is (A).

$f(x) = x^2 e^x$

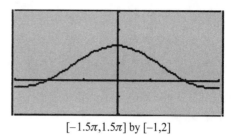

[−1.5π,1.5π] by [−1,2]

Figure S8

Using your calculator, you obtain $f(1) \approx 2.7183$ and $f'(1) \approx 8.15485$.

Equation of tangent line at $x = 1$:
$y - 2.7183 = 8.15485(x - 1)$
$y = 8.15485(x - 1) + 2.7183$
$f(.01) \approx 8.15485(1.1 - 1) + 2.7183 \approx 3.534$.

88. The correct answer is (E).
See Figure S9.

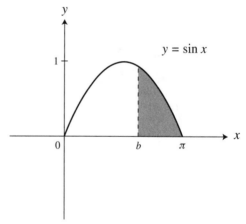

Figure S9

Area = $\displaystyle\int_b^\pi \sin x\, dx = -\cos x\Big]_b^\pi$

$= -\cos\pi - \left(-\cos b\right)$

$= -(-1) + \cos b = 1 + \cos b$

Set $1 + \cos b = 0.2 \Rightarrow \cos b = -0.8 \Rightarrow$
$b = \cos^{-1}(-0.8) \Rightarrow b \approx 2.498$.

89. The correct answer is (D).

$y = x^2; \dfrac{dy}{dx} = 2x$

$y = -\sqrt{x} = -x^{1/2}; \dfrac{dy}{dx} = -\dfrac{1}{2}x^{-1/2} = -\dfrac{1}{2\sqrt{x}}$

Perpendicular tangent lines $\Rightarrow$ slopes are negative reciprocals.

Thus $(2x)\left(-\dfrac{1}{2\sqrt{x}}\right) = -1$

$-\sqrt{x} = -1 \Rightarrow \sqrt{x} = 1$ or $x = 1$.

90. The correct answer is (C).

$x^3 + y^3 = xy$

$3x^2 + 3y^2 \dfrac{dy}{dx} = (1)y + x\dfrac{dy}{dx}$

$3y^2 \dfrac{dy}{dx} - x\dfrac{dy}{dx} = y - 3x^2$

$\dfrac{dy}{dx} = \dfrac{y - 3x^2}{3y^2 - x}$

At $x = 1$, $x^3 + y^3 = xy$ becomes $1 + y^3 = y$
$\Rightarrow y^3 - y + 1 = 0$

Using your calculator, you obtain: $y \approx -1.325$

$\dfrac{dy}{dx}\bigg|_{x=1,\,y=-1.325} \approx \dfrac{-1.325 - 3(1)^2}{3(-1.325)^2 - 1}$

91. The correct answer is (B).

$g(x) = \displaystyle\int_a^x f(t)\,dt \Rightarrow g'(x) = f(x)$

See Figure S10.

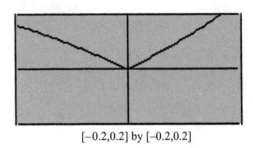

<table>
<tr><td>$g' = f$</td><td>+</td><td>0</td><td>+</td></tr>
</table>

g   incr.   incr.

Figure S10

The graph in (B) is the only one that satisfies the behavior of g.

92. The correct answer is (D).
See Figure S11.

[−0.2,0.2] by [−0.2,0.2]

Figure S11

At $x = 0$, the graph of $g(x)$ shows:
(1) a relative minimum; (2) a change of concavity (3) a cusp (i.e. not differentiable at $x = 0$). Thus, only statements I and II are true.

ANSWERS TO SECTION II QUESTIONS

Answer Key

Part A

1. (a) $y = \dfrac{1}{2}x + 2\ln 2$ (3 pts.)

    (b) 1.436   (1 pt.)

    (c) $y = \ln(e^x + 1) + \ln 2$ (4 pts.)

    (d) 1.438   (1 pt.)

2. (a) 76°   (2 pts.)

    (b) 82.7°   (2 pts.)

    (c) $3.7 \le t \le 8.9$ (2 pts.)

    (d) \$3   (3 pts.)

3. (a) 360   (3 pts.)

    (b) 12 m/sec   (1 pt.)

    (c) 0.407 m/sec²   (2 pts.)

    (d) 0.75 m/sec²   (1 pt.)

    (e) $18 < t < 30$ (2 pts.)

Part B

4. (a) $x = 2$ (2 pts.)

    (b) $x = -5$ (2 pts.)

    (c) $x = -4$, $x = -2$ and $x = 0$ (2 pts.)

    (d) See solution.   (3 pts.)

5. (a) $\dfrac{dy}{dx} = \dfrac{1}{2y + 2}$ (3 pts.)

    (b) $y = -\dfrac{1}{4}x - 3$ (2 pts.)

    (c) $y = 4x - 3$ (2 pts.)

    (d) $(0,1)$ (2 pts.)

6. (a) $\dfrac{32}{3}$ (3 pts.)

    (b) $a = 0$ (1 pt.)

    (c) $b = 4^{2/3}$ (2 pts.)

    (d) $\dfrac{256\pi}{5}$ (3 pts.)

Solutions to Section II Questions

Part A—Calculators are permitted.

1. (a) $\dfrac{dy}{dx} = \dfrac{e^x}{e^x + 1}$

At $x = 0$, $\dfrac{dy}{dx} = \dfrac{e^o}{e^o + 1} = \dfrac{1}{2}$

Equation of tangent line at $x = 0$:

$$y - 2 \ln 2 = \dfrac{1}{2}(x - 0)$$

$$y - 2 \ln 2 = \dfrac{1}{2}x \text{ or } y = \dfrac{1}{2}x + 2 \ln 2.$$

(b) $f(0.1) \approx \dfrac{1}{2}(0.1) + 2 \ln 2 \approx 1.43629 \approx 1.436.$

(c) $\dfrac{dy}{dx} = \dfrac{e^x}{e^x + 1}$

$dy = \dfrac{e^x}{e^x + 1}\,dx$

$\displaystyle\int dy = \int \dfrac{e^x}{e^x + 1}\,dx$

Let $u = e^x + 1$, $du = e^x\,dx$

$\displaystyle\int \dfrac{e^x}{e^x + 1}\,dx = \int \dfrac{1}{u}\,du = \ln|u| + c$

$$= \ln|e^x + 1| + c$$

$y = \ln(e^x + 1) + c$
The point $(0, 2 \ln 2)$ is on the graph of f.
$2 \ln 2 = \ln(e^o + 1) + c$
$2 \ln 2 = \ln 2 + c \Rightarrow c = \ln 2$
$y = \ln(e^x + 1) + \ln 2.$

(d) $f(0.1) = \ln(e^{0.1} + 1) + \ln 2 \approx 1.43754 \approx 1.438$

2. (a) At 1:00 am, $t = 6$.

$$f(6) = 96 - 20 \sin\left(\dfrac{6}{4}\right)$$

$$= 76.05° \approx 76° \text{ Fahrenheit.}$$

(b) Average temperature

$$= \dfrac{1}{12}\int_0^{12}\left[96 - 20 \sin\left(\dfrac{t}{4}\right)\right]dt$$

Using your calculator, you have:

$$\text{Average temperature} = \dfrac{1}{12}(992.80)$$
$$= 82.73 \approx 82.7.$$

(c) Let $y_1 = f(x) = 96 - 20 \sin\left(\dfrac{x}{4}\right)$ and $y_2 = 80$

Using the Intersection function of your calculator, you obtain

$x = 3.70 \approx 3.7$ or $x = 8.85 \approx 8.9$

Thus, heating system is turned on when $3.7 \le t \le 8.9$.

(See Figure S12.)

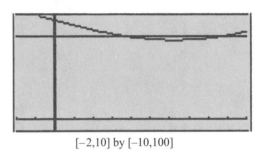

[−2,10] by [−10,100]

Figure S12

(d) Total cost $= (0.25)\displaystyle\int_{3.7}^{8.9}\left(80 - f(t)\right)dt$

$$= (0.25)\int_{3.7}^{8.9}\Big[80 -$$

$$\left(96 - 20 \sin\left(\dfrac{t}{4}\right)\right)\Big]dt$$

$$= (0.25)\int_{3.7}^{8.9}\left(-16 + 20 \sin\left(\dfrac{t}{4}\right)\right)dt.$$

Using your calculator, you have:
$$= (0.25)(13.629) = 3.407$$
$$\approx 3 \text{ dollars.}$$

3. (a) Midpoints of 5 subintervals of equal length are $t = 3, 9, 15, 21,$ and 27.

The length of each subinterval is $\dfrac{30 - 0}{5} = 6$.

Thus $\displaystyle\int_0^{30} v(t)\,dt = 6\big[v(3) + v(9) + v(15)$

$$+ v(21) + v(27)\big]$$
$$= 6[7.5 + 12 + 13.5 + 14$$
$$+ 13] = 6[60] = 360.$$

(b) Average velocity $= \dfrac{1}{30 - 0}\displaystyle\int_0^{30} v(t)\,dt$

$$\approx \frac{1}{30}(360)$$

$$\approx 12 \text{ m/sec.}$$

(c) Average acceleration $= \dfrac{12.2 - 0}{30 - 0} \text{ m/sec}^2$

$$= 0.407 \text{ m/sec}^2.$$

(d) Approximate acceleration at $t = 6$

$$= \frac{v(9) - v(3)}{9 - 3} = \frac{12 - 7.5}{6} = 0.75 \text{ m/sec}^2.$$

(e) Looking at the velocity in the table, you see that the velocity decreases from $t = 18$ to $t = 30$. Thus the acceleration is negative for $18 < t < 30$.

Part B—No calculators.

4. (a) See Figure S13.

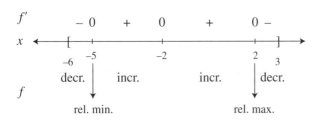

Figure S13

Since f increases on $(-5, 2)$ and decreases on $(2, 3)$, it has a relative maximum at $x = 2$.
(b) Since f decreases on $(-6, -5)$ and increases on $(-5, 2)$, it has a relative minimum at $x = -5$.
(c) See Figure S14.

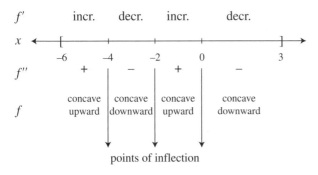

Figure S14

A change of concavity occurs at $x = -4, -2$, and 0, and since f' exists at these x-values, f has a point of inflection at $x = -4$, $x = -2$, and $x = 0$.

(d) See Figure S15.

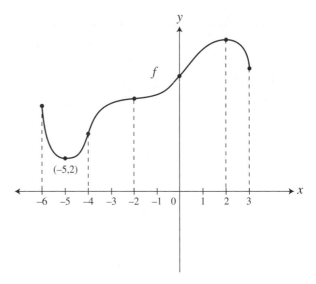

Figure S15

5. (a) Differentiating: $2y\dfrac{dy}{dx} - 1 + 2\dfrac{dy}{dx} = 0$

$$\frac{dy}{dx}(2y + 2) = 1 \Rightarrow \frac{dy}{dx} = \frac{1}{2y + 2}.$$

(b) At $(0, -3)$ $\dfrac{dy}{dx} = \dfrac{1}{2(-3) + 2} = -\dfrac{1}{4}$

$$y - y_1 = m(x - x_1)$$

$$y - (-3) = -\frac{1}{4}(x - 0)$$

$$y + 3 = -\frac{1}{4}x \text{ or } y = -\frac{1}{4}x - 3.$$

(c) $m_{\text{normal}} = \dfrac{-1}{m_{\text{tangent}}}$

At $(0, -3)$, $m_{\text{normal}} = \dfrac{-1}{-\frac{1}{4}} = 4.$

$$y - (-3) = 4\,(x - 0)$$

$$y + 3 = 4x \text{ or } y = 4x - 3.$$

(d) $y = \dfrac{1}{4}x + 3 \Rightarrow m = \dfrac{1}{4}$

Set $\dfrac{dy}{dx} = \dfrac{1}{2y + 2} = \dfrac{1}{4} \Rightarrow y = 1$

$$y^2 - x + 2y - 3 = 0.$$

At $y = 1$, $1^2 - x + 2(1) - 3 = 0 \Rightarrow x = 0.$

Thus, point P is $(0,1)$.

6. See Figure S16.

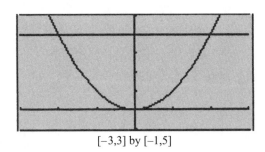

[−3,3] by [−1,5]

Figure S16

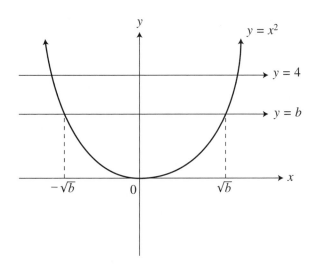

Figure S17

(a) Set $x^2 = 4 \Rightarrow x = \pm 2$

$$\text{Area of } R = \int_{-2}^{2}\left(4 - x^2\right)dx = 4x - \frac{x^3}{3}\Bigg]_{-2}^{2}$$

$$= \left(4(2) - \frac{2^3}{3}\right) - \left(4(-2) - \frac{(-2)^3}{3}\right)$$

$$= \frac{16}{3} - \left(-\frac{16}{3}\right) = \frac{32}{3}.$$

(b) Since $y = x^2$ is an even function, $x = 0$ divides R into two regions of equal area. Thus $a = 0$.

(c) See Figure S17.

$$\text{Area } R_1 = \text{Area } R_2 = \frac{16}{3}$$

$$\text{Area } R_2 = \int_{-\sqrt{b}}^{\sqrt{b}}\left(b - x^2\right)dx$$

$$= 2\int_{0}^{\sqrt{b}}\left(b - x^2\right)dx$$

$$= 2\left[bx - \frac{x^3}{3}\right]_0^{\sqrt{b}} = 2\left[b\left(\sqrt{b}\right) - \frac{\left(\sqrt{b}^{3}\right)}{3}\right]$$

$$= 2\left(b^{3/2} - \frac{b^{3/2}}{3}\right) = 2\left(\frac{2b^{3/2}}{3}\right) = \frac{4b^{3/2}}{3}$$

Set $\dfrac{4b^{3/2}}{3} = \dfrac{16}{3} \Rightarrow b^{3/2} = 4$ or $b = 4^{2/3}$.

(d) Washer Method

$$V = \pi\int_{-2}^{2}\left(4^2 - \left(x^2\right)^2\right)dx = \pi\int_{-2}^{2}\left(16 - x^4\right)dx$$

$$= \pi\left[16x - \frac{x^5}{5}\right]_{-2}^{2} = \frac{256\pi}{5}.$$

SCORING AND INTERPRETATION

Section I–Part A

$$\underline{\hspace{3cm}} \times 1.2 = \underline{\hspace{3cm}}$$
No. Correct   Subtotal A

$$\underline{\hspace{3cm}} \times (0.25) \times 1.2 = \underline{\hspace{3cm}}$$
No. Incorrect   Subtotal B

Part A (Subtotal A – Subtotal B) = $\underline{\hspace{3cm}}$
                      Subtotal C

Section I–Part B

$$\underline{\hspace{3cm}} \times 1.2 = \underline{\hspace{3cm}}$$
No. Correct   Subtotal D

$$\underline{\hspace{3cm}} \times (0.25) \times 1.2 = \underline{\hspace{3cm}}$$
No. Incorrect   Subtotal E

Part B (Subtotal D – Subtotal E) = $\underline{\hspace{3cm}}$
                      Subtotal F

Section II–Part A (Each question is worth 9 points.)

$$\underline{\hspace{2cm}} + \underline{\hspace{2cm}} + \underline{\hspace{2cm}} = \underline{\hspace{3cm}}$$
Q#1   Q#2   Q#3   Subtotal G

Section II–Part B (Each question is worth 9 points.)

$$\underline{\hspace{2cm}} + \underline{\hspace{2cm}} + \underline{\hspace{2cm}} = \underline{\hspace{3cm}}$$
Q#1   Q#2   Q#3   Subtotal H

Total Raw Score (Subtotals C + F + G + H) = ☐

Approximate Conversion Scale:	
Total Raw Score	Approximate AP Grade
75–108	5
60–74	4
45–59	3
31–44	2
0–30	1

Chapter 6

AP Biology

Answer Sheet for Multiple-Choice Questions

1. _____	23. _____	45. _____
2. _____	24. _____	46. _____
3. _____	25. _____	47. _____
4. _____	26. _____	48. _____
5. _____	27. _____	49. _____
6. _____	28. _____	50. _____
7. _____	29. _____	51. _____
8. _____	30. _____	52. _____
9. _____	31. _____	53. _____
10. _____	32. _____	54. _____
11. _____	33. _____	55. _____
12. _____	34. _____	56. _____
13. _____	35. _____	57. _____
14. _____	36. _____	58. _____
15. _____	37. _____	59. _____
16. _____	38. _____	60. _____
17. _____	39. _____	61. _____
18. _____	40. _____	62. _____
19. _____	41. _____	63. _____
20. _____	42. _____	64. _____
21. _____	43. _____	65. _____
22. _____	44. _____	66. _____

67. _____	79. _____	91. _____
68. _____	80. _____	92. _____
69. _____	81. _____	93. _____
70. _____	82. _____	94. _____
71. _____	83. _____	95. _____
72. _____	84. _____	96. _____
73. _____	85. _____	97. _____
74. _____	86. _____	98. _____
75. _____	87. _____	99. _____
76. _____	88. _____	100. _____
77. _____	89. _____	
78. _____	90. _____	

AP BIOLOGY

Section I

Time—1 hour and 20 minutes
100 questions

Directions: For the multiple-choice questions that follow, select the best answer and
fill in the appropriate letter on the answer sheet.

1. Which of the following characteristics would
   allow you to distinguish a prokaryotic cell
   from an animal cell?

   A. Ribosomes
   B. Cell membrane
   C. Chloroplasts
   D. Cell wall
   E. Large central vacuoles

2. Which of the following is a class of virus that
   carries an enzyme called *reverse transcriptase*?

   A. Prion
   B. Viroid
   C. Retrovirus
   D. Plasmid
   E. Pneumococcus

3. ADH, a hormone, is secreted by the

   A. Testes
   B. Kidney
   C. Pituitary
   D. Pancreas
   E. Thyroid

4. A child is diagnosed with Tay-Sachs disease.
   Which of the following organelles is most
   likely affected?

   A. Lysosome
   B. Ribosome
   C. Golgi
   D. Rough endoplasmic reticulum
   E. Peroxisome

5. In humans, the sperm usually fertilizes the
   ovum in the

   A. Cervix
   B. Uterus
   C. Endometrium
   D. Oviduct
   E. Ovary

6. Which of the following structures is derived
   from the ectoderm?

   A. Nerves
   B. Stomach
   C. Heart
   D. Lungs
   E. Liver

7. Which of the following plays a role in a plant's
   ability to avoid transpiration in hot and dry
   areas while successfully completing
   photosynthesis?

   A. Rubisco
   B. Carbon fixation
   C. Chlorophyll
   D. Auxin
   E. Bundle sheath cells

8. Which of the following is the source of oxygen
   produced during photosynthesis?

   A. H_2O
   B. H_2O_2
   C. CO_2
   D. CO
   E. HCO_3^-

9. An accident damages an individual's anterior
   pituitary gland. Production of which of the
   following hormones would not be *directly*
   affected?

   A. LH
   B. Prolactin
   C. Oxytocin
   D. FSH
   E. TSH

10. An organism exposed to wild temperature
    fluctuations shows very little, if any, change
    in its metabolic rate. This organism is most
    probably a

A. Ectotherm
B. Endotherm
C. Thermophyle
D. Ascospore
E. Plasmid

11. Which of the following is a frameshift mutation?

A. CAT HAS HIS → CAT HAS HIT
B. CAT HAS HIS → CAT HSH ISA
C. CAT HAS HIS → CAT HIS HAT
D. CAT HAS HIS → CAT WAS HIT
E. CAT HAS HIS → CCT HAS HIT

12. A researcher conducts a survey of a biome and finds 35 percent more species than she has found in any other biome. Which biome is she most likely to be in?

A. Tundra
B. Tiaga
C. Tropical rain forest
D. Temperate deciduous forest
E. Desert

13. On the basis of the following crossover frequencies, determine the relative location of these four genes:

m & n   →   15%
p & f   →   20%
n & f   →   30%
m & f   →   45%
n & p   →   10%

(A) f   p   m   n

(B) m   n   f   p

(C) m   n   p   f

(D) n   m   p   f

(E) f   m   n   p

14. A man contracts the same flu strain for the second time in a single winter season. The second time he experiences fewer symptoms and recovers more quickly. Which cells are responsible for this rapid recovery?

A. Helper T cells
B. Cytotoxic T cells
C. Memory cells
D. Plasma cells
E. Phagocytes

15. Which of the following are traits that are affected by more than one gene?

A. Heterozygous traits
B. Pleiotropic traits
C. Polygenic traits
D. Blended alleles
E. Codominant traits

16. A lizard lacking a chemical defense mechanism that is colored in the same way as a lizard that has a defense mechanism is displaying

A. Aposometric coloration
B. Cryptic coloration
C. Batesian mimicry
D. Müllerian mimicry
E. Deceptive markings

17. A scientist convinced that a certain cell type is responsible for the initiation of the formation of the notochord transported some of these cells to a different region of the cell. On doing so, she found that a second notochord formed in the new region of the cell. This is an example of

A. Eutrophication
B. Synaptic transmission
C. Homeotic modification
D. Embryonic induction
E. Cytoplasmic reorganization

18. Which of the following is true about the life cycle of a fungus?

A. It is haploid only as a gamete.
B. It alternates between a diploid and a haploid organism.
C. It is diploid only as a zygote.
D. It spends most of its time in the gametophyte stage.
E. Its gametes are formed by meiosis.

19. Crossover would most likely occur in which situation?

A. Two genes (1 and 2) are located right next to each other on chromosome A.
B. Gene 1 is located on chromosome A, and gene 2 is on chromosome B.

C. Genes 1 and 2 code for proteins of similar functions.
D. Genes 1 and 2 are located near each other on the X chromosome.
E. Gene 1 is located on chromosome A; gene 2 is located far away but on the same chromosome.

20. Imagine an organism whose $2n = 96$. Meiosis would leave this organism's cells with how many chromosomes?

A. 192
B. 96
C. 48
D. 24
E. 23

21. A dissacharide is

A. A complex protein found in plants
B. A basic building block of life
C. The group to which glucose belongs
D. A sugar consisting of two monosaccharides
E. A sugar in its simplest form

22. A student conducts an experiment to test the efficiency of a certain enzyme. Which of the following protocols would probably not result in a change in the enzyme's efficiency?

A. Bringing the temperature of the experimental setup from 20°C to 50°C
B. Adding an acidic solution to the setup
C. Adding substrate but not enzyme
D. Placing the substrate and enzyme in a container with double the capacity
E. Adding enzyme but not substrate

23. You observe a species that gives birth to only one offspring at a time and has a relatively long lifespan for its body size. Which of the following is probably also true of this organism?

A. It lives in a newly colonized habitat.
B. It is an aquatic organism.
C. It requires relatively high parental care of offspring.
D. The age at which the offspring themselves can give birth is relatively young.
E. Population sizes fluctuate unpredictably.

24. Which of the following is an example of a detritivore?

A. Cactus

B. Algae
C. Bat
D. Whale
E. Fungus

25. In a certain population of squirrels that is in Hardy–Weinberg equilibrium, black color is a recessive phenotype present in 9 percent of the squirrels, and 91 percent are gray. What percentage of the population is homozygous dominant for this trait?

A. 21 percent
B. 30 percent
C. 49 percent
D. 70 percent
E. 91 percent

26. Refer to question 25 for details on the squirrel population. Which of the following conditions is required to keep this population in Hardy–Weinberg equilibrium?

A. Random mating
B. Genetic drift
C. Mutation
D. Gene flow
E. Natural selection

27. A reaction that includes energy as one of its reactants is called a(n)

A. Exergonic reaction
B. Hydrolysis reaction
C. Endergonic reaction
D. Redox reaction
E. Dehydration reaction

28. A solution that has a concentration of H^+ that is 10,000 times lower than a solution with a pH of 6, itself has a pH of

A. 2
B. 3
C. 4
D. 10
E. 11

29. Which of the following tends to be completely reabsorbed from the glomerular filtrate?

A. Glucose
B. Urea
C. Na^+
D. K^+
E. HCO_3^-

30. Most of the carbon dioxide of our body travels through the blood in the form of

    A. CO_2
    B. CO
    C. HCO_3^-
    D. H_2CO_3
    E. $C_6H_{12}O_6$

31. To which of the following labeled trophic levels would a herbivore most likely be assigned?

    A. A

    B. B

    C. C

    D. D

    E. E

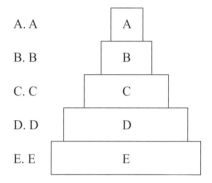

32. A population undergoes a shift in which those who are really tall and those who are really short decrease in relative frequency compared to those of medium size, due to a change in the availability of resources. This is an example of

    A. Directional selection
    B. Stabilizing selection
    C. Disruptive selection
    D. Sympatric speciation
    E. Sexual selection

33. An individual has a disease that reduces the amount of hemoglobin in the blood. Which of the following is probably true of this individual?

    A. Oxygen delivery to cells is compromised.
    B. Cell repair is compromised.
    C. Cells experience O_2 buildup.
    D. The organism has limited defense against viral invasion.
    E. The organism has a reduced number of platelets in the blood.

34. Which of the following is not expelled from the pancreatic duct?

    A. Lipase

B. Amylase
C. Pepsin
D. Trypsin
E. Chymotrypsin

35. Southern blotting is associated with which genetic technique?

    A. Polymerase chain reaction
    B. Protein gel electrophoresis
    C. Synthesis of recombinant DNA
    D. Viral DNA analysis
    E. Pedigree chart analysis

36. Which of the following are major players involved in the process of transduction?

    A. Plasmids
    B. Capsids
    C. Phages
    D. Pili
    E. Vectors

37. Which of the following statements is correct?

    A. Water flows from hypertonic to hypotonic.
    B. Solutes that do not bond to chromatography paper and readily dissolve in chromatography solvent migrate the slowest of all.
    C. Germinating seeds use less oxygen than do nongerminating seeds.
    D. The rate of transpiration increases with an increase in air movement.
    E. Smaller DNA fragments migrate more rapidly than do larger DNA fragments on gel electrophoresis.

38. Which of the following is the difference between C_3 and C_4 plants?

    A. The first step of the Calvin cycle
    B. The elevation at which they live
    C. The kind of chloroplast they contain
    D. The first step of the light reactions
    E. The product of the Calvin cycle

39. Which of the following is *not* true about sex-linked traits?

    A. They occur only in males.
    B. They can be passed from mothers to sons.
    C. Females are frequently carriers.
    D. They are often deleterious.

E. Duchenne's muscular dystrophy is an example.

40. Which of the following is not a form of interspecies interaction?

A. Commensualism
B. Succession
C. Mutualism
D. Parasitism
E. Competition

41. This hormone is known to be responsible for the phototropic response of plants to sunlight.

A. Abscisic acid
B. Auxin
C. Cytokinins
D. Ethylene
E. Gibberellins

42. A scientist decided that right before feeding a cat each day, she would ring a bell in another room and then bring the food into the room. Soon after the experiment began, the cat would begin to salivate in anticipation of the food before the scientist had even entered the room. This is an example of

A. Fixed-action pattern
B. Habituation
C. Imprinting
D. Associative learning
E. Observational learning

43. Two wolves cross paths in the forest. They both immediately begin growling as their fur stands up on its ends, and they circle each other and stare each other down. This interaction is an example of

A. Agonistic behavior
B. Dominance hierarchies
C. Altruistic behavior
D. Inclusive fitness
E. Reciprocal altruism

44. This structure has as one of its functions, the responsibility of acting as a passageway for the transport of water and minerals from soil throughout a plant.

A. Sieve-tube element
B. Phloem
C. Xylem
D. Guard cell
E. Taproot

45. The movement of a moth toward light on a summer night is an example of

A. Kinesis
B. Migration
C. Immigration
D. Taxis
E. Gravitropism

46. Which of the following would not be classified as part of the kingdom Monera?

A. Methanogens
B. Cyanobacteria
C. Halophiles
D. Dinoflagellates
E. Thermoacidophiles

47. Which of the following is *not* a characteristic shared by most members of the kingdom Animalia?

A. Spending some or all of their lives able to move
B. Being multicellular
C. Being heterotrophic
D. Being dominantly haploid
E. Having either radial or bilateral symmetry.

48. Which of the following is involved in the control of water movement in plants?

A. Cortex
B. Epidermis
C. Casparian strip
D. Apical meristems
E. Cutin

49. Which of the following cells are found in mature phloem tissue?

A. Sieve-tube elements
B. Guard cells
C. Tracheids
D. Vessel elements
E. Collenchyma cells

50. An individual has a hard time maintaining normal weight because his metabolic rate is low. There may be a problem with which of the following hormones?

A. ADH

B. Thyroxin
C. Aldosterone
D. GnRH
E. Prolactin

51. Which of the following structures is present in all eukaryotic and prokaryotic cells?

A. Golgi apparatus
B. Nucleus
C. Cell wall
D. Lysosome
E. Riboosome

52. Which of the following organisms would probably spend the most time as a haploid organism?

A. Humans
B. Ferns
C. Whales
D. Angiosperms
E. Fungi

53. Sickle cell anemia is a disease caused by the substitution of an incorrect nucleotide into the DNA sequence for a particular gene. The amino acids are still added to the growing protein chain, but the symptoms of sickle cell anemia result. This is an example of a

A. Frameshift mutation
B. Missense mutation
C. Nonsense mutation
D. Thymine dimer mutation
E. Splicing error.

For questions 54–57, please refer to the following answers:

(A)

(B)

(C)

(D)

(E)

54. This represents the backbone of a structure that is vital to the construction of many cells and is used to produce steroid hormones.

55. This structure plays a vital role in energy reactions.

56. This structure is a purine found in DNA.

57. This structure was synthesized in the ribosome.

For questions 58–61, please refer to the following answers:

A. Glycolysis
B. Chemiosmosis
C. Fermentation
D. Calvin cycle
E. Photolysis

58. When oxygen becomes unavailable, this process regenerates NAD^+, allowing respiration to continue.

59. This process leads to the net production of two pyruvate, two ATP, and two NADH.

60. This process couples the production of ATP with the movement of electrons down the electron transport chain by harnessing the driving force created by a proton gradient.

61. This process has as its products $NADP^+$, ADP, and sugar.

For questions 62–65, please refer to the following answers:

A. Huntington's disease
B. Cri-du-chat syndrome
C. Turner's syndrome
D. Hemophilia
E. Cystic fibrosis

62. This is an example of a sex-linked condition.

63. This is an example of a disease resulting from nondisjunction.

64. This is an example of an autosomal dominant condition.

65. This is an example of a disorder caused by a chromosomal deletion error.

For questions 66–69, please refer to the following answers:

A. Desert
B. Grasslands
C. Tundra
D. Taiga
E. Deciduous forests

66. This biome has cold winters and is known for its pine forests.

67. This biome is the driest of the land biomes and experiences the greatest daily temperature fluctuations.

68. This biome contains trees that drop their leaves during the winter months.

69. This biome contains plants whose roots cannot go deep due to the presence of a permafrost.

For questions 70–73, please refer to the following answers:

A. Oogenesis
B. Spermatogenesis
C. Ovulation
D. Gastrulation
E. Blastulation

70. This process initiates the release of the secondary oocyte to make its way to the uterus.

71. This process leads to the formation of one gamete from each parent cell.

72. This process divides the developing embryo into the ectoderm, mesoderm, and endoderm.

73. This process leads to the formation of four gametes from each parent cell.

For questions 74–77, please use the following answers:

(A)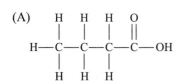

(B)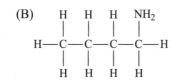

(C)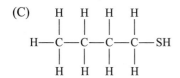

(D)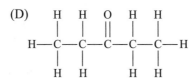

(E)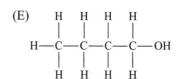

74. This structure contains a hydroxyl group.

75. This structure contains an amino group.

76. This structure contains a carboxyl group.

77. This structure contains a carbonyl group.

Questions 78–80: A behavioral endocrinologist captures male individuals of a territorial bird species over the course of a year to measure testosterone (T) levels. In this population, males may play one of two roles: (1) they may stay in their natal group (the group they were born in) and help raise their younger siblings, or (2) they may leave the natal group to establish a new territory. Use this information and the histograms below to answer the following questions.

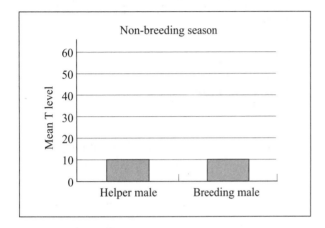

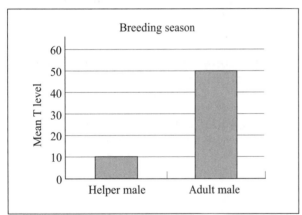

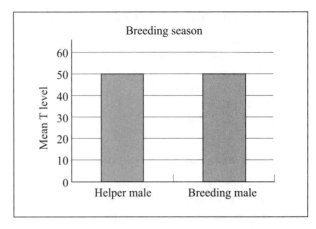

80. Which of the following is the best explanation of the results presented in the above graph, collected from the same population in a different year?

    A. The so-called helper males are actually breeding.
    B. The population has stopped growing.
    C. Females are equally attracted to adult and helper males.
    D. Testosterone level is affected by many processes.
    E. All males are producing the same number of offspring.

Questions 81–84: A researcher grows a population of ferns in her laboratory. She notices, after a few generations, a new variant that has a distinct phenotype. When she tries to breed the original phenotype with the new one, no offspring are produced. When she breeds the new variants, however, offspring that look like the new variant result.

78. Testosterone level in this population may be an example of

    A. Adaptive radiation
    B. An adaptation
    C. Divergent selection
    D. Development
    E. Sperm production

79. What can you infer about the role of testosterone in reproduction in this species?

    A. It is detrimental to breeding.
    B. It aids adult males only.
    C. It ensures that all males reproduce equally.
    D. It aids in breeding.
    E. It has nothing to do with reproduction or breeding.

81. What caused the change in the variant?

    A. Karyotyping
    B. Balance polymorphism
    C. Mutation
    D. Polyploidy
    E. Migration

82. What kind of speciation does this example illustrate?

    A. Allopatric
    B. Sympatric
    C. Isolated
    D. Polyploidy
    E. Migration

83. Which of the following could possibly characterize the new variant?

A. Balanced polymorphism
B. Adaptive radiation
C. Divergent selection
D. Equilibrium
E. Polyploidy

84. Which of the following is likely to exhibit the process described above?

    A. Fallow deer
    B. Fruitflies
    C. Grass
    D. Spotted toads
    E. Blackbirds

For questions 85–87, please refer to the following answers:

85. The DNA placed in this electrophoresis gel separates as a result of what characteristic?

    A. pH
    B. Charge
    C. Size
    D. Polarity
    E. Hydrophobicity

86. If this gel were used in a court case as DNA evidence taken from the crime scene, which of the following suspects appears to be guilty?

    A. Suspect A
    B. Suspect B
    C. Suspect C
    D. Suspect D
    E. Suspect E

87. Which two suspects, while not guilty, could possibly be identical twins?

    A. A and B
    B. A and C
    C. B and C
    D. B and D
    E. B and E

Questions 88–91: The frequency of genotypes for a given trait are given in the accompanying graph. Answer the following questions using this information:

AA	Aa	aa
36%	45%	?%

88. What is the frequency of the recessive homozygote?

    A. 15 percent
    B. 19 percent
    C. 25 percent
    D. 40 percent
    E. 45 percent

89. What would be the approximate frequency of the heterozygote condition if this population were in Hardy–Weinberg equilibrium?

    A. 20 percent
    B. 45 percent
    C. 48 percent
    D. 72 percent
    E. 90 percent

90. Is this population in Hardy–Weinberg equilibrium?

    A. Yes.
    B. No.
    C. Cannot tell from the information given.
    D. Maybe, if individuals are migrating.
    E. No, because mutations must be occurring.

91. Which of the following processes may be occurring in this population, given the allele frequencies?

    A. Directional selection
    B. Homozygous advantage
    C. Hybrid vigor

D. Allopatric speciation
E. Sympatric speciation

Questions 92–94: An eager AP biology student interested in studying osmosis and the movement of water in solutions took a dialysis bag containing a 0.5 M solution and placed it into a beaker containing a 0.6 M solution.

92. After the bag has been sitting in the beaker for a while, what would you expect to have happened to the bag?

A. There will have been a net flow of water out of the bag, causing it to decrease in size.
B. There will be have been a net flow of water into the bag, causing it to swell in size.
C. The bag will be the exact same size because no water will have moved at all.
D. The solute will have moved out of the dialysis bag into the beaker.
E. The solute will have moved from the beaker into the dialysis bag.

93. If this bag were instead placed into a beaker of distilled water, what would be the expected result?

A. There will be a net flow of water out of the bag, causing it to decrease in size.
B. There will be a net flow of water into the bag, causing it to swell in size.
C. The bag will remain the exact same size because no water will move at all.
D. The solute will flow out of the dialysis bag into the beaker.
E. The solute will flow from the beaker into the dialysis bag.

94. Which of the following is true about water potential?

A. It drives the movement of water from a region of lower water potential to a region of higher water potential.
B. Solute potential is the only factor that determines the water potential.
C. Pressure potential combines with solute potential to determine the water potential.
D. Water potential *always* drives water from an area of lower pressure potential to an area of higher pressure potential.
E. Water potential always drives water from a region of lower solute potential to a region of higher solute potential.

Questions 95–97 all use the following pedigree, but are independent of each other:

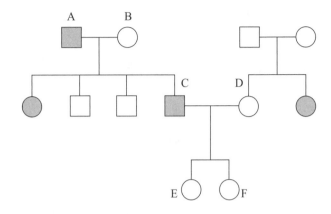

95. If the pedigree is studying an autosomal recessive condition for which the alleles are A and a, what was the probability that a child produced by parents A and B would be heterozygous?

A. 0.0625
B. 0.1250
C. 0.2500
D. 0.3333
E. 0.5000

96. Imagine that a couple (C and D) go to a genetic counselor because they are interested in having children. They tell the counselor that they have a family history of a certain disorder and they want to know the probability of their first-born having this condition. If the condition is autosomal recessive, what is the probability that the child will have it?

A. 0.0625
B. 0.1250
C. 0.2500
D. 0.3333
E. 0.5000

97. Imagine that a couple (C and D) have a child (E) that has the autosomal recessive condition being traced by the pedigree. What is the probability that their second child (F) will have the autosomal recessive condition?

A. 0.0625
B. 0.1250
C. 0.2500
D. 0.3333
E. 0.5000

For questions 98–100, please refer to the following diagram:

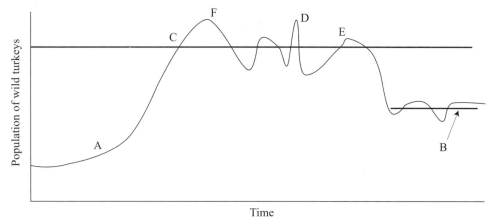

98. The bold line that point *C* intersects is known as the

    A. Biotic potential
    B. Carrying capacity
    C. Limiting factor
    D. Maximum attainable population
    E. Age structure

99. On the basis of what happens at the end of this chart, what is the most likely explanation for the population decline after point *E*?

    A. The population became too dense and it had to decline.

    B. There was a major environmental shift that made survival impossible for many.
    C. Food became scarce, leading to a major famine.
    D. The population had become too large.
    E. The birth rate had surpassed the death rate.

100. What type of growth does the curve seem to represent from point *A* to point *F*?

    A. *K*-selected
    B. *R*-selected
    C. Exponential
    D. Logistic
    E. Unlimited

END OF SECTION I

AP BIOLOGY

Section II

Time—1 hour and 40 minutes
(The first 10 minutes is a reading period. Do not begin writing until the 10-minute period has passed.)

Directions: Answer all the questions. Outline form is not acceptable.
Answers should be in essay form.

1. A murder trial court case ended up ruling against the defendant because of DNA evidence found at the crime scene and analyzed in the forensics lab.

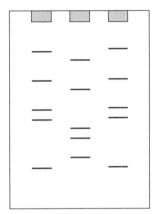

   A. Describe how a gel electrophoresis experiment works and is set up, why things move the way they do, and why the gel would be able to prove, beyond a shadow of a doubt, that the defendant was indeed guilty as charged.
   B. Gel electrophoresis is also used to determine court paternity cases. Describe how a gel could be used to prove whether an individual is the father of a particular baby. Include all the pertinent experimental laboratory procedures in your description.

2. Control mechanisms are a common theme throughout all of biology. Answer *two* of the following three answer choices below, explaining in detail how the specified reactions are controlled.

   A. In the cell cycle, which consists of interphase, mitosis, and cytokinesis, there are plenty of opportunities for control and regulation. Describe *three* control mechanisms vital to this cycle.
   B. Hormones are vital to human physiology; their production and release are tightly regulated by the body. Describe a mechanism by which hormone release is controlled, citing an actual example from human physiology.
   C. An operon is an on/off switch vital to the conservation of energy in many organisms. Describe how, in particular, the lactose operon works, providing an explanation of what exactly turns the switch on and off.

3. Speciation, the process by which new species are formed, can occur by many mechanisms. Explain how *three* of the following are involved in the process of species formation.

   A. Geographic barriers
   B. Polyploidy
   C. Balanced polymorphism
   D. Reproductive isolation

4. Ethology, the study of animal behavior, has given us insight into the nature of animal minds. Pick *three* of the following, define the terms, and discuss real-life examples.

   A. Fixed-action patterns
   B. Dominance hierarchies
   C. Kinesis
   D. Reciprocal altruism
   E. Agonistic behavior

END OF SECTION II

ANSWERS TO MULTIPLE-CHOICE QUESTIONS

Answer Key

1. D	21. D	41. B	61. D	81. C
2. C	22. D	42. D	62. D	82. B
3. C	23. C	43. A	63. C	83. E
4. A	24. E	44. C	64. A	84. C
5. D	25. C	45. D	65. B	85. C
6. A	26. A	46. D	66. D	86. B
7. E	27. C	47. D	67. A	87. B
8. A	28. D	48. C	68. E	88. B
9. C	29. A	49. A	69. C	89. C
10. B	30. C	50. B	70. C	90. B
11. B	31. D	51. E	71. A	91. B
12. C	32. B	52. E	72. D	92. A
13. C	33. A	53. B	73. B	93. B
14. C	34. C	54. A	74. E	94. C
15. C	35. B	55. C	75. B	95. E
16. C	36. C	56. D	76. A	96. D
17. D	37. E	57. B	77. D	97. E
18. C	38. A	58. C	78. B	98. E
19. E	39. A	59. A	79. D	99. B
20. C	40. B	60. B	80. A	100. D

Explanations of Answers to the Multiple-Choice Questions

1. **D**—Cell walls are present in prokaryotes, but not eukaryotic animal cells. Ribosomes and cell membranes are present in both of them. Chloroplasts and large central vacuoles are not seen in either of them. Animal cells have small vacuoles.

2. **C**—The retrovirus is an RNA virus that enters a host and immediately uses its reverse transcriptase enzyme to convert the RNA into DNA so that it can incorporate into the host genome and be replicated. None of the other answer choices carry this enzyme.

3. **C**—Antidiuretic hormone is secreted from the posterior pituitary gland and functions to regulate the body's salt concentration.

4. **A**—Tay-Sachs disease is a storage disease—a disease caused by a missing enzyme from the lysosome. Individuals with this disease are missing an enzyme crucial to the breakdown of a particular lipid. The absence of the enzyme causes the lipid to accumulate in the brain and lead to the symptoms associated with the disease.

5. **D**—The oviduct, also known as the *fallopian tube,* is the usual site of egg fertilization in humans.

6. **A**—The stomach, liver, and lungs are derived from the endoderm. The heart is derived from the mesoderm. The nervous system tissue does indeed come from the ectoderm.

7. **E**—Bundle sheath cells are the extra photosynthetic cell type present in C_4 plants that are able to more efficiently perform photosynthesis in hot and dry environments.

8. **A**—The oxygen released by plants is produced during the light reactions of photosynthesis. The main inputs to the light reactions are water and light. Water is the source of the oxygen.

9. **C**—Oxytocin is produced in the hypothalamus and sent down to the *posterior* pituitary to be released when necessary. All the others are produced in the anterior pituitary.

10. **B**—Endotherms are organisms whose metabolic rates do not respond to shifts in environmental temperature.

11. **B**—A frameshift mutation is one in which the reading frame for the protein construction machinery is shifted. It is a deletion or addition of nucleotides in a number that is *not* a multiple of 3. Often this can read to premature stop codons, which lead to nonfunctional proteins.

12. **C**

13. **C**—We can see from the data that m and f have the highest crossover frequency. They must therefore be farthest apart of any pair along the chromosome. This leaves only answer choice C.

14. **C**—Memory B cells are able to recognize foreign invaders if they come back into our systems and lead to a more rapid and efficient attack on the invader.

15. **C**—Polygenic traits are traits that require the input of multiple genes to determine the phenotype. Skin color is a classic example of a polygenic trait; three genes combine to provide the various shades of skin tone seen in humans.

16. **C**—This is a classic example of batesian mimicry.

17. **D**—*Synaptic transmission* is the term used to describe how nervous impulses travel from place to place in the human body. Homeotic genes are regulatory genes that determine how segments of an organism will develop. Answer D is the best choice as *induction* is defined as the process by which one group of cells influences another group of cells through physical contact or chemical signaling.

18. **C**—Fungi spend a small amount of time as a diploid organism. They are diploid only as a zygote.

19. **E**—Crossover is most likely to occur between two genes that are located far away from each other on the same chromosome.

20. **C**—Meiosis reduces the number of chromosomes in an individual by half: $96 \div 2 = 48$.

21. **D**—A dissacharide is a carbohydrate consisting of two monosaccharide monomers linked together. Common examples include maltose, lactose, and sucrose.

22. **D**—The volume of the container is not a major factor that affects enzyme efficiency.

23. **C**—The original question describes an organism that can be classified as a *K*-selected population. Individuals of this class tend to have fairly constant size, low reproductive rates, and offspring that require extensive care.

24. **E**—A detritivore is an organism that also goes by the nickname "decomposer." Fungi are decomposers.

25. **C**—If 9 percent of the population is homozygous recessive, this means that $q^2 =$ 0.09, and that the square root of $q^2 = 0.30 = q$. This means that $p = 0.70$ since $p + q = 1$. Thus, the percentage of the population that is homozygous dominant: $p^2 = (0.7)^2 = 0.49$ or 49 percent.

26. **A**—All the other answer choices are violations of the Hardy–Weinberg equilibrium.

27. **C**—Exergonic reactions give off energy, and hydrolysis reactions are reactions that use water to break apart a compound. Redox reactions are reactions that involve the movement of electrons. Dehydration reactions are reactions that bring two molecules together, releasing water as a product.

28. **D**—Since the pH scale is a logarithmic scale, a concentration of H^+ that is 10,000 times lower is 10^4 times lower, meaning that the pH value is 4 points *higher* (less acidic) than the pH of 6.

29. **A**—Glucose is usually completely reabsorbed in the kidney unless its concentration exceeds the physical capacity of the nephron to reabsorb the sugar. This is the case in diabetes, a condition in which glucose is lost in a patient's urine.

30. **C**—Bicarbonate ion is the most common form in which the carbon dioxide waste product travels in the bloodstream.

31. **D**—Herbivores tend to be the primary consumers of trophic pyramids, and thus would be assigned to the first level up from the bottom.

32. **B**—Stabilizing selection tends to eliminate the extremes of a population, directional selection is a shift toward one of the extremes, and disruptive selection is the camel-hump selection in which the two extremes are favored over the middle. Sympatric speciation is the formation of new species due to an inability to reproduce that is not caused by geographic separation. Sexual selection is evolution of characters that aid in mate acquisition.

33. **A**—Hemoglobin is the molecule that carries oxygen for the red blood cell and is vital to the survival of our cells.

34. **C**—Pepsin is released in the stomach and is the stomach's main protein digestive enzyme.

35. **B**—Southern blotting is an experiment performed to determine whether a particular sequence of DNA is present in a sample to be examined. Gel electrophoresis is vital to this procedure.

36. **C**—Phages are the bacteria-infecting viruses that are able to carry DNA from one cell to another and are the transport vehicles for DNA during the process of transduction.

37. **E**—Gel electrophoresis is a lab technique used to separate DNA on the basis of size. DNA dropped into wells at the head of the gel will migrate to the other side, with the smaller pieces moving at a faster rate.

38. **A**—Normally in C_3 plants carbon fixation produces two 3-carbon molecules. In C_4 plants, the carbon fixation step produces a 4-carbon molecule, which is converted into malate and sent from the mesophyll cells to the bundle sheath cells where the CO_2 is used to build sugar. This allows the C_4 plant to perform successful photosynthesis in nonideal conditions.

39. **A**—Females can have sex-linked conditions; they are just more common in males because males have only one X chromosome and thus require only one bad copy of the allele to express the condition.

40. **B**—Succession is a ecological process in which landforms evolve over time in response to the environmental conditions. Commensualism is when one organism benefits while the other is unaffected. Mutualism is where both organisms reap benefits from the interaction. Parasitism is when one organism benefits at the other's expense. Competition is the situation in which organisms fight for some limited resource.

41. **B**—Auxin does a lot. Remember this plant hormone for the exam.

42. **D**—This is a Pavlovesque example of associative learning.

43. **A**—Agonistic behaviors result from conflicts over resources, such as food, mates, or territory.

44. **C**—The xylem is the water superhighway for the plant.

45. **D**—Taxis is unfortunate when it causes you to go up in smoke as bugs often do.

46. **D**—Dinoflagellates are part of the kingdom Protista.

47. **D**—Members of the kingdom Animalia tend to be diploid for most of their lives.

48. **C**—The casparian strip blocks water from passing in between the cells of the endodermis of plants. This is one of the mechanisms by which plants control water movement.

49. **A**—Guard cells are the cells responsible for controlling the opening and closing of the stomata in plants. Tracheids and vessel elements are cells found in xylem. Collenchyma cells are live cells that function as providers of flexible and mechanical support in plants.

50. **B**—Thyroxin is the hormone released by the thyroid that controls the body's metabolic rate.

51. **E**—Ribosomes are universally found in both prokaryotes and eukaryotes.

52. **E**—A fungus spends most of its life cycle as a haploid organism.

53. **B**

54. **A**—Cholesterol is one of the lipids that serves as the starting point for the synthesis of sex hormones.

55. **C**

56. **D**—Purines have a double-ring structure; pyrimidines, a single-ring one.

57. **B**—The ribosome is the site of protein synthesis.

58. **C**

59. **A**

60. **B**

61. **D**

62. **D**

63. **C**—An aneuploid condition is one in which there is an abnormal number of chromosomes. Turner's syndrome is a monosomy.

64. **A**

65. **B**

66. **D**

67. **A**

68. **E**

69. **C**

70. **C**

71. **A**

72. **D**

73. **B**

74. **E**

75. **B**

76. **A**

77. **D**

78. **B**—Testosterone level is an adaptive trait in this population, one that has been molded by natural selection (or possibly sexual selection; we cannot determine this from the question) to aid in reproduction. Adaptive radiation is a process by which many speciation events occur in a newly exploited environment and does not apply here. This is not an example of divergent selection because both breeding and non-breeding males have low testosterone levels during at least one part of the year; if the two male types always differed in testosterone level, this population could eventually split into two populations. Development and sperm production may be related to testosterone but are not addressed in this experiment.

79. **D**—Since testosterone levels are increased only during the breeding season, we can infer that testosterone has some role in breeding. Since reproductive males express higher testosterone levels only during the breeding season, we hypothesize that testosterone is beneficial, as opposed to detrimental, to breeding.

80. **A**—Since testosterone seems to be linked with reproduction, we infer from the new data that the "nonbreeding" males are actually breeding, and therefore have elevated testosterone levels. Females, population growth, and number of offspring produced are not considered in this example. Finally, although testosterone does affect many physiological processes, none of these are discussed or illustrated in this example.

81. **C**—Although several processes can affect the frequency of a new phenotype or genotype, once it is in place, the original genetic change must have been the result of a mutation (probably a chromosomal aberration).

82. **B**—No physical barrier separated the two populations; this is therefore an example of sympatric, not allopatric speciation. The other answer choices are not types of speciation.

83. **E**—Polyploidy is the only answer that can describe an *individual*. All the others are processes or states that described *population* events. Polyploidy is the duplication of whole chromosomes that leads to speciation because the new variety can no longer breed with the original.

84. **C**—Polyploidy is much more common in plants; mutations such as the duplication of whole chromosomes are usually lethal to animals.

85. **C**—Gel electrophoresis separates DNA on the basis of size. Smaller samples travel a greater distance down the gel compared to larger samples.

86. **B**—His DNA fingerprint seems to exactly match that of the evidence DNA sample.

87. **B**—A and C seem to share the exact same restriction fragment cut of their DNA. Perhaps they are messing with our head and added the DNA from the same individual twice.

88. **B**—100 – 45 – 36 = 19 percent.

89. **C**—36 percent of the population is AA. Taking the square root of 0.36, we find the frequency of the A allele to be 0.6. This means that the a allele's frequency must be 1- 0.6, or 0.4. From these numbers we can calculate the *expected* Hardy–Weinberg heterozygous frequency as $2pq = 2(A)(a) = 2(0.6)(0.4) = 48.0$ or 48 percent.

90. **B**—The expected heterozygous probability does not match up with the actual. This population is not in Hardy–Weinberg equilibrium.

91. **B**—The homozygous frequency is higher than expected; one explanation for this is that the homozygotes are being selected for.

92. **A**—Water will flow *out* of the bag because the solute concentration of the beaker is hypertonic compared to the dialysis bag. Osmosis passively drives water from a hypotonic region to a hypertonic region.

93. **B**—Water would now flow *into* the bag because the solute gradient has been reversed. Now the beaker is hypotonic compared to the dialysis bag. Water thus moves into the bag.

94. **C**—Water potential = pressure potential + solute potential. Water passively moves from regions with high water potential toward those with lower water potential.

95. **E**—The mother (person B) must be heterozygous Aa because she and her husband (aa) have produced children that have the double recessive condition. This means that person B (the mother) must have contributed an a, and that the cross is Aa × aa—and the probability is ½.

96. **D**—To answer this question, we must first determine the probability that person D is heterozygous. We know she is not aa because she does not have the conditon. Since we know that the father *has* the condition, we know for certain that his genotype is aa. Both of mother D's parents must be heterozygous since neither of them have the condition, but they have produced a child with the condition. The probability that mother D is heterozygous Aa is ⅔. The probability that a couple with the genotypes Aa × aa have a double recessive child is ½. The probability that these 2 will have a child with the condition is ½ × ⅔ = ⅓ = 0.333.

	A	a
A	AA	Aa
a	Aa	aa

97. E—If the couple has a child (person E) with the recessive condition, then we know for certain that mother D must be heterozygous. It is definitely an aa × Aa cross, leaving a 50 percent chance that their child will be aa.

98. B

99. B

100. D

RATING THE FREE-RESPONSE QUESTIONS

Free-Response Grading Outline

1. Gel electrophoresis question

   A. Maximum (5 points)

   - Mentioning that smaller particles travel faster.   (1 point)

   - Mentioning that the fragments of DNA are placed into wells at the head of the gel to begin their migration to the other side. (1 point)

   - Mentioning that the DNA migrates only as electric current is passed through the gel.   (1 point)

   - Mentioning that the DNA migrates from negative charge to positive charge.   (1 point)

   - Mentioning that when DNA samples from different individuals are cut with restriction enzymes, they show variations in the band patterns on gel electrophoresis known as *restriction fragment length polymorphisms* (RFLPs).   (1 point)

   - Mentioning that DNA is specific to each individual, and when it is mixed with restriction enzymes, different combinations of RFLPs will be obtained from person to person.   (1 point)

   - Definition of a DNA fingerprint as the combination of an individual's RFLPs inherited from each parent.   (1 point)

   - Mentioning that if an individual's electrophoresis pattern identically matches those of the crime scene evidence, the DNA has spoken and shown the individual to be the perpetrator, since the probability of two people having an identical set of RFLPs is virtually nonexistent.   (1 point)

   B. (maximum 5 points)

   - Mentioning that DNA samples would need to be taken from the disputed child and the potential parents involved.   (1 point)

   - Definition of a restriction enzyme as an enzyme that cuts DNA at a particular sequence and creates open fragments of DNA called "sticky ends."   (1 point)

   - Mentioning that the DNA from all the different individuals involved must be cut by the same restriction enzyme(s) so that the RFLPs created can be compared to each other.   (1 point)

   - Mentioning that each sample of DNA must be placed into a different well at the top of the gel plate.   (1 point)

   - Mentioning that the DNA will migrate from negative charge to positive charge, once the current is applied, to create an RFLP pattern specific for each individual— this is a look at the DNA fingerprint of an individual.   (1 point)

   - Mentioning that some sort of dye should be added to the DNA samples that will allow for proper viewing of the bands after the current is disconnected. (1 point)

   - Mentioning that one of the two DNA cuts from the child's fingerprint should match up with one of the two DNA cuts from the father's fingerprint and one from the mother's fingerprint as well, because the child inherits one chromosome of each homologous pair from the mother, and one from the father.   (1 point)

2. Controlled mechanisms question

  A. Cell cycle (maximum 5 points—maximum 2 points from each of the three mechanisms)

   - Defining growth factors as factors required by some cells to enter the cell division cycle. In their absence these cells may rest in the quiet G0 phase of the cycle.   (1 point)

   - Mentioning checkpoints, which exist throughout the cell cycle, to ensure that there are enough nutrients and raw materials present to progress into the next stage of the cell cycle.   (1 point)

   - Definition of cyclin as a protein that accumulates during interphase.   ($\frac{1}{2}$ point)

   - Definition of a protein kinase as a protein that controls the activities of other proteins through the addition of phosphate groups.   ($\frac{1}{2}$ point)

   - Definition of cyclin-dependent kinase as the kinase specific to the cell cycle and mentioning its presence at all times throughout the cell cycle.   ($\frac{1}{2}$ point)

   - Definition of MPF, the complex formed when cyclin binds to cyclin-dependent kinase. Mentioning that early in the cell cycle, because the cyclin concentration is low, the concentration of MPF is also low. As the concentration of cyclin reaches a certain threshold level, enough MPF is formed to push the cell into mitosis.   ($\frac{1}{2}$ point)

   - Mentioning that as mitosis proceeds, the level of cyclin declines, decreasing the amount of MPF present, pulling the cell out of mitosis.   ($\frac{1}{2}$ point)

   - Mentioning density-dependent inhibition, causing the growth of cells to slow or stop when a certain density of cells is reached. This is because there are not enough raw materials for the growth and survival of more cells. This causes the cells to enter the G0 phase.   (1 point)

  B. Hormones (maximum 5 points)

   - Mentioning negative feedback, which occurs when a hormone acts to, directly or indirectly, inhibit further secretion of the hormone of interest.   (1 point)

   - Mentioning an example of negative feedback such as insulin, which is secreted by the pancreas. When the blood glucose gets too high, the pancreas is stimulated to produce insulin, which causes cells to use more glucose. As a result of this activity, the blood glucose level declines, halting the production of insulin by the pancreas.   (1 point)

   - Mentioning positive feedback, which occurs when a hormone acts to, directly or indirectly, cause increased secretion of the hormone.   (1 point)

   - Mentioning an example of positive feedback, such as the LH surge that occurs prior to ovulation in females induced by estrogen that leads to further production of estrogen.   (1 point)

   - Definition of a hormone.   ($\frac{1}{2}$ point)

   - Description of how a hormone is able to affect a cell far from its site of release by traveling through the bloodstream.   ($\frac{1}{2}$ point)

   - Mentioning examples of hormone systems in the human body including the proper name, site of release, and function of the hormone.   ($\frac{1}{2}$ point each, for a total of 1 point maximum)

  C. Operon (maximum 5 points)

   - Definition of a promoter region as the base sequence that signals the start site for gene transcription.   ($\frac{1}{2}$ point)

   - Definition of an operator as a short sequence of DNA near the promoter that assists in transcription by interacting with regulatory proteins.   ($\frac{1}{2}$ point)

   - Definition of a repressor as a protein that prevents the binding of RNA polymerase to the promoter site.   ($\frac{1}{2}$ point)

   - Definition of an enhancer as a DNA region located thousands of bases away from the promoter that influences transcription.   ($\frac{1}{2}$ point)

   - Definition of an inducer as a molecule that binds to and inactivates a repressor (lactose for the lac operon).   ($\frac{1}{2}$ point)

   - Definition of the lactose operon as one that services a series of three genes involved in the process of lactose metabolism. This produces the genes that help the bacteria digest lactose.   (1 point)

   - Mentioning that in the absence of lactose, a repressor binds to the promoter region and prevents transcription from occurring. (1 point)

- Mentioning that when lactose is present, there is a binding site on the repressor where lactose attaches, causing the repressor to let go of the promoter region, leaving RNA polymerase free to bind to that site and initiate transcription of the genes. (1 point)

- Mentioning that when the lactose disappears, the repressor again becomes free to bind to the promoter, halting the process yet again. ($\frac{1}{2}$ point)

3. Speciation question (here, the student can obtain 4 points from a couple of the answers; if 4 points are obtained for an answer, a maximum of 3 points can be obtained from each of the other 2 answers).

A. Geographic barriers (maximum 4 points)

- Mentioning how geographic barriers can lead to reproductive isolation of members from the same species. ($\frac{1}{2}$ point)

- Mentioning that if these geographically separated species are moved into regions that have different environments, natural selection might favor different characteristics from the same species in the different environments. (1 point)

- Mentioning that this is an example of allopatric speciation—interbreeding ceases because some sort of barrier separates a single population into two. (1 point)

- Definition of divergent evolution as the evolution of two species farther apart from each other as they are exposed to different environmental challenges. (1 point)

- Mentioning the Galapagos finches as an example of geographic barriers leading to reproductive isolation and divergent evolution. ($\frac{1}{2}$ point)

- Mentioning that if after a long period of time, these divergent species come back together and are unable to reproduce, they have become a new species. (1 point)

B. Polyploidy (maximum 4 points)

- Definition of polyploidy as a condition in which an individual has more than the normal number of sets of chromosomes. (1 point)

- Description of how polyploidy initially occurs—an accident during cell division could double the chromosome number in the offspring, producing a tetraploid ($4n$) organism. (1 point)

- Alternate description of how polyploidy could initially occur—the breeding of two individuals from different species leads to a hybrid that is usually sterile and contains chromosomes that are not able to pair up during meiosis because they are not homologous. (1 point)

- Definition of an autopolyploid—organism with more than two chromosome sets all from the same species. ($\frac{1}{2}$ point)

- Definition of an allopolyploid—organism with more than two chromosome sets that come from more than one species. ($\frac{1}{2}$ point)

- Mentioning that although an individual may be healthy, it cannot reproduce with nonpolyploidic members of its species. (1 point)

- Mentioning that polyploidic individuals are able to mate only with other individuals who have the same polyploidic chromosomal makeup. (1 point)

C. Balanced polymorphism (maximum 3 points)

- Definition of balanced polymorphism—some characters have two or more phenotypic variants, such as tulip color. (1 point)

- Mention of the fact that if one phenotypic variant leads to increased reproductive success, directional selection will eventually eliminate all other varieties because only those who have the particular phenotypic variant of choice will survive to be able to reproduce, and thus only their genes will be passed along. (1 point)

- Mentioning that this requirement for a particular variant of the trait in order to survive reproductively isolates individuals of the same species from each other, opening the door for sympatric speciation. (1 point)

- Mentioning that if the balanced polymorphism causes the two variants to diverge enough to no longer be able to interbreed—speciation has occurred. (1 point)

- Citing an example of balanced polymorphism. (1 point)

D. Reproductive isolation (maximum 4 points)

- Mentioning that any barrier that prevents two species from producing offspring can be categorized as reproductive isolation. ($\frac{1}{2}$ point)

- Definition of prezygotic barriers as reproductive barriers that make the fertilization of the female ovum impossible.   (1 point)

- Mentioning, as an example of prezygotic barriers, any of the following ($\frac{1}{2}$ point each, up to 1 point total for prezygotic barrier examples): (a) *habitat isolation*—two species live in different habitats (they just don't see each other, so they cannot reproduce); (b) *temporal isolation*—two species mate at either different times of the *year* or different times of the day (either way, they are isolated from each other because they do not mate at the same time); (c) *behavioral isolation*—two species have different mating behaviors that do not mix well (members of the other species do not understand the actions of the other as mating signals—a simple communication breakdown); (d) *mechanical isolation*—mating may actually be attempted, but the physical sexual structures do not function together properly (they are incompatible).

- Definition of postzygotic barriers as reproductive barriers that prevent a properly formed hybrid between two species from reproducing themselves.   (1 point)

- Mentioning, as an example of postzygotic barriers, any of the following ($\frac{1}{2}$ point each, up to 1 point total for postzygotic barrier examples): (a) hybrid breakdown—sometimes the first generation of hybrids produced are able to reproduce with each other, but after that the wheels come off and the next generation is infertile; (b) reduced hybrid viability—the two different species are able to mate physically and the hybrid zygote is formed, but problems arise during the development of the hybrid that lead to prenatal death of the individual; (c) reduced hybrid fertility—the two different species are able to mate physically and produce a viable offspring but the offspring is infertile.

4. Ethology question (here, again, the student can obtain 4 points from a couple of the answers, if 4 points are obtained for an answer, a maximum of 3 points can be obtained from each of the other 2 answers).

A. Fixed-action patterns (maximum 3 points)

- Definition of a FAP as an innate behavior that seems to be a programmed response to some stimulus.   (1 point)

- Mentioning that once a FAP starts, it will not stop until it has been completed. (1 point)

- Mentioning that these FAPs exist because they provide some selective advantage to the species and remain for that reason. (1 point)

- Example of a FAP—such as male stickleback fish who attack anything with a red underbelly; graylag geese and the rolling of egg-shaped objects from near their nest, back into their nest; when mama bird returns to the nest with food, the blind baby birds immediately shift to their "I'm hungry" food-begging routine.   (1 point)

B. Dominance hierarchies (maximum 4 points)

- Definition of a dominance hierarchy as a ranking of power among the members of a group of individuals.   (1 point)

- Mentioning that the member with the most power is the "alpha" member.   ($\frac{1}{4}$ point)

- Mentioning that the second-in-command is the "beta" member.   ($\frac{1}{4}$ point)

- Mentioning that a dominance hierarchy is not permanent and is subject to change. In chimpanzee societies, the alpha male can lose his dominance and become subordinate to another chimp over time.   (1 point)

- Mentioning that one selective advantage of these hierarchies is that the order is known by all involved in the group and that this eliminates the energy waste that comes from physical fighting for resources since a pecking order is predetermined and everyone knows when it is their turn to partake.   (1 point)

- Mentioning that dominance hierarchies are a characteristic of group-living animals. (1 point)

C. Kinesis (maximum 3 points)

- Definition of kinesis as a change in the speed of a movement in response to a stimulus.   (1 point)

- Mentioning that an organism will slow down in an environment that it likes, and speed up in an environment that it does not like. (1 point)

- Mentioning an example of kinesis, such as pillbugs, who prefer damp environments. (1 point)

- Mentioning that kinesis is a randomly directed motion. (½ point)

D. Reciprocal altruism (maximum 4 points)

- Definition of altruistic behavior as helping others even though it is at the expense of the individual who is doing the helping. (1 point)

- Definition of reciprocal altruism—animals that behave altruistically toward others who are not relatives in the hope that in the future, perhaps the individual will return the favor. (1 point)

- Mentioning that these interactions are rare and limited to species with stable social groups that allow for future exchanges of this nature. (1 point)

- Mentioning an example of reciprocal altruism, such as bats vomiting food for those who did not get any; a baboon or wolf helping another in a fight. (1 point)

- Some argue that the reciprocally altruistic action must benefit the helper in some way and that true altruism does not exist in nature. (½ point)

E. Agonistic behavior (maximum 3 points)

- Definition of agonistic behavior as a contest of intimidation and submission that provides the winner with access to some resource. (1 point)

- Mentioning that the contest is usually one where two individuals exchange threatening displays in an effort to scare the other into giving up the resource. (1 point)

- Mentioning that individuals involved in these battles rarely come away injured. (1 point)

- Mentioning examples of agonistic resources that lead to these reactions: food, mates, and territory. (Mentioning two will be worth ½ point.)

SCORING AND INTERPRETATION

Multiple-Choice Questions

Number of correct answers: _____
Number of incorrect answers: _____
Number of blank answers: _____

Did you complete this part of the test in the allotted time? <u>Yes/No</u>

Free-Response Questions

1. ____ / 10
2. ____ / 10
3. ____ / 10
4. ____ / 10

Did you complete this part of the test in the allotted time? <u>Yes/No</u>

CALCULATE YOUR SCORE

Multiple-Choice Questions

_____ − _____ × (0.907) = _____
number right　(number wrong × .25)　　　　　　MC raw score

Free-Response Questions

Add up the total points accumulated in the four questions and multiply the sum by 1.50 to obtain the free response raw score: _____ × 1.50 _____
　　　　　　FR points　　　FR raw score

Now combine the raw scores from the multiple-choice and free-response sections to obtain your net raw score for the entire practice exam. Use the ranges listed below to determine your grade for this exam. Don't worry about how I arrived at the following ranges, and remember that they are rough estimates on questions that are not actual AP exam questions . . . do not read too much into them.

Raw Score	Approximate AP Score
84–150	5
65–84	4
48–65	3
29–48	2
0–29	1

Chapter 7

AP U.S. Government and Politics

Answer Sheet for Multiple-Choice Questions

1. _____	16. _____	31. _____	46. _____
2. _____	17. _____	32. _____	47. _____
3. _____	18. _____	33. _____	48. _____
4. _____	19. _____	34. _____	49. _____
5. _____	20. _____	35. _____	50. _____
6. _____	21. _____	36. _____	51. _____
7. _____	22. _____	37. _____	52. _____
8. _____	23. _____	38. _____	53. _____
9. _____	24. _____	39. _____	54. _____
10. _____	25. _____	40. _____	55. _____
11. _____	26. _____	41. _____	56. _____
12. _____	27. _____	42. _____	57. _____
13. _____	28. _____	43. _____	58. _____
14. _____	29. _____	44. _____	59. _____
15. _____	30. _____	45. _____	60. _____

Scoring Formula:

$$\underline{\hspace{3cm}} - \underline{\hspace{4cm}} = \underline{\hspace{2.5cm}}$$
number right — (number wrong × .25) — raw score

AP U.S. GOVERNMENT AND POLITICS

Section I

Time—45 minutes

60 questions

Directions: For the following multiple-choice questions, select the best answer choice and fill in the appropriate blank on the answer sheet.

1. The burning of a United States flag would best be described as

   A. unintended speech
   B. an obscenity
   C. a right that would be prohibited by the First Amendment
   D. symbolic speech
   E. a criminal activity

2. Richard Neustadt, a noted political theorist, has stated that a president's power comes from

   A. having the president's political party control both houses of the Congress during the presidential term
   B. the president's ability to persuade others to do what he or she wants
   C. being outside of politics
   D. not being sensitive to the political surroundings
   E. implementing his or her policies over the party's policies

3. The first African-American to serve on the Supreme Court of the United States was

   A. Thurgood Marshall
   B. John Marshall
   C. Clarence Thomas
   D. Danny Thomas
   E. William O. Douglas

4. How often are members of the House of Representatives elected?

   A. every six years
   B. every five years
   C. every four years
   D. every three years
   E. every two years

5. Which of the following best describes the use of a voting machine?

   A. They are easy to use.
   B. It is easy to "cheat" with a voting machine.
   C. The voting process speeds up by allowing quicker vote counts.
   D. They never make mistakes.
   E. They are cheaper than paper ballots.

6. If the president must nominate a new vice president due to the office being vacated, the nomination must be approved and confirmed by

   A. the Senate
   B. the House of Representatives
   C. both houses of the Congress
   D. the Supreme Court
   E. the Senate and the Supreme Court

7. Interest groups are different from political parties because they

   A. only attempt to influence the president
   B. do not nominate candidates for office
   C. are only concerned with the winning of elections
   D. deal with a wide range of policy issues
   E. are more concerned with the making of policy than influencing policy

8. In the United States Constitution, where is the congressional power of taxation found?

   A. Article I, Section 9
   B. Article II, Section 8
   C. Article I, Section 8
   D. Article VI, Section 2
   E. Article IV, Section 3

9. A list of items that government officials determine as their priorities is best defined as a/an

    A. priority list
    B. agenda
    C. agenda list
    D. policy agenda
    E. political agenda

10. The Full Faith and Credit Clause of the Constitution is the requirement that each state accept the public acts, records, and judicial proceedings of every other state, found in the Constitution in

    A. Article I
    B. Article VI
    C. Article IV
    D. Article III
    E. Article II

11. Which amendment of the United States Constitution applies to unreasonable searches and seizure?

    A. Fourth Amendment
    B. Tenth Amendment
    C. Fifth Amendment
    D. Ninth Amendment
    E. Second Amendment

12. Congressional elections occur during non-presidential election years, that is, every two years. What is a possible significance of an "off-year" election?

    A. The president may be forced to resign.
    B. The political power of Congress increases.
    C. The power base of Congress may change.
    D. The Constitution may change.
    E. There are many new candidates running for office.

13. Most international agreements are made by executive agreement, that is they are agreements between the president of the United States and the head of a foreign government. Executive agreements

    A. are binding agreements on all parties, present and future
    B. require the approval of both houses of the Congress
    C. remove government authority from the Congress

    D. must be approved by the Supreme Court
    E. do not require Senate approval

14. An order from the Supreme Court requesting that a lower court send up its records on a particular case is known as

    A. certificate
    B. writ of certiorari
    C. appeal
    D. brief proposal
    E. writ of power

15. In creating the United States Constitution, the founding fathers felt the key elements of keeping government control out of the hands of the majority and separating the powers of governmental institutions would be necessary for maintaining a strong central government. This idea of government came to be known as the

    A. constitutional form of government
    B. Madisonian model of government
    C. Jeffersonian model of government
    D. Hamiltonian model of government
    E. centralized model of government

16. Which of the following is a proposed plan of reform for the Electoral College when electing the president?
    I. the district plan
    II. the proportional plan
    III. direct population election
    IV. the national bonus plan

    A. I only
    B. II and IV only
    C. I, II, III, and IV
    D. III only
    E. III and IV only

17. Political action committees are extensions of interest groups that

    A. raise money for campaigns
    B. call for the resignation of fraudulent office holders
    C. encourage massive use of propaganda
    D. define public opinion
    E. determine public opinion

18. Which of the following is true about most presidential elections?

    A. Candidates from all parties usually receive some electoral votes.

B. They result in major party realignments.

C. They often center around one important issue.

D. The winner of the popular vote usually wins the majority of the electoral vote.

E. They are nonpartisan elections.

19. The power of television in American politics was best illustrated in which of the following presidential elections with regard to the final result of that election?

A. the Bush–Gore election of 2000

B. the Truman–Dewey election of 1948

C. the Nixon–Kennedy election of 1960

D. the Carter–Ford election of 1976

E. the Reagan–Carter election of 1980

20. An important result of *McCulloch v. Maryland* (1819) was to

A. establish the supremacy of the federal government over the states

B. place limits on the powers of Congress

C. establish the doctrine of judicial review

D. establish the doctrine of dual federalism

E. give greater power to the states

21. Which of the following occurs latest in the passage of a bill in Congress?

A. conference committee

B. referral to committee

C. investigation and hearings

D. debate on the floor

E. committee mark-up

22. Voters casting their ballots for candidates of a presidential candidate's political party because of the popularity of the presidential candidate is best described as

A. same party voting

B. presidential coattail effect

C. party electoral effect

D. the electoral effect

E. presidential party voting

23. Which of the following would best be described as a true statement regarding the Supreme Court of the United States?

A. Judges are nominated by the president and confirmed by the House of Representatives.

B. Judges serve at the will of the president.

C. Judges are appointed for life and can only be removed by impeachment.

D. Judges set their own salaries and benefits.

E. Judges are always from the same political party as the president.

24. Which of the following is the best example of why people do not vote?

I. Religious beliefs forbid participation in government.

II. Many people are happy with their current political system.

III. distrust of the political process

A. I only

B. II only

C. III only

D. I and III

E. I, II, and III

25. Executive departments that include those of cabinet level are created by:

A. Congress

B. the Constitution

C. the president

D. the Supreme Court

E. recommendation of other cabinet-level offices

26. When the House of Representatives sits as one large committee, it is sitting as

A. the full house

B. a quorum

C. a standing committee

D. the Committee of the Whole

E. the Committee at Large

27. Which of the following is a false statement regarding minor parties?

A. Third parties have been useful in introducing new ideas in American politics.

B. Minor parties have played an important role in reforming American politics.

C. Minor parties have usually been successful in getting candidates elected to office.

D. Minor parties may also be classified as ideological parties.

E. Minor parties tend to focus on single issues.

28. Checking with party members on party policy and helping the floor leader to determine if there are enough votes to pass a particular issue is part of the job description of which of the following members of Congress?

    A. minority floor leaders
    B. whips
    C. Speaker of the House
    D. president pro tem
    E. committee chairpersons

29. When the United States government is party to a case, who represents the United States before the Supreme Court?

    A. attorney general
    B. chief justice of the Supreme Court
    C. solicitor general
    D. secretary of justice
    E. general counsel for the president

30. With reference to the executive branch, the 25th Amendment calls for

    A. a system of checks and balances.
    B. direct election of the president
    C. a direct change in the Electoral College
    D. more power to be given to the vice president
    E. presidential succession and disability

31. Which of the following is a reason for the decline in voting?

    A. decrease in the number of eligible voters
    B. decline in parties' ability to mobilize voters
    C. same-day registration in a larger number of states
    D. penalties for nonvoting
    E. increase in party loyalty

32. Which of the following is true of the incumbency effect?

    A. Members of the House of Representatives benefit more than members of the Senate.
    B. Members of the Senate benefit more than members of the House of Representatives.
    C. Members of the House of Representatives and Senate benefit equally.
    D. Incumbency does not benefit either members of the House of Representatives or Senate.
    E. The president benefits from the incumbency effect.

33. Which of the following might be least likely to vote?

    A. high school dropout
    B. wealthy white businessman
    C. woman professional
    D. labor union member
    E. Catholic

34. In the enforcement of federal law, the president has the authority to issue executive orders. These orders have the same effect as a federal law. The issuing of an executive order falls under the president's

    A. law making power
    B. executive order power
    C. ordinance power
    D. judicial power
    E. non-legislative powers

35. After 1950, the success of the civil rights movement was aided most by

    A. African-Americans lowering their expectations
    B. the passage of the 14th Amendment
    C. a shift of the movement to the courts
    D. African-Americans winning election to public office
    E. interest group participation in the civil rights movement

36. As a special interest group, the National Organization for Women was organized for the purpose of

    A. ratifying an equal rights amendment for women
    B. creating more jobs for women
    C. dealing with the abortion issue in America
    D. advocating for state legislation to protect women's rights
    E. promoting a national women's party devoted to the purpose of electing the first woman president

37. Which of the following is not true of federalism?

    A. A resident of one state may not be discriminated against by another state.
    B. The federal government handles matters of national concern.
    C. States may extradite fugitives from one state to another.

D. States must honor another state's public acts, laws, and records.

E. The powers of the federal government are less than the powers of the state governments.

38. The Supreme Court case of *Gideon v. Wainwright* was a significant case in that it

A. caused law enforcement officers to advise the criminally accused of their rights

B. called for attorney rights to be applied at the state level as well as at the federal level

C. called for the accused to be confronted by witnesses against them

D. stated that search warrants were constitutionally required under all circumstances

E. allowed judges to determine what constitutes double jeopardy in a case

39. A bill that has been held up in a committee may be forced out of that committee by which of the following methods?

A. joint resolution

B. House call by the Speaker

C. discharge petition

D. cloture petition

E. cannot be forced out of a committee in either house of Congress

40. Party dealignment might be occurring if

A. government tends to be "divided"

B. one party tends to win control of government more often

C. support for minor parties is declining

D. political parties are becoming more centralized

E. people are voting Republican more often than they are voting Democrat

41. Which of the following is not a check on the power of the federal courts by Congress?

A. changing the tenure of justices

B. confirmation of appointments

C. changing the court's jurisdiction

D. altering the number of justices

E. amending the Constitution

42. The War Powers Resolution of 1973 requires

I. the president to inform Congress within 48 hours of any commitment of American troops abroad

II. the president to keep troops abroad for at least 60 days

III. the president to follow the guidelines of the Constitution regarding war

A. I only

B. II only

C. III only

D. I and II only

E. I, II, and III

43. Which of the following historic Supreme Court cases called for apportionment of representative seats in Congress to be as equal as possible?

A. *Marbury v. Madison*

B. *McCulloch v. Maryland*

C. *Mapp v. Ohio*

D. *Wesberry v. Sanders*

E. *Miranda v. Arizona*

44. A list of cases to be heard is called a/an

A. decisis of cases

B. agenda of cases

C. docket

D. court agenda

E. amicus docket

45. A political liberal tends to

A. support big government business

B. support government spending

C. support society as it once was

D. be extreme and dogmatic about conservative government

E. be reactionary on the issues before them

46. The Constitution of the United States was written as a direct result of

A. the American Revolution

B. orders issued by the Second Continental Congress

C. the failure of state governments under the new federal union

D. the decisions reached at the Annapolis Convention

E. the failure of the Articles of Confederation to provide adequate direction for |the union

47. When voters elect a representative from a district within a state, and that representative is selected from several candidates, what type of election system is that state using?

    A. a general ticket system
    B. a single-member district system
    C. at-large voting
    D. a one-person one-vote system
    E. gerrymandering

48. The president's key foreign and military advisors would be the

    A. State Department
    B. Central Intelligence Agency
    C. Federal Bureau of Investigation
    D. Department of Homeland Security
    E. National Security Council

49. How many presidents of the United States have been impeached?

    A. two
    B. three
    C. one
    D. four
    E. none

50. Originally, the "founding fathers" believed that members of the Senate should be selected by state legislatures. In 1913, a constitutional amendment required senators to be elected by the people of a state. Which of the following amendments called for this change?

    A. 12th Amendment
    B. 16th Amendment
    C. 20th Amendment
    D. 14th Amendment
    E. 17th Amendment

51. Which of the following is not considered to be one of the special or legislative courts in the federal court system?

    A. the Territorial Courts
    B. the United States Tax Court
    C. the United States Claims Court
    D. the Courts of Appeals
    E. the Court of Military Appeals

52. What is the minimum age requirement for a member of the United States Senate?

    A. 35

B. 25
C. 30
D. 21
E. There is no minimum age requirement.

53. The first political parties in America were the Federalist and the Democratic-Republicans. The leaders of these two parties were

    A. John Adams and Andrew Jackson
    B. George Washington and John Adams
    C. Alexander Hamilton and Thomas Jefferson
    D. Alexander Hamilton and Aaron Burr
    E. James Madison and Dewitt Clinton

54. When appointing justices to the Supreme Court, the president considers all of the following except

    A. political ideology
    B. senatorial courtesy
    C. judicial experience
    D. political party of nominee
    E. race, age, and gender of nominee

55. Which of the following is not a constitutional power of the president?

    A. the president invoking the practice of executive privilege
    B. the president creating cabinet-level departments of the executive branch
    C. The president is the recognized leader of a political party.
    D. the president serving as commander of the military
    E. the president signing or vetoing legislation

56. Which of the following is a specific power of the Senate?

    I. tries and convicts impeachment cases
    II. elects vice president when electoral college fails
    III. approves presidential appointments and treaties

    A. I only
    B. II only
    C. I and II
    D. II and III
    E. I, II, and III

57. Which office of the executive branch is responsible for helping the president prepare the national budget?

    A. Office of Budget Affairs
    B. Department of the Treasury
    C. Department of Commerce
    D. Office of Management and Budget
    E. United States Tax Office

58. What type of jurisdiction does the Supreme Court have?

    A. only original
    B. only appellate
    C. only exclusive
    D. original and mutual
    E. original and appellate

59. Which of the following is the most powerful person in the United States Senate?

    A. speaker
    B. vice president
    C. president of the Senate
    D. minority leader
    E. majority leader

60. A major factor influencing whether or not a person approves of a president's job performance is

    A. political party identification
    B. geographic location
    C. race
    D. level of income
    E. gender

END OF SECTION I

AP U.S. GOVERNMENT AND POLITICS
Section II
Time—100 minutes

1. Interest groups often exert vast influences over public policymaking.

   a. Identify three major activities used by interest groups to influence public policymaking.

   b. Explain how each activity identified affects each of the following:

      • legislative branch

      • executive branch

      • judicial branch

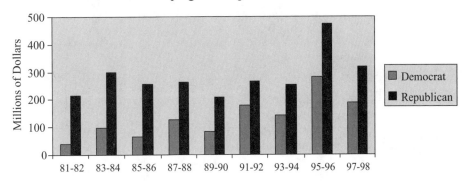

Political Campaign Receipts: 1981-1998

2. Using the data in the graph above and your knowledge of United States government and politics, perform the following tasks:

   a. Identify one significant pattern shown in the graph above.

   b. Discuss two factors that might contribute to the trend you identified.

   c. Discuss one consequence of this trend for the United States political process.

3. Relationships between the president and both Congress and the courts involve the use of strategies designed to achieve the president's public policy goals.

   a. Identify and discuss two strategies the president may use with Congress to achieve public policy goals.

b. Identify and discuss two strategies the president may use with the courts to achieve public policy goals.

c. Identify one method Congress has and one method the courts have which might prevent the president from achieving public policy goals.

4. In both presidential and congressional campaigns, the candidates must get nominated and then elected. Major differences exist between presidential and congressional campaigns.

a. Discuss the process of being nominated to run for presidential or congressional office.

b. Identify and discuss two major differences that exist between presidential and congressional campaigns.

c. Identify two methods that have been used in recent presidential elections to encourage voter participation. Explain how each method has been used to encourage voter participation.

END OF SECTION II

ANSWERS TO MULTIPLE-CHOICE QUESTIONS

Answer Key

1.	D	16.	C	31.	B	46.	E
2.	B	17.	A	32.	A	47.	B
3.	A	18.	D	33.	A	48.	E
4.	E	19.	C	34.	C	49.	A
5.	C	20.	A	35.	C	50.	E
6.	C	21.	A	36.	D	51.	D
7.	B	22.	B	37.	E	52.	C
8.	C	23.	C	38.	B	53.	C
9.	D	24.	E	39.	C	54.	B
10.	C	25.	A	40.	A	55.	B
11.	A	26.	D	41.	A	56.	E
12.	C	27.	C	42.	A	57.	D
13.	E	28.	B	43.	D	58.	E
14.	B	29.	C	44.	C	59.	E
15.	B	30.	E	45.	B	60.	A

Explanations of Answers to the Multiple-Choice Questions

1. **D.** In *Texas v. Johnson* the Supreme Court stated that the burning of the United States flag was a form of symbolic speech, protected under the First Amendment.

2. **B.** Richard Neustadt stated that a president's power comes from the ability to persuade others to do what he or she wants.

3. **A.** The first African-American appointed to the Supreme Court was Thurgood Marshall, appointed by Lyndon Johnson.

4. **E.** Members of the House of Representatives are elected every two years.

5. **C.** Voting machines have allowed for quicker counting of votes, speeding up the process.

6. **C.** If the president nominates a vice president due to a vacancy, the 25th Amendment calls for both houses of Congress to approve the nomination.

7. **B.** Interest groups do not nominate candidates for office.

8. **C.** Congress is given the power to tax in Article I, Section 8.

9. **D.** The policy agenda is a list of items that government officials determine as priorities.

10. **C.** The Full Faith and Credit clause is found in Article IV of the Constitution.

11. **A.** The Fourth Amendment protects against unreasonable searches and seizures.

12. **C.** Often, during off-year elections, the party of the president may lose seats in Congress, changing the base of power.

13. **E.** Executive agreements do not require Senate approval. They are binding only on the parties who make the agreement.

14. **B.** A writ of certiorari (cert) is an order from the Supreme Court requesting a lower court send up its records on a particular case.

15. **B.** The Madisonian model of government proposed a strong central government, separation of powers, and limiting the effects of the majority.

16. **C.** Proposed reforms of the electoral college include the district plan, proportional plan, national bonus plan, and direct popular election.

17. **A.** Political action committees are extensions of interest groups that raise money for political candidates and campaigns.

18. **D.** In most presidential elections, the winner of the popular vote also wins the majority of the electoral vote.

19. **C.** The power of the media, especially television, is best illustrated by the Kennedy–Nixon election in 1960, with the first televised presidential debates.

20. **A.** An important result of *McCulloch v. Maryland* (1819) was to establish the supremacy of the federal government over the states.

21. **A.** The conference committee occurs latest in the passage of a bill through Congress.

22. **B.** Presidential coattails is the phenomenon whereby voters support members of the president's party running for other offices, because of the president's popularity.

23. **C.** Justices to the Supreme Court are appointed for life terms, during good behavior, and can be removed only through impeachment and conviction of the charges.

24. **E.** People may choose not to vote because they are happy with the current government, mistrust government, or because religious reasons may prevent their participation.

25. **A.** Congress creates executive departments.

26. **D.** The House of Representatives sitting as one large committee is the Committee of the Whole.

27. **C.** Minor parties have not been very successful in getting candidates elected to office. No president and only a few members of Congress have been elected from minor parties.

28. **B.** Floor whips check on party members and help the floor leader gather the votes necessary to pass or defeat a bill.

29. **C.** The solicitor general represents the United States government before the Supreme Court.

30. **E.** The 25th Amendment calls for a method to deal with presidential succession and disability.

31. **B.** A decline in the political parties' ability to mobilize voters is a reason for the decline in voter turnout.

32. **A.** The incumbency effect benefits members of the House of Representatives more than members of the Senate.

33. **A.** The high school dropout might be least likely to vote.

34. **C.** The president issuing an executive order is an example of ordinance powers.

35. **C.** The successes of the civil rights movement after 1950 was aided by a shift of the movement to the courts.

36. **D.** The National Organization for Women's goal was to protect women's rights through the passage of legislation.

37. **E.** The powers of the federal government are not less than the powers of the states under federalism.

38. **B.** *Gideon v. Wainwright* provided for attorney rights in state cases. This case was used by the Court to apply the Sixth Amendment to the states through the due process clause of the 14th Amendment.

39. **C.** Bills held up in committee may be forced out of committee by discharge petition.

40. **A.** One sign of party dealignment may be "divided government," with one party controlling the executive branch and the other party controlling one or both houses of Congress.

41. **A.** Changing the tenure of judges is not a check on the power of the federal courts by Congress. Tenure for federal judges is established by the Constitution.

42. **A.** The War Powers Resolution requires the president to inform Congress within 48 hours of any commitment of American troops abroad.

43. **D.** *Wesberry v. Sanders* called for apportionment of representative seats in Congress be as equal as possible.

44. **C.** A docket is a list of cases to be heard by the court.

45. **B.** Liberals tend to support government spending.

46. **E.** The Constitution of the United States was written as a direct result of the failure of the Articles of Confederation to provide adequate direction for the union.

47. **B.** A single-member district allows for only one winner to be elected to represent the voters.

48. **E.** The National Security Council is composed of the president's key foreign and military advisors.

49. **A.** Two presidents, Andrew Johnson and Bill Clinton, were impeached by the House of Representatives; neither was convicted by the Senate. Richard Nixon resigned prior to impeachment charges being voted on by the House of Representatives, therefore he was not impeached.

50. **E.** The 17th Amendment allows for the direct election of senators.

51. **D.** The Courts of Appeals are constitutional courts, not legislative courts.

52. **C.** The minimum age for members of the Senate is 30 years.

53. **C.** The leaders of the Federalists and Democratic Republicans were Alexander Hamilton and Thomas Jefferson, respectively.

54. **B.** Senatorial courtesy is not used by the president when appointing justices to the Supreme Court.

55. **B.** Congress, not the president, creates cabinet-level departments of the executive branch.

56. **E.** Powers of the Senate include trying and convicting impeachment cases, electing the vice president if the electoral college fails, and approving presidential appointments and treaties.

57. **D.** The Office of Management and Budget is the executive branch agency responsible for helping the president prepare the annual budget.

58. **E.** The Supreme Court has both original and appellate jurisdiction.

59. **E.** The most powerful person in the Senate is the majority leader.

60. **A.** Political party identification is a major factor that influences whether a person approves or disapproves of a president's job performance.

RATING THE FREE-RESPONSE ESSAYS

Scoring Rubric for Essay 1

Total Value: 6 points

Part a: 1 point for each correct identification of activities = 3 points
Part b: 1 point for each correct explanation of activities = 3 points

Scoring Rubric for Essay 2

Total Value: 4 points

Part a: 1 point for correct identification of pattern = 1 point
Part b: 1 point for correct identification of each factor = 2 points
Part c: 1 point for correct identification of consequence of trend = 1 point

Scoring Rubric for Essay 3

Total Value: 8 points

Part a: 1 point for correct identification of two strategies = 1 point
        1 point for each correct discussion of strategies = 2 points
Part b: 1 point for correct identification of two strategies = 1 point
        1 point for each correct discussion of strategies = 2 points
Part c: 1 point for each correct identification of methods = 2 points

Scoring Rubric for Essay 4

Total Value: 9 points

Part a: 1 point for each correct discussion of nomination process = 1 point
Part b: 1 point for each correct identification of a difference = 2 points
        1 point for each correct discussion of a difference = 2 points
Part c: 1 point for each correct identification of recent methods = 2 points
        1 point for each correct explanation of recent methods = 2 points

Chapter 8

AP Chemistry

Answer Sheet for Multiple-Choice Questions

1. _____	20. _____	39. _____	58. _____
2. _____	21. _____	40. _____	59. _____
3. _____	22. _____	41. _____	60. _____
4. _____	23. _____	42. _____	61. _____
5. _____	24. _____	43. _____	62. _____
6. _____	25. _____	44. _____	63. _____
7. _____	26. _____	45. _____	64. _____
8. _____	27. _____	46. _____	65. _____
9. _____	28. _____	47. _____	66. _____
10. _____	29. _____	48. _____	67. _____
11. _____	30. _____	49. _____	68. _____
12. _____	31. _____	50. _____	69. _____
13. _____	32. _____	51. _____	70. _____
14. _____	33. _____	52. _____	71. _____
15. _____	34. _____	53. _____	72. _____
16. _____	35. _____	54. _____	73. _____
17. _____	36. _____	55. _____	74. _____
18. _____	37. _____	56. _____	75. _____
19. _____	38. _____	57. _____	

AP CHEMISTRY

Section I

Time —1 hour and 30 minutes

75 questions

Directions: Answer the following questions in the time allowed. You may use a periodic table while taking this exam. Write your answers on the answer sheet.

1. Choose the strongest Lewis base from the following.

   A. Na^+
   B. Fe^{3+}
   C. NH_3
   D. Zn^{2+}
   E. BF_3

2. Which of the following CANNOT behave as both a Brønsted base and a Brønsted acid?

   A. HPO_4^{2-}
   B. $C_2O_4^{2-}$
   C. HSO_4^-
   D. $HC_2O_4^-$
   E. HCO_3^-

3. A species, molecule, or ion, is called a Lewis base if it does which of the following?

   A. It is an electron-pair donor.
   B. It donates an H^+.
   C. It accepts an H^+.
   D. It is an electron-pair acceptor.
   E. It increase the $H^+(aq)$ in water.

4. Which of the following are proper laboratory procedures for a titration?
   I.   Make sure the color change of the indicator persists for at least 30 s.
   II. Allow all materials to cool to room temperature before they are weighed.
   III. Rinse the buret with deionized water before it is filled with titrant for the first titration.

   A. I and III only
   B. I, II, and III
   C. II only
   D. II and III only
   E. I and II only

5. In most of its compounds, this element exists as a monatomic cation.

   A. F
   B. S
   C. N
   D. Ca
   E. Cl

6. In which of the following groups are the species listed correctly in order of increasing radius?

   A. Sr, Ca, Mg
   B. Se^{2-}, S^{2-}, O^{2-}
   C. Mn^{3+}, Mn^{2+}, Mn
   D. I^-, Br^-, Cl^-
   E. K, Ca, Sc

7. Which of the following elements has the lowest electronegativity?

   A. F
   B. I
   C. C
   D. K
   E. Al

8. Which of the following represents the correct formula for hexamminechromium(III) chloride?

   A. $[Cr(NH_3)_6](ClO_3)_3$
   B. $(NH_3)_6Cr_3Cl$
   C. Am_6CrCl_3
   D. $[Cr(NH_3)_6]Cl_3$
   E. $[Cr_3(NH_3)_6]Cl_3$

9. ____ $Fe(OH)_3(s) +$ ____ $H_2SeO_4(aq)$
   $\rightarrow$ ____ $Fe_2(SeO_4)_3(s) +$ ____ $H_2O(l)$

   After the above chemical equation is balanced, the lowest whole-number coefficient for water is

A. 1
B. 6
C. 9
D. 12
E. 3

10. Which of the following best represents the net ionic equation for the reaction of barium hydroxide with an aqueous potassium sulfate solution?

A. $Ba(OH)_2 + KSO_4 \rightarrow BaSO_4 + KOH$
B. $Ba^{2+} + K_2SO_4 \rightarrow BaSO_4 + 2\ K^+$
C. $Ba^{2+} + SO_4^{2-} \rightarrow BaSO_4$
D. $Ba(OH)_2 + SO_4^{2-} \rightarrow BaSO_4 + 2\ OH^-$
E. $Ba(OH)_2 + K_2SO_4 \rightarrow BaSO_4 + 2\ KOH$

11. A sample of magnesium metal is heated in the presence of nitrogen gas. After the sample was heated, some water was added to it. Which of the following statements is false?

A. The magnesium reacted with the nitrogen to produce magnesium nitride.
B. No reaction occurred because nitrogen gas is so unreactive.
C. The solid did not dissolve in the water.
D. After the addition of the water, the distinctive odor of ammonia gas was present.
E. The water converted some of the magnesium nitride to magnesium hydroxide.

12. A student mixes 50.0 mL of 0.10 M $Ni(NO_3)_2$ solution with 50.0 mL of 0.10 M NaOH. A green precipitate forms, and the concentration of the hydroxide ion becomes very small. Which of the following correctly places the concentrations of the remaining ions in order of decreasing concentration?

A. $[Na^+] > [Ni^{2+}] > [NO_3^-]$
B. $[Ni^{2+}] > [NO_3^-] > [Na^+]$
C. $[Na^+] > [NO_3^-] > [Ni^{2+}]$
D. $[NO_3^-] > [Na^+] > [Ni^{2+}]$
E. $[Ni^{2+}] > [Na^+] > [NO_3^-]$

13. The addition of concentrated $Ba(OH)_2(aq)$ to a 1.0 M $(NH_4)_2SO_4$ solution will result in which of the following observations?

A. The odor of ammonia is detected, and a white precipitate forms.
B. The formation of a white precipitate takes place.

C. The solution becomes acidic.
D. The odor of ammonia is detected.
E. An odorless gas forms and bubbles out of the mixture.

14. Manganese, Mn, forms a number of oxides. A particular oxide is 69.6% Mn. What is the simplest formula for this oxide?

A. MnO
B. Mn_2O_3
C. Mn_3O_4
D. MnO_2
E. Mn_2O_7

15. Sodium sulfate forms a number of hydrates. A sample of a hydrate is heated until all the water is removed. What is the formula of the original hydrate if it loses 56% of its mass when heated?

A. $Na_2SO_4.H_2O$
B. $Na_2SO_4.2H_2O$
C. $Na_2SO_4.6H_2O$
D. $Na_2SO_4.8H_2O$
E. $Na_2SO_4.10H_2O$

16. $3\ Cu(s) + 8\ HNO_3(aq) \rightarrow$
$3\ Cu(NO_3)_2(aq) + 2\ NO(g) + 4\ H_2O(l)$

Copper metal reacts with nitric acid according to the above equation. A 0.30-mol sample of copper metal and 100.0 mL of 3.0 M nitric acid are mixed in a flask. How many moles of NO gas will form?

A. 0.20 mol
B. 0.038 mol
C. 0.10 mol
D. 0.075 mol
E. 0.30 mol

17. Gold(III) oxide, Au_2O_3, can be decomposed to gold metal, Au, plus oxygen gas, O_2. How many moles of oxygen gas will form when 2.21 g of solid gold(III) oxide is decomposed? The formula weight of gold(III) oxide is 442.

A. 0.00750 mol
B. 0.0150 mol
C. 0.00500 mol
D. 0.00250 mol
E. 0.0100 mol

18. ____ $C_4H_{11}N(l) +$ ____ $O_2(g) \rightarrow$
____ $CO_2(g) +$ ____ $H_2O(l) +$ ____ $N_2(g)$

When the equation is balanced, the lowest whole number coefficient for CO_2 is

A. 4
B. 16
C. 27
D. 22
E. 2

19. $2 KMnO_4 + 5 H_2C_2O_4 + 3 H_2SO_4 \rightarrow K_2SO_4 + 2 MnSO_4 + 10 CO_2 + 8 H_2O$

How many moles of $MnSO_4$ are produced when 2.0 mol of $KMnO_4$, 5.0 mol of $H_2C_2O_4$, and 1.5 mol of H_2SO_4 are mixed?

A. 2.0 mol
B. 1.5 mol
C. 1.0 mol
D. 3.0 mol
E. 2.5 mol

20. ___ $KClO_3 \rightarrow$ ___ $KCl +$ ___ O_2

After the above equation is balanced, how many moles of O_2 can be produced from 1.0 mol of $KClO_3$?

A. 1.5 mol
B. 3.0 mol
C. 1.0 mol
D. 3.0 mol
E. 6.0 mol

21. $Sr + 2 H_2O \rightarrow Sr(OH)_2 + H_2$

Strontium reacts with water according to the above reaction. What volume of hydrogen gas, at standard temperature and pressure, is produced from 0.100 mol of strontium?

A. 3.36 L
B. 5.60 L
C. 2.24 L
D. 4.48 L
E. 1.12 L

22. A sample of nitrogen gas is placed in a container with constant volume. The temperature is changed until the pressure doubles. Which of the following also changes?

A. density
B. moles
C. average velocity
D. number of molecules
E. potential energy

23. An experiment to determine the molecular weight of a gas begins by heating a solid to produce a gaseous product. The gas passes through a tube and displaces water in an inverted, water-filled bottle. The mass of the solid is measured, as is the volume and the temperature of the displaced water. Once the barometric pressure has been recorded, what other information is needed to finish the experiment?

A. the heat of formation of the gas
B. the density of the water
C. the mass of the displaced water
D. the vapor pressure of the water
E. the temperature to which the solid was heated

24. Determine the final temperature of a sample of hydrogen gas. The sample initially occupied a volume of 6.00 L at 127° C and 875 mm Hg. The sample was heated, at constant pressure, until it occupied a volume of 15.00 L.

A. 318° C
B. 727° C
C. 45° C
D. 160° C
E. 1000° C

25. From the following, choose the gas that probably shows the least deviation from ideal gas behavior?

A. Kr
D. CH_4
C. O_2
D. H_2
E. NH_3

Choose from the following types of energy for questions 26–28.

A. free energy
B. lattice energy
C. kinetic energy
D. activation energy
E. ionization energy

26. The maximum energy available for useful work from a spontaneous reaction

27. The energy needed to separate the ions in an ionic solid

28. The energy difference between the transition state and the reactants

29. 1. $2 ClF(g) + O_2(g) \rightarrow Cl_2O(g) + OF_2(g)$ $\quad \Delta H° = 167.5$ kJ

    2. $2 F_2(g) + O_2(g) \rightarrow 2 OF_2(g)$ $\quad \Delta H° = -43.5$ kJ

    3. $2 ClF_3(l) + 2 O_2(g) \rightarrow Cl_2O(g) + 3 OF_2(g)$ $\quad \Delta H° = 394.1$ kJ

    Using the information given above, calculate the enthalpy change for the following reaction:

    $$ClF(g) + F_2(g) \rightarrow ClF_3(l)$$

    A. −135.1 kJ
    B. +135.1 kJ
    C. 270.2 kJ
    D. −270.2 kJ
    E. 0.0 kJ

30. When lithium sulfate, Li_2SO_4, is dissolved in water, the temperature increases. Which of the following conclusions may be related to this?

    A. Lithium sulfate is less soluble in hot water.
    B. The hydration energies of lithium ions and sulfate ions are very low.
    C. The heat of solution for lithium sulfate is endothermic.
    D. The solution is not an ideal solution.
    E. The lattice energy of lithium sulfate is very low.

31. What is the energy required to completely separate the ions in an ionic solid?

    A. ionization energy
    B. kinetic energy
    C. activation energy
    D. lattice energy
    E. free energy

32. $C_2H_4(g) + H_2O(g) \rightarrow C_2H_5OH(g)$ $\quad \Delta H = -46$ kJ

    Determine ΔH for the above reaction if $C_2H_5OH(l)$ was formed in the above reaction instead of $C_2H_5OH(g)$. The ΔH of vaporization for C_2H_5OH is 43 kJ/mol.

    A. +3 kJ
    B. +89 kJ
    C. −3 kJ
    D. +43 kJ
    E. −89 kJ

33. The ground-state configuration of Ni^{2+} is which of the following?

    A. $1s^22s^22p^63s^23p^63d^84s^2$
    B. $1s^22s^22p^63s^23p^63d^{10}4s^2$
    C. $1s^22s^22p^63s^23p^63d^{10}$
    D. $1s^22s^22p^63s^23p^63d^8$
    E. $1s^22s^22p^63s^23p^63d^54s^2$

34. A ground-state electron in a calcium atom might have which of the following sets of quantum numbers?

    A. $n = 3; l = 2; m_l = 0; m_s = -1/2$
    B. $n = 5; l = 0; m_l = 0; m_s = -1/2$
    C. $n = 4; l = 1; m_l = 0; m_s = -1/2$
    D. $n = 4; l = 0; m_l = 0; m_s = -1/2$
    E. $n = 4; l = 0; m_l = +1; m_s = -1/2$

The following answers are to be used for questions 35–38.

    A. Pauli exclusion principle
    B. electron shielding
    C. the wave properties of matter
    D. Heisenberg uncertainty principle
    E. Hund's rule

35. The diffraction of electrons

36. The maximum number of electrons in an atomic orbital is two.

37. An oxygen atom is paramagnetic in the ground state.

38. The position and momentum of an electron cannot be determined exactly.

39. Magnesium reacts with element X to form an ionic compound. If the ground-state electron configuration of X is $1s^22s^22p^5$, what is the simplest formula for this compound?

    A. Mg_2X_3
    B. MgX_2
    C. MgX_4
    D. Mg_2X_5
    E. MgX

40. VSEPR predicts that a BF_3 molecule will be which of the following shapes?

    A. tetrahedral
    B. trigonal bipyramidal
    C. square pyramid

D. trigonal planar
E. square planar

41. Which of the following is polar?

A. BF_3
B. IF_5
C. CF_4
D. XeF_4
E. AsF_5

42. The only substance listed below that contains ionic, σ, and π bonds is:

A. C_2H_4
B. NaH
C. NH_4Cl
D. $NaC_2H_3O_2$
E. H_2O

43. Which molecule or ion in the following list has the greatest number of unshared electron pairs around the central atom?

A. IF_7
B. NO_3^-
C. BF_3
D. NH_3
E. CBr_4

44. Which of the following processes does not involve breaking an ionic or a covalent bond?

A. $2\,NO(g) + O_2 \rightarrow 2\,NO_2(g)$
B. $NaNO_3(s) \rightarrow Na^+(aq) + NO_3^-(aq)$
C. $Zn(s) \rightarrow Zn(g)$
D. $2\,H_2(g) + O_2(g) \rightarrow 2\,H_2O(g)$
E. $2\,KClO_3(s) \rightarrow 2\,KCl(s) + 3\,O_2(g)$

Choose from the following solids for questions 45–48.

A. composed of atoms held together by delocalized electrons
B. composed of molecules held together by intermolecular dipole–dipole interactions
C. composed of positive and negative ions held together by electrostatic attractions
D. composed of macromolecules held together by strong bonds
E. composed of molecules held together by intermolecular London forces

45. Graphite

46. Ca(s)

47. $CaCO_3(s)$

48. $SO_2(s)$

49. The critical point represents

A. the highest temperature and pressure where the substance may exist as discrete solid and gas phases.
B. the highest temperature and pressure where the substance may exist as discrete liquid and gas phases.
C. the temperature and pressure where the substance exists in equilibrium as solid, liquid, and gas phases.
D. the highest temperature and pressure where the substance may exist as discrete liquid and solid phases.
E. the highest temperature and pressure where a substance can sublime.

50. A sample of a pure liquid is placed in an open container and heated to the boiling point. Which of the following may increase the boiling point of the liquid?

I.   The container is sealed.
II.   The size of the container is increased.
III. More liquid is added.

A. II and III
B. I and III
C. III only
D. II only
E. I only

51. Which point on the diagram below might represent the normal boiling point?

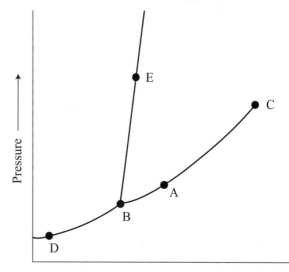

52. What is the total concentration of cations in a solution made by combining 700.0 mL of 3.0 M $(NH_4)_3PO_4$ with 300.0 mL of 2.0 M Na_2SO_4?

   A. 2.7 M
   B. 13 M
   C. 7.5 M
   D. 5.0 M
   E. 2.5 M

53. A stock solution that is 0.30 M in Na_2SO_4 is available. How many moles of solid Na_3PO_4 must be added to 800 mL of this solution to increase the sodium ion concentration to 0.90 M?

   A. 0.060
   B. 0.12
   C. 0.080
   D. 0.16
   E. 0.24

54. If a solution of ethyl ether, $(C_2H_5)_2O$, in ethanol, C_2H_5OH, is treated as an ideal solution. What is the mole fraction of ethyl ether in the vapor over an equimolar solution of these two liquids? The vapor pressure of ethyl ether is 480 mm Hg at 20° C, and the vapor pressure of ethanol is 50 mm Hg at this temperature.

   A. 0.50
   B. 0.76
   C. 0.91
   D. 0.27
   E. 0.09

55. How many milliliters of concentrated ammonia (7.0-molar NH_3) are needed to prepare 0.250 L of 3.0-molar NH_3?

   A. 110 mL
   B. 0.11 mL
   C. 200 mL
   D. 150 mL
   E. 75 mL

56. The plot of ln[A] versus time gives a straight line. This implies the rate law is

   A. rate $= k[A]^2$
   B. rate $= k[A]^{-2}$
   C. rate $= k[A]^0$
   D. rate $= k[A]^{-1}$
   E. rate $= k[A]$

57. The specific rate constant, k, for radioactive lawrencium-256 is 86 h^{-1}. What mass of a 0.0500 ng sample of lawrencium-256 remains after 58 s?

   A. 0.0500 ng
   B. 0.0250 ng
   C. 0.0125 ng
   D. 0.00625 ng
   E. 0.0375 ng

58. The purpose of using a lit match to start the fire in a gas grill is

   A. to supply the free energy for the reaction
   B. to catalyze the reaction
   C. to supply the heat of reaction
   D. to supply the kinetic energy for the reaction
   E. to supply the activation energy for the reaction

59.
Acid	K_a, acid dissociation constant
H_3PO_4	7.2×10^{-3}
$H_2PO_4^-$	6.3×10^{-8}
HPO_4^{2-}	4.2×10^{-13}

Using the above information, choose the best answer for preparing a pH = 7.9 buffer.

   A. K_2HPO_4
   B. K_3PO_4
   C. $K_2HPO_4 + KH_2PO_4$
   D. $K_2HPO_4 + K_3PO_4$
   E. $H_3PO_4 + KH_2PO_4$

60. What is the ionization constant, K_a, for a weak monoprotic acid if a 0.6-molar solution has a pH of 2.0?

   A. 1.7×10^{-4}
   B. 1.7×10^{-2}
   C. $6. \times 10^{-6}$
   D. 2.7×10^{-3}
   E. 3.7×10^{-4}

Questions 61–64 refer to the following aqueous solutions. All concentrations are 1 M.

   A. CH_3NH_2 (methylamine) and LiOH (lithium hydroxide)
   B. $C_2H_5NH_2$ (ethylamine) and $C_2H_5NH_3NO_3$ (ethylammonium nitrate)
   C. CH_3NH_2 (methylamine) and $HC_3H_5O_2$ (propionic acid)
   D. $KClO_4$ (potassium perchlorate) and $HClO_4$ (perchloric acid)

E. $H_2C_2O_4$ (oxalic acid) and KHC_2O_4 (potassium hydrogen oxalate)

61. The most basic solution (highest pH)

62. The solution with a pH nearest 7

63. A buffer with a pH > 7

64. A buffer with a pH < 7

65. At constant temperature, a change in volume will NOT affect the moles of the substances present in which of the following?

A. $2 CO(g) + 2 H_2(g) \rightleftharpoons CO_2(g) + CH_4(g)$
B. $CO(g) + Cl_2(g) \rightleftharpoons COCl_2(g)$
C. $PCl_3(g) + Cl_2(g) \rightleftharpoons PCl_5(g)$
D. $CO(g) + H_2O(g) \rightleftharpoons CO_2(g) + H_2(g)$
E. $2 NH_3(g) \rightleftharpoons N_2(g) + 3 H_2(g)$

66. $HCO_3^- + H_2O \rightleftharpoons H_3O^+ + CO_3^{2-}$

Which species, in the above equilibrium, behave as bases?

I. CO_3^{2-}
II. H_2O
III. HCO_3^-

A. I and III
B. II only
C. I and II
D. I only
E. II and III

67. $CO(g) + 2 H_2(g) \rightleftharpoons CH_3OH(g)$

A 1.00-L flask is filled with 0.70 mol of H_2 and 0.60 mol of CO, and allowed to come to equilibrium. At equilibrium, there are 0.40 mol of CO in the flask. What is the value of K_c, the equilibrium constant, for the reaction?

A. 0.74
B. 3.2
C. 0.0050
D. 5.6
E. 1.2

68. $H_2O(l) + CrO_4^{2-}(aq) + HSnO_2^-(aq) \rightarrow$ $CrO_2^-(aq) + OH^-(aq) + HSnO_3^-(aq)$

What is the coefficient of OH^- when the above reaction is balanced?

A. 10

B. 2
C. 5
D. 4
E. 1

69. $2 Bi^{3+} + 3 SnO_2^{2-} + 6 OH^- \rightarrow 3 SnO_3^{2-}$ $+ 3 H_2O + 2 Bi$

For the above reaction, pick the true statement from the following:

A. The oxidation number of tin changes from +2 to +4.
B. The oxidation number of tin changes from +4 to +2.
C. The Bi^{3+} is oxidized by the tin.
D. The OH^- reduces the Bi^{3+}.
E. The SnO_3^{2-} is formed by the reduction of SnO_2^{2-}.

70. An electrolysis cell was constructed with two platinum electrodes in a 1.00 M aqueous solution of KCl. An odorless gas evolved from one electrode and a gas with a distinctive odor evolved from the other electrode. Choose the correct statement from the following list.

A. The odorless gas was oxygen.
B. The odorless gas was evolved at the anode.
C. The gas with the distinctive odor was evolved at the anode.
D. The odorless gas was evolved at the positive electrode.
E. The gas with the distinctive odor was evolved at the negative electrode.

71. When $^{226}_{88}Ra$ decays, it emits 2 α particles, then a β particle, followed by an α particle. The resulting nucleus is:

A. $^{212}_{83}Bi$
B. $^{222}_{86}Rn$
C. $^{214}_{82}Pb$
D. $^{214}_{83}Bi$
E. $^{212}_{85}At$

72. Which of the following lists the types of radiation in the correct order of increasing penetrating power?

A. α, γ, β
B. β, α, γ
C. α, β, γ
D. β, γ, α
E. γ, β, α

73. Which of the following statements are correct concerning β particles?

    I.   They have a mass number of zero and a charge of −1.

    II.   They are electrons.

    III. They are less penetrating than α particles.

    A. I and II
    B. I and III
    C. II and III
    D. I only
    E. II only

74. If 75% of a sample of pure ^3_1H decays in 24.6 yr, what is the half-life of ^3_1H?

    A. 24.6 yr
    B. 18.4 yr
    C. 12.3 yr
    D. 6.15 yr
    E. 3.07 yr

75. Alkenes are hydrocarbons with the general formula C_nH_{2n}. If a 0.453 g sample of any alkene is combusted in excess oxygen, how many moles of water will form?

    A. 0.0648
    B. 0.452
    C. 0.0133
    D. 0.324
    E. 0.0324

END OF SECTION I

AP CHEMISTRY

Section II

Time—1 hour and 30 minutes

Directions: Answer the following questions in the time allowed. You may use the equation/symbol pages, the list of reduction potentials, and a periodic table while taking this exam. Write the answers on a separate sheet of paper.

Part A. Time — 40 minutes

You may use a calculator for part A.

Question 1.

Compound	K_{sp}
$Cr(OH)_2$	1.0×10^{-17}
$Cr(OH)_3$	6.3×10^{-31}
$Fe(OH)_2$	7.9×10^{-16}
$Pb(OH)_2$	1.1×10^{-20}
$Mg(OH)_2$	6.0×10^{-10}
$Mn(OH)_2$	1.9×10^{-13}
$Sn(OH)_2$	6.3×10^{-27}

Use the K_{sp} data given above to answer the following questions.

a. Excess manganese(II) hydroxide, $Mn(OH)_2$, is added to 100.0 mL of deionized water. What is the pH of the solution?
b. A solution that is 0.10 M in Mg^{2+} and 0.10 M in Fe^{2+} is slowly made basic. What is the concentration of Fe^{2+} when Mg^{2+} begins to precipitate?
c. Two beakers are filled with water. Excess chromium(III) hydroxide is added to one and excess tin(II) hydroxide is added to the other. Which beaker has the higher concentration of metal ions? Calculate the concentration of metal ion in each beaker to support your prediction.
d. Chromium(III) hydroxide, $Cr(OH)_3$, is less soluble than chromium(II) hydroxide, $Cr(OH)_2$. Explain.
e. Calculate the grams of lead(II) hydroxide, $Pb(OH)_2$, that will dissolve in 1.00 L of water.

Answer either question 2 or question 3.

Question 2.

$$2 PCl_3(g) + O_2(g) \rightarrow 2 POCl_3(g)$$

Thermodynamic values related to the above reaction are given in the table below.

Substance	ΔH_f° (kJ/mol)	S° (J/mol K)	Bonds	Bond energies (kJ/mol)
$PCl_3(g)$	−287	312	P–Cl	331
$O_2(g)$	0	205.0	O=O	498
$POCl_3(g)$	−542.2	325	O–O	204

a. Determine the enthalpy change for the above reaction.
b. Estimate the PO bond energy.
c. Is the PO bond a single or a double bond? Justify your answer.
d. Calculate the entropy change for the reaction.
e. Is this reaction spontaneous or nonspontaneous at 25° C? Justify your prediction.

Question 3.

The following materials are made available for the determination of the molar mass of an unknown nonvolatile solid.

analytical balance   thermometer   beaker   support stand and clamp
test tube   stopwatch   hot plate

Phenol (melting point = 43° C and K_f = 7.40° C/m) is available as the solvent. The unknown behaves as a nonelectrolyte in phenol.

a. Plot a cooling curve for phenol on the axes below, and plot the cooling curve for a solution of the unknown in phenol.

Pure Phenol: Solution:

43° C   43° C

Time   Time

b. What information must be obtained from the two graphs in order to calculate the molar mass?
c. What additional information is needed to determine the molar mass of the unknown solid?
d. Show how the above information may be used to calculate the molar mass of the unknown solid.

Part B. Time — 50 minutes

You may not use a calculator for part B.

Question 4.

Choose FIVE of the following eight questions. Place your answers in the appropriate boxes. There is no extra credit for answering more than five. Formulas for reactants and products are needed. Do not include formulas for substances that remain unchanged during the reaction. It is not necessary to balance the equations. Unless otherwise noted, assume all the reactions occur in aqueous solution. If a substance is present as ions in solution, write its formula as an ion.

Example: Hydrochloric acid is added to a lead(II) nitrate solution.

$$Pb^{2+} + Cl^- \rightarrow PbCl_2$$

a. An acidified potassium permanganate solution is added to an iron(II) sulfate solution.
b. Excess potassium cyanide is added to an iron(III) nitrate solution.
c. Concentrated hydrobromic acid is added to a potassium nitrite solution.
d. A clean magnesium strip is immersed in a copper(II) sulfate solution.
e. Dinitrogen pentoxide is mixed with water.
f. Concentrated hydrochloric acid is added to manganese(IV) oxide.
g. Chlorine gas is bubbled through a solution of calcium iodide.
h. An iron(III) nitrate solution is made basic with potassium hydroxide.

Question 5.

Five beakers are placed in a row on a countertop. Each beaker is half filled with a 0.20 M aqueous solution. The solutes, in order, are: (1) potassium sulfate, (2) methyl alcohol, (3) sodium carbonate, (4) ammonium chromate, and (5) barium chloride. The solutions are all at 25° C.

Answer the following questions with respect to the five solutions listed above.

a. Which solution will form a precipitate when ammonium chromate is added to it? Give the formula of the precipitate.
b. Which solution is the most basic? Explain.
c. Which solution will exhibit the lowest boiling point elevation? Explain.
d. Which solution is colored?
e. Which solution will not react with solution (5) barium chloride?

Question 6.

A sample of a solid, weak monoprotic acid, HA, is supplied along with standard sodium hydroxide solution.

The sodium hydroxide solution was standardized with potassium hydrogen phthalate (KHP).

a. List the apparatus required to titrate an HA solution.
b. Sketch a pH versus volume of base added curve for the titration.
c. Sketch the titration curve if the unknown acid was really a diprotic acid.
d. Describe the steps required to determine the molar mass of HA.
e. How would the molar mass of HA be changed if the KHP contained an inert impurity?

Answer either question 7 or question 8.

Question 7.

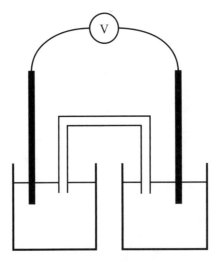

V = voltmeter

The above galvanic cell is constructed with a cadmium electrode in a 1.0 M $Cd(NO_3)_2$ solution in the left compartment and a silver electrode in a 1.0 M $AgNO_3$ in the right compartment. The salt bridge contains a KNO_3 solution. The cell voltage is positive.

a. What is the balanced net-ionic equation for the reaction, and what is the cell potential?
b. Show how to calculate the equilibrium constant for the cell.

c. Write the expression for Q that would be needed in the Nernst equation. Explain why any substances from the net-ionic equation do not appear in Q.
d. Show how to calculate the free energy for the reaction.
e. Identify the anode, the cathode, the oxidizing agent, and the reducing agent.

Question 8.

Relate each of the following to atomic properties and the principles of bonding.

a. The ionization energy of nitrogen atoms is higher than expected.
b. Draw the Lewis electron-dot structures for CO_2 and CO. Explain the polarity of these compounds.
c. The compound C_2H_3F is polar, but compounds with the general formula $C_2H_2F_2$ are sometimes polar and sometimes nonpolar. Show the structures and explain.
d. There are two isomers with the formula C_2H_6O. One of the isomers is more soluble in water than the other. Use the structures of these two compounds to explain the difference in solubility.
e. Why does SiF_4 react with fluoride ion, and CF_4 not react?

END OF SECTION II

ANSWERS TO MULTIPLE-CHOICE QUESTIONS

Answer Key

1. C	20. A	39. B	58. E
2. B	21. C	40. D	59. C
3. A	22. C	41. B	60. A
4. E	23. D	42. D	61. A
5. D	24. B	43. D	62. C
6. C	25. D	44. C	63. B
7. D	26. A	45. D	64. E
8. D	27. B	46. A	65. D
9. B	28. D	47. C	66. C
10. C	29. A	48. B	67. D
11. B	30. A	49. B	68. B
12. D	31. D	50. E	69. A
13. A	32. E	51. A	70. C
14. B	33. D	52. C	71. D
15. E	34. D	53. C	72. C
16. D	35. C	54. C	73. A
17. A	36. A	55. A	74. C
18. B	37. E	56. E	75. E
19. C	38. D	57. C	

Explanations of Answers to the Multiple-Choice Questions

1. **C.** This is the only one that has a pair of electrons to donate.

2. **B.** All can behave as Brønsted bases. Only B cannot behave as an acid.

3. **A.** This is the definition of a Lewis base.

4. **E.** The buret should be rinsed with titrant, not water.

5. **D.** The others are normally monatomic anions.

6. **C.** Increasing sizes indicate decreasing charge, lower position in a column on the periodic table, or position to the left in a period on the periodic table.

7. **D.** The element furthest away from F.

8. **D.** Hexammine = $(NH_3)_6$; chromium(III) = Cr^{3+}; chloride = Cl^-

9. **B.** $2\ Fe(OH)_3(s) + 3\ H_2SeO_4(aq) \rightarrow Fe_2(SeO_4)_3(s) + 6\ H_2O(l)$

10. **C.** The soluble compounds should be separated and the spectator ions eliminated.

11. **B.** Magnesium nitride does form.

12. **D.** Some of the nickel remains, the sodium does not change, and two nitrates are formed per nickel(II) nitrate.

13. **A.** The reactions are: $NH_4^+ + OH^- \rightarrow NH_3 + H_2O$ and $Ba^+ + SO_4^{2-} \rightarrow BaSO_4$

14. **B.** Percentages: (A) 77.8; (B) 69.6; (C) 72.0; (D) 63.2; (E) 49.5

15. **E.** Percentage of water: (A) 11; (B) 20; (C) 43; (D) 50; (E) 56

16. **D.** Nitric acid is the limiting reagent.

17. **A.** $(2.21\ g)(1\ mol/442\ g)(3\ mol\ O_2/2\ mol) = 7.50 \times 10^{-3}\ mol$

18. **B.** $4\ C_4H_{11}N(l) + 27\ O_2(g) \rightarrow 16\ CO_2(g) + 22\ H_2O(l) + 2\ N_2(g)$

19. **C.** Sulfuric acid is the limiting reagent.

20. **A.** $(1.0\ mol\ KClO_3)(3\ mol\ O_2/2\ mol\ KClO_3) = 1.5\ mol$

21. **C.** $(0.100\ mol\ Sr)(1\ mol\ H_2/1\ mol\ Sr)(22.4\ L/mol) = 2.24\ L$

22. **C.** The average velocity is related to temperature.

23. **D.** Water, whenever present, will contribute its vapor pressure.

24. **B.** $T_2 = (V_2T_1)/V_1 = (15.00\ L \times 400\ K)/(6.00\ L) - 273 = 727°C$

25. **D.** Small and nonpolar

26. **A.** Definition

27. **B.** Definition

28. **D.** Definition

29. **A.**

$\frac{1}{2}[2\ ClF(g) + O_2(g) \rightarrow Cl_2O(g) + OF_2(g)]$	$\frac{1}{2}(167.5\ kJ)$
$\frac{1}{2}[2\ F_2(g) + O_2(g) \rightarrow 2\ OF_2(g)]$	$\frac{1}{2}(-43.5\ kJ)$
$\frac{1}{2}[Cl_2O(g) + 3\ OF_2(g) \rightarrow 2\ ClF_3(l) + 2\ O_2(g)]$	$-\frac{1}{2}(394.1\ kJ)$
$ClF(g) + F_2(g) \rightarrow ClF_3(l)$	$-135.1\ kJ$

30. **A.** Exothermic processes shift toward the starting materials when heated.

31. **D.** Definition

32. **E.** Subtract the heat of vaporization from the original value.

33. **D.** Ni^{2+} has 26 electrons. The first electrons to leave are the 4s electrons.

34. **D.** This describes one of the 4s electrons.

35. **C.** Diffraction is a wave phenomenon.

36. **A.** Definition

37. **E.** Electrons fill the orbitals individually before pairing. Unpaired electrons = paramagnetic.

38. **D.** Definition

39. **B.** X is F and forms a −1 ion. Magnesium forms a +2 ion.

40. **D.** BF_3 has three electron pairs around the B.

41. **B.** Using VSEPR, all the others are nonpolar.

42. **D.** Ionic bonding needs a metal and a nonmetal (usually). Only the acetate ion has resonating bonds (σ and π).

43. **D.** All the others have no unshared electron pairs.

44. **C.** Sublimation usually does not involve bond breaking. In any case, Zn is a metal, and it has no ionic or covalent bonds to break.

45. **D.** Both diamond and graphite are covalent network solids.

46. **A.** This is a description of metallic bonding.

47. **C.** This is a description of ionic bonding.

48. **B.** SO_2 consists of polar molecules.

49. **B.** Definition

50. **E.** This will increase the pressure and, therefore, the boiling point.

51. **A.** This is the only point on the liquid–gas transition line.

52. **C.** (0.7000 L)(3.0 mol/L)(3 cations/mol) + (0.3000 L)(2.0 mol)(2 cations/mol)

53. **C.** (0.800 L)(0.90 mol Na^+/L)–(0.800 L)(0.30 mol/L)(2 Na^+/mol)
    $$= 0.24 \text{ mol } Na^+ \text{ needed}$$

    $$(0.24 \text{ mol } Na^+)(1 \text{ mol } Na_3PO_4/3 \text{ mol } Na^+) = 0.080 \text{ mol } Na_3PO_4$$

54. **C.** Equimolar gives a mole fraction of 0.5.

    $$0.5 \times 480 \text{ mm Hg} + 0.5 \times 50 \text{ mm Hg} = 265 \text{ mm Hg (total vapor pressure)}$$

    $$\text{mole fraction ethyl ether} = (0.5 \times 480 \text{ mm Hg})/265 \text{ mm Hg}$$

55. **A.** $V_{con} = M_{dil}V_{dil}/M_{con} = (3.0 \text{ M} \times 250 \text{ mL})/7.0 \text{ M}$

56. **E.** This plot only gives a straight-line for a first-order reaction.

57. **C.** $t_{1/2} = (0.693/86 \text{ h}^-)(3600 \text{ s/h}) = 29$ s. The time is equivalent to two half-lives, so one-fourth of the sample should remain.

58. **E.** Energy is required to initiate the reaction.

59. **C.** The pK_a for $H_2PO_4^-$ is nearest to the pH value needed. Thus, the simplest buffer would involve this ion. The phosphoric acid in E would lower the pH too much.

60. **A.** $K_a = [H^+][A^-]/[HA]$ $[H^+] = [A^-] = 1.0 \times 10^{-2}$ $[HA] = 0.6$

61. **A.** LiOH is a strong base.

62. **C.** A solution of a weak acid and a weak base would be nearly neutral.

63. **B.** Only B and E are buffers. B is basic, and E is acidic.

64. **E.** Only B and E are buffers. B is basic, and E is acidic.

65. **D.** If there are equal numbers of moles of gas on each side of the equilibrium arrow, then volume or pressure changes will not affect the equilibrium.

66. **C.** HCO_3^- behaves as an acid.

67. **D.** The loss of 0.20 mol of CO means that 0.40 mol of H_2 reacted (leaving 0.30 mol) and 0.20 mol of CH_3OH formed. Dividing all the moles by the volume gives the molarity, and:

    $$K_c = (0.20)/(0.40)(0.30)^2 = 5.6$$

68. **B.** $H_2O(l) + 2 CrO_4^{2-}(aq) + 3 HSnO_2^-(aq) \rightarrow$
    $$2 CrO_2^-(aq) + 2 OH^-(aq) + 3 HSnO_3^-(aq)$$

69. **A.** Assigning oxidation numbers and definitions are required.

70. **C.** Hydrogen (odorless) evolves at the cathode, and chlorine (distinctive odor) evolves at the anode.

71. **D.** The mass should be $226 - (4 + 4 + 0 + 4) = 214$. The atomic number should be $88 - (2 + 2 - 1 + 2) = 83$.

72. **C.** Alpha particles are the least penetrating, and gamma rays are the most penetrating.

73. **A.** In nuclear reactions, the mass of a β particle is treated as 0 and a charge of -1. Electrons and β particles are the same.

74. **C.** After one half-life, 50% would remain. After another half-life, this would be reduced by one-half to 25%. The total amount decayed is 75%. Thus, 24.6 years must be two half-lives of 12.3 years each.

75. **E.**

Scoring the Multiple-Choice Questions

Count the answers you got correct. Then count the answers you got wrong (skip those you did not answer). Multiply the number of wrong answers by 0.25 and subtract this value for the number of correct answers. This gives you your score on this set of questions.

ANSWERS, EXPLANATIONS, AND SCORING FOR FREE-RESPONSE QUESTIONS

Question 1.

a. The volume of the solution is irrelevant. The equilibrium $Mn(OH)_2(s) \rightleftharpoons Mn^{2+}(aq) + 2\ OH^-(aq)$ is important. The mass action expression for this equilibrium is: $K_{sp} = [Mn^{2+}][OH^-]^2 = 1.9 \times 10^{-13}$. Setting $[Mn^{2+}] = x$ and $[OH^-] = 2x$, and plugging into the mass action expression gives: $(x)(2x)^2 = 4x^3 = 1.9 \times 10^{-13}$. Solving for x gives $x = 3.6 \times 10^{-5}$, and $[OH^-] = 2x = 7.2 \times 10^{-5}$.

You get 1 point for the correct $[OH^-]$.
    There are two common ways to finish the problem. You do not need to show both.

    (i) $pOH = -\log [OH^-] = -\log 7.5 \times 10^{-5} = 4.14$
         $pH = 14.00 - pOH = 14.00 - 4.14 = 9.86$
    (ii) $[H^+] = K_w / [OH^-] = 1.0 \times 10^{-14} / 7.5 \times 10^{-5} = 1.4 \times 10^{-10}$
         $pH = -\log [H^+] = -\log 1.4 \times 10^{-10} = 9.86$

You get 1 point for the correct pH. If you got the wrong $[OH^-]$ value, but used it correctly, you still get 1 point.

b. The important equilibria are: $M(OH)_2(s) \rightleftharpoons M^{2+}(aq) + 2\ OH^-(aq)$, where $M = Mg$ or Fe. It is necessary to determine the hydroxide ion concentration when the iron begins to precipitate.

$$K_{sp} = [Mg^{2+}][OH^-]^2 = 6.0 \times 10^{-10}$$

$$[OH^-]^2 = K_{sp}/[Mg^{2+}] = 6.0 \times 10^{-10}/0.10 = 6.0 \times 10^{-9}$$

$$[OH^-] = 7.7 \times 10^{-5}$$

Using this value with the magnesium equilibrium gives:

$$K_{sp} = [Fe^{2+}][OH^-]^2 = 7.9 \times 10^{-16}$$

$$[Fe^{2+}] = K_{sp}/[OH^-]^2 = (7.9 \times 10^{-16})/(7.7 \times 10^{-5})^2 = 1.3 \times 10^{-7} \text{ M}$$

You get 1 point for the correct $[OH^-]$ and 1 point for the correct $[Fe^{2+}]$. Alternately, you get 1 point if you did only part of the procedure correctly. There is a maximum of 2 points for this part.

c. Using the appropriate mass action expressions:

$$K_{sp} = [Sn^{2+}][OH^-]^2 = 6.3 \times 10^{-27}$$
$$[Sn^{2+}] = x \text{ and } [OH^-]^2 = 2x$$
$$(x)(2x)^2 = 4x^3 = 6.3 \times 10^{-27}$$

$$x = 1.2 \times 10^{-9} \text{ M} = [Sn^{2+}]$$

$$K_{sp} = [Cr^{3+}][OH^-]^3 = 6.3 \times 10^{-31}$$
$$[Cr^{3+}] = x \text{ and } [OH^-] = 3x$$
$$(x)(3x)^3 = 27x^4 = 6.3 \times 10^{-31}$$

$$x = 1.2 \times 10^{-8} \text{ M} = [Cr^{3+}]$$

The tin(II) hydroxide beaker has the lower metal ion concentration.
    You get 1 point for the correct beaker. You also get 1 point for each metal ion concentration you got correct. Your answers do not need to match exactly, but they should round to the same value.

d. The higher the charge on the cation, the less soluble a substance is.

You get 1 point for this answer.

e. The mass action expression is:

$$K_{sp} = [Pb^{2+}][OH^-]^2 = 1.1 \times 10^{-20}$$
$$[Pb^{2+}] = x \text{ and } [OH^-] = 2x$$
$$(x)(2x)^2 = 4x^3 = 1.1 \times 10^{-20}$$

$$x = 1.4 \times 10^{-7} \text{ M}$$

$$(1.4 \times 10^{-7} \text{ mol/L})(1.00 \text{ L})(241.2 \text{ g/mol}) = 3.4 \times 10^{-5} \text{ g}$$

You get 1 point for the correct answer (or an answer that rounds to this answer). You get 1 point for the setup.

Total your points for the different parts. There is a maximum of 10 points possible.

Question 2.

a. $\Delta H_{rxn}° = [2(-542.2)] - [2(-287) + 1(0)] = -510. \text{ kJ}$

The setup (products − reactants) is worth 1 point, and the answer is worth 1 point. You do not need to get the exact answer, but your answer should round to this one.

b. The answer from part a equals the bonds broken minus the bonds formed. Both phosphorus molecules have three P–Cl bonds, and O_2 has an O=O bond.

$$[(2 \times 3 \times 331) + (498)] - [(2 \text{ PO}) + (2 \times 3 \times 331)] = -510. \text{ kJ}$$

$$\text{PO} = 504 \text{ kJ}$$

The setup (broken – formed) is worth 1 point, and the answer is worth 1 point. You do not need to get the exact answer, but your answer should round to this one.

c. It is a double bond. The value from part b is much higher than the single bond values from the table.

You get 1 point for the correct prediction, and 1 point for the explanation. If you got the wrong answer for part b, you can still get 1 or 2 points if you used the answer correctly on this part.

d. $\Delta S_{rxn}° = [2(325)] - [2(312) + 1(205.0)] = -179 \text{ J/K}$

The setup (products – reactants) is worth 1 point, and the answer is worth 1 point. You do not need to get the exact answer, but your answer should round to this one.

e. The free energy change must be calculated.

$$\Delta G_{rxn}° = \Delta H_{rxn}° - T\Delta S_{rxn}° = -510. \text{ kJ} - (298 \text{ K})(1 \text{ kJ/1000 J})(-179 \text{ J/K}) = -457 \text{ kJ}$$

The negative value means the reaction is spontaneous.

You get 1 point for the prediction that the reaction is spontaneous. The setup (plugging into the equation) is worth 1 point if you remember to change the temperature to Kelvin and the joule to kilojoule conversion. An additional 1 point comes from the answer. If you got the wrong value in either part a or b, but used it correctly, you will still get the point for the answer. The free energy equation is part of the material supplied in the exam booklet.

Question 3.

a.

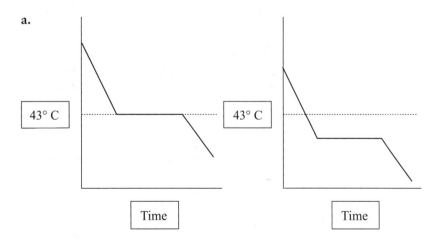

You get 1 point for the first plot. You get 1 point for the second plot only if the level region is definitely below 43° C.

b. The difference in the temperatures of the two level regions (ΔT) is needed.

You get 1 point for this answer.

c. The mass (in grams) of the unknown solid and the mass (in kilograms) of the phenol are required.

You get 1 point for each of these answers.

d. The required equation is: $\Delta T = K_f m$

Calculate the molality of the solution by dividing the change in temperature (ΔT) by the freezing point depression constant (K_f).
   Calculate the moles of the unknown by multiplying the molality of the solution by the kilograms of phenol.
   Calculate the molar mass by dividing the grams of the unknown by the moles of the unknown.
   You get 1 point for each correct calculation you listed.

Total your points. There are 8 possible points.

Question 4.

Only the five answers will be graded. If you do more than five, only the first five will be graded. No extra points will be given for doing more than five. There are no extra points for balancing.

a. $H^+ + MnO_4^- + Fe^{2+} \rightarrow Fe^{3+} + Mn^{2+} + H_2O$

You get 1 point for the correct formulas for the reactants and 2 points for the correct formulas for the products. No variations are allowed.

b. $CN^- + Fe^{3+} \rightarrow [Fe(CN)_6]^{3-}$

You get 1 point for the correct formulas for the reactants and 2 points for the correct formula for the product. No variations are allowed.

c. $H^+ + NO_2^- \rightarrow HNO_2$

You get 1 point for the correct formulas for the reactants and 2 points for the correct formula for the product. No variations are allowed.

d. $Mg + Cu^{2+} \rightarrow Mg^{2+} + Cu$

You get 1 point for the correct formulas for the reactants and 2 points for the correct formulas for the products. No variations are allowed.

e. $N_2O_5 + H_2O \rightarrow HNO_3$

You get 1 point for the correct formulas for the reactants and 2 points for the correct formulas for the products. No variations are allowed.

f. $H^+ + Cl^- + MnO_2 \rightarrow Cl_2 + Mn^{2+} + H_2O$

You get 1 point for the correct formulas for the reactants and 2 points for the correct formulas for the products. No variations are allowed.

g. $Cl_2 + I^- \rightarrow Cl^- + I_2$

You get 1 point for the correct formulas for the reactants and 2 points for the correct formulas for the products. No variations are allowed.

h. $Fe^{3+} + OH^- \rightarrow Fe(OH)_3$

You get 1 point for the correct formulas for the reactants and 2 points for the correct formula for the product. No variations are allowed.

Question 5.

a. Solution (5) barium chloride will give a precipitate. The formula of the precipitate is $BaCrO_4$.

You get 1 point for picking the correct solution, and 1 point for the correct formula for the precipitate.

b. Solution (3) sodium carbonate is the most basic. Since the carbonate ion is the conjugate base of a weak acid, it will undergo significant hydrolysis to produce a basic solution.

You get 1 point for picking the correct solution, and 1 point for the correct formula for the explanation.

c. Solution (2) methyl alcohol will show the least boiling point elevation. Methyl alcohol is the only nonelectrolyte.

You get 1 point for picking the correct solution, and 1 point for the correct formula for the explanation.

d. Solution (4) ammonium chromate is yellow.

You get 1 point for picking the correct solution.

e. Solution (2) methyl alcohol is the only solution that will not form a precipitate with barium chloride.

You get 1 point for picking the correct solution.

Question 6.

a.
*analytical balance	*buret	clamp
desiccator	drying oven	*Erlenmeyer flask
pH meter	pipette	support stand
wash bottle		

You get 1 point if you have ALL the starred items. You get 1 point for the other items. There is a maximum of 2 points. If you only have some of the starred items, your maximum is 1 point.

b.

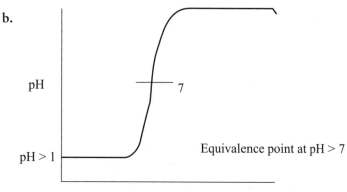

You get 1 point for this graph. You get 1 point for noting that the equivalence point is greater than 7.

c.

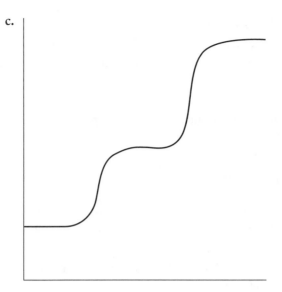

You get 1 point for this graph. You must show two regions.

d. 1. Weigh a sample of HA.
   2. Titrate HA versus standard NaOH to find the volume of NaOH solution required to neutralize the acid.
   3. Multiply the concentration of the NaOH solution times the volume used to get the moles of NaOH.
   4. The moles of HA is the same as the moles of NaOH.
   5. Divide the mass of HA by the moles of HA.

   You get 2 points if you list all five steps. If you miss one or more steps you only get 1 point. You get 0 points if you get none of the steps correct. There are no bonus points for more steps or more details.

e. If the KHP contained an inert impurity, the concentration of the NaOH solution would be too low. If the concentration of the NaOH solution is low, then more solution would be needed for the titration of HA. This would yield a lower number of moles of HA, giving a higher molar mass.

   You get 1 point for the NaOH concentration being low. You get 1 point for predicting a higher molar mass. If you incorrectly predicted the NaOH concentration to be too high, you can get 1 point if you predicted a lower molar mass.

Total your points. There is a maximum of 9 possible points.

Question 7.

a. The following reduction half-reactions are provided on the AP exam:

$$Cd^{2+} + 2\ e^- \rightarrow Cd \qquad E° = -0.40\ V$$

$$Ag^+ + 1\ e^- \rightarrow Ag \qquad E° = +0.80\ V$$

The first reaction needs to be reversed, the silver half-reaction needs to be doubled, and the reactions and voltages added.

$$Cd \rightarrow Cd^{2+} + 2 \, e^- \qquad\qquad\qquad E° = +0.40 \text{ V}$$

$$2(Ag^+ + 1 \, e^- \rightarrow Ag) \qquad\qquad E° = +0.80 \text{ V}$$

$$2 \, Ag^+ + Cd \rightarrow Cd^{2+} + 2 \, Ag \qquad E° = +1.20 \text{ V}$$

You get 1 point for the correct equation. You also get 1 point for the correct cell voltage.

b. Use the equation $\log K = nE°/0.0592$ (This equation is given on the AP exam.)

$$\log K = (2 \times 1.20)/0.0592$$

You get 1 point for plugging the values into the correct equation. You get the point even if you plugged in a wrong answer for $E°$ from part a. The question does not ask you to do any calculations, thus, there are no points for showing any work beyond what is shown.

c. $Q = [Cd^{2+}]/[Ag^+]^2$ This answer is worth 1 point.

The remaining substances (Cd and Ag) are solids. Solids do not appear in Q expressions.

You get 1 point for the explanation.

d. Use the equation $\Delta G° = -nFE°$ (This equation is given on the AP exam.)

$$\Delta G° = -nFE° = -(2)(96500)(1.20)$$

You get 1 point for plugging the values into the correct equation. The question does not ask you to do any calculations, thus, there are no points for showing any work beyond what is shown.

e.
Anode   Cd
Cathode   Ag
Oxidizing Agent Ag^+
Reducing Agent Cd^{2+}

You get 1 point for each correctly identified item.

Total your points. There are 10 possible points.

Question 8.

a. Nitrogen atoms have a half-filled set of p-orbitals. Half-filled sets of orbitals have an increased stability.

You get 1 point for this answer.

b. :Ö::C::Ö: :C:::O:

CO_2 is linear and nonpolar. The different electronegativities of C and O make CO polar.

You get 1 point for each correct Lewis structure and 1 point if you explain both polarities correctly. There is a maximum of 3 points.

You may use a double line between the C and each of the O's in CO_2, and a triple line between the C and O in CO.

c. There is one compound with the formula C_2H_3F, and there are three compounds with the formula $C_2H_2F_2$. The structures are:

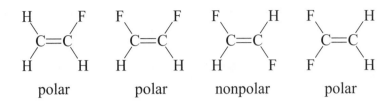

| polar | polar | nonpolar | polar |

The fluorines are the most electronegative atoms present, and the bonds to them are polar covalent. The only nonpolar compound is the result of the polar C–F bonds pulling equally in opposite directions.

You get 1 point for ALL the structures, and 1 point for a correct explanation. There is a maximum of 2 points.

d. The structures are: CH_3–O–CH_3 and CH_3CH_2OH.

The first compound (dimethyl ether) is polar, but not as soluble in water as the second compound (ethanol) which is capable of hydrogen bonding to water.

You get 1 point if you show both structures, and you get 1 point for a correct explanation. The names shown in parentheses are not required.

e. Silicon tetrafluoride is capable of reacting with the fluoride ion (to produce SiF_6^{2-}) because silicon can expand its octet. Carbon tetrafluoride does not react because carbon cannot expand its octet.

An alternate explanation would be that silicon has d orbitals available for reacting and carbon does not.

You get 1 point for either explanation.

Total your points for the problem. There is a maximum of 9 possible points.

Scoring the Free-Response Questions

TOTAL SCORE:

Question 1   _____

Question 2 or 3   _____

Question 4   _____

Question 5   _____

Question 6   _____

Question 7 or 8   _____

Chapter 9

AP Psychology

Answer Sheet for Multiple-Choice Questions

1. _____
2. _____
3. _____
4. _____
5. _____
6. _____
7. _____
8. _____
9. _____
10. _____
11. _____
12. _____
13. _____
14. _____
15. _____
16. _____
17. _____
18. _____
19. _____
20. _____
21. _____
22. _____
23. _____
24. _____
25. _____

26. _____
27. _____
28. _____
29. _____
30. _____
31. _____
32. _____
33. _____
34. _____
35. _____
36. _____
37. _____
38. _____
39. _____
40. _____
41. _____
42. _____
43. _____
44. _____
45. _____
46. _____
47. _____
48. _____
49. _____
50. _____

51. _____
52. _____
53. _____
54. _____
55. _____
56. _____
57. _____
58. _____
59. _____
60. _____
61. _____
62. _____
63. _____
64. _____
65. _____
66. _____
67. _____
68. _____
69. _____
70. _____
71. _____
72. _____
73. _____
74. _____
75. _____

76. _____
77. _____
78. _____
79. _____
80. _____
81. _____
82. _____
83. _____
84. _____
85. _____
86. _____
87. _____
88. _____
89. _____
90. _____
91. _____
92. _____
93. _____
94. _____
95. _____
96. _____
97. _____
98. _____
99. _____
100. _____

AP PSYCHOLOGY

Section I

Time—70 minutes

100 questions

Directions: Each of the questions or incomplete statements below is followed by five suggested answers or completions. Select the one that is best in each case and write your answer neatly on the answer sheet.

1. Which of the following would play a role in quickly alerting you to a gas leak in your car?

   A. olfactory receptors
   B. gustatory receptors
   C. feature detectors
   D. basilar membrane
   E. pacinian corpuscles

2. A population frequently studied to best assess the relative effects of nature vs. nurture is

   A. identical twins
   B. identical quadruplets
   C. adopted children and their adoptive parents
   D. couples who have been married for many years
   E. families with genetic diseases

3. After watching cartoons in which characters hit, punch, and kick other characters, nursery school students engage in more aggressive behavior than after watching *Barney*. This observation best supports

   A. psychoanalytic theory
   B. psychodynamic theory
   C. social learning theory
   D. humanistic theory
   E. opponent process theory

4. The smallest unit of language that carries meaning is a

   A. concept
   B. word
   C. phoneme
   D. morpheme
   E. grammar

5. Nat's therapist tells him to relax, close his eyes, and breathe slowly whenever he begins to experience fear associated with being in an enclosed space. The therapist is using a technique that is central to

   A. person-centered therapy
   B. psychoanalysis
   C. rational–emotive therapy
   D. Gestalt therapy
   E. systematic desensitization

6. Which of the following perspectives is most concerned with self-esteem and actualizing one's potential?

   A. humanistic
   B. behavioral
   C. cognitive
   D. psychodynamic
   E. sociocultural

7. A therapist used the Rorschach inkblot test to help him analyze his patient's problems. He was most likely a

   A. psychoanalyst
   B. person-centered therapist
   C. behavioral psychologist
   D. certified clinical social worker
   E. psychiatrist

8. A pigeon trained to peck at a green light pecks at a yellow light also. This illustrates

   A. generalization
   B. discrimination
   C. extinction
   D. spontaneous recovery
   E. shaping

9. Who would most likely have said, "People are basically good"?

   A. Psychoanalyst Sigmund Freud
   B. Behaviorist B. F. Skinner
   C. Cognitivist Albert Ellis
   D. Humanist Carl Rogers
   E. Gestaltist Fritz Perls

10. More than half of the volume of the human brain is composed of the

   A. cerebral cortex
   B. septum, amygdala, hippocampus, and cingulate cortex
   C. medulla, pons, and cerebellum
   D. hypothalamus and thalamus
   E. olfactory bulbs, optic chiasma, pituitary gland, and reticular formation

11. Joey, a 25 year-old convict, has a history of conduct disorder in elementary school and bullying in junior high. By high school, he was mugging peers and taking whatever he wanted from elderly shoppers without caring if he hurt anyone. Joey is most likely suffering from

   A. antisocial personality disorder
   B. dissociative identity disorder
   C. paranoid schizophrenia
   D. somatoform disorder
   E. amnesia

12. Your little cousin watches you at the computer, and when you get up he immediately tries to use the keyboard. His behavior in this situation can best be explained on the basis of

   A. superstition
   B. classical conditioning
   C. operant aversive conditioning
   D. modeling
   E. discrimination

13. Although Andy wanted to cut class to get to the Yankee opener, he came to class to take a quiz and review for an exam. According to Freud, this behavior evidences a strong

   A. egocentricity
   B. super id
   C. id
   D. superego
   E. libido

14. An unjustifiable and usually negative attitude toward a group and its members is called

   A. prejudice
   B. ethnocentrism
   C. in-group bias
   D. discrimination
   E. scapegoating

15. Which approach emphasizes that therapists can effectively help their clients by offering unconditional positive regard?

   A. Gestalt therapy
   B. cognitive therapy
   C. humanistic therapy
   D. behavior modification
   E. psychoanalysis

16. Some groups of gang members wear head coverings and sunglasses when they assault people. The use of such disguises contributes to

   A. social loafing
   B. cognitive dissonance
   C. learned helplessness
   D. deindividuation
   E. the fundamental attribution error

17. Of the following, which is characteristic of formal operational thinking?

   A. simple motor responses to sensory stimuli
   B. failure to understand reversibility
   C. capacity to deal well with concrete objects, but not hypothetical situations
   D. logical reasoning and systematic planning
   E. magical thinking and egocentrism

18. Which neurotransmitter is most closely associated with both Parkinson's disease and schizophrenia?

   A. acetylcholine
   B. dopamine
   C. serotonin
   D. endorphins
   E. GABA

19. Today, it is unlikely that a psychologist could condition a baby to fear a rat and other small animals in a research study at a university because

   A. no parent would permit a child to participate in such a study

B. the study violates ethical guidelines
C. babies are too young to fear small animals
D. conditioning experiments are no longer done
E. fear of animals is inborn

20. According to Adler, first born children are more likely than subsequent children in a family to be

   A. sociable
   B. funny
   C. responsible
   D. followers
   E. liberal

21. Brenda gets enraged when people criticize her, talks about becoming the first woman president, exaggerates her abilities and talents, takes advantage of classmates, and constantly demands attention in class. When she received a certificate for participating in an essay contest, she told everyone she'd won a prestigious writing award. She most likely would be diagnosed as evidencing

   A. hypochondriasis
   B. disorganized schizophrenia
   C. antisocial personality disorder
   D. narcissistic personality disorder
   E. clinical depression

22. "Psychology is the science of behavior and mental processes" commonly defines psychology. In their definition of psychology, behaviorists would be likely to eliminate
   I. science
   II. behavior
   III. mental processes

      A. I only
      B. II only
      C. III only
      D. I and III only
      E. I, II, and III

23. According to Erikson, a young adult's developmental crisis centers around

   A. intimacy vs. isolation
   B. identity vs. role confusion
   C. autonomy vs. shame and guilt
   D. industry vs. inferiority
   E. generativity vs. stagnation

24. The perceived volume of a tone is mainly determined by its

   A. frequency
   B. timbre
   C. amplitude
   D. overtones
   E. saturation

25. Shannon forgot her pillow when she went camping, so she complained about having to sleep with her head flat the whole night. Her failure to fold up her jeans and sweater to use as a pillow-substitute best illustrates the effects of

   A. the availability heuristic
   B. functional fixedness
   C. confirmation bias
   D. the representativeness heuristic
   E. belief perseverance

26. According to Abraham Maslow, esteem needs must at least be partially met before one is prompted to satisfy

   A. belongingness needs
   B. physiological needs
   C. self actualization needs
   D. love needs
   E. safety needs

27. The most widely used self-report inventory for personality assessment is the

   A. MMPI-2
   B. TAT
   C. WAIS-R
   D. Rorschach
   E. PSAT

28. Behavioral therapy typically alters the patterns of responding of clients by

   A. helping patients identify a hierarchy of anxiety-arousing experiences
   B. vigorously challenging clients' illogical ways of thinking
   C. influencing patients by controlling the consequences of their actions
   D. repeating or rephrasing what a client says during the course of therapy
   E. focusing attention on clients' positive and negative feelings toward their therapists.

29. Scott tried to unscramble the letters NEBOTYA for 20 minutes to spell a word, but was not successful. While walking to class, the answer suddenly came to him that the word was BAYONET. This exemplifies

    A. classical conditioning
    B. operant conditioning
    C. the law of effect
    D. insight
    E. observational learning

30. A disorder characterized by delusions of persecution, hallucinations, and disordered thinking is

    A. paranoid schizophrenia
    B. anorexia nervosa
    C. conversion disorder
    D. hypochondriasis
    E. organic mental disorder

31. Jyoti notes the behavior of people as they wait in line for tickets to rock concerts. Which of the following research methods is she using?

    A. naturalistic observation
    B. survey
    C. controlled experiment
    D. quasi-experiment
    E. case study

32. In daylight, objects that reflect all wavelengths of light appear

    A. black
    B. white
    C. dull
    D. ultraviolet
    E. infrared

33. The Intelligence Quotient is defined as the

    A. chronological age/mental age × 100
    B. performance score/verbal score × 100
    C. mental age/chronological age × 100
    D. verbal score/performance score × 100
    E. range/standard deviation × 100

34. According to Elisabeth Kubler-Ross, the first reaction of a person faced with a terminal illness is

    A. acceptance
    B. anger
    C. bargaining
    D. denial
    E. depression

35. When Jared saw shadows of people on the walls of his bedroom, his blood pressure increased and his breathing rate sped up. These physical reactions were most directly regulated by his

    A. sensorimotor system
    B. somatic nervous system
    C. sympathetic nervous system
    D. pineal gland
    E. parasympathetic nervous system

36. Which psychoactive drugs are most frequently prescribed to relieve pain?

    A. stimulants
    B. depressants
    C. antidepressants
    D. antipsychotics
    E. narcotics

37. During the manic phase of a bipolar disorder, individuals are most likely to experience

    A. high self-esteem
    B. delusions of persecution
    C. uncontrollable grief and despair
    D. visual hallucinations
    E. extreme sleepiness

38. Dan read a list of 30 vocabulary words only once. If he is typical and shows the serial position effect, we would expect that the words he remembers two days later are

    A. at the beginning of the list
    B. in the middle of the list
    C. at the end of the list
    D. distributed throughout the list
    E. unpredictable

39. Tony got accepted to the college he wants to attend, is going to the prom with a girl he really admires, and was hired for the summer job he sought. He has high

    A. self-efficacy
    B. self-doubt
    C. self-handicapping
    D. introversion
    E. deindividuation

40. Species-specific behaviors that cannot be explained as a result of social learning or conditioning, such as Monarch butterflies flying to Mexico to mate, are called

    A. motives
    B. fixed-action patterns
    C. schemas
    D. imprinting
    E. reflexes

41. Tests that have been pre-tested with a sample of the population for whom the test is intended and have a uniform set of instructions and administration procedures are

    A. valid
    B. standardized
    C. reliable
    D. fair
    E. predictive

42. A famous character in a Shakespearean play keeps washing her hands to get them clean of blood that is no longer on them. The repeated washing of her hands is

    A. a delusion
    B. a compulsion
    C. a hallucination
    D. an obsession
    E. an attribution

43. After collecting and analyzing the responses of 2,000 randomly selected study participants, Adeel finds that college juniors who work at paying jobs 15 hours a week get higher grades than juniors who don't have paying jobs or who work full time. Which of the following research methods did Adeel use?

    A. experimental
    B. naturalistic observation
    C. case study
    D. survey
    E. quasi-experimental

44. Which of the following best exemplifies sensory adaptation?

    A. enjoying a song the more you hear it
    B. responding immediately every time the fire alarm is sounded
    C. not realizing how cold the pool is after you are under the water for a few minutes

    D. relying heavily on your hearing when you are walking down a dark corridor
    E. not knowing what other people at a cocktail party are saying while you are attending to one conversation

45. The Diagnostic and Statistical Manual of Mental Disorders (DSM-IV) published by the American Psychiatric Association provides information about all of the following EXCEPT

    A. names of mental disorders
    B. categorization of all mental disorders
    C. primary symptoms of all mental disorders
    D. secondary symptoms of all mental disorders
    E. causes of all mental disorders

46. Dieters often have difficulty losing additional weight after reaching a specific plateau because their bodies function at a lowered metabolic rate according to

    A. VMH theory
    B. opponent process theory
    C. set point theory
    D. the law of effect
    E. drive reduction theory

47. Which of the following scans can *image* brain function?
    I.   CAT
    II. MRI
    III. PET

    A. I only
    B. II only
    C. III only
    D. II and III only
    E. I, II, and III

48. If arrested for committing a crime, whom of the following would be most likely to be declared legally insane?

    A. Aaron, who suffers symptoms of disorganized schizophrenia
    B. Brett, who has been diagnosed with obsessive–compulsive disorder
    C. Clara, who suffers symptoms of zoophobia
    D. Don, who suffers symptoms of hypochondriasis
    E. Ed, who has been diagnosed with narcissistic personality disorder

49. During cooperative learning, all of the students in Group A initially were opposed to the death penalty, whereas two of the students in Group B were opposed to the death penalty and two were in favor of the death penalty. According to research, after an intense discussion within each group about capital punishment, we would expect

    A. both groups would moderate their positions.
    B. Group A would moderate their positions, but Group B would retain their original positions.
    C. Group A would become more firmly entrenched, while Group B members would moderate their positions.
    D. Group A would retain their original positions, but Group B would moderate their positions.
    E. both groups would have every member more firmly entrenched in their positions.

50. Wilder Penfield's studies suggest that some long-lost memories can be elicited through electrical stimulation of the brain. This suggests that forgetting may be a matter of

    A. displacement
    B. gradual decay
    C. retrieval failure
    D. failure to encode the memories
    E. unconscious wishes to forget

51. During World War II, millions of Jews and other minorities were slaughtered because they were blamed for the financial and social problems of Germany. Such scapegoating illustrates

    A. sour grapes rationalization
    B. displacement
    C. sweet lemons rationalization
    D. projection
    E. reaction formation

52. Of the following, which provides the most valid and reliable data about individuals as they progress through various stages of development?

    A. cross-sectional studies
    B. surveys
    C. transactional analysis
    D. longitudinal studies
    E. correlational studies

53. As the time for the AP Psychology exam approached, several students in the class who had not been doing homework or attending classes earlier in the term became more concerned about studying and attending regularly. Their motivation seems to be

    A. intrinsic
    B. extrinsic
    C. instinctive
    D. pessimistic
    E. homeostatic

54. A classically conditioned response can best be eliminated by presentation of

    A. the unconditional stimulus without the conditional stimulus
    B. the conditional stimulus without the unconditional stimulus
    C. a neutral stimulus
    D. conditional stimulus a few seconds before the unconditional stimulus
    E. unconditioned response

55. The scores of Brian's team on the quiz were: 8, 6, 9, 7, 10, 9, 5, 4, 9. The median of the team's scores is

    A. 9
    B. 8
    C. 7.5
    D. 7
    E. 6

56. What type of test is the Advanced Placement Examination in Psychology?

    A. aptitude
    B. projective
    C. achievement
    D. intelligence
    E. individual

57. Functionally, receptors in the retina of the eye differ most from receptors in the cochlea of the ear in the

    A. magnitude of the resting potentials of their membranes
    B. ions involved in their action potentials
    C. types of energy they transduce
    D. number of axons each cell possesses
    E. ability to reproduce

58. Irrelevant thoughts that provide stimulation when your interest is flagging, letting you experience positive emotions, are

    A. nonconscious
    B. unconscious
    C. daydreams
    D. delusions
    E. circadian

59. Which of the following contributes most directly to people's exaggerated perceptions of the likelihood of air travel disasters, nuclear power accidents, and terrorist violence?

    A. belief perseverance
    B. the framing effect
    C. overconfidence
    D. the representativeness heuristic
    E. the availability heuristic

60. According to Whorf's linguistic relativity hypothesis,

    A. we have an innate language acquisition device
    B. apes do not have language because they don't use proper syntax
    C. we tend to observe and imitate models
    D. language determines the way we think
    E. rewarding good behavior increases its frequency

61. A severely overweight rat would most likely result from lesioning of the

    A. hippocampus
    B. thalamus
    C. hypothalamus
    D. amygdala
    E. pineal gland

62. Maria, a bright high school student, fears success. To which of the following colleges would she most likely apply?

    A. Harvard, Stanford, and the local community college
    B. Stanford, Oxford, and the most competitive state college in her state
    C. the local community college and distant community colleges
    D. Harvard, Yale, and Stanford
    E. the most competitive state college in her state and in other states

63. A projective test with ambiguous pictures that are frequently used to assess achievement motivation is the

    A. Thematic Apperception Test
    B. Rorschach inkblot test
    C. WAIS-R
    D. MMPI-2
    E. Stanford-Binet

64. David collected data on 15 research participants. Their scores were: 42, 38, 14, 13, 12, 12, 11, 11, 11, 10, 10, 10, 9, 9, 9. Which of the following statistics best reflects the central tendency of this data set?

    A. standard deviation
    B. correlation coefficient
    C. mode
    D. median
    E. mean

65. The medical model of psychologically disordered behavior is most likely to be criticized for neglecting the importance of

    A. depression
    B. anxiety disorders
    C. neurotransmitters
    D. genetic abnormalities
    E. social circumstances

66. Which of the following explanations of why a 17-year-old drives his car at or below the speed limit best illustrates Kohlberg's conventional level of morality?

    A. "I don't want to get any tickets."
    B. "It's the law."
    C. "I want my parents to approve of my driving."
    D. "I don't want to crash my car."
    E. "With so many people in our society driving cars, I cannot put anyone else or myself in danger by driving at a faster speed than the number of cars, roads, and weather conditions permit."

67. The president of a company brought in an outside consultant to disagree with him about an important decision to be discussed at a meeting of his top level executives in order to avoid

    A. the bystander effect
    B. groupthink
    C. social loafing
    D. the mere exposure effect
    E. the fundamental attribution error

68. Javier wants to study the effects on achievement of taking a course in chemistry in the afternoon, rather than in the morning. A teacher has chemistry classes with the same number of students at 8:30 a.m. and 1:00 p.m., and volunteers to participate with her classes. A major problem in this study would be

    A. poor replication
    B. lack of a hypothesis
    C. confounding variables
    D. difficulty in obtaining informed consent
    E. the placebo effect

69. The heritability for traits of identical twins is

    A. 0
    B. 25
    C. 50
    D. 75
    E. 100

70. "Get cookie," best exemplifies

    A. babbling
    B. cooing
    C. holophrases
    D. telegraphic speech
    E. mental set

71. Research reveals that the most critical factor in Type A behavior associated with heart disease is

    A. anger
    B. competitiveness
    C. sense of time urgency
    D. conscientiousness
    E. motivation

72. Dr. Scarlett conducted experiments in which she electrically stimulates parts of a cat's brain. A cat that became terrified in the presence of a mouse was most likely stimulated in the

    A. limbic system
    B. thalamus
    C. medulla
    D. cerebellum
    E. temporal lobe

73. Which of the following LEAST influences sexual behavior?

    A. hypothalamus
    B. pituitary
    C. gonads
    D. cerebral cortex
    E. reticular formation

74. Ben thinks students will answer questions printed on yellow paper more quickly than those printed on blue paper. All study participants will take three tests with 35 multiple-choice questions each. The independent variable in Ben's experiment is

    A. the color of the paper
    B. the number of questions answered correctly
    C. how long it takes students to answer questions
    D. the total number of questions answered
    E. the difference in results between the experimental and control groups

75. Which of the following best illustrates hostile aggression?

    A. A man slaps his wife because he is angry that she made hamburgers for dinner again.
    B. A sanitation man knocks over some rose bushes when he throws an empty can to the curb.
    C. A waitress breaks several cups and saucers when she drops a tray on the floor.
    D. A careless driver hits and severely injures a pedestrian who is crossing the street.
    E. An adolescent hangs up on an irritating salesperson.

76. Cognitivists claim that classical conditioning results from

    A. an association between the unconditioned stimulus and the unconditioned response
    B. an association between the unconditioned stimulus and the conditioned stimulus
    C. an association between the conditioned stimulus and the unconditioned response
    D. an association between the conditioned stimulus and the conditioned response
    E. an expectation of what is coming following the conditioned stimulus

77. Which is likely to increase as a normal, healthy individual ages from 25 to 75 years of age?

    A. visual acuity
    B. crystallized intelligence

C. ability to reason speedily
D. fluid intelligence
E. intelligence quotient

78. In the rock opera "Tommy," Tommy becomes deaf and blind after witnessing a terrible murder, although there is nothing organically wrong with his ears or eyes. Tommy is suffering from

A. panic disorder
B. post-traumatic stress disorder
C. conversion disorder
D. obsessive–compulsive disorder
E. hypochondriasis

79. Which of the following are included in the peripheral nervous system?

A. brain, spinal cord, cranial nerves
B. cranial nerves, spinal nerves, autonomic ganglia
C. spinal cord, spinal nerves, sense organs
D. medulla, pons, thalamus
E. amygdala, hippocampus, hypothalamus

80. Loss of the ability to understand language results from loss of tissue in which of the following lobes?

A. right frontal
B. right temporal
C. right parietal
D. left frontal
E. left temporal

81. When a 17-year-old student is failing at school, which society would most likely hold the parents accountable?

A. United States of America
B. Canadian
C. Japanese
D. English
E. German

82. Receptors that respond to gravity and keep you informed of your body's location in space are located primarily in the

A. cochlea of the ear
B. macula of the eye
C. olfactory mucosa
D. muscles and joints of the skeleton
E. semicircular canals of the ear

83. Although Jen is a very bright four-year old, she doesn't think her mother's sister has any sisters. This lack of ability reflects

A. conservation
B. introspection
C. transposition
D. magical thinking
E. egocentrism

84. You are given four lists of words to learn: 1, 2, 3, 4. You must learn list 1, then list 2, etc. Which list(s) would cause proactive interference for remembering list 2?

A. list 1 only
B. list 3 only
C. list 4 only
D. lists 3 and 4 only
E. lists 1, 3, and 4

85. Dr. Ramchandran found that his patients who brushed their teeth after lunch had 1/20 the number of cavities in their teeth as those who didn't. After interviewing the dentist, a local news writer reports that brushing teeth after lunch prevents cavities. Based on the dentist's research, which of the following statements is true?

A. If at least 100 patients were studied, the writer's statement is justified.
B. If a minimum of 500 patients were studied, the writer's statement is justified.
C. At least 100 of the patients needed to have brushed their teeth after lunch for the writer's statement to be justified.
D. Dr. Ramchandran's study needs to be replicated for the writer's statement to be justified.
E. No matter how many participants, the writer's statement is not justified.

86. Which of the following endocrine glands is NOT paired with a hormone that it produces?

A. pineal–melatonin
B. hypothalamus–thyroid-stimulating hormone
C. thyroid–thyroxine
D. adrenals–cortisol
E. pancreas–glucagon

87. A recent comparison of the intelligence scores of Asian Americans and African Americans on the Stanford Binet showed that

I. the mean score for Asian Americans was higher than for African Americans
II. some African Americans scored higher than the average Asian Americans
III. some Asian Americans scored lower than the average African Americans

    A. I only
    B. II only
    C. III only
    D. I and II only
    E. I, II, and III

88. A special diet can prevent the expression of the trait for

    A. Tay-Sachs syndrome
    B. PKU (phenylketonuria)
    C. Huntington's disease
    D. Down syndrome
    E. Klinefelter's syndrome

89. Implications of Harlow's study (of baby monkeys reared by artificial mothers) for humans include which of the following?
I. Providing breast milk is the key to developing an attachment between the baby and the mother.
II. An infant can form an attachment with a nurturing father or other caretaker.
III. Lack of nursing at the breast leads to maladjustment of a child.

    A. I only
    B. II only
    C. III only
    D. I and II only
    E. I, II, and III

90. Michelle watches Ray Romano on television, but doesn't recognize him when she walks past him in Manhattan. Which effect on perception does this best illustrate?

    A. convergence
    B. context
    C. proximity
    D. closure
    E. monocular cues

91. Emily scored at the 65th percentile on a standardized achievement test. This indicates which of the following? Her score was

    A. above average
    B. average

    C. below average
    D. just passing
    E. unreliable

92. As a result of an accident, Abdul lost sight in his right eye. To judge the distance of vehicles when he is driving, Abdul is able to rely on cues of
I. accommodation
II. relative size
III. retinal disparity

    A. I only
    B. II only
    C. III only
    D. I and II only
    E. I, II, and III

93. All of the following are positive symptoms of schizophrenia EXCEPT

    A. auditory hallucinations
    B. visual hallucinations
    C. paranoid delusions
    D. flat affect
    E. incoherent speech

94. Today Susan took a pill for her allergy that raised her blood pressure, caused her heart to beat faster, and raised her body temperature. Now caught in traffic, she feels angry. Yesterday, when she took the pill she was with her husband. When her blood pressure rose, her heart speeded up, she got hotter, and she felt amorous. This description exemplifies

    A. the adaptation–level phenomenon
    B. two–factor theory
    C. James–Lange theory
    D. Cannon–Bard theory
    E. homeostatic theory

95. Which of the following reinforcement schedules results in maintenance of behavior that is LEAST resistant to extinction?

    A. continuous
    B. fixed ratio
    C. fixed interval
    D. variable ratio
    E. variable interval

96. When the class listened to a list of words, half the group was directed to listen for sounds while the other half was asked to

gauge the emotional impact of the words. The group who gauged the emotional impact remembered many more words. This is evidence that better retention results with attention to

A. semantic features
B. echoic features
C. shallow processing
D. surface processing
E. rehearsal

97. Alpha waves are most closely associated with

A. the hypnagogic state
B. Stage 2 sleep
C. Stage 3 sleep
D. Stage 4 sleep
E. alertness

98. The focus of structuralists most closely matches the current perspective of

A. psychoanalysis
B. behaviorists
C. cognitivists
D. humanists
E. evolutionists

99. The primary reason why we cannot taste sand or smell platinum is that

A. they are not chemicals
B. they are not soluble in water
C. they are poisonous
D. they have no nutritional value
E. the thresholds for tasting sand and smelling platinum are higher for humans than for amphibians and reptiles

100. After sending a decal to display on a window and greeting cards with their logo, a charity sent the same people envelopes requesting contributions. Many people send contributions. The charity is using a technique known as

A. overcompensation
B. foot-in-the-door phenomenon
C. the bystander effect
D. proximity
E. in-group bias

END OF SECTION I

AP PSYCHOLOGY

Section II

Essays

Time—50 minutes

Directions: Take approximately 50 minutes to answer *both* of the essay questions. According to the College Board directions, "It is not enough to answer a question by merely listing facts. You should present a cogent argument based on your critical analysis of the question posed, using appropriate psychological terminology."

Essay 1:

A. Define each of the following terms:
- superego
- level of moral development
- conformity
- deindividuation
- modelling

B. Discuss how each of the factors (in A) helps determine whether or not an adolescent wearing a Halloween costume and mask will damage property if he doesn't get treats he asks for when "trick or treating" on Halloween.

Essay 2:

A neuroscientist thinks he has developed a drug that can stop the progression of Alzheimer's disease in people who are in the initial stages of the disease. Design a research experiment that will support or refute his hypothesis. In your research design describe the following:

- sample
- assignment
- independent variable
- dependent variable
- experimental group
- control group
- possible confounding variable
- how you would determine whether or not the drug is effective

END OF SECTION II

ANSWERS TO THE MULTIPLE-CHOICE QUESTIONS

Answer Key

1. A	21. D	41. B	61. C	81. C
2. A	22. C	42. B	62. C	82. D
3. C	23. A	43. D	63. A	83. E
4. D	24. C	44. C	64. D	84. A
5. E	25. B	45. E	65. E	85. E
6. A	26. C	46. C	66. B	86. B
7. A	27. A	47. C	67. B	87. E
8. A	28. C	48. A	68. C	88. B
9. D	29. D	49. C	69. A	89. B
10. A	30. A	50. C	70. D	90. B
11. A	31. A	51. B	71. A	91. A
12. D	32. B	52. D	72. A	92. D
13. D	33. C	53. B	73. E	93. D
14. A	34. D	54. B	74. A	94. B
15. C	35. C	55. B	75. A	95. A
16. D	36. E	56. C	76. E	96. A
17. D	37. A	57. C	77. B	97. A
18. B	38. A	58. C	78. C	98. C
19. B	39. A	59. E	79. B	99. B
20. C	40. B	60. D	80. E	100. B

Explanations of Answers to the Multiple-Choice Questions

1. **A.** Olfactory receptors in the nasal passages would "smell" the gas leak and send information to the olfactory bulb, alerting the brain to the danger.

2. **A.** Identical twins. Since they share the same genes, the difference between them would be a result of nurture. Identical quadruplets would be extremely rare and so it would be difficult to find a large enough sample size for a study.

3. **C.** The children's more aggressive behavior following the more violent cartoon supports Albert Bandura's social learning theory of aggression studied in the Bobo doll study.

4. **D.** A morpheme is the smallest unit of language that carries meaning while a phoneme is the smallest unit of language that has no meaning.

5. **E.** Systematic desensitization is a behavior therapy especially effective in the treatment of phobias such as claustrophobia in this question. The patient learns through classical conditioning to replace the fear with relaxation.

6. **A.** Humanistic perspective pioneer Abraham Maslow places self-esteem and finally self-actualization as higher needs in his hierarchy of needs theory of motivation.

7. **A.** The Rorschach inkblot test is a projective test designed to reveal the unconscious mind and is a technique quite useful to the psychoanalyst in therapy.

8. **A.** When the pigeon sees the yellow light instead of the green one, he generalizes his pecking response to a similar stimulus. The pigeon can be taught to discriminate between the two-colored lights, but has not yet been trained to do so.

9. **D.** Carl Rogers is a humanistic psychologist who believes like Maslow that people are born good and that only the conditions of worth placed on the individual by society changes this natural tendency.

10. **A.** Over half of the brain's volume is composed of the cerebral cortex. The cerebral cortex is the section of the brain thought to be responsible for higher thought processing and covers all of the other structures of the brain.

11. **A.** Joey seems to have antisocial personality disorder. He shows no guilt when he hurts others. The condition is first evident in late childhood and the early teen years, as in this case, and the criminal behavior often accelerates over time.

12. **D.** Modeling is a social cognitive process in which new behavior is learned by watching others and then imitating their actions.

13. **D.** Freud's superego operates on the morality principle and, thus, overrides the impulse to cut class in this example and to do the right thing by attending class.

14. **A.** Prejudice is the unjustifiable negative attitude toward a group and its members, while discrimination would be acting upon this attitude.

15. **C.** One technique used by Carl Rogers in his client-centered humanistic therapy is to give unconditional positive regard to his clients to undo the effects of conditions of worth and to allow the individual to realize his positive actualizing potential.

16. **D.** Deindividuation found in group mob behavior is helpful in creating an environment of anonymity, which could also be affected by wearing head coverings and sunglasses.

17. **D.** Piaget's formal operational thought is the final stage of reasoning characterized by hypothetical thought, systematic planning and abstract, logical reasoning abilities.

18. **B.** In patients with Parkinson's disease, damage occurs in the dopamine-rich substantia nigra. With the degeneration of these neurons, movement problems begin to occur. A synthetic drug known as L-dopa is able to alleviate some of their movement problems. Schizophrenics' problems are related to an excessive amount of dopamine.

19. **B.** Watson and Raynor's classic study involving classical conditioning of fear in 9-month-old baby Albert would today violate the APA ethical guidelines that prohibit physical or mental suffering by subjects.

20. **C.** Adler's classic theory of birth order has suggested that since oldest children grow up in a world of adults, they often show responsibility for younger siblings and develop into responsible adults.

21. **D.** Brenda's constant attention-seeking and egotistical attitudes are classic markers of the narcissistic personality.

22. **C.** Behaviorists discount the role of "mentalistic" aspects that cannot be directly observed.

23. **A.** Erikson's sixth stage of psychosocial development occurs during young adulthood and is marked by the crisis of intimacy vs. isolation—a desire to form closer

bonds to others. Many marriages are the result of this growing sense of intimacy and divorce may be a result of the negative fear of isolation and marrying too early.

24. **C.** The height of the wave or its amplitude allows us to perceive loudness from sound waves.

25. **B.** Shannon's inability to think of using her jeans and sweater as a pillow is an example of functional fixedness—not seeing unusual uses of familiar objects.

26. **C.** In his hierarchy of needs, Maslow theorizes that lower level needs must be met before higher level needs can be attained. Self-actualization is the uppermost need and cannot be attempted until esteem needs, the need level below it, are satisfied.

27. **A.** The MMPI-2 is the most widely used self-report inventory for personality assessment.

28. **C.** Behaviorists believe that we learn new behavior through rewards and punishment. Any maladaptive behavior can be changed by altering the consequences of that behavior.

29. **D.** Insight learning is the sudden appearance of a solution when directed thinking is no longer being utilized. As Scott consciously shifted his attention to other matters, the solution to the anagram appeared.

30. **A.** Paranoid schizophrenics suffer from disordered thinking and often have delusions of persecution and hallucinations.

31. **A.** Jyoti is utilizing the naturalistic observation technique frequently used by behaviorists.

32. **B.** White is the perceived quality of reflected wavelengths of all colors.

33. **C.** Used on the old Stanford–Binet intelligence tests, the Intelligence Quotient originally coined by William Stearns represents one's mental age divided by one's chronological age multiplied by 100. One's mental age is a measure of one's intellectual development relative to others.

34. **D.** Kubler-Ross's classic study of 200 terminal cancer patients determined their emotional reactions followed a similar pattern. Denial is followed by the emotions of anger, bargaining, depression, and acceptance.

35. **C.** The sympathetic nervous system is the part of the autonomic nervous system activated in stressful situations. When Jared realizes the shadows are just that, the parasympathetic nervous system will be activated to return the body to homeostasis.

36. **E.** Narcotics or opiates are the classification of drugs most used to relieve patients' pain. Because they are highly addictive, a doctor must prescribe their limited use.

37. **A.** One of the characteristics of the manic high is an inflated ego and sense of euphoria. The patient has little need for sleep during this phase of the condition.

38. **A.** According to the serial positioning effect, words at the beginning of the list are stored in your long-term memory. Words remembered at the end of the list are in one's short-term memory, which lasts only 20+ seconds and would be forgotten 2 days later. Poorest recall would occur for words in the middle of the list.

39. **A.** Tony's sense of self-efficacy or belief in his abilities to accomplish tasks should be maximized by all of these accomplishments.

40. **B.** Fixed action patterns are species-specific innate behaviors unaffected by learning.

41. **B.** To standardize a test, each of the actions mentioned would be taken—pre-testing of a sample population for whom the test is intended under uniform instructions.

42. **B.** Compulsive hand washing is a common experience of those suffering from obsessive–compulsive disorder. A compulsion is an irresistible impulse to repeat some action over and over even though it serves no useful purpose.

43. **D.** The survey technique is being utilized here. It is a research method that obtains large samples of responses through questionnaire or interview. No variables have been manipulated as in an experiment.

44. **C.** Sensory adaptation is the lessening of perception of a stimulus with repeated stimulation, like the temperature of the pool water. You perceive the pool water as cold when you first jump in, but the nerve firing decreases over time with repeated stimulation and you no longer notice it.

45. **E.** DSM-IV is a diagnostic guide used by mental health professionals to diagnose patients. It lists symptoms of these disorders, but does not list the causes of mental disorders.

46. **C.** According to set point theory, an individual's regulated weight is balanced by adjusting food intake and metabolic rate.

47. **C.** Only the PET scan images function of the brain. The CAT and MRI both show the structures of the brain in good detail. The fMRI, like the PET, can show both structure and function.

48. **A.** Because Aaron seems to be suffering from a psychosis or break with reality, he may not have been able to tell the difference between right and wrong when he committed the crime. Each of the other disorders fall under the umbrella of psycho-neuroses, which are not as disabling.

49. **C.** Group A is likely to become more entrenched. This is an example of group polarization.

50. **C.** Penfield's studies suggest that the old memories are still present and probably have not been stimulated or needed to be retrieved recently.

51. **B.** Displacement, a Freudian defense mechanism, allows us to express feeling towards a group or individual perceived to be less threatening to us, rather than the direct target or ourselves.

52. **D.** Longitudinal studies follow the same group of people for a longer period of time. They are tested at several points, thus providing reliable data about age effects. Cross sectional studies unfortunately suffer from the cohort effect and are not as valid for measuring these effects.

53. **B.** Their goal seems more related to successful completion of the course with a passing grade than learning the material. Grades represent extrinsic rewards, while learning for pleasure would be measured by intrinsic, internal satisfaction, and rewards.

54. **B.** Repeated presentations of the conditioned stimulus without the unconditioned stimulus brings about extinction in classical conditioning. The new conditioned response will disappear.

55. **B.** The median is a measure of central tendency achieved by ordering the numbers consecutively and determining the middle number. Here there are nine numbers, so the 5th number, 8, is the median of the scores.

56. **C.** Because the AP exam in Psychology is supposed to measure what you have learned in a course already taken, it is an achievement test.

57. **C.** Transduction is the conversion of physical stimuli into changes in the activity of receptor cells of sensory organs. The rods and cones are stimulated by photons of light while the hair cells in the cochlea are stimulated by sound waves.

58. **C.** When our interest decreases, we often daydream about seemingly irrelevant ideas.

59. **E.** The availability heuristic is a tendency to estimate the probability of certain events in terms of how readily they come to mind. Each time any of these events do occur, the media publicizes the information very thoroughly.

60. **D.** Although largely discredited, Whorf believed that language determines the way we think. He cited studies of bilingual people who said that they experienced a different sense of self when thinking in two different languages.

61. **C.** A lesion in the ventromedial hypothalamus would cause a rat to continue to eat. It is theorized to be the "satiety" center, or off button, for hunger sensation, so if it was lesioned, the rat would continue to eat as long as the food supply was available.

62. **C.** Matina Horner's studies concluded that bright women fear success because it is correlated with masculinity in our culture. Maria would attend a community college rather than a very competitive college. Those with fear of success tend to select easy or noncompetitive goals.

63. **A.** David McClelland and others used the TAT to assess achievement motive in their subjects. The stories that subjects told interpreting the pictures displayed were rated for achievement themes.

64. **D.** In data sets that have a few outliers like the 42 and 38 here, the median is a better measure of central tendency than the arithmetic mean.

65. **E.** The medical model attributes mental illness to faulty processes in neurochemistry, brain structures, and genetics. Social circumstances would not be considered as causative factors.

66. **B.** According to Kohlberg, most teens follow a conventional level of morality. Stage IV, or the law and order stage, says that you understand the need for laws and, thus, conform to them for the good of the community.

67. **B.** Irving Janis described the dangerous implications of groupthink during the disastrous Bay of Pigs invasion. The top executives may want to preserve group harmony, so they would tend to self-censor opposing viewpoints to the president's. Bringing in outside consultants to play devil's advocate will increase the likelihood that more possibilities will be explored and the pros and cons will be discussed before the decision is made.

68. **C.** Although Javier teaches the same subject at both time periods, confounding variables, such as the overall GPA of both groups, left uncontrolled are likely to give him faulty results.

69. **A.** Heritability is the percentage of variation among individuals that is caused by genes. Since identical twins have exactly the same genes, none of their differences can be attributed to heredity.

70. **D.** Telegraphic speech, or shortened two-word sentences, are characteristic of children's language development, starting at around age 2.

71. **A.** Though Type A individuals tend to have each of these traits, further research showed that the Type A traits of anger, hostility, and cynicism were the ones most correlated with heart disease.

72. **A.** The limbic system is considered to be emotion central of the central nervous system. The amygdala is a structure within the limbic system that has been found to be very active in strong emotional responses, such as fear.

73. **E.** The reticular formation arouses our attention, but not specifically our sexual behavior. It keeps us alert to incoming stimuli and filters out stimuli when we are asleep. Each of the other answers are more directly involved in some action of sexual behavior, especially in humans.

74. **A.** The independent variable is what is manipulated in an experiment. The color of paper, either yellow or blue, is manipulated to determine its effects on the speed at which questions are answered, the dependent variable.

75. **A.** Hostile aggression is defined as inflicting pain upon an unwilling victim. The man is slapping his wife out of anger and consciously choosing to display it in this fashion.

76. **E.** Upon further investigation of Pavlov's findings in classical conditioning, Rescorla and others found that conditioning occurs because of the expectation that follows the conditioned stimulus more so than just their pairing in time. This revised cognitive view is called the contingency model of conditioning.

77. **B.** In late adult development, fluid intelligence or abstract, flexible reasoning declines somewhat, but most people's crystallized intelligence for concrete information continues to increase.

78. **C.** Tommy's blindness and deafness are the result of a conversion disorder. Excessive anxiety over witnessing the murder has caused these symptoms, which have no organic basis.

79. **B.** The peripheral nervous system is made up of everything outside the central nervous system, which includes the brain and spinal cord. Each of the other answers includes aspects of the central nervous system.

80. **E.** The inability to understand language suggests damage to Wernicke's area, located in the left temporal lobe. If the problem had been an inability to speak or find words, damage to Broca's area in the left frontal lobe would have been the likely cause.

81. **C.** The Japanese culture is a collectivist society, which would blame the group or parents specifically for a child's behavior. The other countries are individualistic societies, which would tend to blame the behavior on the individual, especially a 17-year-old capable of intelligent thought.

82. **D.** Body awareness and positioning are regulated by the kinesthetic or propriocentric sense, whose receptors are found in the muscles and joints of the skeleton.

83. **E.** Jen's egocentrism allows her to see things from only her own point of view and, thus, her failure to understand that her mother's sister is also her aunt's sister.

84. **A.** Proactive interference is forgetting new information because of prior information that blocks its encoding. In this case then, list 1 interferes with your recall of list 2.

85. **E.** Unfortunately, the newspaper took Dr. Ramchandran's finding and made correlational data into cause and effect data, which can only be determined by a controlled experiment.

86. **B.** The pituitary gland secretes thyroid-stimulating hormone. The hypothalamus produces releasing factors.

87. **E.** All three of these findings are possible. Though the mean score may be higher for Asian Americans, the range of scores *within* a particular group (African Americans) is always much greater than is the mean score *between* two different groups (African Americans and Asian Americans). Neither of these tells us how any one individual will do.

88. **B.** Each of the other answers involves a genetic disorder that is irreversible. PKU is a recessive trait that results in severe, irreversible brain damage unless the baby is fed a special diet low in phenylalanine.

89. **B.** Harlow's study showed that contact comfort (touch) was more important than the feeding situation for normal physical and psychological development.

90. **B.** Context is an important stimulus variable in determining what we perceive.

91. **A.** Average ranking would be 50th percentile, so 65th percentile is above that point. Emily scored better than 64 out of every 100 students who took that test.

92. **D.** Accommodation is a change in the shape of the lens that occurs when an object moves closer or further away and relative size is a monocular cue for depth. Abdul would use both of these to judge the distance of vehicles when he is driving. Retinal disparity requires binocular vision.

93. **D.** Positive symptoms indicate the presence of symptoms and negative symptoms the absence of symptoms. A flat affect is a lack or absence of an emotional response to stimuli.

94. **B.** Schachter and Singer's two-factor theory says that when physiologically aroused for no apparent immediate reason, we tend to look to environmental factors for an explanation. Susan's change in emotional response was caused more by the situation she found herself in.

95. **A.** Although continuous reinforcement is used for the quickest learning, it also suffers from being the fastest to extinguish as well. Variable schedules of reinforcement are the more resistant to extinction.

96. **A.** By gauging the emotional impact of the words, the class was making a connection to them and, thus, ensuring more meaning (semantic), deeper processing, and greater retention in long-term memory.

97. **A.** The hypnagogic state occurs as we are about to fall asleep, when we are very relaxed and alpha waves are present.

98. **C.** The focus of structuralists like Wundt and Titchener was on the units of consciousness and identification of elements of thought using introspection with other people. This is very similar to the present day cognitive exploration of the thinking process.

99. **B.** Sand and platinum are not soluble in water and, thus, cannot be tasted or smelled.

100. **B.** By accepting the gift of the greeting cards, many recipients felt obligated to send a donation when it was requested later. This is known as the foot-in-the-door technique of compliance often used by organizations.

RATING THE ESSAYS

Scoring Rubric for Essay 1

This is a 10-point rubric. Five points are given for proper definitions of the terms and 5 points are given for applying each to the scenario correctly: 1 point for definition of each term and 1 point for application to scenario.

Point 1: Defining superego as the third part of Freud's personality triad, also known as the conscience of the personality, which operates on the morality principle

Point 2: Suggesting that the superego would prevent adolescents from damaging the property because of the guilt it would inflict and the pride they would feel in resisting that temptation

Point 3: Defining the level of moral development as referencing the Kohlberg's theory of moral development, divided into the pre-conventional, conventional, and post-conventional stages of morality

Point 4: Suggesting that adolescents are probably at the conventional stage of morality and that if they were at stage 3 of conformity, they would obey the group norm, which may be to damage the property. Similarly, if they were operating at stage 4 of the law and order stage, they would be more likely to determine that it was unjust to destroy other peoples' property.

Point 5: Defining conformity as the adoption of attitudes and behaviors shared by a particular group

Point 6: Suggesting that the group would probably agree with each others' decision to destroy or not, depending on the "leader" of the pack or majority decision

Point 7: Defining deindividuation as a feeling of high arousal and anonymity when in group situations, which may lead to antisocial acts

Point 8: Depending on the size of the group, but also based on the wearing of masks and costumes that help to shield them from identification, it is more likely that the group will tend to destroy the property, justifying their behavior based on the fact that they didn't get the treats they asked for

Point 9: Defining modeling as a learning process of watching and imitating a specific behavior displayed

Point 10: In this situation, again going along with the leader. If some of the adolescents begin to destroy the property, others are likely to observe and imitate that behavior as well.

Sample Essay

Sigmund Freud proposed a three part theory of personality including the id, the ego, and the superego. The superego, or third part, develops last and operates on the morality principle. Most school-age children know the difference between right and wrong and their conscience, what Freud called the superego, makes them feel guilty when they disobey authority figures. If the superego has overpowered the id, the adolescents will probably not destroy the property because of their guilt.

These adolescents are probably operating at the conventional level of morality according to Kohlberg's moral development theory. His theory says that at different stages, individuals judge right and wrong based on their intellectual reasoning ability. In stage 3, they would base their decision on seeking approval from other members of the group, and in stage 4 they would base their decision on the laws of society.

Young adolescents might very well reason that it is okay to damage the person's property since they didn't get the treats they asked for. Seeking approval of their peers, the majority rules. However, if the adolescents were in the law and order stage, they might decide that damaging other's property was unlawful and, thus, would resist the temptation to break the law.

Conformity is very similar to the principle of Kohlberg's stage 3 reasoning. It is adopting the attitudes and behaviors of groups that you belong to. Not wanting to be excluded from the group, members tend to go along. In this situation, one might jump to the conclusion that teens would be likely to damage property of those who did not give them treats. Conforming behavior operates on group norms and whatever the majority decided to do in this situation; the others would be likely to follow.

Deindividuation is a state of high arousal in a large group situation. Antisocial acts are more likely to occur because of the anonymity of the individual group members. On this Halloween night, groups of adolescents who are already in costumes and masks, thus, shielding their identity, would be more likely to damage property because of the emotional arousal felt in this situation. They are out seeking "treats," and angered by the refusal to comply with their request, they might turn to destructive measures. Individually, most of the adolescents would probably not do this, but collectively and because of the anonymity of the situation, they would be more likely to be carried away by the emotions of the situation.

Finally, modeling is defined as a learning method in which someone observes someone else doing a specific behavior and then imitates that behavior. Bandura says that others tend to model those they consider of equal or greater status. If there were one or more leaders in this group, whatever behavior they initiated would likely be imitated by others who were watching. With adolescents who may tend to take risks, Halloween night might be an opportunity to vandalize by those who had already "learned" this behavior and for others to imitate what they had seen, thus damaging the property of those who did not treat them.

Scoring Rubric for Essay 2

This is a 10-point rubric: 2 points assigned for the design of the experiment and 8 points for the individual components asked for in the question.

Design an experiment:

2 points for identification of two of the following: research question, hypothesis, ethics.

Question: Will a new drug stop the progression of Alzheimer's disease in people who are in the initial stages of the disease?

Hypothesis: If the new drug is given to a sample of people in the early stages of Alzheimer's, then it will stop the progression.

Ethics: Since this drug is experimental, patients who volunteer and show a baseline memory loss will be told that they may or may not be given the drug. Should it be found to be effective, with possible side effects noted, those receiving the placebo will be allowed to take the drug as well. The potential harm would be discussed with patients and informed consent must be given for participation. Patients may withdraw at any point during the experiment.

1 point for **Sample**—a subgroup of the population of Alzheimer's patients that participates in the study; could be obtained by volunteers from a newspaper solicitation in major cities or from lists of patients with Alzheimer's from gerontologists in the area. You want it to be representative of all early-stage patients.

1 point for **Assignment**—division of the sample into groups such that every individual has an equal chance of being put in either the drug or placebo group. Group matching would be important.

1 point for identifying the **independent variable**—drug/no drug or placebo

1 point for identifying the **dependent variable**—effects of the drug on Alzheimer's symptoms; degree of progression of symptoms.

1 point for identifying the **experimental group**—participants who receive the drug

1 point for identifying the **control group**—participants who receive a placebo or no drug group

1 point for mentioning possible **confounding variables**—sex of patients and varying ages; misdiagnosis; other medical conditions during the trial period; not taking the dosage as prescribed.

1 point for describing how you would determine **effectiveness**—comparison of two group baseline scores and final results after the experimental period. Inferential statistics such, as t test or ANOVA, to determine significance of results. p value of .05 or less will be considered significant.

Sample Essay

For the purpose of this essay, my neuroscientist will be Dr. Hylton and her new drug will be called Lacetyl. Her research question is whether her new drug is effective and her hypothesis is that if she administers the drug for a period of 6 weeks or more, then patients with early symptoms of Alzheimer's will not get worse. Collecting a representative sample is her first problem.

Since Alzheimer's is usually definitively diagnosed with an autopsy to determine whether or not neural tangles and plaques are present, she must solicit elderly patients (age 75 or older) who are showing early symptoms and then carefully screen them to rule out other conditions. Tests might include not only blood and urine tests, but also cognitive functioning tasks, especially dealing with memory loss. She might solicit volunteers through newspaper ads, but because of the problem with diagnosis, she may wish to contact gerontologists or specialists dealing with patients with Alzheimer's and solicit volunteers from them. Since impairment should be limited in the early stages, potential risks should be discussed with the volunteers, their written consent forms should be signed, and their identity should be kept anonymous. To prevent bias on her part, Dr. Hylton would create a double-blind condition in which neither she nor the patients will know whether or not they are taking the drug or the placebo. To prevent confounds, group matching will be used to assign the patients, with both groups representing a similar range of initial functioning.

The independent variable in this experiment is the drug and the dependent variable is its effectiveness in improving patients' symptoms. The experimental group receives the drug and the control group the placebo. It might also be beneficial to have a second control group that receives no drug at all. The drug would be administered daily and weekly tests of urine, blood, and cognitive tasks would be repeated for a period of 6 weeks. Any potential negative side effects would be noted and the experiment would be halted immediately if these proved dangerous to any subjects receiving the drug.

Potential confounds are many. If a prescription is given, the patients may forget to take the medication. Sex, age, race, and other demographic variables not controlled in the sample could also prove a problem. Other medical conditions during testing and improper diagnosis in the first place could throw off our results. Obviously, when this study is concluded, replication would be necessary.

To determine whether Lacetyl is effective or not, baseline results would be compared in subjects and the differences between the results in the placebo and drug groups compared. Using inferential statistics, we would try to determine whether or not there was a significant difference between the two groups by using t tests or ANOVA. If her p value is .05 or less, then she will conclude that the drug is effective and await further studies and replication.

SCORING AND INTERPRETATION

Now that you've finished the exam and scored your answers, you can examine your results. You can *roughly* equate your results to an AP test score. To put an approximate AP score on the results of your practice test, follow these steps:

1. Count the number of Section I questions you answered correctly.

    Number correct _____

2. Count the number you answered incorrectly.

    Number not correct _____

3. Multiply the number *answered* incorrectly by .25.

    × .25 _____

4. Subtract the product in #3 from the number answered correctly in #1.

    _____

    Copy this Section I score on the line to the right.

    Section I weighted score: _____

5. Using the score rubrics,

    A. determine your score for Essay 1

    _____

    B. determine your score for Essay 2

    _____

    C. add the scores for Essays 1 and 2

    _____

    D. multiply your essay total by 2.5

    _____

    Copy this Section II score on the line to the right.

    Section II weighted score: _____

6. Add your scores for Section I and Section II.

    Total composite score: _____

7. Since scoring cuts vary from test to test, this is only a very rough estimate. Match your score from #6 with these:

Composite Score Range	Rough Estimate of AP Score
100–150	5
85–99	4
63–84	3
45–62	2
0–44	1

Chapter 10

AP Statistics

Answer Sheet for Multiple-Choice Questions

1.	_____		21.	_____	
2.	_____		22.	_____	
3.	_____		23.	_____	
4.	_____		24.	_____	
5.	_____		25.	_____	
6.	_____		26.	_____	
7.	_____		27.	_____	
8.	_____		28.	_____	
9.	_____		29.	_____	
10.	_____		30.	_____	
11.	_____		31.	_____	
12.	_____		32.	_____	
13.	_____		33.	_____	
14.	_____		34.	_____	
15.	_____		35.	_____	
16.	_____		36.	_____	
17.	_____		37.	_____	
18.	_____		38.	_____	
19.	_____		39.	_____	
20.	_____		40.	_____	

AP STATISTICS

Section I

Time—1 hour and 30 minutes

40 questions

Directions: Solve each of the following problems. Decide which is the best of the choices given and answer in the appropriate place on the answer sheet. No credit will be given for anything written on the exam. Do not spend too much time an any one problem.

1. A poll was conducted in the San Francisco Bay Area after the San Francisco Giants lost the World Series to the Anaheim Angels about whether the team should get rid of a pitcher who lost two games during the series. Five hundred twenty five adults were interviewed by telephone, and 55% of those responding indicated that the Giants should get rid of the pitcher. It was reported that the survey had a margin of error of 3.5%. Which of the following best describes what is meant by a 3.5% margin of error?

   A. About 3.5% of the respondents were not Giants fans, and their opinions had to be discarded.
   B. It's likely that the true percentage that favor getting rid of the pitcher is between 51.5% and 58.5%
   C. About 3.5% of those contacted refused to answer the question.
   D. About 3.5% of those contacted said they had no opinion on the matter.
   E. About 3.5% thought their answer was in error and are likely to change their mind.

2. In a highly academic suburban school system, 45% of the girls and 40% of the boys take advanced placement classes. There are 2200 girls and 2100 boys enrolled in the high schools of the district. What is the expected number of students who take advanced placement courses in a random sample of 150 students?

   A. 128
   B. 64
   C. 78
   D. 90
   E. 75

3. One of the values in a normal distribution is 43 and its z score is 1.65. If the mean of the distribution is 40, what is the standard deviation of the distribution?

   A. 3
   B. −1.82
   C. .55
   D. 1.82
   E. −.55

4. Two plans are being considered for determining resistance to fading of a certain type of paint. Some 1500 homes of 9500 homes in a large city are known to have been painted with the paint in question. The plans are:

   Plan A: (i)   Random sample 100 homes from all the homes in the city.
            (ii) Record the amount of fade over a 2-year period.

(iii) Generate a confidence interval for the average amount of fade for all 1500 homes with the paint in question.

Plan B: (i) Random sample 100 homes from the 1500 homes with the paint in question.

(ii) Record the amount of fade over a 2-year period.

(iii) Generate a confidence interval for the average amount of fade for all 1500 homes with the paint in question.

A. Choose Plan A over Plan B
B. Either plan is good—the confidence intervals will be the same.
C. Neither plan is good—neither addresses the concerns of the study.
D. Choose Plan B over Plan A
E. You can't make a choice—there isn't enough information given to evaluate the two plans.

5. Which of the following is *not* a property of the sample standard deviation (s)?

A. sensitive to the variability of the distribution
B. independent of the mean
C. resistant to extreme data values
D. independent of the median
E. all of the above are properties of s

6. The weights of professional football players are approximately normally distributed with a mean of 245 lbs. with a standard deviation of 20 lbs. If Thor is at the 80th percentile in weight for football players, which of the following is closest to his weight in pounds?

A. 265
B. 255
C. 252
D. 270
E. 262

7. In a famous study from the late 1920s, the Western Electric Company wanted to study the effect of lighting on productivity. They discovered that worker productivity increased with each change of lighting, whether the lighting was increased or decreased. The workers were aware that a study was in progress. What is the most likely cause of this phenomena? (This effect is known as the Hawthorne Effect.)

A. Response bias
B. Absence of a control group
C. Lack of randomization
D. Sampling variability
E. Undercoverage

8. Chris is picked up by the police for stealing hubcaps, but claims that he is innocent, and it is a case of mistaken identity. He goes on trial, and the judge somberly informs the jury that Chris is innocent until proved guilty. That is, they should find him guilty only if there is overwhelming evidence to reject the assumption of innocence. What risk is involved in the jury making a type-I error?

A. He is guilty, but the jury finds him innocent, and he goes free.
B. He is innocent, and they find him innocent, and he goes free.
C. He is innocent, but the jury finds him guilty, and he goes to jail.
D. He is guilty, and they find him guilty, and he goes to jail.
E. He is guilty, and they correctly reject the assumption of innocence.

9. Given $P(A) = .4$, $P(B) = .3$, $P(B|A) = .2$. What are $P(A \text{ and } B)$ and $P(A \text{ or } B)$?

   A. $P(A \text{ and } B) = .12$, $P(A \text{ or } B) = .58$
   B. $P(A \text{ and } B) = .08$, $P(A \text{ or } B) = .62$
   C. $P(A \text{ and } B) = .12$, $P(A \text{ or } B) = .62$
   D. $P(A \text{ and } B) = .08$, $P(A \text{ or } B) = .58$
   E. $P(A \text{ and } B) = .08$, $P(A \text{ or } B) = .70$

10. As part of a training program to improve sales efficiency, 10 trainees were given a pretest and a post-test on the sales skills emphasized in the program. The results were as follows:

Trainee	Pretest Score	Post-test Score
A	15	17
B	17	17
C	18	21
D	12	16
E	19	18
F	21	21
G	16	19
H	15	19
I	14	15
J	18	20

   What number of degrees of freedom are involved with the appropriate t test for determining if there is a real difference between the mean pre- and post-test scores?

   A. 9
   B. 10
   C. 18
   D. 19
   E. 20

11. A researcher is interested in establishing a cause-and-effect relationship between exercise level and percentage of body fat. Which of the following should she use?

   A. A survey with a stratified random sample
   B. An observational study
   C. A census
   D. A controlled experiment
   E. A longitudinal study

12. You are going to conduct an experiment to determine which of four different brands of cat food promotes growth best in kittens ages 4 months to 1 year. You are concerned that the effect might vary by the breed of the cat, so you divide the cats into three different categories by breed. This gives you eight kittens in each category. You randomly assign two of the kittens in each category to one of the four foods. The design of this study is best described as:

   A. Randomized block, blocked by breed of cat and type of cat food
   B. Randomized block, blocked by type of cat food
   C. Matched pairs where each two cats are considered a pair
   D. A controlled design in which the various breed of cats are the controls
   E. Randomized block, blocked by breed of cat

13.

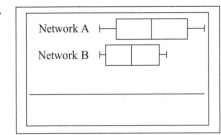

The boxplots above compare the television ratings for two competing networks. What conclusion(s) can you draw from the boxplots?

I.   Network A has more shows than Network B
II. Network A has a greater range of ratings than Network B
III. Network A is higher rated than Network B

    A. I and II only
    B. II and III only
    C. I and III only
    D. I, II, and III
    E. III only

14. A least-squares regression line for predicting performance on a college entrance exam based on high school grade point average (GPA) is determined to be $Score = 273.5 + 91.2 \,(GPA)$. One student in the study had a high school GPA of 3.0 and a score of 510. What is the residual score for this student?

    A. 26.2
    B. 43.9
    C. −37.1
    D. −26.2
    E. 37.1

15. The following table gives the probabilities of various outcomes for a gambling game.

Outcome	Lose $1	Win $1	Win $2
Probability	.6	.25	.15

What is the player's expected return on a bet of $1?

    A. $.05
    B. −$.60
    C. −$.05
    D. −$.10
    E. You can't answer this question because this isn't a complete probability distribution.

16. A kennel club argues that 50% of dog owners in their area own Golden Retrievers, 40% own Shepherds of one kind or another, and 10% own a variety of other breeds. A random sample of 50 dogs from the area turns up the data in the following table:

Golden Retriever	Shepherd	Other
27	22	1

What is the value of the χ^2 statistic for the goodness-of-fit test on these data?

A. 3.56
B. 2.12
C. 4.31
D. 3.02
E. 2.78

17. A poll is taken to measure the proportion of voters who plan to vote for a former actor for governor. A 95% confidence interval is constructed based on a sample survey. The interval constructed is <.35, .42>. Which of the following best describes how to interpret this interval?

A. The probability is .95 that about 40% of the voters will vote for the former actor.
B. The probability is .95 that between 35% and 42% of the population will vote for the former actor.
C. At least 35%, but not more than 42%, of the voters will vote for the former actor.
D. The sample result is likely to be in the interval <.35, .42>
E. It is likely that the true proportion of voters who will vote for the former actor is between 35% and 42%

18. Harvey found out that his z score on a college readiness test, compared to others who took the same test was 1.25. Which of the following best describes how you might interpret this value?

A. Harvey's score was 125.
B. Harvey's score was 1.25 standard deviations above the mean of all people taking the test.
C. Only 1.25% of the people taking the test had scores higher than Harvey.
D. Harvey scored 1.25 points above the mean of all people taking the test.
E. Harvey's score was 1.25 times the mean score of all people taking the test.

19. You want to compare the number of home runs hit in the American League to the number of home runs hit in the National League each year over the past 25 years. Which of the following is likely to be most useful in graphically demonstrating the differences between the two leagues?

A. Parallel boxplots
B. Scatterplot of American League vs. National League
C. Back-to-back stemplots
D. Side-by-side histograms
E. Cumulative frequency plots

Questions 20 and 21 refer to the following information:

At a local community college, 90% of students take English. 80% of those who don't take English take art courses, while only 50% of those who do take English take art.

20. What is the probability that a student takes art?

A. .80
B. .53
C. .50
D. 1.3
E. .45

21. What is the probability that a student who takes art doesn't take English?

    A. .08
    B. .10
    C. .8
    D. .85
    E. .15

22. A teacher was recording grades for her class of 32 AP Statistics students. She accidentally recorded one score much too high (she put a "1" in front, so the score was 192 instead of 92). The corrected score was still greater any other grade in the class. Which of the following sample statistics remained the same after the correction was made?

    A. Mean
    B. Standard Deviation
    C. Range
    D. Variance
    E. Interquartile range

23. A study of 15 people ages 5 through 77 was conducted to determine the amount of leisure time people of various ages have. The results are shown in the following table.

Time = 7.85 + 0.0094 Age				
Predictor	Coef	St Dev	t ratio	P
Constant	7.845	3.032	2.59	.023
Age	0.00935	0.07015	0.13	.896
s = 5.628	R-sq = 0.1%	R-sq(adj) = 0.0%		

Which of the following is the 99% confidence interval for the true slope of the regression line?

    A. $.00935 \pm 3.012(.07015)$
    B. $.00935 \pm 2.977(5.628)$
    C. $7.845 \pm 3.012(.07015)$
    D. $.00935 \pm 2.977(.07015)$
    E. $.00935 \pm 3.012(5.628)$

24. You want to conduct a survey to determine the types of exercise equipment most used by people at your health club. You plan to base your results on a sample of 40 members. Which of the following methods will generate a simple random sample of 40 of the members?

    A. Mail out surveys to every member and use the first 40 that are returned as your sample.
    B. Randomly pick a morning and survey the first 40 people who come in the door that day.
    C. Divide the number of members by 40 to get a value k. Choose one of the first kth names on the list using a random number generator. Then choose every kth name on the list after that name.
    D. Put each member's name on a slip of paper and randomly select 40 slips.
    E. Get the sign-in lists for each day of the week, Monday through Friday. Randomly choose 8 names from each day for the survey.

25. In a large population, 55% of the people get a physical examination at least once every two years. A SRS of 100 people are interviewed and the sample proportion is computed. The mean and standard deviation of the sampling distribution of the sample proportion are

    A. 55, 4.97
    B. .55, .002
    C. 55, 2
    D. .55, .0497
    E. You cannot determine the standard deviation from the information given.

26. In a test of the null hypothesis H_0: $p = .35$, with $\alpha = .01$, against the alternative hypothesis H_A: $p < .35$, a large random sample produces a z score of -2.05. Based on this, which of the following conclusions can be drawn?

    A. It is likely that $p < .35$
    B. $p < .35$ only 2% of the time.
    C. If the z score were positive instead of negative, we would be able to reject the null hypothesis.
    D. We do not have sufficient evidence to claim that $p < .35$.
    E. 1% of the time we will reject the alternative hypothesis in error.

27. A wine maker advertises that the mean alcohol content of the wine produced by his winery is 11%. A 95% confidence interval, based on a random sample of 100 bottles of wine yields a confidence interval for the true alcohol content of <10.5, 10.9>. Could this interval be used as part of a hypothesis test of the null hypothesis H_0: $p = .11$ vs. the alternative hypothesis H_A: $p \neq .11$ at the .05 level of confidence?

    A. No, you cannot use a confidence interval in a hypothesis test.
    B. Yes, because .11 is not contained in the 95% confidence interval, a two-sided test at the .05 level of significance would provide good evidence that the true mean content is different from 11%.
    C. No, because we do not know that the distribution is approximately normally distributed.
    D. Yes, because .11 is not contained in the 95% confidence interval, a two-sided test at the .05 level of significance would fail to reject the null hypothesis.
    E. No, confidence intervals can only be used in one-sided confidence intervals.

28. The weights of a large group of college football players is approximately normally distributed. It was determined that 10% of the players weigh less than 154 pounds and 5% weigh more than 213 pounds. What are the mean and standard deviation of the distribution of weights of football players?

    A. 183.5, 19.44
    B. 185.8, 22.36
    C. 179.8, 20.17
    D. 167.3, 18.66
    E. 170.9, 19.85

29. An advice columnist asks readers to write in about how happy they are in their marriage. The results indicate that 79% of those responding would not marry the same partner if they had it to do all over again. Which of the following statements are true?

    A. It's likely that this result is an accurate reflection of the population.

B. It's likely that this result is higher than the true population proportion because persons unhappy in their marriages are most likely to respond.

C. It's likely that this result is lower than the true population proportion because persons unhappy in their marriages are unlikely to respond.

D. It's likely that the results are not accurate because people tend to lie in voluntary response surveys.

E. There is really no way of predicting whether the results are biased or not.

30. A national polling organization wishes to generate a 98% confidence interval for the proportion of voters who will vote for candidate Iam Sleazy in the next election. The poll is to have a margin of error of no more than 3%. What is the minimum sample size needed for this interval?

A. 6032
B. 1508
C. 39
D. 6033
E. 1509

31. In a test of the hypothesis $H_0: p = .7$ against $H_A: p > .7$, the power of the test when $p = .8$ would be greatest for which of the following?

A. $n = 30, \alpha = .10$
B. $n = 30, \alpha = .05$
C. $n = 25, \alpha = .10$
D. $n = 25, \alpha = .05$
E. It cannot be determined with the information given.

32. A school survey of students concerning which band to hire for the next school dance shows 70% of students in favor of hiring The Greasy Slugs. What is the probability that, in a random sample of 200 students, at least 150 will favor hiring The Greasy Slugs?

A. $\binom{200}{150}(.7)^{150}(.3)^{50}$

B. $\binom{200}{150}(.3)^{150}(.7)^{50}$

C. $P\left(z > \dfrac{.75 - .70}{\sqrt{\dfrac{.7(.3)}{200}}}\right)$

D. $P\left(z > \dfrac{.75 - .70}{\sqrt{\dfrac{.7(.3)}{150}}}\right)$

E. $P\left(z > \dfrac{.70 - .75}{\sqrt{\dfrac{.7(.3)}{200}}}\right)$

33. Which of the following describes an experiment but not an observational study?

   A. A cause-and-effect relationship can be demonstrated.
   B. The cost of conducting it is excessive.
   C. More advanced statistics are needed for analysis after the data are gathered.
   D. By law, the subjects must be informed that they are part of a study.
   E. Possible confounding variables are more difficult to control.

34. A least-squares regression line, $\hat{y} = a + bx$ is to be constructed for two variables x and y. As part of the process it is determined that $r = .77$, $\bar{x} = 3.5$, $s_x = .32$, $\bar{y} = 17.8$, and $s_y = 3.6$. What is the slope of the regression line?

   A. 5.09
   B. .068
   C. 11.25
   D. 8.66
   E. 3.92

35. For which one of the following distributions is the mean most likely to be less than the median?

A.

D.
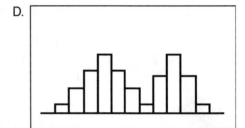

B.

E.
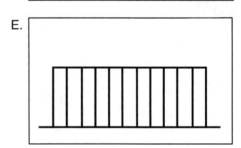

C.
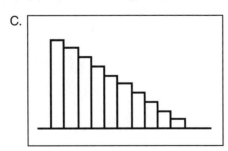

36. In an experiment, the purpose of randomization is to

   A. equalize blocks in a block design
   B. reduce variability by repeating the experiment on many subjects
   C. control for variables not under study that might affect the response
   D. control for common characteristics
   E. make sure each subgroup is fairly represented

37. Which of the following statements is correct?

   I.   The area under a probability density curve for a continuous random variable is 1.
   II. A random variable is a numerical outcome of a random event.
   III. The sum of the probabilities for a discrete random variable is 1.

      A. II only
      B. I and II
      C. I and III
      D. II and III
      E. I, II, and III

38. A 99% confidence interval for the weights of high school wrestlers is given as <125, 160>. Which of the following statements about this interval is true?

   A. At least 99% of the weights of high school wrestlers are in the interval <125,160>.
   B. The probability is .99 that the true mean weight of high school wrestlers is in the interval <125,160>.
   C. Ninety-nine percent of all samples of this size will yield a confidence interval of <125,160>.
   D. The procedure used to generate this confidence interval will capture the true mean weight of high school wrestlers 99% of the time.
   E. The probability is .99 that a randomly selected wrestler will weight between 125 and 160 pounds.

39. A group of 12 students take both the SAT Math and the SAT Verbal. The least-squares regression line for predicting Verbal Score from Math Score is determined to be *Verbal Score* = 106.56 + .74 (*Math Score*). Furthermore, s_b = .11. Determine a 95% confidence interval for the slope of the regression line.

   A. $.74 \pm .245$
   B. $.74 \pm .242$
   C. $.74 \pm .240$
   D. $.74 \pm .071$
   E. $.74 \pm .199$

40. A weight loss clinic claims an average weight loss over 3 months of at least 15 pounds. A random sample of 50 of the clinic's patrons shows a mean weight loss of 14 pounds with a standard deviation of 2.8 pounds. Assuming the distribution of weight losses is approximately normally distributed, what is the appropriate test for this situation, the value of the test statistic, and the associated P value?

   A. z test; $z = -2.53$; $P = .0057$
   B. t test; $t = -2.53$; $.01 < P < .02$
   C. z test; $z = 2.53$; $P = .0057$
   D. t test; $t = 2.53$; $.005 < P < .01$
   E. z test; $z = 2.53$; $P = .9943$

END OF SECTION I

AP STATISTICS

Section II

Time—1 hour and 30 minutes

GENERAL INSTRUCTIONS

There are two parts to this section of the examination. Together, they are worth 50% of the total grade. Part A consists of five equally weighted problems that represent 75% of the total weight of this section. Spend about 65 minutes on this part of the exam. Part B consists of one longer problem that represents 25% of the total weight of this section. Spend about 25 minutes on this part of the exam. You are not necessarily expected to complete all parts of every questions. Statistical tables and formulas are provided.

- Be sure to write clearly and legibly. If you make an error, you may save time by crossing it out rather than trying to erase it. Erased or crossed-out work will not be graded.
- Show all your work. Indicate clearly the methods you use because you will be graded on the correctness of your methods as well as the accuracy of your final answers. Correct answers without support work may not receive credit.

Statistics, Section II, Part A, Questions 1–5

Spend about 65 minutes on this part of the exam; percentage of Section II grade: 75.

Directions: Show all your work. Indicate clearly the methods you use because you will be graded on the correctness of your methods as well as on the accuracy of your results and explanation.

1. David was comparing the number of vocabulary words children know about transportation at various ages. He fit a least squares regression line to the data. The residual plot and part of the computer output for the regression are given below.

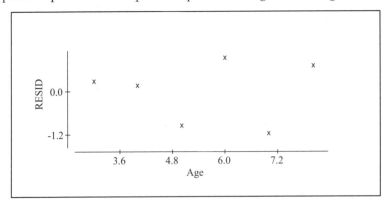

Predictor	Coef	St Dev	t ratio	P
Constant	3.371	1.337	2.52	.065
Words	2.1143	0.2321	9.11	.001
s = 0.9710	R-sq = 95.4%		R-sq(adj) = 94.3%	

    a. Is a line an appropriate model for these data? Explain.
    b. What is the equation of the least-square regression line for predicting the number of words from age.
    c. What is the predicted number of words for a child of 7.5 years of age?
    d. Interpret the slope of the regression line in the context of the problem.

2. Students at Dot.Com Tech are allowed to sign up for one math class each semester. The numbers in each grade level signing up for various classes for next semester are given in the following table.

	Geometry	Algebra II	Analysis	AB Calculus	Total
10th Grade	125	74	23	3	225
11th Grade	41	92	72	25	230
12th Grade	12	47	99	62	220
Total	178	213	194	90	675

    a. What is the probability that a student will take calculus?
    b. What is the probability that a 12th grader will take either analysis or calculus?
    c. What is the probability that a person taking algebra II is a 10th grader?
    d. Consider the events, "A student takes geometry" and "A student is a 10th grader." Are these events independent? Justify your answer.

3. The state in which you reside is undergoing a significant budget crisis that will affect education. Your school is trying to decide how many sections of upper-level mathematics classes to offer next year. It is very expensive to offer sections that aren't full, so the school doesn't want to offer any more sections than it absolutely needs to. The assistant principal in charge of scheduling selects a random sample of 60 current sophomores and juniors. Fifty-five of them return the survey, and 48 indicate that they intend to take math during the coming year. If 80% or more of the students actually sign up for math, the school will need to add a section.

    a. On the basis of the survey data, would you recommend to the assistant principal that an additional class of upper division mathematics be scheduled? Give appropriate statistical evidence to support your recommendation.
    b. Five of the 60 who received surveys failed to return them. If they had returned them, how might it have affected the assistant principal's decision? Explain.

4. It is known that the symptoms of adult depression can be treated effectively with either therapy, antidepressants, or a combination of the two. A pharmaceutical company wants to test a new antidepressant against an older medication that has been on the market for several years. One hundred fifty volunteers who have been diagnosed with depression, and who have not been taking any medication for it, are available for the study. This group contains 72 men and 78 women. Sixty of the volunteers have been in therapy for their depression for at least 3 months.

    a. Design a completely randomized experiment to test the new medication. Include a brief explanation of the randomization process.
    b. Could the experiment you designed in part (a) be improved by blocking? If so, design an improved study that involves blocking. If not, explain why not.

5. The 1970 draft lottery was suspected to be biased toward birthdays later in the year. Because there are 366 possible birthdays, in a fair drawing we would expect to find, each month, an equal number of selections less than or equal to 183 and greater than or equal to 184. The following table shows the data from the 1970 draft lottery.

	Number Selected ≤ 183	Number Selected ≥ 184	Totals
January	12	19	31
February	12	17	29
March	10	21	31
April	11	19	30
May	14	17	31
June	14	16	30
July	14	17	31
August	19	12	31
September	17	13	30
October	13	18	31
November	21	9	30
December	26	5	31
Totals	**183**	**183**	**366**

Do these data give evidence that the 1970 draft lottery was not fair? Give appropriate statistical evidence to support your conclusion.

Statistics, Section II, Part B, Question 6

Spend about 25 minutes on this part of the exam; percentage of Section II grade: 25.

Directions: Show all of your work. Indicate clearly the methods you use because you will be graded on the correctness of your methods as well as on the accuracy of your results and explanation.

6. A lake in the Midwest has a restriction on the size of trout caught in the lake. The average length of trout over the years has been 11 inches with a standard deviation of .6 inches. The lengths are approximately normally distributed. Because of over-fishing during the past few years, any fish under 11.5 inches in length must be released.

   a. What is the probability that a fisherman will get lucky and catch a fish she can keep? Round your answer to the nearest tenth.
   b. Design a simulation to determine the probability how many fish the fisherman must catch, on average, in order to be able to take home five trout for dinner.
   c. Use the table of random digits on the following page to conduct five trials of your simulation. Show your work directly on the table.
   d. Based on your simulation, what is your estimate of the average number of fish that need to be caught in order to catch five she can keep?

79692	51707	73274	12548	91497	11135	81218	79572	06484	87440
41957	21607	51248	54772	19481	90392	35268	36234	90244	02146
07094	31750	69426	62510	90127	43365	61167	53938	03694	76923
59365	43671	12704	87941	51620	45102	22785	07729	40985	92589

e. What is the theoretical expected number of fish that need to be caught in order to be able to keep five of them.

END OF SECTION II

ANSWERS TO THE MULTIPLE-CHOICE QUESTIONS

Answer Key

1. B	11. D	21. E	31. A
2. B	12. E	22. E	32. C
3. D	13. B	23. A	33. A
4. D	14. C	24. D	34. D
5. C	15. B	25. A	35. A
6. E	16. A	26. D	36. C
7. A	17. E	27. B	37. E
8. C	18. B	28. C	38. D
9. B	19. C	29. B	39. A
10. A	20. B	30. E	40. A

Explanations of Answers to the Multiple-Choice Questions

1. **B.** The confidence level isn't mentioned in the problem, but polls often use 95%. If that is the case, we are 95% confident that the true value is within 3.5% of the sample value.

2. **B.** There are 4300 students, 51% (2200) of whom are girls and 49% (2100) of whom are boys. The expected number of girls taking AP courses is $(.51)(.45)(150) = 34.4$. The expected number of boys taking AP courses is $(.49)(.40)(150) = 29.4$. Altogether, $34.4 + 29.4 = 63.8$, or about 64.

3. **D.** $z = 1.65 = \dfrac{43 - 40}{\sigma} \rightarrow \sigma = \dfrac{3}{1.65} = 1.82$.

4. **D.** Choosing your sample from only the homes in your population of interest gives you a larger sample on which to base your confidence interval. If you use Plan A, you will end up with many homes painted with different paint than the paint of interest.

5. **C.**

6. **E.** The 80th percentile means that the area to the left of Thor's weight is .8. This corresponds to a z score of .84 (found using a *Table of Standard Normal Probabilities*). Thus,

$$z_x = .84 = \frac{x - 245}{20} \rightarrow x = 261.8, \text{or } 262.$$

7. **A.** There is a natural tendency on the part of a subject in an experiment to want to please the researcher. It is likely that the employees were increasing their production because they wanted to behave in the way they thought they were expected to.

8. **C.** A type-I error occurs when a true hypothesis is incorrectly rejected. In this case, that means that the assumption of innocence is rejected, and he is found guilty.

9. **B.** $P(A \text{ and } B) = P(A) \cdot P(A \mid B) = (.4)(.2) = .08.$ $P(A \text{ or } B) = P(A) + P(B) - P(A \text{ and } B) = .4 + .3 - .08 = .62.$

10. **A.** This is a matched pairs test. The data for the test are the differences between the post- and pretest scores for each trainee. Thus, it is a one-sample t test with $n - 1 = 10 - 1 = 9$ degrees of freedom.

11. **D.** You can *infer* cause-and-effect with other kind of studies, but the only way to be sure is to control the situation in such a way as to be sure that the only difference between the groups is the variable under study and that means a controlled experiment.

12. **E.** Be clear on the difference between the treatment (type of cat food in this problem) and the blocking variable (breed of cat).

13. **B.** The box is longer for Network A and the ends of the whiskers are further apart than Network B → Network A has a greater range of ratings than Network B. The 3rd quartile, the median, and the 1st quartile of Network A are higher than Network B, which can be interpreted to mean that Network A is higher rated than Network B. I is not correct because there is no way to tell how many values are in a boxplot.

14. **C.** The predicted score for the student is $273.5 + (91.2)(3) = 547.1$. The residual is actual score − predicted score = $510 - 547.1 = -37.1$

15. **B.** The expected value is $(-1)(.6) + (1)(.25) + (2)(.15) = -.05$

16. **A.** The expected values are $.5 \times 50 = 25$ Golden Retrievers, $.4 \times 50 = 20$ Shepherds; and $.1 \times 50 = 5$ Other.

$$\chi^2 = \frac{(27 - 25)^2}{25} + \frac{(22 - 20)^2}{20} + \frac{(1 - 5)^2}{5} = 3.56$$

17. **E.** We are 95% confident that the true proportion who will vote for the former actor is in the interval <.35, .42>. This means that the true proportion is likely to be in this interval.

18. **B.** A z score

$$z = \frac{x - \overline{x}}{s}$$

tells you how many standard deviations (s) a given score (x) is above or below the mean of the data ($\overline{x}$). A z score of 1.25 means that his score was 1.25 standard deviations above the mean.

19. **C.** Back-to-back stemplots are an excellent way of comparing small datasets without losing the actual values in the set. Boxplots can also be used but aren't as useful in this situation because the original data are lost.

20. **B.** The following tree diagram illustrates the situation:

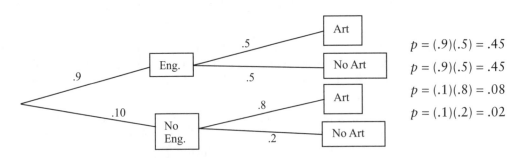

$$p = (.9)(.5) = .45$$
$$p = (.9)(.5) = .45$$
$$p = (.1)(.8) = .08$$
$$p = (.1)(.2) = .02$$

Now, p(student takes art) $= .45 + .08 = .53$

21. **E.** P(doesn't take English | Does take art)

$$= \frac{.08}{.45 + .08} = .15$$

22. **E.** Choices A, B, and D are based on the mean and are not resistant to changes in the maximum value of the dataset. The range now stretches from the minimum value to 92 instead of 192.

23. **A.** $df = n - 2 = 15 - 2 = 13 \rightarrow t^* = 3.012$. The standard error of the slope of the regression line, s_b, is .07015. The confidence interval, therefore, is $.00935 \pm 3.012(.07015)$.

24. **D.** To be a simple random sample, every possible sample of size 40 must be equally likely. Only D meets this standard.

25. **A.** $\mu_X = 100(.55) = 55$, $\sigma_X = \sqrt{100(.55)(.45)} = 4.97$

26. **D.** To reject the null at the .05 level of significance, we would need to have $z < -2.33$

27. **B.** A confidence interval can be used in place of a significance test in a hypothesis test with a two-sided alternative. In this case, the evidence supports the alternative.

28. **C.** Because 10% of the scores are less than 154, we have

$$z_{154} = -1.28 = \frac{154 - \mu}{\sigma}$$

and because 5% of the scores are above 213,

$$z_{213} = 1.645 = \frac{213 - \mu}{\sigma}.$$

We now have two equations in two unknowns

$$-1.28 = \frac{154 - \mu}{\sigma} \text{ and } 1.645 = \frac{213 - \mu}{\sigma}.$$

Doing the algebra to solve for μ and σ, we find $\mu = 179.8$ and $\sigma = 20.17$.

29. **B.** The tendency in voluntary response surveys is for people who feel most strongly about an issue to respond. If people are happy in their marriage, they are less likely to respond.

30. **E.** The upper critical z for a 98% confidence interval is $z^* = 2.33$. The sample size needed is

$$n = \left(\frac{2.33}{2(.03)} \right)^2 = 1508.03.$$

We need to round up to 1509 so that the maximum error is .03.

31. **A.** Power can be increased by increasing n, increasing α, moving the alternative further away from the null, reducing the variability. This choice provides the best combination of large n and large α.

32. **C.**

33. **A.**

34. **D.**

$$b = r \frac{s_y}{s_x} = (.77)\left(\frac{3.6}{.32} \right) = 8.66.$$

35. **A.** The mean is pulled in the direction of skewness.

36. **C.**

37. **E.**

38. **D.** A confidence level is a statement about the procedure used to generate the interval, not about any one interval.

39. **A.** A 95% confidence interval, at $12 - 2 = 10$ degrees of freedom ($t^* = 2.228$) is $.74 \pm (2.228)(.11) = .74 \pm .245$

40. **A.**

$$z = \frac{14 - 15}{2.8/\sqrt{50}} = -2.53 \rightarrow P \text{ value} = .0057.$$

If this were done as a t test, and it could be because the population is approximately normally distributed, then $t = -2.53 \rightarrow .005 < P < .01$ for 49 degrees of freedom— you would have to use 40 degrees of freedom in the table.

SOLUTIONS TO FREE-RESPONSE QUESTIONS

Solution to #1

a. A line is a good model for the data for two reasons: $r^2 = .954 \rightarrow r = .98$, so there is a strong linear correlation between the variables. Also, the residual plot shows no obvious pattern, indicating that the line is a good model for the data.

b. $Words = 3.371 + 2.1143(Age)$.

c. $Words = 3.371 + 2.1143(7.5) = 19.2$.

d. For each year a child grows, the number of words he or she knows about transportation is predicted to grow by 2.1.

Solution to #2

a. P(a student takes calculus) $= 90/675 = .133$.

b. P(a student takes analysis or calculus given that they are in the 12th grade)

$$= \frac{99 + 62}{220} = \frac{161}{220} = .732.$$

c. P(a student is in the 10th grade given that they are taking algebra II)

$$= \frac{74}{213} = .347.$$

d. Let A = "A student takes geometry" and B = "A student is a 10th grader." A and B are independent events if and only if $P(A) = P(A|B)$.

$$P(A) = \frac{178}{675} = .264.$$

$$P(A|B) = \frac{125}{225} = .556.$$

Thus, the events are not independent.

Solution to #3

a. Let p = the true proportion of students who will sign up for upper division mathematics classes during the coming year.

$H_0: p \le .80$
$H_A: p > .80$

We want to use a one-proportion z test, at the .05 level of significance. We note that we are given that the sample was a random sample, and that $np = 55(.8) = 44$ and $55(1 - .8) = 11$ are both larger than 5 (or 10). Thus the conditions needed for this test are satisfied.

$$p = \frac{48}{55} = .873.$$

$$z = \frac{.873 - .80}{\sqrt{\dfrac{.8(1 - .8)}{55}}} = 1.35 \rightarrow P \text{ value} = 1 - .9115 = .0885$$

Because $P > a$, we cannot reject the null hypothesis. The survey evidence is not strong enough to justify adding another section of upper division mathematics.

b. If all five of the other students returned their surveys, there are two worst-case scenarios: all five say they will sign up; all five say they will not sign up. If all five say they will not sign up, then an even lower percentage say they need the class (48/60 rather than 48/55) and our decision to not offer another class would not change.

If all five say they will sign up, then

$$p = \frac{53}{60} = .883.$$

$$z = \frac{.883 - .80}{\sqrt{\dfrac{.8(1 - .8)}{60}}} = 1.61 \rightarrow P \text{ value} = 1 - .9463 = .0537$$

At the 5% level of significance, this is still not quite enough to reject the null. However, it's very close, and the assistant principal might want to generate some additional data before making a final decision.

Solution to #4

a. Randomly divide your 150 volunteers into two groups. One way to do this would be to put each volunteer's name on a slip of paper, put the papers into a box, and begin drawing them out. The first 75 names selected would be in group A, and the other 75 would be in group B. Alternatively, you could flip a coin for each volunteer. If it came up heads, the volunteer goes into group A; if tails, the volunteer goes into group B. The second method would likely end up in unequal size groups.

Administer one group the new medication (treatment group), and administer the old medication to the other group (control) for a period of time. After enough time has passed, have each volunteer evaluated for reduction in the symptoms of depression. Compare the two groups.

b. Because we know that being in therapy can affect the symptoms of depression, block by having the 60 people who have been in therapy be in one block and the 90 who have not been in therapy be in the other block. Then, within each block, conduct an experiment as described in part (a).

Solution to #5

H_0: Month of birth and draft number are independent.
H_A: Month of birth and draft number are not independent.

This is a two-way table with 12 rows and 2 columns. A chi-square test of independence is appropriate. The numbers of expected values are given in the table below:

	Expected Number Selected ≤ 183	Expected Number Selected ≥ 184
January	15.5	15.5
February	14.5	14.5
March	15.5	15.5
April	15	15
May	15.5	15.5
June	15	15
July	15.5	15.5
August	15.5	15.5
September	15	15
October	15.5	15.5
November	15	15
December	15.5	15.5

Because all expected values are greater than 5, the conditions for the chi-square goodness-of-fit test are met.

$$\chi^2 = \frac{(12 - 15.5)^2}{15.5} + \frac{(19 - 15.5)^2}{15.5} + \cdots + \frac{(26 - 15.5)^2}{15.5}$$

$$+ \frac{(5 - 15.5)^2}{15.5} = 31.14$$

$df = (12 - 1)(2 - 1) = 11 \rightarrow .001 < P \text{ value} < .0025$

$\left[\text{On the TI-83, } P = .00105.\right]$

Because the P value is so small, we have evidence to reject the null and conclude that birth month and draft number are not independent. That is, month of birth is related to draft numbers. Observation of the data indicates that the lottery was biased against people born later in the year.

Solution to #6

a. The situation described is pictured below.

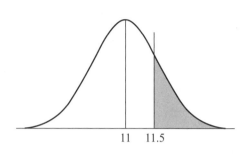

$$P(x > 11.5) = P\left(z_{11.5} = \frac{11.5 - 11}{.6} = .83\right)$$

$= 1 - .7967 = .2033$. Rounding to the nearest tenth, $P(x > 11.5) = .2$

[*On the calculator* $P(x > 11.5)$
$= normalcdf(11.5, 1000, 11, .6)$
$= .2023$.]

b. Because the probability that the fish is large enough to keep is .2, let the digits 0 and 1 represent a fish that is large enough to keep and the digits 2,3,4,5,6,7,8, and 9 represent fish that must be released. Begin at the first line of the table and count the number of digits required until five of the digits 0, 1 are found.

c. On the random number table below, successes (a large enough fish) are in boldface. Backslashes separate the various trials. The number of catches it took to get five sufficiently large fish is indicated under each separate trial.

79692 5**1**7**0**7 73274 **1**2548 9**1**497 **1\11**35 8**1**2**1**8 79572 **0**\6484 8744**0**
                      (26 fish)   *(15 fish)*
4**1**957 2**1**6**0**7 5**1**\248 54772 **1**948**1** 9**0**392 35268 36234 9**0**244 **0**2**1**46
(21 fish)   *(35 fish)*
07**0**94 3**1**75**0**\ 69426 625**1**0 9**0**127 43365 6**1**167 53938 **0**3694 76923
(13 fish)
59365 4367**1** 127**0**4 8794**1** 5**1**62**0** 45**1**02 22785 07729 4**0**985 92589

d. Based on the five trials, an estimate of the average number of catches required to get five fish of minimum size is $(26 + 15 + 21 + 35 + 13)/5 = 22$.

e. The expected number of fish we would need to catch in order to keep one of them with $P = .2$ is $1/.2 = 5$ fish. The expected wait to catch five fish we can keep is then $5(5) = 25$.

SCORING AND INTERPRETATION

Section I: Multiple Choice

$$[\underline{\hspace{3cm}} - (1/4 \times \underline{\hspace{3cm}})] \times 1.25 = \underline{\hspace{3cm}} = \underline{\hspace{3cm}}$$

| Number correct (out of 40) | Number wrong | Multiple-Choice Score (if less than zero, enter zero) | Weighted Section I Score (Do not round) |

Section II: Free Response

Question 1	_____	×	1.875 =	_____
	(out of 4)			(Do not round)
Question 2	_____	×	1.875 =	_____
	(out of 4)			(Do not round)
Question 3	_____	×	1.875 =	_____
	(out of 4)			(Do not round)
Question 4	_____	×	1.875 =	_____
	(out of 4)			(Do not round)
Question 5	_____	×	1.875 =	_____
	(out of 4)			(Do not round)
Question 6	_____	×	3.125 =	_____
	(out of 4)			(Do not round)

Sum = _____
Weighted
Section II Score
(Do not round)

Composite Score

_____ + _____ = _____
Weighted   Weighted   Composite Score
Section I   Section II   (round to nearest
Score   Score   whole number)

Composite Score Range	Rough Estimate of AP Score
68–100	5
53–67	4
40–52	3
29–39	2
0–28	1

The above score breaks are based on the most recent information available. They will give you an approximate idea of how your results on the practice Statistics exam would be scored. However, bear in mind that the breaks are recalculated each year. Also, note that these breaks are for composite scores and are not based on percentage correct.

Chapter 11

AP Physics B

Answer Sheet for Multiple-Choice Questions

1. _____	19. _____	37. _____	55. _____
2. _____	20. _____	38. _____	56. _____
3. _____	21. _____	39. _____	57. _____
4. _____	22. _____	40. _____	58. _____
5. _____	23. _____	41. _____	59. _____
6. _____	24. _____	42. _____	60. _____
7. _____	25. _____	43. _____	61. _____
8. _____	26. _____	44. _____	62. _____
9. _____	27. _____	45. _____	63. _____
10. _____	28. _____	46. _____	64. _____
11. _____	29. _____	47. _____	65. _____
12. _____	30. _____	48. _____	66. _____
13. _____	31. _____	49. _____	67. _____
14. _____	32. _____	50. _____	68. _____
15. _____	33. _____	51. _____	69. _____
16. _____	34. _____	52. _____	70. _____
17. _____	35. _____	53. _____	
18. _____	36. _____	54. _____	

AP PHYSICS B

Section I

Time—90 minutes

70 questions

You may refer to the Constants sheet found in the Appendix. However, you may not use the Equations sheet, and you may not use a calculator on this portion of the exam.

1. A ball is thrown off of a 25-m-high cliff. Its initial velocity is 25 m/s, directed at an angle of 53° above the horizontal. How much time elapses before the ball hits the ground? (sin 53° = 0.80; cos 53° = 0.60; tan 53° = 1.3)

    (A) 3.0 s
    (B) 5.0 s
    (C) 7.0 s
    (D) 9.0 s
    (E) 11.0 s

2. A ball is dropped off of a cliff of height h. Its velocity upon hitting the ground is v. At what height above the ground is the ball's velocity equal to $v/2$?

    (A) $\dfrac{h}{4}$

    (B) $\dfrac{h}{2}$

    (C) $\dfrac{h}{\sqrt{2}}$

    (D) $\dfrac{h}{8}$

    (E) $\dfrac{h}{2\sqrt{2}}$

3. A golf cart moves with moderate speed as it reaches the base of a short but steep hill. The cart coasts up the hill (without using its brake or gas pedal). At the top of the hill the car just about comes to rest; but then the car starts to coast down the other side of the hill. Consider the forward motion of the cart to be positive. Which of the following velocity–time graphs best represents the motion of the cart?

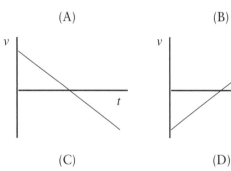

(A) (B)

(C) (D)

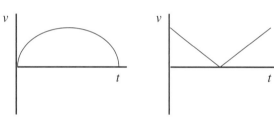

(E)

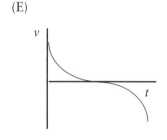

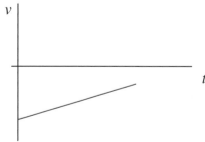

4. The velocity–time graph above represents a car on a freeway. North is defined as the positive direction. Which of the following describes the motion of the car?

(A) The car is traveling north and slowing down.
(B) The car is traveling south and slowing down.
(C) The car is traveling north and speeding up.
(D) The car is traveling south and speeding up.
(E) The car is traveling northeast and speeding up.

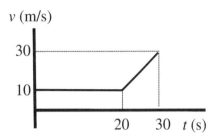

5. A car was caught in heavy traffic. After 20 s of moving at constant speed, traffic cleared a bit, allowing the car to speed up. The car's motion is represented by the velocity–time graph above. What was the car's acceleration while it was speeding up?

(A) 0.5 m/s^2
(B) 1.0 m/s^2
(C) 1.5 m/s^2
(D) 2.0 m/s^2
(E) 3.0 m/s^2

6. A block of mass m sits on the ground. A student pulls up on the block with a tension T, but the block remains in contact with the ground. What is the normal force on the block?

(A) $T + mg$
(B) $T - mg$
(C) mg
(D) $mg - T$
(E) T

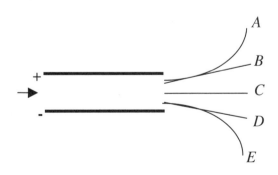

7. A proton moving at constant velocity enters the region between two charged plates, as shown above. Which of the paths shown correctly

indicates the proton's trajectory after leaving the region between the charged plates?

(A) *A*
(B) *B*
(C) *C*
(D) *D*
(E) *E*

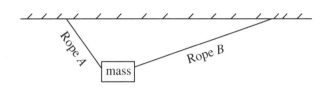

8. A mass hangs from two ropes at unequal angles, as shown above. Which of the following makes correct comparisons of the horizontal and vertical components of the tension in each rope?

	Horizontal tension	Vertical tension
(A)	greater in rope *B*	greater in rope *B*
(B)	equal in both ropes	greater in rope *A*
(C)	greater in rope *A*	greater in rope *A*
(D)	equal in both ropes	equal in both ropes
(E)	greater in rope *B*	equal in both ropes

9. A free-body diagram includes vectors representing the individual forces acting on an object. Which of these quantities should NOT appear on a free-body diagram?

(A) tension of a rope
(B) mass times acceleration
(C) kinetic friction
(D) static friction
(E) weight

10. An object rolls along level ground to the right at constant speed. Must there be any forces pushing this object to the right?

(A) Yes: the *only* forces that act must be to the right.
(B) Yes: but there could also be a friction force acting to the left.
(C) No: no forces can act to the right.
(D) No: while there can be forces acting, no force MUST act.
(E) The answer depends on the speed of the object.

11. A person stands on a scale in an elevator. He notices that the scale reading is lower than his usual weight. Which of the following could possibly describe the motion of the elevator?

    (A) It is moving down at constant speed.
    (B) It is moving down and slowing down.
    (C) It is moving up and slowing down.
    (D) It is moving up and speeding up.
    (E) It is moving up with constant speed.

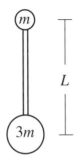

12. A mass m is attached to a mass $3m$ by a rigid bar of negligible mass and length L. Initially, the smaller mass is located directly above the larger mass, as shown above. How much work is necessary to flip the rod 180° so that the larger mass is directly above the smaller mass?

    (A) $4mgL$
    (B) $2mgL$
    (C) mgL
    (D) $4\pi mgL$
    (E) $2\pi mgL$

13. A ball rolls horizontally with speed v off of a table a height h above the ground. Just before the ball hits the ground, what is its speed?

    (A) $\sqrt{2gh}$
    (B) $v\sqrt{2gh}$
    (C) $\sqrt{v^2 + 2gh}$
    (D) v
    (E) $v + \sqrt{2gh}$

Questions 14 and 15

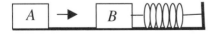

Block B is at rest on a smooth tabletop. It is attached to a long spring, which in turn is anchored to the wall. Block A slides toward and collides with block B. Consider two possible collisions:

Case I: block A bounces back off of block B.
Case II: block A sticks to block B.

14. Which of the following is correct about the speed of block B immediately after the collision?

    (A) It is faster in case II than in case I ONLY if block B is heavier.
    (B) It is faster in case I than in case II ONLY if block B is heavier.
    (C) It is faster in case II than in case I regardless of the mass of each block.
    (D) It is faster in case I than in case II regardless of the mass of each block.
    (E) It is the same in either case regardless of the mass of each block.

15. Which is correct about the period of the ensuing oscillations after the collision?

    (A) The period is greater in case II than in case I if block B is heavier.
    (B) The period is greater in case I than in case II if block B is heavier.
    (C) The period is greater in case II than in case I regardless of the mass of each block.
    (D) The period is greater in case I than in case II regardless of the mass of each block.
    (E) The period is the same in either case.

16. A ball collides with a stationary block on a frictionless surface. The ball sticks to the block. Which of the following would NOT increase the force acting on the ball during the collision?

    (A) increasing the time it takes the ball to change the block's speed
    (B) arranging for the ball to bounce off of the block rather than stick
    (C) increasing the speed of the ball before it collides with the block
    (D) increasing the mass of the block
    (E) anchoring the block in place so that the ball/block combination cannot move after collision

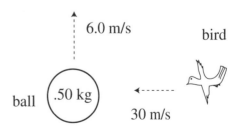

17. A 0.30-kg bird is flying from right to left at 30 m/s. The bird collides with and sticks to a 0.50-kg ball which is moving straight up with speed 6.0 m/s. What is the magnitude of the

momentum of the ball/bird combination immediately after collision?

(A) 12.0 Ns
(B) 9.5 Ns
(C) 9.0 Ns
(D) 6.0 Ns
(E) 3.0 Ns

18. A car slows down on a highway. Its engine is providing a forward force of 1000 N; the force of friction is 3000 N. It takes 20 s for the car to come to rest. What is the car's change in momentum during these 20 s?

(A) 10,000 kg·m/s
(B) 20,000 kg·m/s
(C) 30,000 kg·m/s
(D) 40,000 kg·m/s
(E) 60,000 kg·m/s

19. Which of the following quantities is NOT a vector?

(A) magnetic field
(B) electric force
(C) electric current
(D) electric field
(E) electric potential

20. Which of the following must be true of an object in uniform circular motion?

(A) Its velocity must be constant.
(B) Its acceleration and its velocity must be in opposite directions.
(C) Its acceleration and its velocity must be perpendicular to each other.
(D) It must experience a force away from the center of the circle.
(E) Its acceleration must be negative.

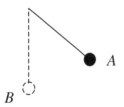

21. A ball of mass m on a string swings back and forth to a maximum angle of 30° to the vertical, as shown above. Which of the following vectors represents the acceleration, **a**, of the mass at point A, the highest point in the swing?

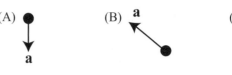

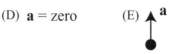

22. A planet of mass m orbits in a circle around a sun. The speed of the planet in its orbit is v; the distance from the planet to the sun is d. What is the magnitude and direction of the net force experienced by the planet?

(A) $\dfrac{v^2}{d}$, toward the sun.

(B) $m\dfrac{v^2}{d}$, toward the sun.

(C) $m\dfrac{v^2}{d}$, away from the sun.

(D) $m\dfrac{v^2}{d}$, along the orbital path.

(E) $\dfrac{v^2}{d}$, along the orbital path.

23. A mass m on a spring oscillates on a horizontal surface with period T. The total mechanical energy contained in this oscillation is E. Imagine that instead a new mass $4m$ oscillates on the same spring with the same amplitude. What is the new period and total mechanical energy?

	Period	Total Mechanical Energy
(A)	T	E
(B)	$2T$	E
(C)	$2T$	$2E$
(D)	T	$4E$
(E)	$2T$	$16E$

24. A satellite orbits the moon in a circle of radius R. If the satellite must double its speed but maintain a circular orbit, what must the new radius of its orbit be?

(A) $2R$
(B) $4R$
(C) ½ R
(D) ¼ R
(E) R

25. The Space Shuttle orbits 300 km above the Earth's surface; the Earth's radius is 6400 km. What is the gravitational acceleration experienced by the Space Shuttle?

    (A) 4.9 m/s²
    (B) 8.9 m/s²
    (C) 9.8 m/s²
    (D) 10.8 m/s²
    (E) zero

26. A cube of ice (specific gravity 0.90) floats in a cup of water. Several hours later, the ice cube has completely melted into the glass. How does the water level after melting compare to the initial water level?

    (A) The water level is 10% higher after melting.
    (B) The water level is 90% higher after melting.
    (C) The water level unchanged after melting.
    (D) The water level is 10% lower after melting.
    (E) The water level is 90% lower after melting.

27. A strong hurricane may include 50 m/s winds. Consider a building in such a hurricane. If the air inside the building is kept at standard atmospheric pressure, how will the outside air pressure compare to the inside air pressure?

    (A) Outside pressure will be the same.
    (B) Outside pressure will be about 2% greater.
    (C) Outside pressure will be about 2% lower.
    (D) Outside pressure will be about twice inside pressure.
    (E) Outside pressure will be about half inside pressure.

28. A heavy block sits on the bottom of an aquarium. Which of the following must be correct about the magnitude of the normal force exerted on the block by the aquarium bottom?

    (A) The normal force is equal to the block's weight.
    (B) The normal force is less than the block's weight.
    (C) The normal force is greater than the block's weight.
    (D) The normal force is equal to the buoyant force on the block.
    (E) The normal force is greater than the buoyant force on the block.

29. The density of water near the ocean's surface is $\rho_o = 1.025 \times 10^3$ kg/m³. At extreme depths, though, ocean water becomes slightly more dense. Let ρ represent the density of ocean water at the bottom of a trench of depth d. What can be said about the gauge pressure at this depth?

    (A) The pressure is greater than $\rho_o g d$, but less than $\rho g d$.
    (B) The pressure is greater than $\rho g d$.
    (C) The pressure is less than $\rho_o g d$.
    (D) The pressure is greater than $\rho_o g d$, but could be less than or greater than $\rho g d$.
    (E) The pressure is less than $\rho g d$, but could be less than or greater than $\rho_o g d$.

30. A 1.0-m-long brass pendulum has a period of 2.0 s on a very cold (−10°C) day. On a very warm day, when the temperature is 30°C, what is the period of this pendulum?

    (A) 1.0 s
    (B) 1.4 s
    (C) 1.8 s
    (D) 2.2 s
    (E) 4.0 s

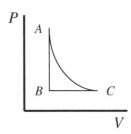

31. The state of a gas in a cylinder is represented by the PV diagram shown above. The gas can be taken through either the cycle $ABCA$, or the reverse cycle $ACBA$. Which of the following statements about the work done on or by the gas is correct?

    (A) In both cases, the same amount of net work is done *by* the gas.
    (B) In both cases, the same amount of net work is done *on* the gas.
    (C) In cycle $ABCA$ net work is done *on* the gas; in cycle $ACBA$ the same amount of net work is done *by* the gas.
    (D) In cycle $ABCA$ net work is done *by* the gas; in cycle $ACBA$ the same amount of net work is done *on* the gas.
    (E) In both cycles net work is done *by* the gas, but more net work is done by the gas in $ACBA$ than in $ABCA$.

32. At room temperature, the rms speed of nitrogen molecules is about 500 m/s. By what factor must the absolute temperature T of the Earth change

for the rms speed of nitrogen to reach escape velocity, 11 km/s?

(A) T must decrease by a factor of 50.
(B) T must increase by a factor of 22.
(C) T must increase by a factor of 50.
(D) T must increase by a factor of 200.
(E) T must increase by a factor of 500.

33. One mole of He (atomic mass 4 amu) occupies a volume of 0.022 m³ at room temperature and atmospheric pressure. How much volume is occupied by one mole of O_2 (atomic mass 32 amu) under the same conditions?

(A) 0.022 m³
(B) 0.088 m³
(C) 0.176 m³
(D) 0.352 m³
(E) 0.003 m³

34. On average, how far apart are N_2 molecules at room temperature?

(A) 10^{-21} m
(B) 10^{-15} m
(C) 10^{-9} m
(D) 10^{-3} m
(E) 1 m

35. Which of the following is NOT a statement or consequence of the second law of thermodynamics, the law dealing with entropy?

(A) The net work done by a gas cannot be greater than the sum of its loss of internal energy and the heat added to it.
(B) Even an ideal heat engine cannot be 100% efficient.
(C) A warm ball of putty cannot spontaneously cool off and rise.
(D) A system cannot become more ordered unless some net work is done to obtain that order.
(E) Heat does not flow naturally from a low to high temperature.

36. Experimenter A uses a very small test charge q_0, and experimenter B uses a test charge $2q_0$ to measure an electric field produced by stationary charges. A finds a field that is

(A) greater than the field found by B
(B) the same as the field found by B
(C) less than the field found by B
(D) either greater or less than the field found by B, depending on the accelerations of the test charges

(E) either greater or less than the field found by B, depending on the masses of the test charges

37. Two isolated particles, A and B, are 4 m apart. Particle A has a net charge of $2Q$, and B has a net charge of Q. The ratio of the magnitude of the electrostatic force on A to that on B is

(A) 4:1
(B) 2:1
(C) 1:1
(D) 1:2
(E) 1:4

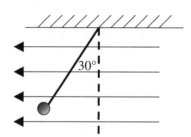

38. A uniform electric field points right to left. A small metal ball charged to +2 mC hangs at a 30° angle from a string of negligible mass, as shown above. The tension in the string is measured to be 0.1 N. What is the magnitude of the electric field? (sin 30° = 0.50; cos 30° = 0.87; tan 30° = 0.58).

(A) 25 N/C
(B) 50 N/C
(C) 2500 N/C
(D) 5000 N/C
(E) 10,000 N/C

39. 1.0 nC is deposited on a solid metal sphere of diameter 0.30 m. What is the magnitude of the electric field at the center of the sphere?

(A) zero
(B) 25 N/C
(C) 100 N/C
(D) 200 N/C
(E) 400 N/C

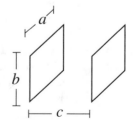

40. The parallel plate capacitor above consists of identical rectangular plates of dimensions $a \times b$, separated by a distance c. To cut the capacitance of this capacitor in half, which of these quantities should be doubled?

(A) a
(B) b
(C) c
(D) ab
(E) abc

41. Two identical capacitors are connected in parallel to an external circuit. Which of the following quantities must be the same for both capacitors?

    I. the charge stored on the capacitor
    II. the voltage across the capacitor
    III. the capacitance of the capacitor

(A) I only
(B) II only
(C) II and III only
(D) I and III only
(E) I, II, and III

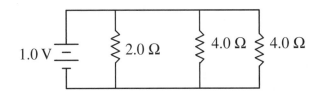

42. Three resistors are connected to a 1.0 V battery, as shown in the diagram above. What is the current through the 2.0 Ω resistor?

(A) 0.25 A
(B) 0.50 A
(C) 1.0 A
(D) 2.0 A
(E) 4.0 A

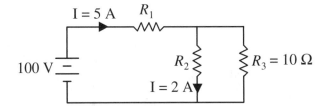

43. What is the voltage drop across R_3 in the circuit diagrammed above?

(A)   10 V
(B)   20 V
(C)   30 V
(D)   50 V
(E) 100 V

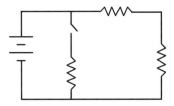

44. Three resistors are connected to an ideal battery as shown in the diagram above. The switch is initially closed. When the switch is open, what happens to the total voltage, current, and resistance in the circuit?

	Voltage	Current	Resistance
(A)	increases	increases	increases
(B)	does not change	does not change	does not change
(C)	does not change	decreases	increases
(D)	does not change	increases	decreases
(E)	decreases	decreases	decreases

45. On which of the following physics principles does Kirchoff's loop rule rest?

(A) conservation of charge
(B) conservation of mass
(C) conservation of energy
(D) conservation of momentum
(E) conservation of angular momentum

Questions 46 and 47

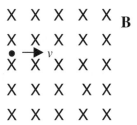

A uniform magnetic field **B** is directed into the page. An electron enters this field with initial velocity v to the right.

46. Which of the following best describes the path of the electron while it is still within the magnetic field?

(A) It moves in a straight line.
(B) It bends upward in a parabolic path.
(C) It bends downward in a parabolic path.
(D) It bends upward in a circular path.
(E) It bends downward in a circular path.

47. The electron travels a distance *d*, measured along its path, before exiting the magnetic field. How much work is done on the electron by the magnetic field?

    (A) *evBd*
    (B) zero
    (C) −*evBd*
    (D) *evBd* sin (d/2π)
    (E) −*evBd* sin (d/2π)

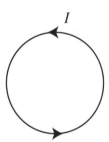

48. The circular wire shown above carries a current *I* in the counterclockwise direction. What will be the direction of the magnetic field at the center of the wire?

    (A) into the page
    (B) out of the page
    (C) down
    (D) up
    (E) counterclockwise

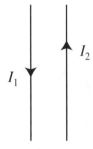

49. Two parallel wires carry currents in opposite directions, as shown above. In what direction will the right-hand wire (the wire carrying current I_2) experience a force?

    (A) left
    (B) right
    (C) into the page
    (D) out of the page
    (E) The right-hand wire will experience no force.

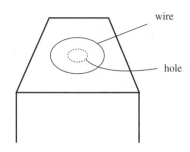

50. A loop of wire surrounds a hole in a table, as shown above. A bar magnet is dropped, north end down, from above the table through the hole. Let the positive direction of current be defined as counterclockwise as viewed from above. Which of the following graphs best represents the induced current **I** in the loop?

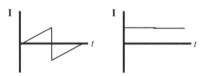

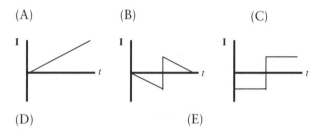

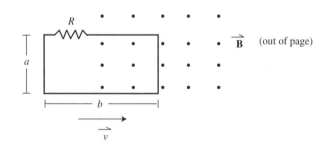

51. A rectangular loop of wire has dimensions $a \times b$ and includes a resistor *R*. This loop is pulled with speed *v* from a region of no magnetic field into a uniform magnetic field **B** pointing through the loop, as shown above. What is the magnitude and direction of the current through the resistor?

    (A) *Bav/R*, left-to-right
    (B) *Bbv/R*, left-to-right
    (C) *Bav/R*, right-to-left
    (D) *Bbv/R*, right-to-left
    (E) *Bba/R*, right-to-left

52. A proton moves in a straight line. Which of the following combinations of electric or magnetic fields could NOT allow this motion?

    (A) only an electric field pointing in the direction of the proton's motion
    (B) only a magnetic field pointing opposite the direction of the proton's motion
    (C) an electric field and a magnetic field, each pointing perpendicular to the proton's motion
    (D) only a magnetic field pointing perpendicular to the proton's motion
    (E) only a magnetic field pointing in the direction of the proton's motion

53. A guitar string is plucked, producing a standing wave on the string. A person hears the sound wave generated by the string. Which wave properties are the same for each of these waves, and which are different?

	Wavelength	Velocity	Frequency
(A)	same	different	same
(B)	same	same	same
(C)	same	different	different
(D)	different	same	different
(E)	different	different	same

54. A traveling wave passes a point. At this point, the time between successive crests is 0.2 s. Which of the following statements can be justified?

    (A) The wavelength is 5 m.
    (B) The frequency is 5 Hz.
    (C) The velocity of the wave is 5 m/s.
    (D) The wavelength is 0.2 m.
    (E) The wavelength is 68 m.

55. What is the frequency of sound waves produced by a string bass whose height is 2 m?

    (A) 1 Hz
    (B) 0.01 Hz
    (C) 100 Hz
    (D) 10 Hz
    (E) 1000 Hz

56. What property of a light wave determines the color of the light?

    (A) frequency
    (B) wavelength
    (C) velocity
    (D) amplitude
    (E) The medium through which the light wave travels

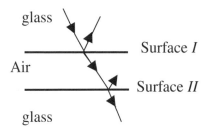

57. Light traveling through glass hits a thin film of air, as shown above. For which of the following beams of light does the light wave change phase by 180°?

    (A) the light reflected off of surface *I*
    (B) the light transmitted through surface *I*
    (C) the light reflected off of surface *II*
    (D) the light transmitted through surface *II*
    (E) both the light reflected off of surface *I* **and** the light reflected off of surface *II*

58. Light from a coherent source passes through a diffraction grating, producing an interference pattern on a screen. Three of the bright spots produced on the screen are 2.2 cm away from one another, as shown above. Now, a new diffraction grating is substituted, whose distance between lines is half of the original grating's. Which of the following shows the new interference pattern?

    (A)

    (B)

    (C)

    (D)

    (E)

59. Which colors of visible light have the *largest* frequency, wavelength, and energy per photon?

	Frequency	Wave-length	Energy per photon
(A)	red	violet	violet
(B)	red	violet	red
(C)	violet	red	violet
(D)	violet	red	red
(E)	violet	violet	violet

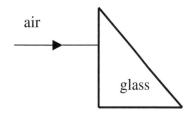

60. White light is incident on the triangular glass prism shown above. Why is it that blue and red light can be seen separately when the light exits the prism?

   (A) The blue light speeds up more inside the glass.
   (B) Some of the red light reflects at each interface.
   (C) The light changes its frequency within the glass.
   (D) The blue light bends farther away from normal at the left-hand interface.
   (E) The blue light bends farther away from normal at the right-hand interface.

61. A convex lens projects a clear, focused image of a candle onto a screen. The screen is located 30 cm away from the lens; the candle sits 20 cm from the lens. Later, it is noticed that this same lens can also project a clear, focused image of the lighted windows of a building. If the building is located 60 m away, what is the distance between the lens and the image of the building?

   (A) 12 cm
   (B) 24 cm
   (C) 40 cm
   (D) 80 cm
   (E) 90 cm

   I. concave mirror
   II. convex mirror
   III. concave lens
   IV. convex lens

62. Which of the optical instruments listed above can produce a virtual image of an object that is smaller than the object itself?

   (A) I only
   (B) II only
   (C) III only
   (D) II and III only
   (E) I and IV only

63. Which of the following does NOT describe a ray that can be drawn for a concave mirror?

   (A) an incident ray through the mirror's center, reflecting right back through the center
   (B) an incident ray through the center point, reflecting through the focal point
   (C) an incident ray through the focal point, reflecting parallel to the principal axis
   (D) an incident ray parallel to the principal axis, reflecting through the focal point
   (E) an incident ray to the intersection of the principal axis with the mirror, reflecting at an equal angle.

64. Monochromatic light is incident on a photoelectric surface with work function W. The intensity, I, of the incident light is gradually increased. Which of the following graphs could represent the kinetic energy KE of electrons ejected by the photoelectric surface as a function of the intensity?

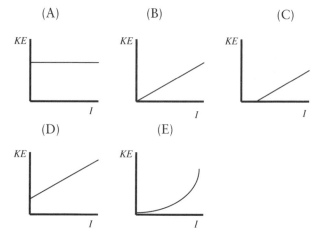

Questions 65 and 66

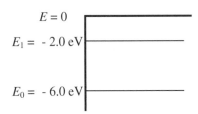

The energy levels of a hypothetical atom are shown above.

65. What wavelength of light must be absorbed to excite electrons from E_0 to E_1?

(A) 1240 nm
(B) 620 nm
(C) 100 nm
(D) 210 nm
(E) 310 nm

66. If E_0 and E_1 are the only atomic energy levels available to the electrons, how many lines will be in the emission spectrum of this atom?

(A) zero
(B) one
(C) two
(D) three
(E) four

67. Monochromatic light is incident on a photoelectric surface of work function 3.5 eV. Electrons ejected from the surface create a current in a circuit. It is found that this current can be neutralized using a stopping voltage of 1.0 V. What is the energy contained in one photon of the incident light?

(A) 1.0 eV
(B) 2.5 eV
(C) 3.5 eV
(D) 4.5 eV
(E) 5.5 eV

68. Which of the following observations provides evidence that massive particles can have a wave nature?

(A) When burning hydrogen is observed through a spectrometer, several discrete lines are seen rather than a continuous spectrum.
(B) When a beam of electrons is passed through slits very close together and then projected on to a phosphorescent screen, several equally spaced bright spots are observed.
(C) When waves on the surface of the ocean pass a large rock, the path of the waves is bent.
(D) When alpha particles are passed through gold foil, most of the alpha particles go through the foil undeflected.
(E) When light is reflected off of a thin film, bright and dark fringes are observed on the film.

69. In which of the following nuclear processes does both the atomic number Z as well as the atomic mass A remain unchanged by the process?

(A) uranium fission
(B) alpha decay
(C) beta$^+$ decay
(D) beta$^-$ decay
(E) gamma decay

70. A thorium nucleus emits an alpha particle. Which of the following fundamental physics principles can be used to explain why the direction of the daughter nucleus's recoil must be in the opposite direction of the alpha emission?

I. Newton's third law
II. conservation of momentum
III. conservation of energy

(A) II only
(B) III only
(C) I and II only
(D) II and III only
(E) I, II, and III

END OF SECTION I

AP PHYSICS B

Section II

Time—90 minutes

You may refer to the Constants sheet and Equations sheet in the Appendix during this portion of the exam. You may also use a calculator during this portion of the exam.

(Note: In some years, the Physics B free-response section will be reduced to 6 rather than 7 questions, still with a 90-minute time frame. We'll leave the seventh question in there for you for extra practice.)

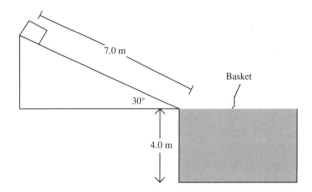

1. (15 points) A package is at rest on top of a frictionless, 7.0 m long, 30° inclined plane, as shown above. The package slides down the plane, then drops 4.0 vertical meters into a waiting basket.

    (a) How long does it take the package to reach the bottom of the plane?
    (b) What is the magnitude and direction of the velocity of the package when it reaches the bottom of the plane?
    (c) What is the TOTAL time it takes for the package both to slide down the plane and then to hit the bottom of the basket?
    (d) How far, horizontally, from the left-hand edge of the basket will the package hit the bottom?
    (e) If the basket were 8.0 m deep rather than 4.0 m deep, how would the answer to part (d) change? Check one box, and justify your answer without reference to an explicit numerical calculation.
    ☐ The horizontal distance would be doubled.
    ☐ The horizontal distance would be more than doubled.
    ☐ The horizontal distance would be increased, but less than doubled.

2. (15 points)

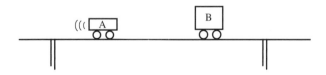

Two carts with different masses collide on a level track on which friction is negligible. Cart B is at rest before the collision. After the collision, the carts bounce off of one another; cart A moves backward, while cart B goes forward.

Consider these definitions of variables:

- m_A, the mass of cart A
- m_B, the mass of cart B
- v_A, the speed of cart A before collision
- v_A', the speed of cart A after collision
- v_B', the speed of cart B after collision

(a) Using only the variables listed above, write an expression for the fraction of momentum conserved in this collision.

(b) Using only the variables listed above, write an expression for the fraction of kinetic energy conserved in the collision.

(c) Which of the expressions you derived in parts (a) and (b) should always be equal to 100%? Justify your answer.

(d) You are given the following equipment:
   one sonic motion detector
   one stopwatch
   one meter stick

Describe a procedure that would allow an experimenter to measure the speeds of the carts before and after collision (keeping in mind that cart B is at rest before collision). Remember to be explicit about the placement of the motion detector; explain clearly how each speed can be determined from your measurements.

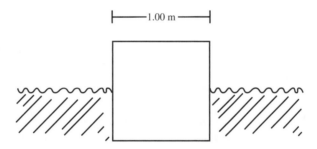

Side View

3. (15 points) A large cube with a side of length 1.00 m is floating on top of a lake. Resting undisturbed, it floats exactly half submerged, as shown above. The density of water is 1000 kg/m³.

(a) Determine the mass of the cube.

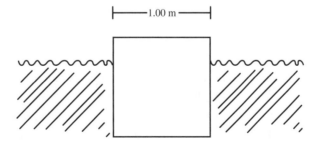

A crane pushes the cube down into the water until it is ³⁄₄ underwater, as shown; the cube is then released from rest.

(b) Determine the magnitude and direction of the net force on the cube at the moment when it is released.

(c) After release, the cube oscillates up and down in simple harmonic motion, just as if it were attached to an ideal spring of "effective spring constant" k. Determine this effective spring constant.

(d) Determine the frequency of the resulting harmonic motion.

(e) If instead, the block is released after being pushed ⁴/₅ of the way into the water, which of the following is correct about the frequency of the new harmonic motion? Check one of the three boxes below, then justify your answer.

☐ The frequency will be greater than before.
☐ The frequency will be smaller than before.
☐ The frequency will be the same as it was before.

4. (15 points)

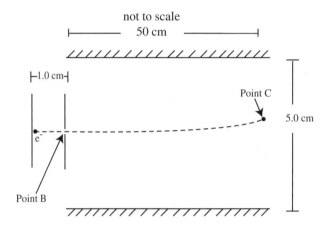

An electron starts from rest and is accelerated between two metal plates over a distance of 1.0 cm through a potential difference of 500 V. The electron exits the plates at point *B*, as shown in the diagram above. Neglect any relativistic effects.

(a) What is the velocity of this electron once it reaches point *B*?

(b) Once the electron has left point *B*, it enters directly between a second set of 50-cm-long parallel plates. These are arranged horizontally, separated by 5 cm, and with a 100 V potential difference between them.
    i. What are the magnitude and direction of the electric force, F_E, on the electron?
    ii. Determine the time it takes for the electron to travel the 50 cm through these plates to point *C*.
    iii. Determine the speed of the electron at point *C*.

(c) While the electron is traveling, it is simultaneously in the gravitational field of the Earth. Explain why it is legitimate to neglect the influence of the gravitational field; include a calculation in your explanation.

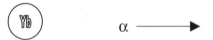

5. (10 points)

An α-particle is emitted with velocity 1.7×10^7 m/s to the right by an initially motionless Ytterbium nucleus with mass number $A = 173$, as shown above. Ytterbium has atomic number $Z = 70$.

(a) Determine the mass number A and atomic number Z of the resulting Erbium nucleus.

(b) Calculate the magnitude of the momentum of the resulting Erbium nucleus.

Radiation beam incident on Erbium nucleus initially moving to the left

After the decay, a beam of radiation of frequency 450 Hz is incident upon the Erbium nucleus opposite the direction of motion. Each photon in the beam is reflected back by the Erbium. Approximately 10^{25} photons strike the nucleus each second.

(c) Calculate how much time the light would have to be incident on the nucleus to stop its motion.

6. (10 points)

An accident occurred in a parking lot. Police lieutenants examined the scene of this accident and found that one of the involved cars, which just about came to a stop before the collision, made skid marks 80 m long. The coefficient of kinetic friction between the rubber tires and the dry pavement was about 0.80; a typical car has a mass of 700 kg.

(a) Draw a free-body diagram representing the forces on the car as it skidded. Assume the car was moving to the right.
(b) Assuming a level road, estimate how fast this car was initially traveling.
(c) The driver was cited for speeding. Explain why.
(d) In court, the driver explains that his car is particularly heavy—it has a mass not of 700 kg, but of 2100 kg. Thus, he suggests that calculations showing he was speeding are invalid. Explain whether the driver's argument makes sense.

7. (10 points) A light ray traveling in air is incident upon a glass ($n = 1.5$) trapezoid as shown above.

(a) Draw and label the normal to the surface at the point at which the light enters the glass.
(b) Determine the angle θ_2 at which the light enters the glass; draw the transmitted ray on the above diagram and label θ_2 on your drawing.
(c) Will the light ray leave the glass out of the bottom edge or the right-hand edge?
   — If the light leaves through the bottom edge, at what angle will it enter the air? Show all calculations and draw the transmitted ray.
   — If the light leaves through the right-hand edge, explain why it will not leave through the bottom edge. Show all calculations and draw the path of the ray through the glass.

END OF SECTION II

ANSWERS TO THE MULTIPLE-CHOICE QUESTIONS

Answer Key

1. B	15. C	29. A	43. C	57. C
2. A	16. A	30. D	44. D	58. C
3. D	17. B	31. C	45. C	59. C
4. B	18. D	32. E	46. D	60. E
5. D	19. E	33. A	47. B	61. A
6. D	20. C	34. C	48. B	62. D
7. D	21. C	35. A	49. B	63. B
8. B	22. B	36. B	50. D	64. A
9. B	23. B	37. C	51. C	65. E
10. D	24. D	38. A	52. D	66. D
11. C	25. B	39. A	53. E	67. D
12. B	26. C	40. C	54. B	68. B
13. C	27. C	41. E	55. C	69. E
14. D	28. B	42. B	56. A	70. C

Explanations of Answers to the Multiple-Choice Questions

1. **B.** Only the vertical motion affects the time in the air. Set up kinematics, with up positive:

$$v_o = 25 \sin 53° \text{ m/s} = 20 \text{ m/s}.$$

$$v_f = ?$$

$$\Delta x = -25 \text{ m}.$$

$$a = -10 \text{ m/s}^2.$$

$$t = \textit{what we're looking for}.$$

Use *** ($v_f^2 = v_o^2 + 2a\Delta x$), then * ($v_f = v_o + at$):

$$v_f^2 = (20 \text{ m/s})^2 + 2(-10 \text{ m/s}^2)(-25 \text{ m}).$$

$$v_f^2 = (400) + (500).$$

$v_f = -30$ m/s, negative because ball moves down at the end.

So * says -30 m/s = 20 m/s + (-10)t; $t = 5.0$ s.

2. **A.** Set up a kinematics chart with down positive:

$$v_o = 0 \text{ because dropped}.$$

$$v_f = v, \text{ given}.$$

$$\Delta x = h.$$

$$a = g.$$

$$t = \text{unknown}.$$

Using *** ($v_f^2 = v_o^2 + 2a\Delta x$) with the variables shown above, $v^2 = 2gh$ so $v = \sqrt{2gh}$. We want to know where the

speed is $v/2$, or $\sqrt{2gh}/2$. Reset the kinematics chart and solve:

$$v_o = 0 \text{ because dropped}.$$

$$v_f = \sqrt{2gh}/2.$$

$$\Delta x = \textit{what we're looking for}.$$

$$a = g.$$

$$t = \text{unknown}.$$

Using ***, $2gh/2 = 2g\Delta x$; $\Delta x = h/4$.

3. **D.** The car must slow down as it goes up the hill. Only A, B, and D start with nonzero speed that approaches zero speed. The speed reaches zero and then the cart speeds up again *in the same direction*. Only D keeps the motion in the same direction after the pause.

4. **B.** Because north is positive, and the velocity is always in the negative section of the graph, the car must move to the south. Because the speed is getting closer to zero, the car slows down.

5. **D.** Acceleration is the slope of the v–t graph. Here, we only want the slope while the car speeds up: (30–10)m/s / (30–20)s = 2.0 m/s².

6. **D.** The free-body diagram looks like this:

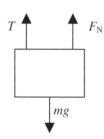

Because the block is in equilibrium, $F_N + T = mg$. Solving, $F_N = mg - T$.

7. **D.** While in the region between the plates, the positively charged proton is attracted to the negative plate, so bends downward. But after leaving the plates, there is no more force acting on the proton. Thus, the proton continues in motion in a straight line by Newton's first law.

8. **B.** Consider the horizontal and vertical forces separately. The only horizontal forces are the horizontal components of the tensions. Because the block is in equilibrium, these horizontal tensions must be *equal*, meaning only choices B and D can be right. But the ropes can't have equal horizontal AND vertical tensions, otherwise they'd hang at equal angles. So D can't be the correct choice, and B must be.

9. **B.** Tension, friction, and weight are specific forces that can pull or drag an object. But "mass times acceleration" is what we set the sum of all forces equal to—*ma* is not itself a force.

10. **D.** If the object is rolling straight at constant speed, it is in equilibrium (regardless of its speed), and the net force on it is zero. But zero net force can be obtained either by rightward forces canceling leftward forces, or by no forces acting at all.

11. **C.** Consider the free-body diagram of the person:

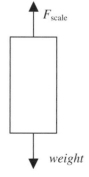

Call up positive, and F_{scale} − weight = ma. The scale reading is less than his normal weight, so the acceleration is negative; i.e., *down*. Downward acceleration means either something speeds up while moving downward, or slows down while moving upward.

12. **B.** Work done by gravity depends only on vertical displacement, not on the total distance moved. The displacement of each mass is L. Work is force (here, weight) times this displacement. It takes $3mgL$ of work to raise the bottom mass, but while that's done, the small mass moves down; this means that negative mgL of work was done to lower the small mass. The total work necessary, then, is $3mgL + (−mgL) = 2mgL$.

13. **C.** Speed means the magnitude of the velocity vector, *not* just the vertical velocity; so you can't just use vertical kinematics. You find the final velocity in both directions, and add the vectors. It's easier, though, to use energy. Call point A the top of the table, point B the floor. $PE_A + KE_A = PE_B + KE_B$; $mgh + \frac{1}{2}mv^2 = 0 + \frac{1}{2}mv_B^2$. Cancel the m and solve for v_B, and you get to

$$\sqrt{v^2 + 2gh}.$$

14. **D.** Momentum must be conserved in the collision. If block A bounces, it changes its momentum by a larger amount than if it sticks. This means that block B picks up more momentum (and thus more speed) when block A bounces. The mass of the blocks is irrelevant because the comparison here is only between bouncing and not bouncing. So B goes faster in case I regardless of mass.

15. **C.** The period depends only on the mass attached to the spring, not at all on the speed. When block A sticks, more mass is attached, and the period is longer according to

$$T = 2\pi\sqrt{\frac{m}{k}}.$$

Which mass is bigger is irrelevant; two blocks will always be heavier than one block.

16. **A.** The relevant equation here is for impulse: $\Delta p = F\Delta t$. The force on the block can be increased either by increasing the momentum change or by decreasing the time of collision.

E decreases collision time; B, C, and D all increase the momentum change. But A *increases* the collision time, thereby decreasing the force.

17. **B.** The system has momentum 3 N·s up, and 9 N·s left. The magnitude of the momentum vector is the Pythagorean sum of 3 and 9 N·s. Without calculating, we know the answer must be more than 9 and less than 12 N·s.

18. **D.** Change in momentum is $F\Delta t$. What does that force represent? The *net* force, which here is 2000 N to the left. 2000 N times 20 s is 40,000 N·s, equivalent to 40,000 kg·m/s.

19. **E.** Fields are vectors because they cause forces, and force is a vector. Current is a vector because charge can flow in either direction in a wire. However, electric potential is related (by $PE = qV$) to potential energy, and all forms of energy are scalar quantities.

20. **C.** The velocity of an object in circular motion is NOT constant because the direction of motion changes. The acceleration and net force must be toward the center of the circle. Because the object's velocity vector is tangent to the circle, acceleration and velocity must be perpendicular to each other.

21. **C.** At point *A* the mass is momentarily at rest, just before it retraces its path back to the bottom. Acceleration is a *change* in velocity. Velocity is zero now, and in a moment will be along the circular path of the pendulum. So acceleration must point in the direction of this velocity change.

22. **B.** Centripetal acceleration is v^2/r, and is always center *seeking;* here this must be toward the sun. But the problem asks for the net force, which is mass times acceleration.

23. **B.** The period of a mass on a spring is

$$T = 2\pi\sqrt{\frac{m}{k}},$$

so multiplying the mass by 4 multiplies the period by 2. The total mechanical energy is equal to the potential energy at the maximum displacement. Here, because the amplitude (i.e., the maximum displacement) doesn't change, the total mechanical energy is also unchanged.

24. **D.** In an orbit, the centripetal force is provided by gravity, $mv^2/r = Gmm/r^2$. Solving for the radius of the orbit, $r = Gm/v^2$. (Here m is the mass of the planet; the mass of the satellite cancels out.) Doubling the speed, which is squared and in the denominator, divides the radius of the orbit by 4.

25. **B.** Don't try to calculate the answer by saying $mg = Gmm/r^2$! Not only would you have had to memorize the mass of the Earth, but you have no calculator and you only have a minute or so, anyway. So think: the acceleration must be less than 9.8 m/s^2 because that value is calculated at the surface of the Earth, and the Shuttle is farther from Earth's center than that. But the added height of 300 km is a small fraction (~5%) of the Earth's radius. So the gravitational acceleration will not be THAT much less. The best choice is thus 8.9 m/s^2. (By the way, acceleration is not zero—if it were, the Shuttle would be moving in a straight line, and not orbiting.)

26. **C.** Ice is 90% as dense as liquid water. So 90% of its volume is under the water, *displacing* water. Okay, when the ice melts, the new liquid takes up only 90% of the space it originally occupied. This liquid's volume is equal to the amount of volume originally displaced by the ice, so the water level does not rise.

27. **C.** Use Bernoulli's equation with the flowing fluid. Consider inside and outside the building as the two positions. The y terms are equal, so get rid of them. Call the velocity inside the building zero. We're left with $\frac{1}{2}\rho v^2_1 + P_1 = P_2$, where 2 means inside the building and 1 is outside. So: pressure outside is less than pressure inside. By how much? Well, if you happened to remember that the density of air is about 1 kg/m^3, you can make the calculation. But just look at the choices. Ambient pressure doesn't even drop by half when you go to the top of a mountain! So the answer is that pressure drops by a couple percentage points.

28. **B.** The free-body diagram of the mass includes the buoyant force AND the normal force up, and mg down. Because the block is in equilibrium, $F_N + F_B = mg$. So the normal force is *less* than mg and certainly not equal to the weight.

29. **A.** For a fluid of uniform density, the pressure at depth d is ρgd because of the weight of the water above depth d. But here, because the density of the water gets bigger, the weight of the water is greater. So the pressure should be *greater* than $\rho_0 gd$. The pressure is *less* than ρgd, because ρ is the maximum density.

30. **D.** Don't use the length expansion equation here, because we don't know the expansion coefficient for brass. Rather, just know that the change in an object's length is always a very small fraction of the original length. By

$$T = 2\pi\sqrt{\frac{1}{g}},$$

a slightly bigger length gives a slightly longer period.

31. **C.** The net work done on or by a gas is the area inside the cycle on the *PV* diagram, so the amount of net work is the same in either direction. In ABCA more work is done ON the gas than by the gas because there's more area under the curve when the volume compresses than when volume expands. By the same logic, in ACBA more work is done BY the gas than on the gas.

32. **E.** RMS velocity is given by

$$v_{rms} = \sqrt{\frac{3k_bT}{m}}.$$

Use round numbers to make calculations easier. v_{rms} would have to be multiplied by a bit more than 20 to reach escape velocity. So the temperature would have to be multiplied by more than 20^2, or more than 400 times.

33. **A.** By the ideal gas law, $V = Nk_bT/P$. Because all of the terms on the right don't change when we discuss oxygen rather than helium, the volume should be the same.

34. **C.** No time or calculator to do the calculation here, but the answer choices allow for an order of magnitude estimate. A molecule is about 1 Angstrom, or 10^{-10} m, across. The separation between molecules must be bigger than this. But molecules certainly aren't a millimeter apart from one another! The only choice that makes sense is C.

35. **A.** B, D, and E are all alternative statements of the second law (Entropy is a measure of disorder, not an important thing to know). C is a consequence of that law—even though energy would be conserved if the putty cooled off and jumped, this action is never observed. **A**, the correct choice, is a statement of the FIRST law

of thermodynamics, which itself is a statement of conservation of energy.

36. **B.** An electric field exists regardless of the amount of charge placed in it, and regardless of whether any charge at all is placed in it. So both experimenters must measure the same field (though they will measure different forces on their test charges).

37. **C.** Ah, the Newton's third law question. Whether we're talking about cars or charges, the force on object A due to object B is always the same as the force on object B due to object A. Thus the forces described must be equal.

38. **A.** The charge is in equilibrium, so the horizontal component of the tension must equal the electric force. This horizontal tension is 0.1 N times sin 30° (not cosine because 30° was measured from the *vertical*), or 0.05 N. The electric force is *qE*, where *q* is 0.002 C. So the electric field is 0.050 N/0.002 C . . . reduce the expression by moving the decimal to get 50/2, or 25 N/C.

39. **A.** In a *metal* sphere, charge is free to move, so the charge ends up on the surface evenly distributed. The electric fields due to each of these charges cancel at the center because for every charge causing a field pointing one way, another charge on the other side of the sphere will cause an equal field pointing the other way. (It's worth knowing that the electric field ANYWHERE inside a conductor is always zero; the justification for this is done in Physics C with Gauss's law.)

40. **C.** Capacitance of a parallel plate capacitor is $\varepsilon_o A/d$, where *A* is the area of the plates and *d* is the separation between plates. To halve the capacitance, we must halve the area or double the plate separation. The plate separation in the diagram is labeled *c*, so double distance *c*.

41. **E.** Hooked in parallel means that the *voltage* for each capacitor must be the same. The capacitors are identical, so the capacitance of each is the same. Thus, by $Q = CV$, the charge on each must be the same, too.

42. **B.** Voltage is always the same across parallel resistors. Because the 2.0 Ω resistor is hooked directly to the battery, the voltage across it is 1.0 V. By Ohm's law, $I = V/R = 0.50$ amps.

43. **C.** The 5 A of current splits into two paths. The path through R_2 takes 2 A, so the path through R_3 takes 3 A. Now use Ohm's law: $V = (3\ A)(10\ \Omega) = 30\ V$.

44. **D.** The voltage must stay the same because the battery by definition provides a constant voltage. Closing the switch adds an extra parallel branch to the network of resistors. Adding a parallel resistor REDUCES the total resistance. By Ohm's law, if voltage stays the same and resistance decreases, total current must increase.

45. **C.** Kirchoff's loop rule says that the sum of voltage changes around a closed circuit loop is zero. When a charge gains or loses voltage, it is also gaining or losing *energy*. The fact that the charge must end up with the same energy it started with is a statement of energy conservation.

46. **D.** A charge in a uniform magnetic field takes a circular path because the magnetic force changes direction, so it's always perpendicular to the charge's velocity. Here the magnetic force by the right-hand rule is initially up.

47. **B.** Work is force times parallel displacement. Because the magnetic force is always perpendicular to the particle's direction of motion, no work can be done by the magnetic field.

48. **B.** The magnetic field caused by a straight wire wraps around the wire by the right-hand rule. Consider just little parts of the curvy wire as if the parts were momentarily straight. The part of the wire at the top of the page produces a B field out of the page in the region inside the loop; the parts of the wire at the bottom of the page or on the side of the page also produce B fields out of the page inside the loop. These fields reinforce each other at the center, so the net B field is out of the page.

49. **B.** The magnetic field produced by I_1 is out of the page at the location of wire 2. The current I_2 is thus moving in a magnetic field; the force on that current-carrying wire is given by ILB and the right-hand rule, which shows a rightward force.

50. **D.** Lenz's law dictates that the direction of induced current is in the direction of decreasing flux by the right-hand rule. The magnetic field from the bar magnet points out of the north end, which is down. When the magnet gets closer to the loop of wire, the field gets stronger, so flux increases in the down direction; therefore, the direction of decreasing flux is the other way, up; and the right-hand rule gives an initial current counterclockwise. As the magnet falls away from the loop, the field still points down (into the south end), but the flux decreases, so now the current flows clockwise. Only choice **D** shows counterclockwise current changing to clockwise current.

51. **C.** For a rectangular loop of wire, the induced EMF is Blv. l represents the length dimension the remains constant in the field, here the side a. The amount of current is thus the EMF divided by R, or Bav/R. Induced current direction is given by the right-hand rule from the direction of decreasing flux. The flux is out of the page and decreasing, so current flows counterclockwise, giving a right-to-left current in the resistor.

52. **D.** An electric field exerts a force on all charged particles in the direction of the field; thus situation (A) would slow the proton down, but not change its direction. Magnetic fields only apply a force if they are perpendicular to a charge's velocity, so (B) and (E) cannot change the proton's direction. A magnetic field perpendicular to motion DOES change a proton's direction, but if a suitable electric field is also included, then the electric force can cancel the magnetic force. So choice **D** is the only one that must change the direction of the proton.

53. **E.** The two waves described move through different media (one through the string, one through the air), so must have different speeds. But, because the sound wave was generated by the string wave, the waves have the same frequencies. By $v = \lambda f$, the wavelength must be different for each as well.

54. **B.** The time between crests is the period of the wave. Period is 1/frequency. So the frequency is $1/(0.2\ s)$, which is 5 Hz.

55. **C.** Use $v = \lambda f$. But you might not remember the precise speed of sound, 340 m/s. So what? This is an order of magnitude problem. Frequency is speed over wavelength. The wavelength of the string base is actually *twice* the height (because it's a standing wave fixed at both ends), or 4 m; so 340 m/s/4 m is closest to 100 Hz. You could also figure this out by thinking about the meaning of the frequencies. Of the choices, only 100 Hz and 1000 Hz are in the audible range.

56. **A.** Frequency determines color. Think about seeing underwater. You see the same colors in clear water that you do in air. But underwater, the speed of the light waves is slower, and the wavelength is shorter. So if wavelength or wave speed determined color, you would see different colors underwater. (Amplitude determines brightness, and the medium through which the wave travels just determines wave speed.)

57. **C.** Light waves change phase by 180° when they are reflected off a material with higher index of refraction; this only happens in the diagram when light reflects off of the bottom surface.

58. **C.** For simplicity's sake, let's assume that the light is not refracted through huge angles, so we can say that $x = m\lambda L/d$, where x is the distance between spots. d is the distance between lines in the grating. So if d is cut in half, x is doubled; the spots are twice as far away. The size of the spots themselves should not change.

59. **C.** $E = hf$, so the higher frequency light also has higher energy per photon. But wavelength varies inversely with frequency by $v = \lambda f$, so bigger frequency means smaller wavelength. You should know either that red light has the longest wavelength, or that violet light has the highest frequency.

60. **E.** (A) is wrong—light *slows down* in glass. (C) is wrong—waves do *not* change frequency when changing media. (D) is wrong—light doesn't change direction at all when hitting an interface directly from the normal. Choice (B) is wrong because, while some red light does reflect at each interface, this doesn't help explain anything about seeing light upon exiting the prism. However, blue light does experience a larger index of refraction than red, so it bends farther from normal when it hits an interface at an angle.

61. **A.** The light from the building that is very far away will be focused at the focal point of the lens. The first part of the problem lets you figure out the focal point using the lensmaker's equation, $1/f = 1/30$ cm $+ 1/20$ cm, so $f = 60/5 = 12$ cm.

62. **D.** All can produce virtual images. However, the converging instruments (the concave mirror and convex lens) can only show virtual images if the object is inside the focal point; these images are larger than the object itself. (Think of a magnifying glass and the inside of a spoon.) The convex mirror and concave lens are diverging instruments, which can ONLY produce smaller, upright images. (Think of a Christmas tree ornament.)

63. **B.** All mirror rays through the center reflect right back through the center.

64. **A.** The frequency of incident photons affects the energy of ejected electrons; the intensity of the beam (number of photons per second) is irrelevant. Thus, the KE vs. intensity graph is simply a horizontal line.

65. **E.** To jump from E_o to E_1 the electron needs to absorb 4.0 eV of energy. So the necessary wavelength is given by 1240 eV·nm / 4.0 eV, or 310 nm. ($E = hc/\lambda$, and $hc = 1240$ eV, as stated on the Constant Sheet.)

66. **D.** The electron can transition from E_0 to E_1 or from E_0 out of the atom. Or, the electron can transition from E_1 out of the atom. This makes three transitions, so three spectral lines.

67. **D.** The stopping voltage is applied to a beam of electrons. Because 1 eV is the energy of 1 electron moved through 1 V of potential difference, these electrons initially had 1 eV of kinetic energy (that was converted into potential energy in order to stop the electrons). These electrons needed 3.5 eV to escape the atom, plus 1 eV for their kinetic energy; this makes a total of 4.5 eV needed from each photon.

68. **B.** In choices A and E, it is light exhibiting wave properties; light is not made up of massive particles. C involves surface waves on the ocean, not the wave behavior of water molecules themselves. Choice D describes Rutherford's experiment, which demonstrated the existence of the atomic nucleus. So choice **B** is correct: a beam of electrons is a beam of *massive* particles. The experiment described demonstrates both diffraction (bending) and interference, both of which are wave properties.

69. **E.** Only gamma decay keeps atomic mass and number the same, because a gamma particle is just a high energy photon; a photon has neither mass nor charge.

70. **C.** Newton's third law requires the daughter nucleus to experience a force opposite to the force exerted on the alpha particle; thus, the daughter must move backward. Conservation of momentum requires the net momentum to be zero after the decay as well as before; this only happens if the daughter moves backward to cancel the alpha's forward momentum. But energy is a scalar, and has no direction. Conservation of energy can be satisfied no matter which way the particles move.

RATING THE FREE-RESPONSE SOLUTIONS

Notes on grading your free-response section.

For answers that are numerical, or in equation form:

*For each part of the problem, look to see if you got the right answer. If you did, and you showed any reasonable (and correct) work, give yourself full credit for that part. It's okay if you didn't explicitly show EVERY step, as long as some steps are indicated, and you got the right answer. However:

*If you got the WRONG answer, then look to see if you earned partial credit. Give yourself points for each step toward the answer as indicated in the rubrics below. Without the correct answer, you must show each intermediate step explicitly in order to earn the point for that step. (See why it's so important to show your work?)

*If you're off by a decimal place or two, not to worry—you get credit anyway, as long as your approach to the problem was legitimate. This isn't a math test. You're not being evaluated on your rounding and calculator-use skills.

*You do not have to simplify expressions in variables all the way. Square roots in the denominator are fine; fractions in nonsimplified form are fine. As long as you've solved properly for the requested variable, and as long as your answer is algebraically equivalent to the rubric's, you earn credit.

*Wrong, but consistent: Often you need to use the answer to part (a) in order to solve part (b). But you might have the answer to part (a) wrong. If you follow the correct procedure for part (b), plugging in your incorrect answer, then you will usually receive *full credit* for part (b). The major exceptions are when your answer to part (a) is unreasonable (say, a car moving at 10^5 m/s, or a distance between two cars equal to 10^{-100} meters), or when your answer to part (a) makes the rest of the problem trivial or irrelevant.

For answers that require justification:

*Obviously your answer will not match the rubric word-for-word. If the general gist is there, you get credit.

*But the reader is not allowed to interpret for the student. If your response is vague or ambiguous, you will NOT get credit.

*If your response consists of both correct and incorrect parts, you will usually not receive credit. It is not possible to try two answers, hoping that one of them is right. (See why it's so important to be concise?)

1.

(a)

1 pt: It's a frictionless plane, so the only force parallel to the incline is a component of gravity, $mg\sin30°$.

1 pt: Set this force equal to ma, so $a = g\sin30 = 5\text{m/s}^2$ down the plane.

1 pt: Set up kinematics, with $v_o = 0$, and $\Delta x = 7.0$ m. Solve for time using ** $(\Delta x = v_o t + \frac{1}{2}at^2)$.

1 pt: The result is $t = 1.7$ s.

(b)

1 pt: Use the kinematics from part (a), but use * $(v_f = v_o + at)$ to get $v_f = 8.5$ m/s.

1 pt: The direction must be down the plane, or 30° below the horizontal.

(c)

1 pt: Only the vertical motion will affect the time to hit the bottom. (This point awarded for any clear attempt to use vertical kinematics.)

1 pt: In the vertical direction, $v_o =$ $(8.5 \text{ m/s})\sin30°$; $\Delta x = 4.0$ m and acceleration is $g = 10$ m/s^2.

1 pt: You can use ** $(\Delta x = v_o t + \frac{1}{2}at^2)$ and a quadratic to solve for time; it's probably easier to solve for v_f first using *** $(v_f^2 = v_o^2 + 2a\Delta x)$. v_f works out to 9.9 m/s. Use * $(v_f = v_o + at)$ to get $t = 0.6$ s.

1 pt: But this time is only the time after the package left the incline. To find the total time, the 1.7 s on the plane must be added to get 2.3 s total.

(d)

1 pt: In the horizontal direction, the package maintains constant speed after leaving the plane.

1 pt: So the horizontal distance is the horizontal velocity (equal to 8.5 m/s[cos 30°]) times the 0.6 seconds the ball fell.

1 pt: The package lands 4.4 m from the left-hand edge.

(e)

1 pt: The horizontal distance would be increased, but less than doubled.

1 pt: The package speeds up as it falls; therefore, the package doesn't take as much time to fall the additional 4 m as it did to fall the original 4 m. The horizontal velocity doesn't change, so the package can't go as far in this additional time.

2.

(a)

1 pt: The total momentum of both carts before collision is $m_A v_A$, because cart B has no speed before collision.

1 pt: The total momentum after collision is $m_A(-v_A') + m_B v_B'$, the negative sign arising because cart A moves backward after collision.

1 pt: So the fraction of momentum conserved is the total momentum after collision divided by the total momentum before collision, $[m_B v_B' - m_A v_A'] / [m_A v_A]$.

(b)

1 pt: The total kinetic energy of both carts before collision is $\frac{1}{2}m_A(v_A)^2$.

1 pt: The total kinetic energy after collision is $\frac{1}{2}m_A(v_A')^2 + \frac{1}{2}m_B(v_B')^2$. (The negative sign on v_A' disappears when velocity is squared.)

1 pt: So the fraction of KE conserved is the total KE after collision divided by the total KE before collision, $[\frac{1}{2}m_A(v_A')^2 + \frac{1}{2}m_B(v_B')^2] / [\frac{1}{2}m_A(v_A)^2]$.

(c)

1 pt: Only the expression in part (a) should always be 100%.

1 pt: Momentum is conserved in all collisions, but kinetic energy can be converted into heat and other forms of energy.

(d)

1 pt: The motion detector can be used to measure the speed of cart A before collision.

1 pt: The detector should be placed at the left edge of the track

1 pt: The speed can be read directly from the detector's output.

1 pt: The motion detector can be used in the same manner to measure the speed of cart A after collision.

1 pt: The stopwatch can be used to measure cart B's speed after collision. Time how long the cart takes to reach the end of the track after the collision.

1 pt: The meter stick can be used to measure the distance cart B traveled in this time

1 pt: Because the track is frictionless, the cart moves at constant speed equal to the distance traveled over the time elapsed.

3.

(a)

1 pt: The buoyant force on this cube is equal to the weight of the water displaced.

1 pt: Half of the block displaces water; half of the block's volume is 0.5 m³.

1 pt: Using the density of water, the mass of 0.5 m³ of water is 500 kg, which has weight 5000 N.

1 pt: Because the cube is in equilibrium, the buoyant force must also equal the weight of the cube. The cube thus has weight 5000 N, and mass 500 kg.

(b)

1 pt: Again, the buoyant force is equal to the weight of the displaced water. This time 0.75 m³ are displaced, making the buoyant force 7500 N.

1 pt: The weight of the mass is 5000 N, so the net force is the up minus down forces, or 2500 N.

(c)

1 pt: When an object is in simple harmonic motion, the net force is equal to kx, where x is the displacement from the equilibrium position.

1 pt: Using the information from part (b), when the displacement from equilibrium is 0.25 m, the net force is 2500 N.

1 pt: So the "spring constant" is 2500 N / 0.25 m = 10,000 N/m.

(d)

1 pt: The period of a mass in simple harmonic motion is

$$T = 2\pi\sqrt{\frac{m}{k}}.$$

1 pt: Plugging in the mass and spring constant from parts (a) and (c), the period is 1.4 s.

1 pt: Frequency is $1/T$ by definition, so the frequency is 0.71 Hz.

(e)

1 pt: The frequency would be the same.

1 pt: The period of a mass in simple harmonic motion is independent of the amplitude.

1 additional point: For correct units on at least three answers in parts (a), (b), (c), or (d), and no incorrect units.

4.

(a)

1 pt: Over a potential difference of 1000 V, the electron converts $qV = 8.0 \times 10^{-17}$ J of potential energy into kinetic energy.

1 pt: Set this energy equal to $\frac{1}{2}mv^2$ and solve for v;

1 pt: you get 1.3×10^7 m/s. (alternate solution is to approach this part of the problem like part (b); full credit is earned if the solution is correct.)

(b) i.

1 pt: The electric field due to parallel plates is V/d. This works out to 100 V/0.05 m = 2000 N/C. (d represents the distance between plates.)

1 pt: The force on the electron is $qE = 3.2 \times 10^{-16}$ N.

1 pt: The force is directed upward, toward the positive plate.

ii.

1 pt: The electron experiences no forces in the horizontal direction, so it maintains a constant horizontal velocity of 1.3×10^7 m/s.

1 pt: Using distance = velocity × time, it takes 3.8×10^{-8} s to travel the 0.5 m between the plates.

iii.

1 pt: The velocity at point C has both a horizontal and vertical component. The horizontal velocity is still 1.3×10^7 m/s.

1 pt: But in the vertical direction, the electron speeds up from rest. (This point is given for

ANY recognition that the vertical direction must be treated separately from the horizontal direction.)

1 pt: Its acceleration is given by the force in part (b) i over its mass: $a = 3.2 \times 10^{-16}$ N / 9.1×10^{-31} kg, $= 3.5 \times 10^{14}$ m/s².

1 pt: Now use a Kinematics Chart to find the vertical speed at point C, with $v_o = 0$ and time given in part (b) ii; this gives 1.3×10^7 m/s.

1 pt: The speed is the magnitude of the velocity vector. The electron's velocity has components to the right and up; add these using the Pythagorean theorem to get 1.8×10^7 m/s.

(c)

1 pt: The electric force, from part (b) i, was 10^{-16} N. The gravitational force is $mg = 10^{-30}$ N.

1 pt: So the gravitational force is many orders of magnitude smaller than the electric force, and is, thus, negligible.

5.

(a)

1 pt: The alpha particle consists of two protons and two neutrons. So the atomic number Z of the Erbium must be two fewer than that of the Ytterbium, $Z = 68$.

1 pt: The mass number A includes both protons *and* neutrons, so must be four fewer in the Erbium than in the Ytterbium, $A = 169$.

(b)

1 pt: Initial momentum of the whole system was zero; so the alpha and the Erbium must have equal and opposite momenta after decay.

1 pt: The alpha's momentum is (4 amu) $(1.7 \times 10^7$ m/s) $= 1.4 \times 10^8$ amu·m/s (or 1.3×10^{-19} kg·m/s); the Erbium has this same amount of momentum.

(c)

1 pt: The momentum p of each incident photon is given by $E = pc$, where E is the energy of the photon, equal to hc/λ. Set the two expressions for energy equal to each other.

1 pt: It is found that the momentum of each photon is $p = h/\lambda = (6.6 \times 10^{-34}$ J·s)/ $(450 \times 10^{-9}$ m) $= 1.5 \times 10^{-27}$ N·s. (Note that this answer is in standard units because we plugged in h and λ in standard units.)

1 pt: Each photon is reflected backward, so each photon *changes* momentum by 1.5×10^{-27} N·s $- (-1.5 \times 10^{-27}$ N·s) $= 3.0 \times 10^{-27}$ N·s.

1 pt: The nucleus has 1.3×10^{-19} N·s of momentum to start with, as found in (b); this point is awarded for both recognizing to use the momentum from part (b) *and* for putting that momentum in standard units.

1 pt: The nucleus loses 3.0×10^{-27} N·s with each photon; so divide to find that 4.3×10^{7} photons will bring the nucleus to rest.

1 pt: Dividing this by the 10^{25} photons each second, only 4×10^{-18} seconds are required to stop the nucleus.

6.

(a)

1 pt: The normal force acts up and the weight of the car acts down; friction acts to the left, opposite velocity.

1 pt: There are no forces acting to the right.

(b)

1 pt: Here, the normal force is equal to the car's weight, mg.

1 pt: The force of friction is μF_N, which is μmg.

1 pt: The net work is done by friction and is equal to the force of friction times the 80 m displacement. Net work done on the car is thus $\mu mg(80 \text{ m})$.

1 pt: Net work is equal to change in kinetic energy . . . because the car comes to rest, the change in KE is equal to the KE when the car was initially moving.

1 pt: So $\mu mg(80 \text{ m}) = \frac{1}{2}mv^2$, and $v = 36$ m/s. (alternate solution: Use $F_{net} = ma$, where F_{net} is the force of friction $= \mu mg$. Solve for acceleration, then use kinematics with final velocity = zero and displacement = 80 m. The answer should still work out to 36 m/s.)

(c)

1 pt: 36 m/s is something like 80 miles per hour . . . in a parking lot?!?!

(d)

1 pt: No, the driver's argument does *not* make sense.

1 pt: In the equation to determine the initial speed of the car, as shown in part (b), the mass cancels out (because it shows up both in the friction force and in the kinetic energy term). So this calculation is valid for any mass car.

7.

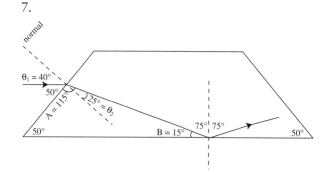

(a)

1 pt: The normal to the surface is, by definition, *perpendicular* to the surface, as shown in the diagram above.

(b)

1 pt: Snell's law is used to determine the angle of transmission: $n_1 \sin \theta_1 = n_2 \sin \theta_2$.

1 pt: Here $n_1 = 1.0$ (for air) and $n_2 = 1.5$.

1 pt: The angle of incidence θ_1 must be measured to the normal.

1 pt: From geometry θ_1 is found to be 40°. So the transmission angle is 25°.

1 pt: This angle must be labeled with respect to the normal, as shown in the diagram above.

(c)

1 pt: The light will leave through the right-hand edge.

1 pt: Using geometry, the angle of incidence of the light on the bottom surface can be found. In the above diagram, the angle labeled A is 115° because it is the 90° angle to the normal plus the 25° angle of transmission. So angle B must be 15° because there are 180° total in a triangle. Therefore, the angle of incidence of the light ray to the bottom surface is 75°.

1 pt: Using Snell's law, the angle of transmission θ_2 is undefined, so total internal reflection must occur. (Or, the critical angle for total internal reflection between glass and air is $\sin \theta_c = 1/1.5$, so $\theta_c = 42°$; 75° is thus bigger than the critical angle, so total internal reflection occurs.)

1 pt: for a diagram showing reflection (with an angle of reflection approximately equal to the angle of incidence) at the bottom surface

SCORING AND INTERPRETATION

Multiple Choice: Number Correct_____

                               Number Wrong _____

Total = right − ($\frac{1}{4}$) wrong _____(70 max)

Free Response: Question 1_____(15 max)

                               Question 2_____(15 max)

                               Question 3_____(15 max)

                               Question 4_____(15 max)

                               Question 5_____(10 max)

                               Question 6_____(10 max)

                               Question 7_____(10 max)

Total Free Response_____(90 max)

1.286 × Multiple Choice +
Free Response = Raw Score_____(180 max)

Composite Score Range	Rough Estimate of AP Score
112–180	5
84–111	4
52–83	3
38–51	2
0–37	1

Chapter 12

AP Physics C

Answer Sheet for Mechanics Multiple-Choice Questions

1. _____	13. _____	25. _____
2. _____	14. _____	26. _____
3. _____	15. _____	27. _____
4. _____	16. _____	28. _____
5. _____	17. _____	29. _____
6. _____	18. _____	30. _____
7. _____	19. _____	31. _____
8. _____	20. _____	32. _____
9. _____	21. _____	33. _____
10. _____	22. _____	34. _____
11. _____	23. _____	35. _____
12. _____	24. _____	

AP PHYSICS C

Section I—Mechanics

Time—45 minutes

35 questions

You may refer to the Constants sheet found in the Appendix. However, you may not use the Equations sheet, and you may not use a calculator on this portion of the exam.

1. A cannon is mounted on a truck that moves forward at a speed of 5 m/s. The operator wants to launch a ball from a cannon so the ball goes as far as possible before hitting the level surface. The muzzle velocity of the cannon is 50 m/s. What angle from the horizontal should the operator point the cannon?

   (A) 5°
   (B) 41°
   (C) 45°
   (D) 49°
   (E) 85°

2. A car moving with speed v reaches the foot of an incline of angle θ. The car coasts up the incline without using the engine. Neglecting friction and air resistance, which of the following is correct about the magnitude of the car's horizontal acceleration a_x and vertical acceleration a_y?

   (A) $a_x = 0$; $a_y < g$
   (B) $a_x = 0$; $a_y = g$
   (C) $a_x < g$; $a_y < g$
   (D) $a_x < g$; $a_y = g$
   (E) $a_x < g$; $a_y > g$

3. A bicycle slows down with an acceleration whose magnitude increases linearly with time. Which of the following velocity–time graphs could represent the motion of the bicycle?

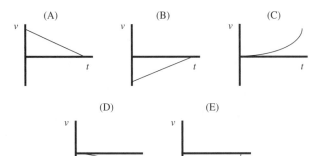

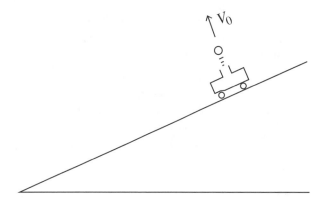

4. A cart is sliding down a low friction incline. A device on the cart launches a ball, forcing the ball perpendicular to the incline, as shown above. Air resistance is negligible. Where will the ball land relative to the cart, and why?

   (A) The ball will land in front of the cart, because the ball's acceleration component parallel to the plane is greater than the cart's acceleration component parallel to the plane.
   (B) The ball will land in front of the cart, because the ball has a greater magnitude of acceleration than the cart.
   (C) The ball will land in the cart, because both the ball and the cart have the same component of acceleration parallel to the plane.
   (D) The ball will land in the cart, because both the ball and the cart have the same magnitude of acceleration.
   (E) The ball will land behind the cart, because the ball slows down in the horizontal direction after it leaves the cart.

5. The quantity "jerk," j, is defined as the time derivative of an object's acceleration,

$$j = \frac{da}{dt} = \frac{d^3x}{dt^3}.$$

What is the physical meaning of the area under a graph of jerk vs. time?

(A) The area represents the object's acceleration.
(B) The area represents the object's change in acceleration.
(C) The area represents the object's change in velocity.
(D) The area represents the object's velocity.
(E) The area represents the object's change in position.

6. A particle moves along the x-axis with a position given by the equation $x(t) = 5 + 3t$, where x is in meters, and t is in seconds. The positive direction is east. Which of the following statements about the particle is FALSE.

(A) The particle is east of the origin at $t = 0$.
(B) The particle is at rest at $t = 0$.
(C) The particle's velocity is constant.
(D) The particle's acceleration is constant.
(E) The particle will never be west of position $x = 0$.

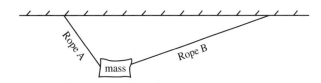

7. A mass hangs from two ropes at unequal angles, as shown above. Which of the following makes correct comparisons of the horizontal and vertical components of the tension in each rope?

	Horizontal Tension	Vertical Tension
(A)	greater in rope B	greater in rope B
(B)	equal in both ropes	greater in rope A
(C)	greater in rope A	greater in rope A
(D)	equal in both ropes	equal in both ropes
(E)	greater in rope B	equal in both ropes

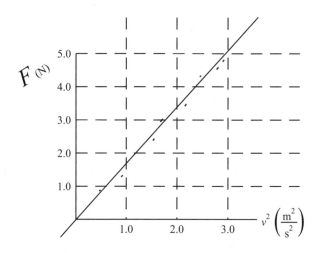

8. The force of air resistance F on a mass is found to obey the equation $F = bv^2$, where v is the speed of the mass, for the range of speeds investigated in an experiment. A graph of F vs. v^2 is shown above. What is the value of b?

(A) 0.83 kg/m
(B) 1.7 kg/m
(C) 3.0 kg/m
(D) 5.0 kg/m
(E) 1.0 kg/m
(F) zero

9. A box sits on an inclined plane without sliding. As the angle of the plane (measured from the horizontal) increases, the normal force

(A) increases linearly
(B) decreases linearly
(C) does not change
(D) decreases nonlinearly
(E) increases nonlinearly

10. Which of the following conditions are necessary for an object to be in static equilibrium?

I. The vector sum of all torques on the object must equal zero.
II. The vector sum of all forces on the object must equal zero.
III. The sum of the object's potential and kinetic energies must be zero.

(A) I only
(B) II only
(C) III only
(D) I and II only
(E) I, II, and III

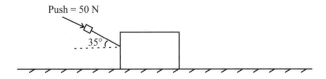

11. A student pushes a big 16-kg box across the floor at constant speed. He pushes with a force of 50 N angled 35° from the horizontal, as shown in the diagram above. If the student pulls rather than pushes the box at the same angle, while maintaining a constant speed, what will happen to the force of friction?

(A) It must increase.
(B) It must decrease.
(C) It must remain the same.
(D) It will increase only if the speed is greater than 3.1 m/s.
(E) It will increase only if the speed is less than 3.1 m/s.

12. Consider a system consisting only of the Earth and a bowling ball, which moves upward in a parabola 10 m above Earth's surface. The downward force of Earth's gravity on the ball, and the upward force of the ball's gravity on the Earth, form a Newton's third law force pair. Which of the following statements about the ball is correct?

(A) The ball must be in equilibrium since the upward forces must cancel downward forces.
(B) The ball accelerates toward the Earth because the force of gravity on the ball is greater than the force of the ball on the Earth.
(C) The ball accelerates toward the Earth because the force of gravity on the ball is the only force acting on the ball.
(D) The ball accelerates away from Earth because the force causing the ball to move upward is greater than the force of gravity on the ball.
(E) The ball accelerates away from Earth because the force causing the ball to move upward plus the force of the ball on the Earth are together greater than the force of gravity on the ball.

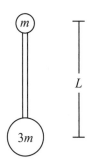

13. A mass m is attached to a mass $3m$ by a rigid bar of negligible mass and length L. Initially, the smaller mass is located directly above the larger mass, as shown above. How much work is necessary to flip the rod 180° so that the larger mass is directly above the smaller mass?

(A) $4mgL$
(B) $2mgL$
(C) mgL
(D) $4\pi mgL$
(E) $2\pi mgL$

14. A ball rolls horizontally with speed v off of a table a height h above the ground. Just before the ball hits the ground, what is its speed?

(A) $\sqrt{2gh}$
(B) $v\sqrt{2gh}$
(C) $\sqrt{v^2 + 2gh}$
(D) v
(E) $v + \sqrt{2gh}$

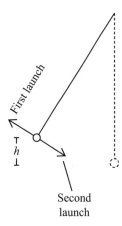

15. A pendulum is launched into simple harmonic motion in two different ways, as shown above, from a point that is a height h above its lowest point. During both launches, the bob is given an initial speed of 3.0 m/s. On the first launch, the

initial velocity of the bob is directed upward along the pendulum's path, and on the second launch it is directed downward along the pendulum's path. Which launch will cause the pendulum to swing with the larger amplitude?

(A) the first launch
(B) the second launch
(C) Both launches produce the same amplitude.
(D) The answer depends on the initial height h.
(E) The answer depends on the length of the supporting rope.

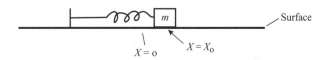

16. The mass M is moving to the right with velocity v_o at position $x = x_o$. Neglect friction. The spring has force constant k. What is the total mechanical energy of the block at this position?

(A) $\frac{1}{2}mv_o^2$
(B) $\frac{1}{2}mv_o^2 + \frac{1}{2}kx_o^2$
(C) $\frac{1}{2}mv_o^2 + \frac{1}{2}kx_o^2 + mgx_o$
(D) $mgx_o + \frac{1}{2}mv_o^2$
(E) $mgx_o + \frac{1}{2}kx_o^2$

17. A sphere, a cube, and a cylinder, all of equal mass, are released from rest from the top of a short incline. The surface of the incline is extremely slick, so much so that the objects do not rotate when released, but rather slide with negligible friction. Which reaches the base of the incline first?

(A) the sphere
(B) the cube
(C) the cylinder
(D) All reach the base at the same time.
(E) The answer depends on the relative sizes of the objects.

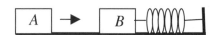

18. Block B is at rest on a smooth tabletop. It is attached to a long spring, which is in turn anchored to the wall. Block A slides toward and collides with block B. Consider two possible collisions:

Collision I: block A bounces back off of block B.
Collision II: block A sticks to block B.

Which of the following is correct about the speed of block B immediately after the collision?

(A) It is faster in case II than in case I ONLY if block B is heavier.
(B) It is faster in case I than in case II ONLY if block B is heavier.
(C) It is faster in case II than in case I regardless of the mass of each block.
(D) It is faster in case I than in case II regardless of the mass of each block.
(E) It is the same in either case regardless of the mass of each block.

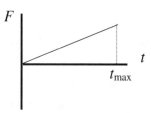

19. A 0.30-kg bird is flying from right to left at 30 m/s. The bird collides with and sticks to a 0.50-kg ball which is moving straight up with speed 6.0 m/s. What is the magnitude of the momentum of the ball/bird combination immediately after collision?

(A) 12.0 Ns
(B) 9.5 Ns
(C) 9.0 Ns
(D) 6.0 Ns
(E) 3.0 Ns

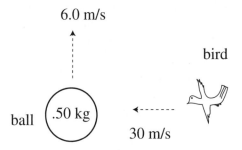

20. The force F on a mass is shown above as a function of time t. Which of the following methods can be used to determine the impulse experienced by the mass?

I. multiplying the average force by t_{max}
II. calculating the area under the line on the graph
III. taking the integral $\int_{0}^{t_{max}} F \cdot dt$

(A) II only
(B) III only
(C) II and III only
(D) I and II only
(E) I, II, and III

21. A projectile is launched on level ground in a parabolic path so that its range would normally be 500 m. When the projectile is at the peak of its flight, the projectile breaks into two pieces of equal mass. One of these pieces falls straight down, with no further horizontal motion. How far away from the launch point does the other piece land?

    (A) 250 m
    (B) 375 m
    (C) 500 m
    (D) 750 m
    (E) 1000 m

Questions 22 and 23

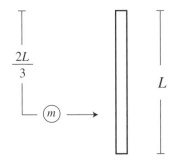

A rigid rod of length L and mass M is floating at rest in space far from a gravitational field. A small blob of putty of mass $m < M$ is moving to the right, as shown above. The putty hits and sticks to the rod a distance $2L / 3$ from the top end.

22. How will the rod/putty contraption move after the collision?

    (A) The contraption will have no translational motion, but will rotate about the rod's center of mass.
    (B) The contraption will have no translational motion, but will rotate about the center of mass of the rod and putty combined.
    (C) The contraption will move to the right and rotate about the position of the putty.
    (D) The contraption will move to the right and rotate about the center of mass of the rod and putty combined.
    (E) The contraption will move to the right and rotate about the rod's center of mass.

23. What quantities are conserved in this collision?

    (A) linear and angular momentum, but not kinetic energy
    (B) linear momentum only
    (C) angular momentum only

    (D) linear and angular momentum, and linear but not rotational kinetic energy
    (E) linear and angular momentum, and linear and rotational kinetic energy

24. A car rounds a banked curve of uniform radius. Three forces act on the car: a friction force between the tires and the road, the normal force from the road, and the weight of the car. Which provides the centripetal force which keeps the car in circular motion?

    (A) the friction force alone
    (B) the normal force alone
    (C) the weight alone
    (D) a combination of the normal force and the friction force
    (E) a combination of the friction force and the weight

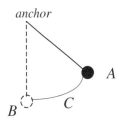

25. A ball of mass m anchored to a string swings back and forth to a maximum position A, as shown above. Point C is partway back to the vertical position. What is the direction of the mass's acceleration at point C?

    (A) along the mass's path toward point B
    (B) toward the anchor
    (C) away from the anchor
    (D) between a line toward the anchor and a line along the mass's path
    (E) along the mass's path toward point A

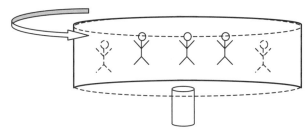

26. In a carnival ride, people of mass m are whirled in a horizontal circle by a floorless cylindrical room of radius r, as shown in the diagram above. If the coefficient of friction between the people and the tube surface is μ, what minimum

speed is necessary to keep the people from sliding down the walls?

(A) $\sqrt{\mu r g}$

(B) $\sqrt{\dfrac{rg}{\mu}}$

(C) $\sqrt{\dfrac{\mu}{rg}}$

(D) $\sqrt{\dfrac{1}{\mu rg}}$

(E) $\sqrt{\mu m g}$

Questions 27 and 28

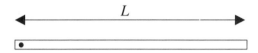

The uniform, rigid rod of mass m, length L, and rotational inertia I shown above is pivoted at its left-hand end. The rod is released from rest from a horizontal position.

27. What is the linear acceleration of the rod's center of mass the moment after the rod is released?

(A) $\dfrac{mgL^2}{2I}$

(B) $\dfrac{mgL^2}{4I}$

(C) $\dfrac{mgL^2}{I}$

(D) $\dfrac{mgL}{2I}$

(E) $\dfrac{2mgL^2}{I}$

28. What is the linear speed of the rod's center of mass when the mass passes through a vertical position?

(A) $\sqrt{\dfrac{mgL^3}{8I}}$

(B) $\sqrt{\dfrac{mg\pi L^3}{4I}}$

(C) $\sqrt{\dfrac{mg\pi L^3}{8I}}$

(D) $\sqrt{\dfrac{mgL^3}{4I}}$

(E) $\sqrt{\dfrac{mgL^3}{2I}}$

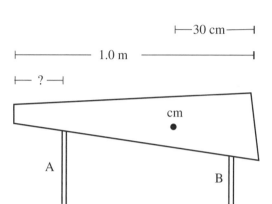

29. The 1.0-m-long nonuniform plank, shown above, has weight 1000 N. It is to be supported by two rods, A and B, as shown above. The center of mass of the plank is 30 cm from the right edge. Each support bears half the weight of the plank. If support B is 10 cm from the right-hand edge, how far from the left-hand edge should support A be?

(A) 0 cm
(B) 10 cm
(C) 30 cm
(D) 50 cm
(E) 70 cm

30. A mass m on a spring oscillates on a horizontal surface with period T. The total mechanical energy contained in this oscillation is E. Imagine that instead a new mass $4m$ oscillates on the same spring with the same amplitude. What is the new period and total mechanical energy?

	Period	Total Mechanical Energy
(A)	T	E
(B)	$2T$	E
(C)	$2T$	$2E$
(D)	T	$4E$
(E)	$2T$	$16E$

31. A mass m is attached to a horizontal spring of spring constant k. The spring oscillates in simple harmonic motion with amplitude A. What is

the maximum speed of this simple harmonic oscillator?

(A) $2\pi\sqrt{\dfrac{m}{k}}$

(B) $2\pi A\sqrt{\dfrac{m}{k}}$

(C) $2\pi A\sqrt{\dfrac{k}{m}}$

(D) $A\sqrt{\dfrac{k}{m}}$

(E) $A\sqrt{\dfrac{m}{k}}$

32. An empty bottle goes up and down on the surface of the ocean, obeying the position function $x = A\cos(\omega t)$. How much time does this bottle take to travel once from its lowest position to its highest position?

(A) $\dfrac{2\pi}{\omega}$

(B) $\dfrac{\pi}{\omega}$

(C) $\dfrac{4\pi}{\omega}$

(D) $\dfrac{\pi}{2\omega}$

(E) $\dfrac{\pi}{4\omega}$

33. The Space Shuttle orbits 300 km above the Earth's surface; the Earth's radius is 6400 km. What is the acceleration due to Earth's gravity experienced by the Space Shuttle?

(A) 4.9 m/s^2
(B) 8.9 m/s^2
(C) 9.8 m/s^2
(D) 10.8 m/s^2
(E) zero

34. An artificial satellite orbits Earth just above the atmosphere in a circle with constant speed. A small meteor collides with the satellite at point P in its orbit, increasing its speed by 1%, but not changing the instantaneous direction of the satellite's velocity. Which of the following describes the satellite's new orbit?

(A) The satellite now orbits in an ellipse, with P as the farthest approach to Earth.
(B) The satellite now orbits in an ellipse, with P as the closest approach to Earth.
(C) The satellite now orbits in a circle of larger radius.
(D) The satellite now orbits in a circle of smaller radius.
(E) The satellite cannot maintain an orbit, so it flies off into space.

35. Mercury orbits the sun in about one-fifth of an Earth year. If 1 au is defined as the distance from the Earth to the sun, what is the approximate distance between Mercury and the sun?

(A) (1/25) au
(B) (1/9) au
(C) (1/5) au
(D) (1/3) au
(E) (1/2) au

STOP. End of mechanics Section I.

Answer Sheet for Electricity and Magnetism Multiple-Choice Questions

36. _____   48. _____   60. _____

37. _____   49. _____   61. _____

38. _____   50. _____   62. _____

39. _____   51. _____   63. _____

40. _____   52. _____   64. _____

41. _____   53. _____   65. _____

42. _____   54. _____   66. _____

43. _____   55. _____   67. _____

44. _____   56. _____   68. _____

45. _____   57. _____   69. _____

46. _____   58. _____   70. _____

47. _____   59. _____

AP PHYSICS C

Section I—Electricity and Magnetism

Time—45 minutes

35 questions

You may refer to the Constants sheet found in the Appendix. However, you may not use the Equations sheet, and you may not use a calculator on this portion of the exam.

36. Experimenter A uses a very small test charge q_o, and experimenter B uses a test charge $2q_o$ to measure an electric field produced by two parallel plates. A finds a field that is

(A) greater than the field found by B
(B) the same as the field found by B
(C) less than the field found by B
(D) either greater or less than the field found by B, depending on the accelerations of the test charges
(E) either greater or less than the field found by B, depending on the masses of the test charges

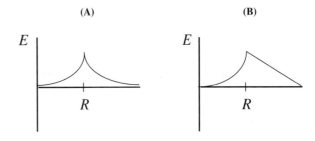

37. A solid conducting sphere has radius R and carries positive charge Q. Which of the following graphs represents the electric field E as a function of the distance r from the center of the sphere?

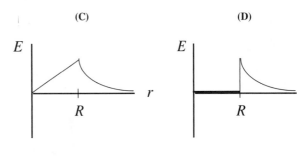

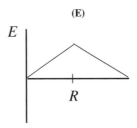

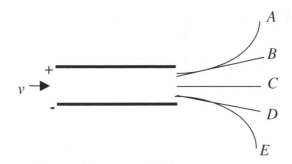

(A) 25 N/C
(B) 50 N/C
(C) 2500 N/C
(D) 5000 N/C
(E) 10,000 N/C

38. An electron moving at constant velocity enters the region between two charged plates, as shown above. Which of the paths above correctly shows the electron's trajectory after leaving the region between the charged plates?

    (A) A
    (B) B
    (C) C
    (D) D
    (E) E

39. Two isolated particles, A and B, are 4 m apart. Particle A has a net charge of 2Q, and B has a net charge of Q. The ratio of the magnitude of the electric force on A to that on B is

    (A) 4:1
    (B) 2:1
    (C) 1:1
    (D) 1:2
    (E) 1:4

41. A thin semicircular conductor of radius R holds charge $+Q$. What is the magnitude and direction of the electric field at the center of the circle?

    (A) $\dfrac{kQ}{R^2}$ · ↑

    (B) $\dfrac{kQ}{R^2}$ · ↓

    (C) $\dfrac{kQ}{\pi R^2}$ · ↑

    (D) $\dfrac{kQ}{\pi R^2}$ · ↓

    (E) The electric field is zero at the center.

42. Above an infinitely large plane carrying charge density σ, the electric field points up and is equal to $\sigma / 2\varepsilon_o$. What is the magnitude and direction of the electric field below the plane?

    (A) $\sigma / 2\varepsilon_o$, down
    (B) $\sigma / 2\varepsilon_o$, up
    (C) σ / ε_o, down
    (D) σ / ε_o, up
    (E) zero

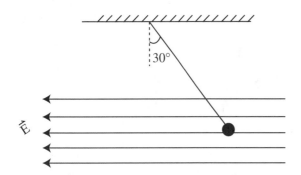

40. A uniform electric field points to the left. A small metal ball charged to –2 mC hangs at a 30° angle from a string of negligible mass, as shown above. The tension in the string is measured to be 0.1 N. What is the magnitude of the electric field? (sin 30° = 0.50; cos 30° = 0.87; tan 30° = 0.58).

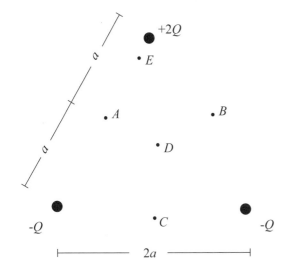

43. Three charges are arranged in an equilateral triangle, as shown above. At which of these points is the electric potential smallest?

   (A) A
   (B) B
   (C) C
   (D) D
   (E) E

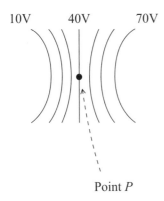

Point P

44. The diagram shows a set of equipotential surfaces. At point P, what is the direction of the electric field?

   (A) left
   (B) right
   (C) up the page
   (D) down the page
   (E) either left or right, which one cannot be determined

45. A metal sphere carries charge Q; a nonconducting sphere of equal size carries the same charge Q, uniformly distributed throughout the sphere. These spheres are isolated from each other. Consider the electric field at the center of the spheres, within the spheres, and outside the spheres. Which of these electric fields will be the same for both spheres, and which will be different?

	At the Center	Elsewhere Within the Sphere	Outside the Sphere
(A)	Same	Same	Same
(B)	Same	Same	Different
(C)	Same	Different	Same
(D)	Different	Different	Same
(E)	Different	Different	Different

46. Under what conditions is the net electric flux through a closed surface proportional to the enclosed charge?

   (A) under any conditions
   (B) only when the enclosed charge is symmetrically distributed
   (C) only when all nearby charges are symmetrically distributed
   (D) only when there are no charges outside the surface
   (E) only when enclosed charges can be considered to be point charges

47. A hollow metal ring of radius r carries charge q. Consider an axis straight through the center of the ring. At what points along this axis are the electric field equal to zero?

   (A) only at the center of the ring
   (B) only at the center of the ring, and a very long distance away
   (C) only a very long distance away
   (D) only at the center of the ring, a distance r away from the center, and a very long distance away
   (E) everywhere along this axis

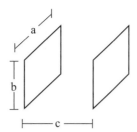

48. A parallel plate capacitor consists of identical rectangular plates of dimensions $a \times b$, separated by a distance c. To cut the capacitance of this capacitor in half, which of these quantities should be doubled?

    (A) a
    (B) b
    (C) c
    (D) ab
    (E) abc

49. Two identical capacitors are hooked in parallel to an external circuit. Which of the following quantities must be the same for both capacitors?

    I. the charge stored on the capacitor
    II. the voltage across the capacitor
    III. the capacitance of the capacitor
    (A) I only
    (B) II only
    (C) II and III only
    (D) I and III only
    (E) I, II, and III

50. A 2-µF capacitor is connected directly to a battery. When the capacitor is fully charged, it stores 600 µC of charge. An experimenter replaces the 2-µF capacitor with three 18-µF capacitors in series connected to the same battery. Once the capacitors are fully charged, what charge is stored on each capacitor?

    (A) 100 µC
    (B) 200 µC
    (C) 600 µC
    (D) 1200 µC
    (E) 1800 µC

51. A spherical conductor carries a net charge. How is this charge distributed on the sphere?

    (A) The charge is evenly distributed on the surface.
    (B) The charge resides on the surface only; the distribution of charge on the surface depends on what other charged objects are near the sphere.

(C) The charge moves continually within the sphere.
(D) The charge is distributed uniformly throughout the sphere.
(E) The charge resides within the sphere; the distribution of charge within the sphere depends on what other charged objects are near the sphere.

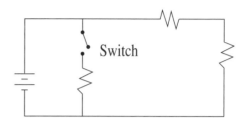

52. Three resistors are connected to a battery as shown in the diagram above. The switch is initially open. When the switch is closed, what happens to the total voltage, current, and resistance in the circuit?

	Voltage	Current	Resistance
(A)	increases	increases	increases
(B)	does not change	does not change	does not change
(C)	does not change	decreases	increases
(D)	does not change	increases	decreases
(E)	decreases	decreases	decreases

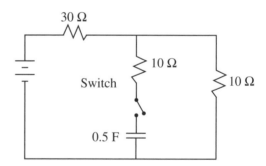

53. In the circuit shown above, the 0.5 F capacitor is initially uncharged. The switch is closed at time $t = 0$. What is the time constant (the time for the capacitor to charge to 63% of its maximum charge) for the charging of this capacitor?

    (A) 5 s
    (B) 10 s
    (C) 20 s
    (D) 30 s
    (E) 40 s

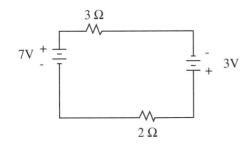

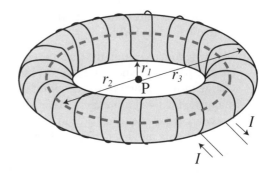

54. In the circuit shown above, what is the current through the 3 Ω resistor?

(A) 0 A
(B) 0.5 A
(C) 1.0 A
(D) 1.5 A
(E) 2.0 A

55. A light bulb rated at 100 W is twice as bright as a bulb rated at 50 W when both are connected in parallel directly to a 100-V source. Now imagine that these bulbs are instead connected in series with each other. Which is brighter, and by how much?

(A) The bulbs have the same brightness.
(B) The 100-W bulb is twice as bright.
(C) The 50-W bulb is twice as bright.
(D) The 100-W bulb is four times as bright.
(E) The 50-W bulb is four times as bright.

57. Wire is wound around an insulated circular donut, as shown above. A current I flows in the wire in the direction indicated by the arrows. The inner, average, and outer radii of the donut are indicated by r_1, r_2, and r_3, respectively. What is the magnitude and direction of the magnetic field at point P, the center of the donut?

(A) zero

(B) $\dfrac{\mu_o I}{2r_1}$.

(C) $\dfrac{\mu_o I}{2r_2}$.

(D) $\dfrac{\mu_o I}{2r_3}$.

(E) $\dfrac{\mu_o I}{2\pi r_2}$.

B

X X X X X
X X X X X
• → v
X X X X X
X X X X X
X X X X X

56. A uniform magnetic field **B** is directed into the page. An electron enters this field with initial velocity v to the right. Which of the following best describes the path of the electron while it is still within the magnetic field?

(A) It moves in a straight line.
(B) It bends upward in a parabolic path.
(C) It bends downward in a parabolic path.
(D) It bends upward in a circular path.
(E) It bends downward in a circular path.

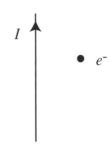

58. A wire carries a current toward the top of the page. An electron is located to the right of the wire, as shown above. In which direction should the electron be moving if it is to experience a magnetic force toward the wire?

(A) into the page
(B) out of the page
(C) toward the bottom of the page
(D) toward the top of the page
(E) to the right

59. Which of the following statements about electric and magnetic fields is FALSE:

    (A) A charge moving along the direction of an electric field will experience a force, but a charge moving along the direction of a magnetic field will not experience a force.
    (B) All charges experience a force in an electric field, but only moving charges can experience a force in a magnetic field.
    (C) A positive charge moves in the direction of an electric field; a positive charge moves perpendicular to a magnetic field.
    (D) All moving charges experience a force parallel to an electric field and perpendicular to a magnetic field.
    (E) A negative charge experiences a force opposite the direction of an electric field; a negative charge experiences a force perpendicular to a magnetic field.

60. Which of these quantities decreases as the inverse square of distance for distances far from the objects producing the fields?

    (A) the electric field produced by a finite-length charged rod
    (B) the electric field produced by an infinitely long charged cylinder
    (C) the electric field produced by an infinite plane of charge
    (D) the magnetic field produced by an infinitely long straight current carrying wire
    (E) the magnetic field produced by a wire curled around a torus

61. A proton enters a solenoid. Upon entry, the proton is moving in a straight line along the axis of the solenoid. Which of the following is a correct description of the proton's motion within the solenoid?

    (A) The proton will be bent in a parabolic path.
    (B) The proton will be bent in a circular path.
    (C) The proton will continue in its straight path at constant velocity.
    (D) The proton will continue in its straight path and slow down.
    (E) The proton will continue in its straight path and speed up.

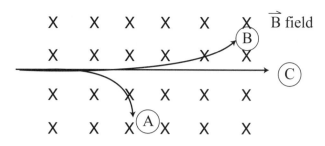

62. A uniform magnetic field points into the page. Three subatomic particles are shot into the field from the left-hand side of the page. All have the same initial speed and direction. These particles take paths A, B, and C, as labeled in the diagram above. Which of the following is a possible identity for each particle?

	A	B	C
(A)	antiproton	proton	electron
(B)	antiproton	positron	neutron
(C)	proton	electron	neutron
(D)	positron	antiproton	neutron
(E)	electron	proton	neutron

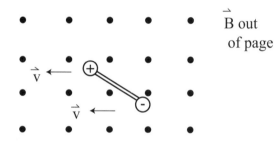

63. The electric dipole shown above consists of equal-magnitude charges and has an initial leftward velocity v in a uniform magnetic field pointing out of the page, as shown above. The dipole experiences

    (A) a clockwise net torque, and a net force to the left
    (B) a counterclockwise net torque, and a net force to the left
    (C) no net torque, and a net force to the left
    (D) a counterclockwise net torque, and no net force
    (E) a clockwise net torque, and no net force

64. A beam of electrons has speed 10^7 m/s. It is desired to use the magnetic field of the earth, 5×10^{-5} T, to bend the electron beam into a circle. What will be the radius of this circle?

    (A) 1 nm
    (B) 1 μm
    (C) 1 mm
    (D) 1 m
    (E) 1 km

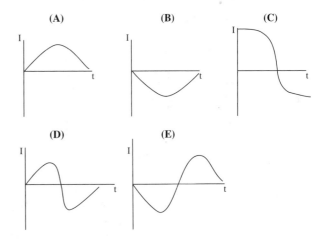

    I dL   •   P

65. A very small element of wire of length dL carries a current I. What is the direction of the magnetic field produced by this current element at point P, shown above?

    (A) to the right
    (B) toward the top of the page
    (C) into the page
    (D) out of the page
    (E) there is no magnetic field produced at point P by this element.

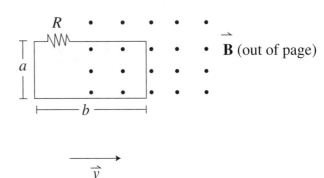

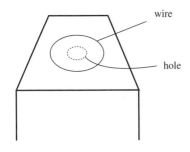

66. A loop of wire surrounds a hole in a table, as shown above. A bar magnet is dropped, north end down, from far above the table through the hole. Let the positive direction of current be defined as counterclockwise as viewed from above. Which of the following graphs best represents the induced current **I** in the loop?

67. A rectangular loop of wire has dimensions $a \times b$ and includes a resistor R. This loop is pulled with speed v from a region of no magnetic field into a uniform magnetic field **B** pointing through the loop, as shown above. What is the magnitude and direction of the current through the resistor?

    (A) Bav/R, left-to-right
    (B) Bbv/R, left-to-right
    (C) Bav/R, right-to-left
    (D) Bbv/R, right-to-left
    (E) Bba/R, right-to-left

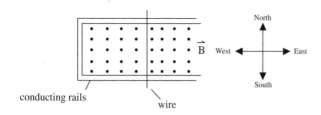

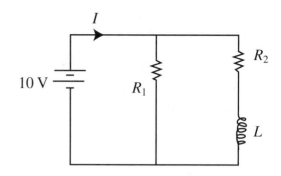

68. A conducting wire sits on smooth metal rails, as shown above. A variable magnetic field points out of the page. The strength of this magnetic field is increased linearly from zero. Immediately after the field starts to increase, what will be the direction of the current in the wire and the direction of the wire's motion?

	Current in the Wire	Motion of the Wire
(A)	north	no motion
(B)	north	east
(C)	north	west
(D)	south	west
(E)	south	east

70. If the two equal resistors R_1 and R_2 are connected in parallel to a 10-V battery with no other circuit components, the current provided by the battery is I. In the circuit shown above, an inductor of inductance L is included in series with R_2. What is the current through R_2 after the circuit has been connected for a long time?

(A) zero
(B) $(1/4) I$
(C) $(1/2) I$
(D) I
(E) $I \dfrac{R_1 + R_2}{LR_2}$

STOP. End of electricity and magnetism Section I.

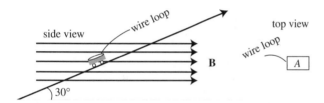

69. A uniform magnetic field **B** points parallel to the ground. A toy car is sliding down a frictionless plane inclined at 30°. A loop of wire of resistance R and cross-sectional area A lies in the flat plane of the car's body, as shown above. What is the magnetic flux through the wire loop?

(A) zero
(B) $BA \cos 30°$
(C) $BA \cos 60°$
(D) BA
(E) $(BA \cos 60°)/R$

END OF SECTION I

AP PHYSICS C

Section II—Mechanics

Time—45 minutes

You may refer to the Constants sheet and Equations sheet in the Appendix. You may also use a calculator on this portion of the exam.

CM1

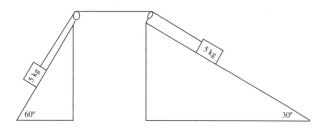

Two 5-kg masses are connected by a light string over two massless, frictionless pulleys. Each block sits on a frictionless inclined plane, as shown above. The blocks are released from rest.

(a) Determine the magnitude of the acceleration of the blocks.
(b) Determine the tension in the rope.

Now assume that the 30° incline is rough, so that the coefficient of friction between the block and the plane is 0.10. The 60° incline is still frictionless.

(c) Determine the magnitude of the acceleration of the blocks.
(d) Determine the tension in the rope.

CM2

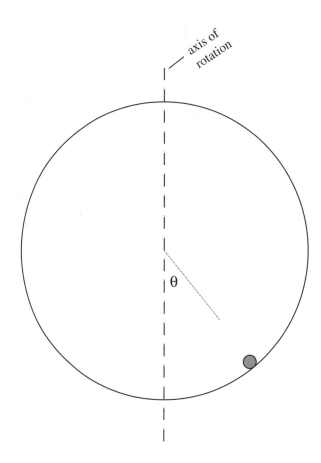

A hollow glass sphere of radius 8.0 cm rotates about a vertical diameter with frequency 5 revolutions per second. A small wooden ball of mass 2.0 g rotates inside the sphere, as shown in the diagram above.

(a) Draw a free-body diagram indicating the forces acting on the wooden ball when it is at the position shown in the picture above.
(b) Calculate the angle θ, shown in the diagram above, to which the ball rises.
(c) Calculate the linear speed of the wooden ball as it rotates.
(d) The wooden ball is replaced with a steel ball of mass 20 g. Describe how the angle θ to which the ball rises will be affected. Justify your answer.

CM3

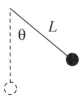

A heavy ball of mass m is attached to a light but rigid rod of length L. The rod is pivoted at the top and is free to rotate in a circle in the plane of the page, as shown above.

(a) The mass oscillates to a maximum angle θ. On the picture of the mass m below, draw a vector representing the direction of the NET force on the mass while it is at angle θ. Justify your choice of direction.

●

(b) Is the magnitude of the net force at the maximum displacement equal to $mg\sin\theta$ or $mg\cos\theta$? Choose one and justify your choice.
(c) Derive an expression for the ball's potential energy U as a function of the angle θ. Assume that a negative angle represents displacement from the vertical in the clockwise direction.
(d) On the axes below, sketch a graph of the mass's potential energy U as a function of the angle θ for angles between −90° and +360°. Label maximum and minimum values on the vertical axis.

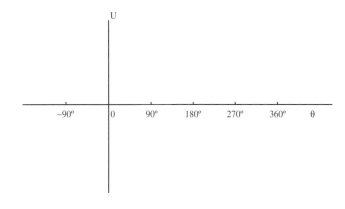

(e) The pendulum is considered a classic example of simple harmonic motion when it undergoes small-amplitude oscillation. With specific reference to the graph you made in part (d), explain why the assumption of simple harmonic motion is valid.

STOP. End of mechanics Section II.

AP PHYSICS C

Section II—Electricity and Magnetism

Time—45 minutes

You may refer to the Constants sheet and Equations sheet in the Appendix. You may also use a calculator on this portion of the exam.

CE&M 1

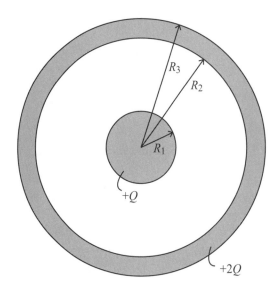

A metal sphere of radius R_1 carries charge $+Q$. A concentric spherical metal shell, of inner radius R_2 and outer radius R_3, carries charge $+2Q$.

(a) Let r represent the distance from the center of the spheres. Calculate the electric field as a function of r in each of the following four regions:

    1. between $r = 0$ and $r = R_1$
    2. between $r = R_1$ and $r = R_2$
    3. between $r = R_2$ and $r = R_3$
    4. between $r = R_3$ and $r = \infty$

(b) How much charge is on each surface of the outer spherical shell? Justify your answer.
(c) Determine the electric potential of the outer spherical shell.
(d) Determine the electric potential of the inner spherical shell.

CE&M 2

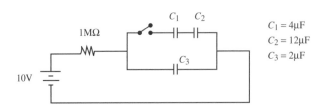

$C_1 = 4\mu F$
$C_2 = 12\mu F$
$C_3 = 2\mu F$

A 1 MΩ resistor is connected to the network of capacitors shown above. The circuit is hooked to a 10-V battery. The capacitors are initially uncharged. The battery is connected and the switch is closed at time $t = 0$.
(a) Determine the equivalent capacitance of C_1, C_2, and C_3.
(b) Determine the charge on and voltage across each capacitor after a long time has elapsed.

(c) On the axes below, sketch the total charge on C_3 as a function of time.

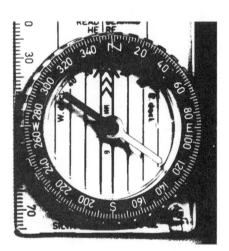

(d) After the capacitors have been fully charged, the switch is opened, disconnecting C_1 and C_2 from the circuit. What happens to the voltage across and charge on C_3? Justify your answer.

CE&M 3

In the laboratory, far from the influence of other magnetic fields, the Earth's magnetic field has a value of 5.00×10^{-5} T. A compass in this lab reads due north when pointing along the direction of Earth's magnetic field.

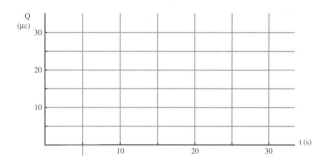

A long, straight current-carrying wire is brought close to the compass, deflecting the compass to the position shown above, 48° west of north.

(a) Describe one possible orientation of the wire and the current it carries that would produce the deflection shown.

(b) Calculate the magnitude B_{wire} of the magnetic field produced by the wire that would cause the deflection shown.

(c) The distance d from the wire to the compass is varied, while the current in the wire is kept constant; a graph of B_{wire} vs. d is produced. On the axes below, sketch the shape of this graph.

(d) It is desired to adjust this plot so that the graph becomes a straight line. The vertical axis is to remain B_{wire}, the magnetic field produced by the wire. How could the quantity graphed on the horizontal axis be adjusted to produce a straight line graph? Justify your answer.

(e) The current carried by the wire is 500 mA. Determine the slope of the line on the graph suggested in part (d).

STOP. End of electricity and magnetism Section II.

ANSWERS TO THE MULTIPLE-CHOICE QUESTIONS

Answer Key

1.	D	15.	C	29.	D	43.	C	57.	A
2.	D	16.	B	30.	B	44.	A	58.	C
3.	E	17.	D	31.	D	45.	C	59.	C
4.	C	18.	D	32.	B	46.	A	60.	A
5.	B	19.	B	33.	B	47.	B	61.	C
6.	B	20.	E	34.	B	48.	C	62.	E
7.	B	21.	D	35.	D	49.	E	63.	E
8.	B	22.	D	36.	B	50.	E	64.	D
9.	D	23.	A	37.	D	51.	B	65.	E
10.	D	24.	D	38.	B	52.	D	66.	D
11.	B	25.	D	39.	C	53.	C	67.	A
12.	C	26.	B	40.	A	54.	E	68.	D
13.	B	27.	B	41.	D	55.	C	69.	C
14.	C	28.	D	42.	A	56.	E	70.	C

Explanations of Answers to the Multiple-Choice Mechanics Questions

1. **D.** A projectile has its maximum range when it is shot at an angle of 45° relative to the ground. The cannon's initial velocity relative to the ground in this problem is given by the vector sum of the man's 5 m/s forward motion and the cannon's 50 m/s muzzle velocity. To get a resultant velocity of 45°, the man must shoot the cannon at only a slightly higher angle, as shown in the diagram below.

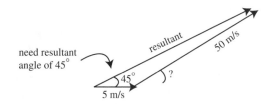

2. **C.** The car stays on the plane, and slows down as it goes up the plane. Thus, the net acceleration is in the direction down the plane, which has both a nonzero horizontal and vertical component. The car is not in free fall, so its vertical acceleration is less than g.

3. **E.** Acceleration is the slope of the v–t graph. Because acceleration increases, the slope of the v–t graph must get steeper, eliminating choices A and B. The bike slows down, so the speed must get closer to zero as time goes on, eliminating choices C and D.

4. **C.** The cart's acceleration is $g\sin\theta$, down the plane, the ball's acceleration is g, straight down. (So the magnitudes of acceleration are different and choice D is wrong.) The component of the ball's acceleration along an axis parallel to the plane is also $g\sin\theta$, equal to the ball's acceleration component.

5. **B.** The area under a jerk–time graph is the quantity $j\,dt$. The derivative

$$j = \frac{da}{dt}$$

can be interpreted as a change in acceleration over a time interval,

$$j = \frac{\Delta a}{\Delta t}.$$

Solving algebraically, $j\,\Delta t$ is Δa, meaning the change in acceleration.

6. **B.** At $t = 0$, $x = +5$ m, so the particle is east of the origin to start with. The velocity is given by the derivative of the position function, $v(t) = 3$ m/s. This is a constant velocity; the acceleration is thus zero (and constant), but at $t = 0$ the velocity is also 3 m/s, so choice B is false.

7. **B.** Consider the horizontal and vertical forces separately. The only horizontal forces are the horizontal components of the tensions. Because the block is in equilibrium, these horizontal tensions must be *equal*, meaning only choices B and D can be right. But the ropes can't have equal horizontal AND vertical tensions, otherwise they'd hang at equal angles. So D can't be the right choice, and B must be right.

8. **B.** The equation $F = bv^2$ is of the form $y = mx$, the equation of a line. Here F is the vertical axis, v^2 is the horizontal axis, so b is the slope of the line. Looking at the graph, the slope is 5.0 N / 3.0 m^2/s^2, = 1.7 kg/m.

9. **D.** Because no forces act perpendicular to the incline except for the normal force and the perpendicular component of weight, and there is no acceleration perpendicular to the incline, the normal force is equal to the perpendicular component of weight, which is $mg\cos\theta$. As the angle increases, the cosine of the angle decreases. This decrease is nonlinear because a graph of F_n vs. θ would show a curve, not a line.

10. **D.** In equilibrium, the net force and the net torque must both be zero. *Static* equilibrium means the object is stationary, so kinetic energy must be zero. However, potential energy can take on any value—a sign suspended above a roadway is in static equilibrium, yet has potential energy relative to Earth's surface.

11. **B.** The friction force is equal to the coefficient of friction times the normal force. The coefficient of friction is a property of the surfaces in contact, and thus will not change here. However, the normal force decreases when the cart is pulled rather than pushed—the surface must apply more force to the box when there is a downward component to the applied force than when there is an upward component. Speed is irrelevant because equilibrium in the vertical direction is maintained regardless.

12. **C.** The ball accelerates *toward* the Earth because, although it is moving upward, it must be slowing down. The only force acting on the ball is Earth's gravity. Yes, the ball exerts a force on the Earth, but that force acts on the Earth, not the ball. According to Newton's 3rd law, force pairs always act on different object, and thus can never cancel.

13. **B.** The work done on an object by gravity is independent of the path taken by the object and is equal to the object's weight times its vertical displacement. Gravity must do $3mgL$ of work to raise the large mass, but must do $mg(-L)$ of work to lower the small mass. The net work done is thus $2mgL$.

14. **C.** Use conservation of energy. Position 1 will be the top of the table; position 2 will be the ground. $PE_1 + KE_1 = PE_2 + KE_2$. Take the PE at the ground to be zero. Then $\frac{1}{2}mv_2^2 = \frac{1}{2}mv_1^2 + mgh$. The *m*s cancel. Solving for v_2, you get choice C. (Choice E is wrong because it's illegal algebra to take a squared term out of a square root when it is added to another term.)

15. **C.** Consider the conservation of energy. At the launch point, the potential energy is the same regardless of launch direction. The kinetic energy is also the same because KE depends on speed alone and not direction. So, both balls have the same amount of kinetic energy to convert to potential energy, bringing the ball to the same height in every cycle.

16. **B.** Total mechanical energy is defined as kinetic energy plus potential energy. The KE here is $\frac{1}{2}mv_0^2$. The potential energy is provided entirely by the spring—gravitational potential energy requires a *vertical* displacement, which doesn't occur here. The PE of the spring is $\frac{1}{2}kx_0^2$.

17. **D.** When an object rotates, some of its potential energy is converted to rotational rather than linear kinetic energy, and thus it moves more slowly than a non-rotating object when it reaches the bottom of the plane. However, here none of the objects rotate! The acceleration does not depend on mass or size.

18. **D.** Momentum must be conserved in the collision. If block A bounces, it changes its momentum by a larger amount than if it sticks. This means that block B picks up more momentum (and thus more speed) when block A bounces. The mass of the blocks is irrelevant because the comparison here is just between bouncing and not bouncing. So B goes faster in collision I regardless of mass.

19. **B.** The momentum of the bird before collision is 9 N·s to the left; the momentum of the ball is initially 3 N·s up. The momentum after collision is the *vector* sum of these two initial momentums. With a calculator you would use the Pythagorean theorem to get 9.5 N·s; without a calculator you should just notice that the resultant vector must have magnitude less than 12 N·s (the algebraic sum) and more than 9 N·s.

20. **E.** Impulse is defined on the equation sheet as the integral of force with respect to time, so III is right. The meaning of this integral is to take the area under a *F* vs. *t* graph, so II is right. Because the force is increasing linearly, the average force will be halfway between zero and the maximum force, and the rectangle formed by this average force will have the same area as the triangle on the graph as shown, so I is right.

21. **D.** The center of mass of the projectile must maintain the projectile path and land 500 m from the launch point. The first half of the projectile fell straight down from the peak of its flight, which is halfway to the maximum range, or 250 m from the launch point. So the second half of equal mass must be 250 m beyond the center of mass upon hitting the ground, or 750 m from the launch point.

22. **D.** By conservation of linear momentum, there is momentum to the right before collision, so there must be momentum to the right after collision as well. A free-floating object rotates about its center of mass; because the putty is attached to the rod, the combination will rotate about its combined center of mass.

23. **A.** Linear and angular momentum are conserved in *all* collisions (though often angular momentum conservation is irrelevant). Kinetic energy, though, is only conserved in an elastic collision. Because the putty sticks to the rod, this collision cannot be elastic. Some of the kinetic energy must be dissipated as heat.

24. **D.**

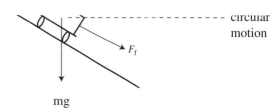

The centripetal force must act toward the center of the car's circular path. This direction is NOT down the plane, but rather is purely horizontal. The friction force acts down the plane and thus has a horizontal component; the normal force acts perpendicular to the plane and has a horizontal component. So BOTH F_n and F_f contribute to the centripetal force.

25. **D.** The mass's acceleration has two components here. Some acceleration must be centripetal (i.e., toward the anchor) because the mass's path is circular. But the mass is also speeding up, so it must have a tangential component of acceleration toward point *B*. The vector sum of these two components must be in between the anchor and point *B*.

26. **B.** The free-body diagram for a person includes F_n toward the center of the circle, *mg* down and the force of friction up:

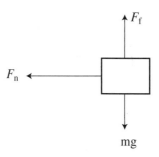

Because the person is not sliding down, $mg = F_f$. And because the motion of the person is circular, the normal force is a centripetal force, so $F_n = mv^2/r$. The force of friction by definition is μF_n. Combining these equations, we have $mg = \mu mv^2/r$; solve for v to get answer choice B. Note: Without any calculation, you could recognize that only choices A and B have units of speed, so you would have had a good chance at getting the answer right just by guessing one of these two!

27. **B.** Use Newton's second law for rotation, $\tau_{net} = I\alpha$. The only torque about the pivot is the rod's weight, acting at the rod's center; this torque is thus $mgL/2$. So the angular acceleration, α, of the rod is $mgL/2I$. But the question asks for a linear acceleration, $a = r\alpha$, where r is the distance to the center of rotation. That distance here is $L/2$. So combining, you get $a = (L/2)(mgL/2I) = mgL^2/4I$.

28. **D.** We cannot use rotational kinematics here because the net torque, and thus the angular acceleration, is not constant. Use conservation of energy instead. The potential energy at the release point is $mg(L/2)$ ($L/2$ because the rod's center of mass is that far vertically above it's lowest point). This potential energy is converted entirely into rotational kinetic energy $\frac{1}{2}I\omega^2$. The rod's angular velocity ω is equal to $v/(L/2)$, where v is the linear speed of the center of mass that we're solving for. Plugging in, you get $mgL/2 = \frac{1}{2}I(v^2/[L/2]^2)$. Solving for v, choice D emerges from the mathematics.

29. **D.** Choose any point at all as the fulcrum; say, the center of mass. Pillar B supports 500 N, and is located 20 cm from the fulcrum, producing a total counterclockwise torque of 10,000 N·cm. Pillar A also supports 500 N; call its distance from the fulcrum "x". So $10,000 = 500x$, and $x = 20$ cm. This means pillar A is located 20 cm left of the center of mass, or **50 cm** from the left edge.

30. **B.** The period of a mass on a spring is

$$2\pi\sqrt{\frac{m}{k}}$$

with the mass under the square root. So when the mass is quadrupled, the period is only multiplied by two. The total mechanical energy is the sum of potential plus kinetic energy. At the greatest displacement from equilibrium (i.e., at the amplitude), the mass's speed is zero and all energy is potential; potential energy of a spring is $\frac{1}{2}kx^2$ and does not depend on mass. So, because the amplitude of oscillation remains the same, the total mechanical energy does not change.

31. **D.** The maximum potential energy of the mass is at the amplitude, and equal to $\frac{1}{2}kA^2$. This is entirely converted to kinetic energy at the equilibrium position, where the speed is maximum. So set $\frac{1}{2}kA^2 = \frac{1}{2}mv_{max}^2$. Solving for v_{max}, you get choice D. (Note: Only choices C and D have units of velocity! So guess between these if you have to!)

32. **B.** The bottle's lowest position is $x = -A$, and its highest position is $x = +A$. When $t = 0$, $\cos(0) = 1$ and the bottle is at $x = +A$. So, find the time when the cosine function goes to -1. This is when $\omega t = \pi$, so $t = \pi/\omega$.

33. **B.** Don't try to calculate the answer by saying $mg = Gmm/r^2$! Not only would you have had to memorize the mass of the Earth, but you have no calculator and you only have a minute or so, anyway. So think: the acceleration must be less than 9.8 m/s^2, because that value is calculated at the surface of the Earth, and the shuttle is farther from earth's center than that. But the added height of 300 km is a small fraction (~5%) of the Earth's radius. So the gravitational acceleration will not be THAT much less. The best choice is thus 8.9 m/s^2. (By the way, acceleration is not zero—if it were, the Shuttle would be moving in a straight line, and not orbiting.)

34. **B.** The orbit can no longer be circular—circular orbits demand a specific velocity. Because the satellite gains speed while at its original distance from the planet, the orbit is now elliptical. Because the direction of the satellite's motion is still tangent to the former circular path, in the next instant the satellite will be farther from Earth than at point P, eliminating answer choice A. The satellite will not "fly off into space" unless it reaches escape velocity, which cannot be 1% greater than the speed necessary for a low circular orbit.

35. **D.** Kepler's third law states that for all planets in the same system, their period of orbit is proportional to the average distance from the sun cubed. Using units of years and au, for Earth, $(1 \text{ year})^2 = (1 \text{ au})^3$. For Mercury, we have $(\frac{1}{5} \text{ year})^2 = (? \text{ au})^3$. Solving for the question mark, you find that the distance from Mercury to the sun is the cube root of $\frac{1}{25}$ au, which is closest to $\frac{1}{3}$ au.

Explanations of Answers to the Multiple-Choice Electricity and Magnetism Questions

36. **B.** An electric field exists regardless of the amount of charge placed in it, and regardless of whether any charge at all is placed in it. So both experimenters must measure the same field (though they will measure different forces on their test charges).

37. **D.** You could use Gauss's law to show that the field outside the sphere has to decrease as $1/r^2$, eliminating choices B and E. But it's easier just to remember that an important result of Gauss's law is that *electric field inside a conductor is always zero everywhere*, so D is the only possibility.

38. **B.** While in the region between the plates, the negatively charged proton is attracted to the positive plate, so bends upward. But after leaving the plates, there is no more force acting on the electron. Thus, the electron continues in motion in a straight line by Newton's first law.

39. **C.** This is a Newton's third law problem! The force of A on B is equal (and opposite) to the force of B on A. Or, we can use Coulomb's law: The field due to A is $k(2Q)/(4\text{ m})^2$. The force on B is $QE = k2QQ/(4\text{ m})^2$. We can do the same analysis finding the field due to B and the force on A to get the same result.

40. **A.** The charge is in equilibrium, so the horizontal component of the tension must equal the electric force. This horizontal tension is 0.1 N times sin 30° (not cosine because 30° was measured from the *vertical*), or 0.05 N. The electric force is qE, where q is 0.002 C. So the electric field is 0.050 N/0.002 C. Reduce the expression by moving the decimal to get 50/2, or 25 N/C.

41. **D.** The answer could, in principle, be found using the integral form of Coulomb's law. But you can't do that on a one-minute multiple-choice problem. The electric field will point down the page—the field due to a positive charge points away from the charge, and there's an equal amount of charge producing a rightward field as a leftward field, so horizontal fields cancel. So, is the answer B or D? Choice B is not correct because electric fields add as vectors. Only the vertical component of the field due to each little charge element contributes to the net electric field, so the net field must be *less than* kQ/R^2.

42. **A.** Use the symmetry of the situation to see the answer. Because the infinitely large plane looks the same on the up side as the down side, its electric field must look the same, too—the field must point away from the plane and have the same value.

43. **C.** Another way to look at this question is, "where would a small positive charge end up if released near these charges?" because positive charges seek the smallest potential. The positive charge would be repelled by the $+2Q$ charge and attracted to the $-Q$ charges, so would end up at point C. Or, know that potential due to a point charge is kq/r. Point C is closest to both $-Q$ charges, so the r terms will be smallest, and the negative contribution to the potential will be largest; point C is farthest from the $+2Q$ charge, so the r term will be large, and the positive contribution to the potential will be smallest.

44. **A.** A positive charge is forced from high to low potential, which is generally to the left; and the force on a positive charge is in the direction of the electric field. At point P itself the electric field is directly to the left because an electric field is always perpendicular to equipotential surfaces.

45. **C.** The charge on the metal sphere distributes uniformly on its surface. Because the nonconducting sphere also has a uniform charge distribution, by symmetry the electric fields will cancel to zero at the center. Outside the spheres we can use Gauss's law: $E \cdot A = Q_{enclosed}/\varepsilon_0$. Because the charge enclosed by a Gaussian surface outside either sphere will be the same, and the spheres are the same size, the electric field will be the same everywhere outside either sphere. But within the sphere? A Gaussian surface drawn inside the conducting sphere encloses no charge, while a Gaussian surface inside the nonconducting sphere does enclose some charge. The fields inside must *not* be equal.

46. **A.** That's what Gauss's law says: Net flux through a closed surface is equal to the charge enclosed divided by ε_0. Though Gauss's law is only *useful* when all charge within or without a Gaussian surface is symmetrically distributed, Gauss's law is *valid* always.

47. **B.** The electric field at the center of the ring is zero because the field caused by any charge element is canceled by the field due to the charge on the other side of the ring. The electric field decreases as $1/r^2$ by Coulomb's law, so a long distance away from the ring the field goes to zero. The field is nonzero near the ring, though, because each charge element creates a field pointing away from the ring, resulting in a field always along the axis.

48. **C.** Capacitance of a parallel plate capacitor is $\varepsilon_o A/d$, where A is the area of the plates, and d is the separation between plates. To halve the capacitance, we must halve the area or double the plate separation. The plate separation in the diagram is labeled c, so double distance c.

49. **E.** We are told that the capacitors are identical, so their capacitances must be equal. They are hooked in parallel, meaning the voltages across them must be equal as well. By $Q = CV$, the charge stored by each must also be equal.

50. **E.** First determine the voltage of the battery by $Q = CV$. This gives $V = 600\ \mu C/2\ \mu F = 300$ V. This voltage is hooked to the three series capacitors, whose equivalent capacitance is 6 μF (series capacitors add inversely, like parallel resistors). So the total charge stored now is $(6\ \mu F)(300\ V) = 1800\ \mu C$. This charge is *not* split evenly among the capacitors, though! Just as the current through series resistors is the same through each and equal to the total current through the circuit, the charge on series capacitors is the same and equal to the total.

51. **B.** The charge does reside on the surface, and, if the conductor is alone, will distribute evenly. But, if there's another nearby charge, then this charge can repel or attract the charge on the sphere, causing a redistribution.

52. **D.** The voltage must stay the same because the battery by definition provides a constant voltage. Closing the switch adds a parallel branch to the network of resistors. Adding a parallel resistor *reduces* the total resistance. By Ohm's law, if voltage stays the same and resistance decreases, total current must increase.

53. **C.** The time constant for an RC circuit is equal to RC. The resistance used is the resistance encountered by charge that's flowing to the capacitor; in this case, 40 Ω. So RC = 20 s.

54. **E.** Assume that the current runs counterclockwise in the circuit, and use Kirchoff's loop rule. Start with the 7-V battery and trace the circuit with the current: $+ 7V - I(3\Omega) + 3V - I(2\Omega) = 0$. Solve for I to get 2.0 A.

55. **C.** The intrinsic property of the light bulb is *resistance*; the power dissipated by a bulb depends on its voltage and current. When the bulbs are connected to the 100-V source, we can use the expression for power $P = V^2/R$ to see that the bulb rated at 50 watts has twice the resistance of the other bulb. Now in series, the bulbs carry the same current. Power is also I^2R; thus the 50-watt bulb with twice the resistance dissipates twice the power, and is twice as bright.

56. **E.** The electron bends downward by the right-hand rule for a charge in a B field—point to the right, curl fingers into the page, and the thumb points up the page. But the electron's negative charge changes the force to down the page. The path is a circle because the direction of the force continually changes, always pointing perpendicular to the electron's velocity. Thus, the force on the electron is a centripetal force.

57. **A.** This is one of the important consequences of Ampere's law. The magnetic field inside the donut is always along the axis of the donut, so the symmetry demands of Ampere's law are met. If we draw an "Amperean Loop" around point P but inside r_1, this loop encloses no current; thus the magnetic field must be zero.

58. **C.** The magnetic field due to the wire at the position of the electron is into the page. Now use the other right-hand rule, the one for the force on a charged particle in a magnetic field. If the charge moves down the page, then the force on a positive charge would be to the right, but the force on a (negative) electron would be left, toward the wire.

59. **C.** A positive charge experiences a force in the direction of an electric field, and perpendicular to a magnetic field; but the direction of a force is not necessarily the direction of motion.

60. **A.** The electric field due to *any* finite-sized charge distribution drops off as $1/r^2$ a long distance away because if you go far enough away, the charge looks like a point charge. This is not true for infinite charge distributions, though.

The magnetic field due to an infinitely long wire is given by

$$\frac{\mu_\circ I}{2\pi r},$$

not proportional to $1/r^2$; the magnetic field produced by a wire around a torus is zero outside the torus by Ampere's law.

61. **C.** The magnetic field produced by a single loop of wire at the center of the loop is directly out of the loop. A solenoid is a conglomeration of many loops in a row, producing a magnetic field that is uniform and along the axis of the solenoid. So, the proton will be traveling parallel to the magnetic field. By $F = qvB\sin\theta$, the angle between the field and the velocity is zero, producing no force on the proton. The proton continues its straight-line motion by Newton's first law.

62. **E.** By the right-hand rule for the force on a charged particle in a magnetic field, particle C must be neutral, particle B must be positively charged, and particle A must be negatively charged. Charge B must be more massive than charge A because it resists the change in its motion more than A. A proton is positively charged and more massive than the electron; the neutron is not charged.

63. **E.** The force on the positive charge is upward; the force on the negative charge is downward. These forces will tend to rotate the dipole clockwise, so only A or E could be right. Because the charges and velocities are equal, the magnetic force on each = qvB and is the same. So, there is no net force on the dipole. (Yes, no net force, even though it continues to move to the left.)

64. **D.** The centripetal force keeping the electrons in a circle is provided by the magnetic force. So set $qvB = mv^2/r$. Solve to get $r = (mv)/(qB)$. Just look at orders of magnitude now: $r = (10^{-31}$ kg$)(10^7$ m/s$)/(10^{-19}$ C$)(10^{-5}$ T$)$. This gives r $10^{24}/10^{24} = 10^0$ m ~ 1 m.

65. **E.** An element of current produces a magnetic field that wraps around the current element, pointing out of the page above the current and into the page below. But right in front (or anywhere along the axis of the current), the current element produces no magnetic field at all.

66. **D.** A long way from the hole, the magnet produces very little flux, and that flux doesn't change much, so very little current is induced. As the north end approaches the hole, the magnetic field points down. The flux is *increasing* because the field through the wire gets stronger with the approach of the magnet; so, point your right thumb upward (in the direction of *decreasing* flux) and curl your fingers. You find the current flows counterclockwise, defined as positive. Only A or D could be correct. Now consider what happens when the magnet leaves the loop. The south end descends away from the loop. The magnetic field still points down, into the south end of the magnet, but now the flux is *decreasing*. So point your right thumb down (in the direction of decreasing flux) and curl your fingers. Current now flows clockwise, as indicated in choice D. (While the magnet is going through the loop current goes to zero because the magnetic field of the bar magnet is reasonably constant near the center of the magnet.)

67. **A.** You remember the equation for the induced EMF in a moving rectangular loop, $\varepsilon = Blv$. Here l represents the length of the wire that doesn't change within the field; dimension a in the diagram. So the answer is either A or C. To find the direction of induced current, use Lenz's law: The field points out of the page, but the flux through the loop is *increasing* as more of the loop enters the field. So, point your right thumb into the page (in the direction of decreasing flux) and curl your fingers; you find the current is clockwise, or left-to-right across the resistor.

68. **D.** Start by finding the direction of the induced current in the wire using Lenz's law: the magnetic field is out of the page. The flux *increases* because the field strength increases. So point your right thumb into the page, and curl your fingers to find the current flowing clockwise, or south in the wire. Now use the right-hand rule for the force on moving charges in a magnetic field (remembering that a current is the flow of positive charge). Point down the page, curl your fingers out of the page, and the force must be to the west.

69. **C.** There is clearly nonzero flux because the field does pass through the wire loop. The flux is not BA, though, because the field does not go *straight* through the loop—the field hits the loop at an angle. So is the answer $BA \cos 30°$, using the angle of the plane; or $BA \cos 60°$, using the

angle from the vertical? To figure it out, consider the extreme case. If the incline were at zero degrees, there would be zero flux through the loop. Then the flux would be $BA \cos 90°$, because $\cos 90°$ is zero, and $\cos 0°$ is one. So don't use the angle of the plane, use the angle from the vertical, $BA \cos 60°$.

70. **C.** The inductor resists changes in current. But after a long time, the current reaches steady state, meaning the current does not change; thus the inductor, after a long time, might as well be just a straight wire. The battery will still provide current I, of which half goes through each equal resistor.

RATING THE FREE-RESPONSE SOLUTIONS

Notes on grading your free-response section.

For answers that are numerical, or in equation form:

*For each part of the problem, look to see if you got the right answer. If you did, and you showed any reasonable (and correct) work, give yourself full credit for that part. It's okay if you didn't explicitly show EVERY step, as long as some steps are indicated and you got the right answer. However:

*If you got the WRONG answer, then look to see if you earned partial credit. Give yourself points for each step toward the answer as indicated in the rubrics below. Without the correct answer, you must show each intermediate step explicitly in order to earn the point for that step. (See why it's so important to show your work?)

*If you're off by a decimal place or two, not to worry—you get credit anyway, as long as your approach to the problem was legitimate. This isn't a math test. You're not being evaluated on your rounding and calculator-use skills.

*You do not have to simplify expressions in variables all the way. Square roots in the denominator are fine; fractions in nonsimplified form are fine. As long as you've solved properly for the requested variable, and as long as your answer is algebraically equivalent to the rubric's, you earn credit.

*Wrong, but consistent: Often you need to use the answer to part (a) in order to solve part (b). But you might have the answer to part (a) wrong. If you follow the correct procedure for part (b), plugging in your incorrect answer, then you will usually receive *full credit* for part (b). The major exceptions are when your answer to part (a) is unreasonable (say, a car moving at

10^5 m/s, or a distance between two cars equal to 10^{-100} meters), or when your answer to part (a) makes the rest of the problem trivial or irrelevant.

For answers that require justification:

*Obviously your answer will not match the rubric word-for-word. If the general gist is there, you get credit.

*But the reader is not allowed to interpret for the student. If your response is vague or ambiguous, you will NOT get credit.

*If your response consists of both correct and incorrect parts, you will usually not receive credit. It is not possible to try two answers, hoping that one of them is right. (See why it's so important to be concise?)

CM1

(a)

1 pt: Write Newton's second law for the direction along the plane for each block. Call the mass of each identical block m.

1 pt: For the right block, $T - mg\sin 30 = ma$.

1 pt: For the left block $mg\sin 60 - T = ma$.

1 pt: Here the directions chosen are consistent, so that forces that accelerate the system to the left are positive. (However, you earn this point as long as directions are consistent.)

1 pt: Solve these equations simultaneously (it's easiest just to add them together).

1 pt: $a = 1.8$ m/s². (An answer of $a = -1.8$ m/s² is incorrect because the magnitude of a vector cannot be negative.)

(Alternatively, you can just recognize that *mg*sin60 pulls left, while *mg*cos60 pulls right, and use Newton's second law directly on the combined system. Be careful, though, because the mass of the ENTIRE system is 10 kg, not 5 kg!)

(b)

1 pt: Just plug the acceleration back into one of the original Newton's second law equations from part (a).

1 pt: You get $T = 35$ N.

(c)

For parts (c) and (d), points are awarded principally for showing the difference that friction makes in the solution. You earn credit for properly accounting for this difference, even if your overall solution is wrong, as long as you followed a similar process to parts (a) and (b).

1 pt: Following the solution for part (a), this time the right block's equation becomes $T - mg\sin30 - \mu F_n$, where μ is the coefficient of friction, given as 0.10.

1 pt: The normal force is equal to $mg\cos30$.

1 pt: The left block's equation is the same as before, $mg\sin60 - T = ma$.

1 pt: Eliminating T and solving, we get 1.4 m/s². This is reasonable because we get a smaller acceleration when friction is included, as expected. [This answer point is awarded for ANY acceleration that is less than that calculated in part (a).]

(d)

1 pt: Plugging back into one of the equations in part (c), we find $T = 36$ N this time, or whatever tension is consistent with part (c).

1 pt: Awarded for ANY tension greater than that found in part (b).

1 pt: For proper units on at least one acceleration and one tension, and no incorrect units.

CM2

(a)

1 pt: The weight of the ball acts down.

1 pt: The normal force acts up and left, perpendicular to the surface of the glass.

1 pt: No other forces act.

(b)

1 pt: The normal force can be broken into vertical and horizontal components, where the vertical is $F_n\cos\theta$ and the horizontal is $F_n\sin\theta$. (The vertical direction goes with cosine here because θ is measured from the vertical.)

1 pt: The net vertical force is zero because the ball doesn't rise or fall on the glass. Setting up forces equal to down, $F_n\cos\theta = mg$.

1 pt: The horizontal force is a centripetal force, so $F_n\sin\theta = mv^2/r \sin\theta$.

1 pt: For using $r\sin\theta$ and not just r. (Why? Because you need to use the radius of the actual circular motion, which is not the same as the radius of the sphere.)

1 pt: The tangential speed "v" is the circumference of the circular motion divided by the period. Since period is $1/f$, and because the radius of the circular motion is $r\sin\theta$, this speed $v = 2\pi r\sin\theta f$.

1 pt: Now divide the vertical and horizontal force equations to get rid of the F_n term:

$$\sin\theta/\cos\theta = v^2/r\sin\theta g.$$

1 pt: Plug in the speed and the sin θ terms cancel, leaving $\cos\theta = g/4\pi r f^2$.

1 pt: Plugging in the given values (including $r = 0.08$ m), $\theta = 67°$.

(c)

1 pt: From part (a), the linear speed is $2\pi r \sin\theta f$.

1 pt: Plugging in values, the speed is 2.3 m/s. (If you didn't get the point in part (a) for figuring out how to calculate linear speed, but you do it right here, then you can earn the point here.)

(d)

1 pt: The angle will not be affected.

1 pt: Since the mass of the ball does not appear in the equation to calculate the angle in part (b), the mass does not affect the angle.

CM3

F_{net}

(a)

1 pt: The net force is at an angle down and to the left, perpendicular to the rod.

1 pt: Because the ball is instantaneously at rest, the direction of the velocity in the next instant must also be the direction of the acceleration; this direction is along the arc of the ball's motion.

(b)

1 pt: The magnitude of the net force is $mg\sin\theta$.

1 pt: It's easiest to use a limiting argument: When $\theta = 90°$, then the net force would be simply the weight of the ball, mg. $mg\sin 90° = mg$, while $mg\cos 90° = $ zero; hence the correct answer.

(c)

1 pt: The force on the mass is $-mg\sin\theta$, the negative arising because the force is always opposite the displacement.

1 pt: Potential energy is derived from force by $U = -\int F dx$.

1 pt: The distance displaced $x = L\theta$.

1 pt: The differential dx becomes $L\,d\theta$.

1 pt: The integral becomes $\int mgL\sin\theta\,d\theta$, which evaluates to $-mgL\cos\theta$. (Here the constant of integration can be taken to be any value at all because the zero of potential energy can be chosen arbitrarily.) [Alternate solution: Using geometry, it can be found that the height of the bob above the lowest point is $L - L\cos\theta$. Thus, the potential energy is $mgh = mg(L - L\cos\theta)$.

This gives the same answer, but has defined the arbitrary constant of integration as mgL.]

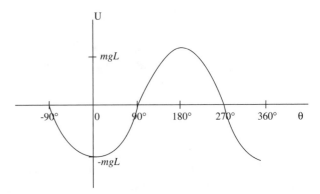

(d)

1 pt: The graph should look like some sort of sine or cosine function, oscillating smoothly.

1 pt: The graph should have an amplitude of mgL, though the graph can be shifted arbitrarily up or down on the vertical axis.

1 pt: The graph should have a minimum at $\theta = 0$.

1 pt: The graph should have a maximum at $\theta = 180°$.

(e)

1 pt: For simple harmonic motion, the restoring force must be linearly proportional to the displacement, like $F = -kx$. This yields an energy function that is quadratic: $-\int(-kx)\cdot dx$ integrates to give $U = \frac{1}{2}kx^2$. The graph of the energy of a simple harmonic oscillator is, thus, parabolic.

1 pt: Near the $\theta = 0$ position, the graph in part (e) is shaped much like a parabola, only deviating from a parabolic shape at large angles; so the pendulum is a simple harmonic oscillator as long as the energy graph approximates a parabola.

CE&M 1

(a)

1 pt: Inside a conductor, the electric field must always be zero. $E = 0$.

1 pt: Because we have spherical symmetry, use Gauss's law.

1 pt: The area of a Gaussian surface in this region is $4\pi r^2$. The charge enclosed by this surface is Q.

1 pt: So, $E = Q_{enclosed}/\varepsilon_o A = Q/4\pi\,\varepsilon_o r^2$.

1 pt: Inside a conductor, the electric field must always be zero. $E = 0$.

2 pts: Just as in part 2, use Gauss's law, but now the charged enclosed is $3Q$. $E = 3Q/4\pi \varepsilon_o r^2$.

(b)

1 pt: $-Q$ is on the inner surface.

1 pt: $+3Q$ is on the outer surface.

1 pt: Because $E = 0$ inside the outer shell, a Gaussian surface inside this shell must enclose zero charge, so $-Q$ must be on the inside surface to cancel the $+Q$ on the small sphere. Then to keep the total charge of the shell equal to $+2Q$, $+3Q$ must go to the outer surface.

(c)

1 pt: Because we have spherical symmetry, the potential due to both spheres is $3Q/4\pi \varepsilon_o r$, with potential equal to zero an infinite distance away.

1 pt: So at position R_3, the potential is $3Q/4\pi \varepsilon_o R_3$. (Since $E = 0$ inside the shell, V is the same value everywhere in the shell.)

(d)

1 pt: Integrate the electric field between R_1 and R_2 to get $V = Q/4\pi \varepsilon_o r + a$ constant of integration.

1 pt: To find that constant, we know that $V(R_2)$ was found in part (c), and is $3Q/4\pi \varepsilon_o R_3$. Thus, the constant is

$$\frac{3Q}{4\pi\varepsilon_o R_3} - \frac{Q}{4\pi\varepsilon_o R_2}.$$

1 pt: Then, potential at $R_1 = Q/4\pi \varepsilon_o R_1 +$ the constant of integration.

CE&M 2

(a)

1 pt: The series capacitors add inversely,

$$\frac{1}{4\mu F} + \frac{1}{12\mu F} = \frac{1}{C_{eq}},$$

so C_{eq} for the series capacitors is 3 μF.

1 pt: The parallel capacitor just adds in algebraically, so the equivalent capacitance for the whole system is 5 μF.

(b)

1 pt: After a long time, the resistor is irrelevant; no current flows because the fully charged capacitors block direct current.

1 pt: The voltage across C_3 is 10 V (because there's no voltage drop across the resistor without any current).

1 pt: By $Q = CV$ the charge on C_3 is 20 μC.

1 pt: Treating C_1 and C_2 in series; the equivalent capacitance is 3 μF, the voltage is 10 V (in parallel with C_3).

1 pt: The charge on the equivalent capacitance of C_1 and C_2 is 30 μC; thus the charge on $C_1 = 30$ μC, and the charge on C_2 is also 30 μC (charge on series capacitors is the same).

1 pt: Using $Q = CV$, the voltage across C_1 is 7.5 V.

1 pt: Using $Q = CV$, the voltage across C_2 is 2.5 V.

(c)

1 pt: For a graph that starts at $Q = 0$.

1 pt: For a graph that asymptotically approaches 20 μC (or whatever charge was calculated for C_3 in part b).

1 pt: For calculating the time constant of the circuit, $RC = 5$ s.

1 pt: For the graph reaching about 63% of its maximum charge after one time constant.

(d)

1 pt: For recognizing that the voltage does not change.

1 pt: For explaining that if voltage changed, than Kirchoff's voltage rule would not be valid around a loop including C_3 and the battery (or explaining that voltage is the same across parallel components, so if one is disconnected the other's voltage is unaffected).

CE&M 3

(a)

1 pt: For placing the wire along a north–south line.

1 pt: The wire could be placed above the compass, with the current traveling due north. (The wire also could be placed underneath the compass, with current traveling due south.)

(b)

1 pt: The **B** field due to Earth plus the **B** field caused by the wire, when added together as vectors, must give a resultant direction of 48° west of north.

1 pt: Placing these vectors tail-to-tip, as shown below, $\tan 48° = \mathbf{B}_{wire}/\mathbf{B}_{Earth}$.

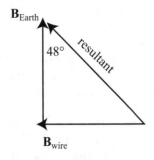

1 pt: So $\mathbf{B}_{wire} = \mathbf{B}_{Earth}\tan 48° = 5.6 \times 10^{-5}$ T.

(c)

1 pt: The magnetic field due to a long, straight, current-carrying wire is given by

$$\mathbf{B} = \frac{\mu_o I}{2\pi r},$$

where r is the distance from the wire to the field point, represented in this problem by d.

1 pt: So $\mathbf{B}$ is proportional to $1/d$; this results in a hyperbolic graph.

1 pt: This graph should be asymptotic to both the vertical and horizontal axes.

(d)

1 pt: Place $1/d$ on the horizontal axis.

2 pts: The equation for the field due the wire can be written

$$\mathbf{B} = \left(\frac{\mu_o I}{2\pi}\right)\left(\frac{1}{d}\right).$$

Everything in the first set of parentheses is constant. So, this equation is of the form $y = mx$, which is the equation of a line, if $1/d$ is put on the x-axis of the graph. (1 point can be earned for a partially complete explanation. On this problem, no points can be earned for justification if the answer is incorrect.)

(e)

1 pt: The slope of the graph, from the equation above, is

$$\frac{\mu_o I}{2\pi r},$$

1 pt: For plugging in values correctly, including 0.5 A or 500 mA.

1 pt: For units on the slope equivalent to magnetic field times distance (i.e., T·m, T·cm, mT·m, etc.)

1 pt: For a correct answer, complete with correct units: 1.0×10^{-7} Tm, or 1.0×10^{-4} mT·m.

SCORING AND INTERPRETATION

Mechanics

Multiple Choice: Number Correct_____
                      Number Wrong _____

Total = Right – ($\frac{1}{4}$) Wrong _____(35 max)

Free Response: Question 1_____(15 max)
                   Question 2_____(15 max)
                   Question 3_____(15 max)

        Total Free Response_____(45 max)

$1.286 \times$ Multiple Choice + Free Response =
Raw Score _____(90 max)

Composite Score Range	Rough Estimate of AP Score
56–90	5
40–55	4
29–39	3
15–28	2
0–14	1

Electricity and Magnetism

Multiple Choice: Number Correct_____
                      Number Wrong _____

Total = Right – ($\frac{1}{4}$) Wrong _____(35 max)

Free Response: Question 1_____(15 max)
                   Question 2_____(15 max)
                   Question 3_____(15 max)

        Total Free Response_____(45 max)

$1.286 \times$ Multiple Choice + Free Response =
Raw Score _____(90 max)

Composite Score Range	Rough Estimate of AP Score
52–90	5
39–51	4
26–38	3
15–25	2
0–14	1

Reference Materials

In the past, many of the following tables, formulas, and equations have been supplied for use during specified sections of the respective exams. Visit www.collegeboard.com/ap and search the subjects you are studying to determine exactly which materials will be provided and when you will be permitted to refer to them.

CHEMISTRY

Periodic Table of the Elements[1]

Classical group numbers	IA	IIA	IIIB	IVB	VB	VIB	VIIB		VIII		IB	IIB	IIIA	IVA	VA	VIA	VIIA	0
Modern group numbers	1	2	3	4	5	6	7	8	9	10	11	12	13	14	15	16	17	18

Periods

Key:
1 — Atomic number
H — Symbol
1.0080 — Atomic mass

Period 1
- 1 H 1.0080
- 2 He 4.00260

Period 2
- 3 Li 6.941
- 4 Be 9.01218
- 5 B 10.81
- 6 C 12.011
- 7 N 14.0067
- 8 O 15.9994
- 9 F 18.9984
- 10 Ne 20.179

Period 3
- 11 Na 22.9898
- 12 Mg 24.305
- 13 Al 26.9815
- 14 Si 28.086
- 15 P 30.9738
- 16 S 32.06
- 17 Cl 35.453
- 18 Ar 39.948

Period 4
- 19 K 39.102
- 20 Ca 40.08
- 21 Sc 44.9559
- 22 Ti 47.90
- 23 V 50.9414
- 24 Cr 51.996
- 25 Mn 54.9380
- 26 Fe 55.847
- 27 Co 58.9332
- 28 Ni 58.71
- 29 Cu 63.546
- 30 Zn 65.37
- 31 Ga 69.72
- 32 Ge 72.59
- 33 As 74.9216
- 34 Se 78.96
- 35 Br 79.904
- 36 Kr 83.80

Period 5
- 37 Rb 85.4678
- 38 Sr 87.62
- 39 Y 88.9059
- 40 Zr 91.22
- 41 Nb 92.9064
- 42 Mo 95.94
- 43 Tc 98.9062
- 44 Ru 101.07
- 45 Rh 102.9055
- 46 Pd 106.4
- 47 Ag 107.868
- 48 Cd 112.40
- 49 In 114.82
- 50 Sn 118.69
- 51 Sb 121.75
- 52 Te 127.60
- 53 I 126.9045
- 54 Xe 131.30

Period 6
- 55 Cs 132.9055
- 56 Ba 137.34
- 57 La° 138.9055
- 72 Hf 178.49
- 73 Ta 180.9479
- 74 W 183.85
- 75 Re 186.2
- 76 Os 190.2
- 77 Ir 192.22
- 78 Pt 195.09
- 79 Au 196.9665
- 80 Hg 200.59
- 81 Tl 204.37
- 82 Pb 207.2
- 83 Bi 208.9806
- 84 Po (210)
- 85 At (210)
- 86 Rn (222)

Period 7
- 87 Fr (223)
- 88 Ra 226.0254
- 89 Ac† (227)
- 104 Unq (261)
- 105 Unp (262)
- 106 Unh (263)

° Lanthanides:
- 58 Ce 140.12
- 59 Pr 140.9077
- 60 Nd 144.24
- 61 Pm (145)
- 62 Sm 150.4
- 63 Eu 151.96
- 64 Gd 157.25
- 65 Tb 158.9254
- 66 Dy 162.50
- 67 Ho 164.9303
- 68 Er 167.26
- 69 Tm 168.9342
- 70 Yb 173.04
- 71 Lu 174.97

† Actinides:
- 90 Th 232.0381
- 91 Pa 232.0359
- 92 U 238.029
- 93 Np 237.0482
- 94 Pu (242)
- 95 Am (243)
- 96 Cm (247)
- 97 Bk (249)
- 98 Cf (251)
- 99 Es (254)
- 100 Fm (253)
- 101 Md (256)
- 102 No (254)
- 103 Lr (257)

[1]Family and period labels are not provided on the periodic table supplied with the AP Chemistry exam. Become familiar with these labels so that you can function effectively without them.

Keywords and Equations

Basics

T = temperature	n = moles	m = mass	P = pressure
V = volume	D = density	v = velocity	**M** = molar mass
KE = kinetic energy	t = time		

Boltzmann's constant, $k = 1.38 \times 10^{-23}$ J K^{-1}
electron charge = -1.6022×10^{-19} coulombs
1 electron volt per atom = 96.5 kJ mol^{-1}

$K = {}^{\circ}C + 273$ $D = m/V$

Gases

u_{rms} = root mean square speed
r = rate of effusion
STP = 0.000° C and 1.000 atm
$PV = nRT$
$(P + n^2a/V^2)(V - nb) = nRT$
$P_A = P_{total} \times X_A$, where X_A = moles A /total moles
$P_{total} = P_A + P_B + P_C + \cdots$
$P_1V_1/T_1 = P_2V_2/T_2$

$u_{rms} = \sqrt{3kT/m} = \sqrt{3RT/M}$

KE per molecule = $\frac{1}{2} mv^2$

KE per mol = $\frac{3}{2}$ RTn

$r_1/r_2 = \sqrt{M_2/M_1}$

1 atm = 760 mm Hg
        = 760 torr

Thermodynamics

S° = standard entropy	H° = standard enthalpy
G° = standard free energy	q = heat
c = specific heat capacity	C_p = molar heat capacity at constant pressure

$\Delta S^{\circ} = \Sigma\, S^{\circ}$ products $- \Sigma\, S^{\circ}$ reactants
$\Delta H^{\circ} = \Sigma\, \Delta H_f^{\circ}$ products $- \Sigma\, \Delta H_f^{\circ}$ reactants
$\Delta G^{\circ} = \Sigma\, \Delta G_f^{\circ}$ products $- \Sigma\, \Delta G_f^{\circ}$ reactants
$\Delta G^{\circ} = \Delta H^{\circ} - T\Delta S^{\circ}$
        $= -RT \ln K = -2.303\ RT \log K$
        $= -n\ F\ E^{\circ}$
$\Delta G = \Delta G^{\circ} + RT \ln Q = \Delta G^{\circ} + 2.303\ RT \log Q$
$q = mc\Delta T$
$C_p = \Delta H/\Delta T$

Light and Electrons

E = energy ν = frequency λ = wavelength

p = momentum v = velocity n = principal quantum number

m = mass $\Delta E = h\nu$ or $E = h\nu$ $c = \lambda\nu$ $\lambda = h/mv$ $p = mv$

$E_n = (-2.178 \times 10^{-18}/n^2)$ J

Solutions

Π = osmotic pressure

i = van't Hoff factor

K_f = molal freezing-point depression constant

K_b = molal boiling-point elevation constant

K_f for water = 1.86 K kg mol^{-1}

K_b for water = 0.512 K kg mol^{-1}

$\Delta T_f = iK_f \times$ molality

$\Delta T_b = iK_b \times$ molality

$\Pi = (nRT/V)\,i$

$\pi = MRT$

Kinetics

$$\text{Rate} = k[A]^m [B]^n \ldots$$

$$\ln \frac{[A]_0}{[A]_t} = kt \text{ or } \ln[A]_t - \ln[A]_O = -kt \text{ (first order)}$$

$$\frac{1}{[A]_t} - \frac{1}{[A]_0} = kt \quad \text{(second order)}$$

$$t_{1/2} = \frac{\ln 2}{k} = \frac{0.693}{k}$$

$$k = Ae^{-E_a/RT} \text{ or } \ln k = \frac{-E_a}{R}\left(\frac{1}{T}\right) + \ln A$$

E_a = activation energy

k = rate constant

A = frequency factor

Electrochemistry

I = current (amperes)   q = charge (coulombs)

$E°$ = standard reduction potential   K = equilibrium constant

1 faraday (F) = 96,500 coulombs (C)

Faraday's constant, F = 96,500 coulombs per mole of electrons

$$I = q/t \qquad \log K = \frac{nE°}{0.0592}$$

$$E_{cell} = E°_{cell} - \left(\frac{RT}{nF}\right) \ln Q = E°_{cell} - \left(\frac{0.0592}{n}\right) \log Q \text{ at } 25°C$$

Equilibrium

Q = reaction quotient

$$Q = \frac{[C]^c[D]^d}{[A]^a[B]^b}, \text{ where } aA + bB \rightleftharpoons cC + dD$$

equilibrium constants:

K_a (weak acid) K_b (weak base) K_w (water)

K_p (gas pressure) K_c (molar concentrations)

$$K_a = \frac{[H^+][A^-]}{[HA]} \qquad K_b = \frac{[OH^-][HB^+]}{[B]}$$

$K_w = [OH^-][H^+] = 1.0 \times 10^{-14} = K_a \times K_b$ at $25°C$

$pH = -\log [H^+]$, $pOH = -\log [OH^-]$

$14 = pH + pOH$

$$pH = pK_a + \log \frac{[A^-]}{[HA]}$$

$$pOH = pK_b + \log \frac{[HB^+]}{[B]}$$

$pK_a = -\log K_a$, $pK_b = -\log K_b$

$K_p = K_c(RT)^{\Delta n}$, where Δn = moles product gas − moles reactant gas

Experimental

Beer's Law: A = abc (A = absorbance; a = molar absorbtivity; b = path length; c = concentration)

STATISTICS

Formulas

Descriptive Statistics

$$\bar{x} = \frac{\sum x_i}{n}$$

$$s_x = \sqrt{\frac{1}{n-1} \sum \left(x_i - \bar{x} \right)^2}$$

$$s_p = \sqrt{\frac{\left(n_1 - 1 \right)s_1^2 + \left(n_2 - 1 \right)s_2^2}{\left(n_1 + 1 \right) + \left(n_2 - 1 \right)}}$$

$$\hat{y} = b_0 + b_1 x$$

$$b_1 = \frac{\sum \left(x_i - \bar{x} \right)\left(y_1 - \bar{y} \right)}{\sum \left(x_i - \bar{x} \right)^2}$$

$$b_0 = \bar{y} - b_1 \bar{x}$$

$$r = \frac{1}{n-1} \sum \left(\frac{x_i - \bar{x}}{s_x} \right)\left(\frac{y_i - \bar{y}}{s_y} \right)$$

$$b_1 = r \frac{s_y}{s_x}$$

$$s_{b_1} = \frac{\sqrt{\dfrac{\sum \left(y_i - \hat{y} \right)^2}{n-2}}}{\sqrt{\sum \left(x_i - \bar{x} \right)^2}}$$

Probability

$$P(A \cup B) = P(A) + P(B) - P(A \cap B)$$

$$P(A|B) = \frac{P(A \cap B)}{P(B)}$$

$$E(X) = \mu_x = \sum x_i p_i$$

$$Var(X) = \sigma_x^2 = \sum (x_i - \mu_x)^2 p_i$$

If X has a binomial distribution with parameters n and p, then:

$$P(X = k) = \binom{n}{k} p^k (1 - p)^{n-k}$$

$$\mu_x = nk$$

$$\sigma_x = \sqrt{np(1 - p)}$$

$$\mu_{\hat{p}} = p$$

$$\sigma_{\hat{p}} = \sqrt{\frac{p(1 - p)}{n}}$$

If $\bar{x}$ is the mean of a random sample of size n from an infinite population with mean μ and standard deviation σ, then

$$\mu_{\bar{x}} = \mu$$

$$\sigma_{\bar{x}} = \frac{\sigma}{\sqrt{n}}$$

Inferential Statistics

Standardized test statistic: $\dfrac{\text{statistic} - \text{parameter}}{\text{standard deviation of statistic}}$

Confidence interval: statistic $\pm$ (critical value) • (standard deviation of statistic)

Single-Sample

Statistic	Standard Deviation
Sample Mean	$\dfrac{\sigma}{\sqrt{n}}$
Sample Proportion	$\sqrt{\dfrac{p(1-p)}{n}}$

Two-Sample

Statistic	Standard Deviation
Difference of sample means $(\sigma_1 \neq \sigma_2)$	$\sqrt{\dfrac{\sigma_1^2}{n_1} + \dfrac{\sigma_2^2}{n_2}}$
Difference of sample means $(\sigma_1 = \sigma_2)$	$\sigma\sqrt{\dfrac{1}{n_1} + \dfrac{1}{n_2}}$
Difference of sample proportions $(p_1 \neq p_2)$	$\sqrt{\dfrac{p_1(1-p_1)}{n_1} + \dfrac{p_2(1-p_2)}{n_2}}$
Difference of sample proportions $p_1 = p_2$	$\sqrt{p(1-p)}\sqrt{\dfrac{1}{n_1} + \dfrac{1}{n_2}}$

$$\text{Chi-square test statistic} = \sum \frac{(\text{observed} - \text{expected})^2}{\text{expected}}$$

Tables

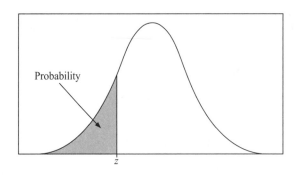

Table entry for *z* is the
probability lying below *z*.

Probability

z

TABLE A   Standard Normal Probabilities

z	.00	.01	.02	.03	.04	.05	.06	.07	.08	.09
−3.4	.0003	.0003	.0003	.0003	.0003	.0003	.0003	.0003	.0003	.0002
−3.3	.0005	.0005	.0005	.0004	.0004	.0004	.0004	.0004	.0004	.0003
−3.2	.0007	.0007	.0006	.0006	.0006	.0006	.0006	.0005	.0005	.0005
−3.1	.0010	.0009	.0009	.0009	.0008	.0008	.0008	.0008	.0007	.0007
−3.0	.0013	.0013	.0013	.0012	.0012	.0011	.0011	.0011	.0010	.0010
−2.9	.0019	.0018	.0018	.0017	.0016	.0016	.0015	.0015	.0014	.0014
−2.8	.0026	.0025	.0024	.0023	.0023	.0022	.0021	.0021	.0020	.0019
−2.7	.0035	.0034	.0033	.0032	.0031	.0030	.0029	.0028	.0027	.0026
−2.6	.0047	.0045	.0044	.0043	.0041	.0040	.0039	.0038	.0037	.0036
−2.5	.0062	.0060	.0059	.0057	.0055	.0054	.0052	.0051	.0049	.0048
−2.4	.0082	.0080	.0078	.0075	.0073	.0071	.0069	.0068	.0066	.0064
−2.3	.0107	.0104	.0102	.0099	.0096	.0094	.0091	.0089	.0087	.0084
−2.2	.0139	.0136	.0132	.0129	.0125	.0122	.0119	.0116	.0113	.0110
−2.1	.0179	.0174	.0170	.0166	.0162	.0158	.0154	.0150	.0146	.0143
−2.0	.0228	.0222	.0217	.0212	.0207	.0202	.0197	.0192	.0188	.0183
−1.9	.0287	.0281	.0274	.0268	.0262	.0256	.0250	.0244	.0239	.0233
−1.8	.0359	.0351	.0344	.0336	.0329	.0322	.0314	.0307	.0301	.0294
−1.7	.0446	.0436	.0427	.0418	.0409	.0401	.0392	.0384	.0375	.0367
−1.6	.0548	.0537	.0526	.0516	.0505	.0495	.0485	.0475	.0465	.0455
−1.5	.0668	.0655	.0643	.0630	.0618	.0606	.0594	.0582	.0571	.0559
−1.4	.0808	.0793	.0778	.0764	.0749	.0735	.0721	.0708	.0694	.0681
−1.3	.0968	.0951	.0934	.0918	.0901	.0885	.0869	.0853	.0838	.0823
−1.2	.1151	.1131	.1112	.1093	.1075	.1056	.1038	.1020	.1003	.0985
−1.1	.1357	.1335	.1314	.1292	.1271	.1251	.1230	.1210	.1190	.1170
−1.0	.1587	.1562	.1539	.1515	.1492	.1469	.1446	.1423	.1401	.1379
−0.9	.1841	.1814	.1788	.1762	.1736	.1711	.1685	.1660	.1635	.1611
−0.8	.2119	.2090	.2061	.2033	.2005	.1977	.1949	.1922	.1894	.1867
−0.7	.2420	.2389	.2358	.2327	.2296	.2266	.2236	.2206	.2177	.2148
−0.6	.2743	.2709	.2676	.2643	.2611	.2578	.2546	.2514	.2483	.2451
−0.5	.3085	.3050	.3015	.2981	.2946	.2912	.2877	.2843	.2810	.2776
−0.4	.3446	.3409	.3372	.3336	.3300	.3264	.3228	.3192	.3156	.3121
−0.3	.3821	.3783	.3745	.3707	.3669	.3632	.3594	.3557	.3520	.3483
−0.2	.4207	.4168	.4129	.4090	.4052	.4013	.3974	.3936	.3897	.3859
−0.1	.4602	.4562	.4522	.4483	.4443	.4404	.4364	.4325	.4286	.4247
−0.0	.5000	.4960	.4920	.4880	.4840	.4801	.4761	.4721	.4681	.4641

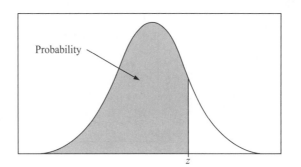

Table entry for z is the
probability lying below z.

TABLE A   Standard Normal Probabilities (*continued*)

z	.00	.01	.02	.03	.04	.05	.06	.07	.08	.09
0.0	.5000	.5040	.5080	.5120	.5160	.5199	.5239	.5279	.5319	.5359
0.1	.5398	.5438	.5478	.5517	.5557	.5596	.5636	.5675	.5714	.5753
0.2	.5793	.5832	.5871	.5910	.5948	.5987	.6026	.6064	.6103	.6141
0.3	.6179	.6217	.6255	.6293	.6331	.6368	.6406	.6443	.6480	.6517
0.4	.6554	.6591	.6628	.6664	.6700	.6736	.6772	.6808	.6844	.6879
0.5	.6915	.6950	.6985	.7019	.7054	.7088	.7123	.7157	.7190	.7224
0.6	.7257	.7291	.7324	.7357	.7389	.7422	.7454	.7486	.7517	.7549
0.7	.7580	.7611	.7642	.7673	.7704	.7734	.7764	.7794	.7823	.7852
0.8	.7881	.7910	.7939	.7967	.7995	.8023	.8051	.8078	.8106	.8133
0.9	.8159	.8186	.8212	.8238	.8264	.8289	.8315	.8340	.8365	.8389
1.0	.8413	.8438	.8461	.8485	.8508	.8531	.8554	.8577	.8599	.8621
1.1	.8643	.8665	.8686	.8708	.8729	.8749	.8770	.8790	.8810	.8830
1.2	.8849	.8869	.8888	.8907	.8925	.8944	.8962	.8980	.8997	.9015
1.3	.9032	.9049	.9066	.9082	.9099	.9115	.9131	.9147	.9162	.9177
1.4	.9192	.9207	.9222	.9236	.9251	.9265	.9279	.9292	.9306	.9319
1.5	.9332	.9345	.9357	.9370	.9382	.9394	.9406	.9418	.9429	.9441
1.6	.9452	.9463	.9474	.9484	.9495	.9505	.9515	.9525	.9535	.9545
1.7	.9554	.9564	.9573	.9582	.9591	.9599	.9608	.9616	.9625	.9633
1.8	.9641	.9649	.9656	.9664	.9671	.9678	.9686	.9693	.9699	.9706
1.9	.9713	.9719	.9726	.9732	.9738	.9744	.9750	.9756	.9761	.9767
2.0	.9772	.9778	.9783	.9788	.9793	.9798	.9803	.9808	.9812	.9817
2.1	.9821	.9826	.9830	.9834	.9838	.9842	.9846	.9850	.9854	.9857
2.2	.9861	.9864	.9868	.9871	.9875	.9878	.9881	.9884	.9887	.9890
2.3	.9893	.9896	.9898	.9901	.9904	.9906	.9909	.9911	.9913	.9916
2.4	.9918	.9920	.9922	.9925	.9927	.9929	.9931	.9932	.9934	.9936
2.5	.9938	.9940	.9941	.9943	.9945	.9946	.9948	.9949	.9951	.9952
2.6	.9953	.9955	.9956	.9957	.9959	.9960	.9961	.9962	.9963	.9964
2.7	.9965	.9966	.9967	.9968	.9969	.9970	.9971	.9972	.9973	.9974
2.8	.9974	.9975	.9976	.9977	.9977	.9978	.9979	.9979	.9980	.9981
2.9	.9981	.9982	.9982	.9983	.9984	.9984	.9985	.9985	.9986	.9986
3.0	.9987	.9987	.9987	.9988	.9988	.9989	.9989	.9989	.9990	.9990
3.1	.9990	.9991	.9991	.9991	.9992	.9992	.9992	.9992	.9993	.9993
3.2	.9993	.9993	.9994	.9994	.9994	.9994	.9994	.9995	.9995	.9995
3.3	.9995	.9995	.9995	.9996	.9996	.9996	.9996	.9996	.9996	.9997
3.4	.9997	.9997	.9997	.9997	.9997	.9997	.9997	.9997	.9997	.9998

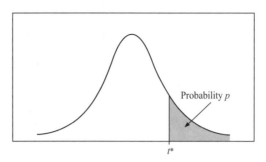

Table entry for p and C is the point t^* with probability p lying above it and probability C lying between $-t^*$ and t^*.

Probability p

t^*

TABLE B t Distribution Critical Values

df	.25	.20	.15	.10	.05	.025	.02	.01	.005	.0025	.001	.0005
							Tail probability p					
1	1.000	1.376	1.963	3.078	6.314	12.71	15.89	31.82	63.66	127.3	318.3	636.6
2	.816	1.061	1.386	1.886	2.920	4.303	4.849	6.965	9.925	14.09	22.33	31.60
3	.765	.978	1.250	1.638	2.353	3.182	3.482	4.541	5.841	7.453	10.21	12.92
4	.741	.941	1.190	1.533	2.132	2.776	2.999	3.747	4.604	5.598	7.173	8.610
5	.727	.920	1.156	1.476	2.015	2.571	2.757	3.365	4.032	4.773	5.893	6.869
6	.718	.906	1.134	1.440	1.943	2.447	2.612	3.143	3.707	4.317	5.208	5.959
7	.711	.896	1.119	1.415	1.895	2.365	2.517	2.998	3.499	4.029	4.785	5.408
8	.706	.889	1.108	1.397	1.860	2.306	2.449	2.896	3.355	3.833	4.501	5.041
9	.703	.883	1.100	1.383	1.833	2.262	2.398	2.821	3.250	3.690	4.297	4.781
10	.700	.879	1.093	1.372	1.812	2.228	2.359	2.764	3.169	3.581	4.144	4.587
11	.697	.876	1.088	1.363	1.796	2.201	2.328	2.718	3.106	3.497	4.025	4.437
12	.695	.873	1.083	1.356	1.782	2.179	2.303	2.681	3.055	3.428	3.930	4.318
13	.694	.870	1.079	1.350	1.771	2.160	2.282	2.650	3.012	3.372	3.852	4.221
14	.692	.868	1.076	1.345	1.761	2.145	2.264	2.624	2.977	3.326	3.787	4.140
15	.691	.866	1.074	1.341	1.753	2.131	2.249	2.602	2.947	3.286	3.733	4.073
16	.690	.865	1.071	1.337	1.746	2.120	2.235	2.583	2.921	3.252	3.686	4.015
17	.689	.863	1.069	1.333	1.740	2.110	2.224	2.567	2.898	3.222	3.646	3.965
18	.688	.862	1.067	1.330	1.734	2.101	2.214	2.552	2.878	3.197	3.611	3.922
19	.688	.861	1.066	1.328	1.729	2.093	2.205	2.539	2.861	3.174	3.579	3.883
20	.687	.860	1.064	1.325	1.725	2.086	2.197	2.528	2.845	3.153	3.552	3.850
21	.686	.859	1.063	1.323	1.721	2.080	2.189	2.518	2.831	3.135	3.527	3.819
22	.686	.858	1.061	1.321	1.717	2.074	2.183	2.508	2.819	3.119	3.505	3.792
23	.685	.858	1.060	1.319	1.714	2.069	2.177	2.500	2.807	3.104	3.485	3.768
24	.685	.857	1.059	1.318	1.711	2.064	2.172	2.492	2.797	3.091	3.467	3.745
25	.684	.856	1.058	1.316	1.708	2.060	2.167	2.485	2.787	3.078	3.450	3.725
26	.684	.856	1.058	1.315	1.706	2.056	2.162	2.479	2.779	3.067	3.435	3.707
27	.684	.855	1.057	1.314	1.703	2.052	2.158	2.473	2.771	3.057	3.421	3.690
28	.683	.855	1.056	1.313	1.701	2.048	2.154	2.467	2.763	3.047	3.408	3.674
29	.683	.854	1.055	1.311	1.699	2.045	2.150	2.462	2.756	3.038	3.396	3.659
30	.683	.854	1.055	1.310	1.697	2.042	2.147	2.457	2.750	3.030	3.385	3.646
40	.681	.851	1.050	1.303	1.684	2.021	2.123	2.423	2.704	2.971	3.307	3.551
50	.679	.849	1.047	1.299	1.676	2.009	2.109	2.403	2.678	2.937	3.261	3.496
60	.679	.848	1.045	1.296	1.671	2.000	2.099	2.390	2.660	2.915	3.232	3.460
80	.678	.846	1.043	1.292	1.664	1.990	2.088	2.374	2.639	2.887	3.195	3.416
100	.677	.845	1.042	1.290	1.660	1.984	2.081	2.364	2.626	2.871	3.174	3.390
1000	.675	.842	1.037	1.282	1.646	1.962	2.056	2.330	2.581	2.813	3.098	3.300
∞	.674	.841	1.036	1.282	1.645	1.960	2.054	2.326	2.576	2.807	3.091	3.291
	50%	60%	70%	80%	90%	95%	96%	98%	99%	99.5%	99.8%	99.9%
						Confidence level C						

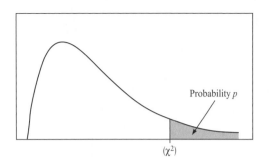

Table entry for p is the point (χ^2) with probability p lying above it.

Probability p

(χ^2)

TABLE C χ^2 Critical Values

df	\multicolumn{12}{c}{Tail probability p}
	.25	.20	.15	.10	.05	.025	.02	.01	.005	.0025	.001	.0005
1	1.32	1.64	2.07	2.71	3.84	5.02	5.41	6.63	7.88	9.14	10.83	12.12
2	2.77	3.22	3.79	4.61	5.99	7.38	7.82	9.21	10.60	11.98	13.82	15.20
3	4.11	4.64	5.32	6.25	7.81	9.35	9.84	11.34	12.84	14.32	16.27	17.73
4	5.39	5.99	6.74	7.78	9.49	11.14	11.67	13.28	14.86	16.42	18.47	20.00
5	6.63	7.29	8.12	9.24	11.07	12.83	13.39	15.09	16.75	18.39	20.51	22.11
6	7.84	8.56	9.45	10.64	12.59	14.45	15.03	16.81	18.55	20.25	22.46	24.10
7	9.04	9.80	10.75	12.02	14.07	16.01	16.62	18.48	20.28	22.04	24.32	26.02
8	10.22	11.03	12.03	13.36	15.51	17.53	18.17	20.09	21.95	23.77	26.12	27.87
9	11.39	12.24	13.29	14.68	16.92	19.02	19.68	21.67	23.59	25.46	27.88	29.67
10	12.55	13.44	14.53	15.99	18.31	20.48	21.16	23.21	25.19	27.11	29.59	31.42
11	13.70	14.63	15.77	17.28	19.68	21.92	22.62	24.72	26.76	28.73	31.26	33.14
12	14.85	15.81	16.99	18.55	21.03	23.34	24.05	26.22	28.30	30.32	32.91	34.82
13	15.98	16.98	18.20	19.81	22.36	24.74	25.47	27.69	29.82	31.88	34.53	36.48
14	17.12	18.15	19.41	21.06	23.68	26.12	26.87	29.14	31.32	33.43	36.12	38.11
15	18.25	19.31	20.60	22.31	25.00	27.49	28.26	30.58	32.80	34.95	37.70	39.72
16	19.37	20.47	21.79	23.54	26.30	28.85	29.63	32.00	34.27	36.46	39.25	41.31
17	20.49	21.61	22.98	24.77	27.59	30.19	31.00	33.41	35.72	37.95	40.79	42.88
18	21.60	22.76	24.16	25.99	28.87	31.53	32.35	34.81	37.16	39.42	42.31	44.43
19	22.72	23.90	25.33	27.20	30.14	32.85	33.69	36.19	38.58	40.88	43.82	45.97
20	23.83	25.04	26.50	28.41	31.41	34.17	35.02	37.57	40.00	42.34	45.31	47.50
21	24.93	26.17	27.66	29.62	32.67	35.48	36.34	38.93	41.40	43.78	46.80	49.01
22	26.04	27.30	28.82	30.81	33.92	36.78	37.66	40.29	42.80	45.20	48.27	50.51
23	27.14	28.43	29.98	32.01	35.17	38.08	38.97	41.64	44.18	46.62	49.73	52.00
24	28.24	29.55	31.13	33.20	36.42	39.36	40.27	42.98	45.56	48.03	51.18	53.48
25	29.34	30.68	32.28	34.38	37.65	40.65	41.57	44.31	46.93	49.44	52.62	54.95
26	30.43	31.79	33.43	35.56	38.89	41.92	42.86	45.64	48.29	50.83	54.05	56.41
27	31.53	32.91	34.57	36.74	40.11	43.19	44.14	46.96	49.64	52.22	55.48	57.86
28	32.62	34.03	35.71	37.92	41.34	44.46	45.42	48.28	50.99	53.59	56.89	59.30
29	33.71	35.14	36.85	39.09	42.56	45.72	46.69	49.59	52.34	54.97	58.30	60.73
30	34.80	36.25	37.99	40.26	43.77	46.98	47.96	50.89	53.67	56.33	59.70	62.16
40	45.62	47.27	49.24	51.81	55.76	59.34	60.44	63.69	66.77	69.70	73.40	76.09
50	56.33	58.16	60.35	63.17	67.50	71.42	72.61	76.15	79.49	82.66	86.66	89.56
60	66.98	68.97	71.34	74.40	79.08	83.30	84.58	88.38	91.95	95.34	99.61	102.7
80	88.13	90.41	93.11	96.58	101.9	106.6	108.1	112.3	116.3	120.1	124.8	128.3
100	109.1	111.7	114.7	118.5	124.3	129.6	131.1	135.8	140.2	144.3	149.4	153.2

PHYSICS B & C

Constants

1 amu	u	1.7×10^{-27} kg
mass of proton	m_p	1.7×10^{-27} kg
mass of neutron	m_n	1.7×10^{-27} kg
mass of electron	m_e	9.1×10^{-31} kg
charge of proton	e	1.6×10^{-19} C
Avogadro's number	N	6.0×10^{-23} mol^{-1}
Universal gas constant	R	8.3 J / (mol·K)
Boltzmann's constant	k_B	1.4×10^{-23} J / K
Speed of light	c	3.0×10^{8} m/s
Planck's constant	h	6.6×10^{-34} J·s
	h	4.1×10^{-15} eV·s
Planck's constant·speed of light	hc	1.99×10^{-25} J·m
	hc	1.24×10^{3} eV·nm
Permittivity of free space	ε_o	8.9×10^{-12} C^2 / N·m^2
Coulomb's law constant	k	9.0×10^{9} N·m^2 / C^2
Permeability of free space	μ_o	$4\pi \times 10^{-7}$ T·m / A
Universal gravitation constant	G	6.7×10^{-11} N·m^2 / C^2
Earth's free fall acceleration	g	9.8 m/s
1 atmosphere of pressure	atm	1.0×10^{5} Pa
1 electron-volt	eV	1.6×10^{-19} J

PHYSICS B

Equations

Note: Remember, your textbook might use slightly different symbols

Newtonian Mechanics

$$v_f = v_o + at$$
$$x - x_0 = v_0 t + \tfrac{1}{2} at^2$$
$$v_f^2 = v_0^2 + 2a(x - x_0)$$
$$F_{net} = ma$$
$$F_f = \mu F_n$$
$$a_c = \frac{v^2}{r}$$
$$\tau = F \cdot d$$
$$p = mv$$

$$I = \Delta p = F \cdot \Delta t$$
$$KE = \tfrac{1}{2} mv^2$$
$$PE_g = mgh$$
$$W = F \cdot \Delta x$$
$$P = \frac{W}{\Delta t}$$
$$P = F \cdot v$$
$$F = -kx$$
$$PE_s = \tfrac{1}{2} kx^2$$

$$T = 2\pi\sqrt{\frac{m}{k}}$$
$$T = 2\pi\sqrt{\frac{L}{g}}$$
$$T = \frac{1}{f}$$
$$F_G = G\frac{M_1 M_2}{r^2}$$
$$PE_G = G\frac{M_1 M_2}{r}$$

Electricity and Magnetism

$$F = \frac{1}{4\pi\varepsilon_0} \frac{q_1 q_2}{r^2}$$

$$F = qE$$

$$PE_E = qV = \frac{1}{4\pi\varepsilon_0} \frac{q_1 q_2}{r}$$

$$E = \frac{V}{d}$$

$$V = \frac{1}{4\pi\varepsilon_0} \sum \frac{q_i}{r_i}$$

$$Q = CV$$

$$C = \varepsilon_0 \frac{A}{d}$$

$$PE_C = \frac{1}{2} CV^2$$

$$I = \frac{\Delta Q}{\Delta t}$$

$$R = \rho \frac{L}{A}$$

$$V = IR$$

$$P = IV$$

$$C_p = \sum C_i$$

$$\frac{1}{C_s} = \sum \frac{1}{C_i}$$

$$R_s = \sum R_i$$

$$\frac{1}{R_p} = \sum \frac{1}{R_i}$$

$$F = qvB \sin \theta$$

$$F = ILB \sin \theta$$

$$B = \frac{\mu_0 I}{2\pi r}$$

$$\phi_m = BA \cos \theta$$

$$\varepsilon = -N \frac{\Delta\phi}{\Delta t}$$

$$\varepsilon = Blv$$

Fluid Mechanics and Thermal Physics

$$P = P_o + \rho g h$$

$$F_b = \rho V g$$

$$A_1 v_1 = A_2 v_2$$

$$P_1 + \rho g y_1 + \tfrac{1}{2}\rho v_1^2 = P_2 + \rho g y_2 + \tfrac{1}{2}\rho v_2^2$$

$$\Delta L = \alpha L_0 \Delta T$$

$$P = \frac{F}{A}$$

$$PV = nRT$$

$$KE_{avg} = \frac{3}{2} k_B T$$

$$v_{rms} = \sqrt{\frac{3 k_B T}{m}}$$

$$W = -p\Delta V$$

$$\Delta U = Q + W$$

$$e = \frac{W}{Q_H}$$

$$e_{ideal} = \frac{T_H - T_C}{T_H}$$

Waves and Optics

$$v = \lambda f$$

$$\frac{1}{f} = \frac{1}{d_o} + \frac{1}{d_i}$$

$$d \sin \theta = m\lambda$$

$$n = \frac{c}{v}$$

$$n_1 \cdot \sin \theta_1 = n_2 \cdot \sin \theta_2$$

$$m = \frac{h_i}{h_o} = \frac{d_i}{d_0}$$

$$x = \frac{m\lambda L}{d}$$

$$\sin \theta_c = \frac{n_2}{n_1}$$

$$f = \frac{r}{2}$$

Atomic and Nuclear Physics

$$E = hf = pc$$

$$\lambda = \frac{h}{p}$$

$$KE = hf - W$$

$$E = (\Delta m)c^2$$

PHYSICS C

Equations

You'll notice that the C equation sheet often expresses relationships in calculus terms. Don't let that confuse you; for example, though impulse is expressed as an integral of force with respect to time, you should also interpret that as force times time if the force is constant, or as the area under a force vs. time graph.

Remember, your textbook might use slightly different symbols

Mechanics

$$v_f = v_o + at$$

$$p = \frac{dW}{dt}$$

$$\omega_f = \omega_0 + \alpha t$$

$$x - x_o = v_o t + \tfrac{1}{2} at^2$$

$$P = F \cdot v$$

$$\Delta\theta = \omega_0 t + \tfrac{1}{2} \alpha t^2$$

$$v_f^2 = v_0^2 + 2a(x - x_o)$$

$$PE_g = mgh$$

$$F = -kx$$

$$F_{net} = ma$$

$$a_c = \frac{v^2}{r} = \omega^2 r$$

$$PE_s = \tfrac{1}{2} kx^2$$

$$F = \frac{dp}{dt}$$

$$\tau = F \cdot d$$

$$T = \frac{2\pi}{\omega} = \frac{1}{f}$$

$$I = \Delta p = \int F \cdot dt$$

$$\tau_{net} = I\alpha$$

$$T = 2\pi \sqrt{\frac{m}{k}}$$

$$p = mv$$

$$I = \int r^2 dm = \sum m_i r_i^2$$

$$T = 2\pi \sqrt{\frac{L}{g}}$$

$$F_f = \mu F_n$$

$$M x_{cm} = \sum m_i x_i$$

$$F_G = G \frac{M_1 M_2}{r^2}$$

$$W = \int F \cdot dx$$

$$v = r\omega$$

$$PE_G = G \frac{M_1 M_2}{r}$$

$$KE = \tfrac{1}{2} mv^2$$

$$L = I\omega = mvr$$

$$KE = \tfrac{1}{2} I\omega^2$$

$$F = \frac{1}{4\pi\varepsilon_o} \frac{q_1 q_2}{r^2}$$

$$\frac{1}{C_s} = \sum \frac{1}{C_i}$$

$$F = ILB \sin \theta$$

$$F = qE$$

$$I = \frac{dQ}{dt}$$

$$B_s = \mu_o n L$$

$$\oint E{\cdot}dA = \frac{Q_{enclosed}}{\varepsilon_0}$$

$$PE_C = \frac{1}{2} CV^2$$

$$\phi_m = \int B{\cdot}dA$$

$$E = -\frac{dv}{dr}$$

$$R = \rho \frac{L}{A}$$

$$\varepsilon = \frac{d\phi_m}{dt}$$

$$PE_E = qV = \frac{1}{4\pi\varepsilon_o} \frac{q_1 q_2}{r}$$

$$V = IR$$

$$\varepsilon = Blv$$

$$V = \frac{1}{4\pi\varepsilon_o} \sum \frac{q_i}{r_i}$$

$$R_s = \sum R_i$$

$$\varepsilon = -L \frac{dI}{dt}$$

$$Q = CV$$

$$\frac{1}{R_p} = \sum \frac{1}{R_i}$$

$$PE_L = \frac{1}{2} LI^2$$

$$C = \kappa \varepsilon_0 \frac{A}{d}$$

$$P = IV$$

$$C_p = \sum C_i$$

$$F = qvB \sin \theta$$

$$\oint B{\cdot}dl = \mu_0 I_c$$

Appendix B

Web Sites

www.collegeboard.com/student/testing/ap/about.htm
This Web site is designed for students. It offers information about the Advanced Placement program, including registration procedures, fees, and a calendar. Searching the subject(s) in which you are interested (e.g., AP Biology) will lead you to a course outline, sample queestions, scoring, and much more.

dir.groups.yahoo.com/dir/
Yahoo offers a directory of clubs and chat rooms on a wide array of interests. Search the subject(s) you wish to pursue on the home page (e.g., AP U.S. History) and you will locate a number of small groups of students who are eager to share insights about the upcoming exam.